SUBMARINE OPERATIONAL EFFECTIVENESS IN THE 20TH CENTURY

SUBMARINE OPERATIONAL EFFECTIVENESS IN THE 20TH CENTURY

PART TWO (1939 - 1945)

BY

CAPTAIN JOHN F. O'CONNELL, USN (RET.)

iUniverse, Inc.
Bloomington

Submarine Operational Effectiveness in the 20th Century
Part Two (1939 - 1945)

iUniverse books may be ordered through booksellers or by contacting:

iUniverse
1663 Liberty Drive
Bloomington, IN 47403
www.iuniverse.com
1-800-Authors (1-800-288-4677)

ISBN: 978-1-4620-4257-9 (sc)
ISBN: 978-1-4620-4261-6 (ebk)

Printed in the United States of America

iUniverse rev. date: 08/13/2011

Dedicated to

My daughter Mary Eileen O'Connell,
Who has her late mother's beauty and charm,
And who has displayed more courage in adversity
Than most of the submariners
I have known

CONTENTS

INTRODUCTION

A previous volume, Part One (1900-1939), dealt with the introduction of the submarine weapon system and its exploitation during World War I (1914-1918) and the Spanish Civil War (1936-1939). It reported the development of submarine arms in various European nations, Japan and the United States, ending on the verge of World War II in 1939.

This volume, Part Two, covers 1939 through 1945, concentrating on two major strategic submarine campaigns. The first was by Nazi Germany against Great Britain in the Atlantic and Indian Oceans; and the second by the United States against the Empire of Japan in the western Pacific Ocean. Both the United Kingdom and Japan were island nations, heavily dependent upon sea commerce to feed their populations and industry. Their opponents set out to starve them of food stuffs and raw materials. Germany was ultimately unsuccessful in its U-boat campaign; while the United States was successful in isolating Japan from its food and raw materials sources overseas.

In 1939 the ranking of number of submarines in commission, by major nation, was as follows:

USSR	218
Italy	115
USA	99
France	77
Great Britain	70
Japan	62
Germany	57[1]

Based on pure numbers the reader might expect that Soviet submarines would roll up the largest scores of ships sunk during WW II, and Germany the least. The actual results were reversed. Soviet submarines, despite their large numbers, accomplished very little. Germany, starting the war at a disadvantage in numbers of submarines, quickly swelled their ranks and embarked on an unrestricted submarine campaign that might have prevented an invasion of France by the Allies in 1944.

Italy with the second largest number of submarines did not fare well. She did not learn much from her submarine adventures during the Spanish Civil War, and suffered large losses to British ASW forces soon after entering the war in 1940. Italian submarines participated in the Battle of the Atlantic and some of their commanding officers ran up a number of sinking's but were no match for their German counterparts. Admiral Doenitz considered Italian submarines incapable of meaningful participation in the Atlantic wolf pack battles and assigned them operating areas in the southern part of the North Atlantic to keep them separate from the U-boat operating areas which were his main concern.

The United States entered the war on 8 December 1941 after the surprise Japanese carrier air strike at Pearl Harbor. That same day a totally unexpected order was issued from Washington, ***"Execute unrestricted air and submarine warfare against the Empire of Japan"***. Never was a submarine service less prepared to carry out such an order. Nevertheless it began an effort that grew by leaps and bounds and eventually by late 1944 succeeded in establishing a submarine blockade of the Japanese home islands. The U.S. submarine blockade effectively defeated Japan although its leaders were unwilling to accept reality, and determined to fight to the bitter end.

France's naval efforts were aborted by her early surrender in 1940. Some French submarines went over and operated under British control. Great Britain's submarine service performed admirably under difficult conditions in the North Sea and the Mediterranean Sea as well as the Indian Ocean.

Japan had a capable and competent submarine service but its activities were not well directed during much of the Pacific War. Some twenty-four IJN submarines were in Hawaiian operational waters at the time of the surprise attack on Pearl Harbor. None achieved any sinking's and one was sunk by air ASW forces.

IJN focus for its submarine arm was on reconnaissance and attack against major U.S. surface ships. During 1942 IJN submarines were successful in attacking U.S. naval vessels including scarce and extremely valuable aircraft carriers, but after that they fell far behind. Like other elements of the Japanese Fleet they were intended to inflict attrition on

American forces venturing west into Asian waters. An IJN submarine scored big at the Battle of Midway in June 1942 when it sank damaged aircraft carrier USS Yorktown (CV-5). In the Battle of the Santa Cruz Islands, in September of the same year USS Wasp (CV-7) was hit by three torpedoes from IJN submarine I-19 and later sank. They were generally not employed against soft targets, merchant ships that resupplied U.S. fighting forces in the far reaches of the western Pacific. A result of that lack of activity meant that there was not the same need to convoy in the Pacific that existed in the Atlantic.

Germany started small and finished big. She began with only 57 U-boats but commissioned 1,096 more during the war.[2] The Battle of the Atlantic focused on the efforts of U-boats to stop trans-Atlantic commerce that was necessary to keep Great Britain in the war and to build up forces in the British Isles for an invasion of occupied France. Germany almost succeeded but was finally beaten in early 1943 by a huge ASW effort primarily by Great Britain and Canada, with assistance by the United States.

PREFACE

The question of how to measure "effectiveness" of a submarine campaign is not simple. What operations are considered in making a judgment?

Since the submarine is primarily a weapons system the true test is how effective it is in war. But the equation is complicated. It involves both the submarine, designed to capture or sink ships, and the antisubmarine warfare (ASW) efforts used by the defenders. A relatively simple submarine might fare very well against limited opposition, but fail when subjected to an intense ASW campaign.

Is the submarine in question a failure if the submarine campaign ultimately fails? Or must we measure the extent of the ASW campaign necessary to defeat it in order to evaluate the subject submarine class's effectiveness? The author has judged the German U-boat campaign as very effective even though it was ultimately defeated, whereas the American submarine campaign destroyed Japan's merchant marine.

The effectiveness of a submarine in wartime depends upon a number of elements. They include the basic design, the supporting infrastructure of the host nation including submarine tenders (depot ships) and submarine bases, the ASW environment in which it operates, the selection and training of the submarine crew, "work up" practices of the submarine operating authority and other factors including the strategy selected and submarine operational practices. The list goes on and on.

In a boyhood game of "guns" the winner is usually the boy with the loudest voice who first shouts "*Bang, bang, you're dead, I won*". Submarine effectiveness is not so easily decided. The devil is in the details and they must be laid out and examined carefully to truly decide if the submarine weapon system in question was effective or not, and why. That at least is the author's excuse for including so many details about the conflicts in which submarines were employed.

Chapter One—German U-boats

Germany began World War II with its attack on Poland on September 1, 1939. At the time Rear Admiral Karl Doenitz was in command of the U-boat arm. He continued in that command throughout the war, rising in rank and functional naval authority before finally being named as Hitler's successor as head of state in 1945. Interestingly Karl Doenitz had first conceived the tactics and strategy of his WW II U-boat campaign while sitting behind barbed wire in a British prisoner-of-war camp in 1918 and 1919.

At the end of September 1918 then Lieutenant Doenitz set out on a patrol in the Mediterranean Sea in command of UB-68. He had discussed possible tactics to deal with the Allied convoy system with Lieutenant-Commander Steinbauer, a *Pour le Merite* award holder, and they had agreed to conduct coordinated surface attacks at night at sea on convoys. The other U-boat could not sail on time because of repair status. Doenitz proceeded on his own after Steinbauer failed to show up at their planned rendezvous about 50 nm SE of Cape Passero in Sicily. He made several solitary attacks on a convoy proceeding from Suez to Malta but was forced to the surface and had to scuttle his boat. He was taken prisoner and sent to a prison camp.[3]

Germany had announced that an unrestricted submarine campaign would begin on 1 February 1917. Its strategic goal was to force Great Britain to the negotiating table. U-boats were already effectively conducting an unrestricted campaign in the Mediterranean Sea. The United States complained about sinking without warning of ships in the Atlantic, and these complaints caused the German Admiralty to modify its Atlantic U-boat operating rules from time to time. In the Med, where few U.S. flagged ships sailed, they didn't worry because there were no U.S. complaints.

Shipping losses mounted in early 1917: in February 520,412 tons; in March 564,497 tons; and in April 860,497 tons. In April 1917 Great

Britain had only six weeks grain supply in the British Isles. German authorities believed that their rate of sinking's would be so great that by the fall of 1917 Great Britain would be forced to enter negotiations with the Central Powers. That would end the British blockade which was doing so much economic damage to Germany. With Great Britain out of the war, Germany could deal with the French.

Great Britain had employed convoy to transport the British Expeditionary Force to France at the start of the war. Convoy was also used for troop transport all during the war, and for the vital cross-Channel coal trade to France. However it had not been implemented for ordinary merchant traffic. Faulty operations analysis led the Royal Navy to believe that a convoy was much more likely to be sighted by a submarine than an individual ship—untrue, and that grouping many ships together would merely increase the number of ships an individual submarine could sink at one time—also unlikely, since armed escorts would immediately drive a surfaced submarine down or keep it submerged while the bulk of the convoy steamed away. A further note—British submarines had stopped the Swedish iron ore trade with Germany in the Baltic Sea during 1915. However, the following year the German Navy instituted strict convoy procedures and in 1916 British submarines were unable to interfere with iron ore shipping.

The Admiralty finally agreed to run some test merchant convoys in May 1917 from Gibraltar to the British Isles and from Norfolk, Virginia to the British Isles. Based upon their successes convoy was instituted widely in August of 1917. Ship losses rapidly dropped. Great Britain no longer faced being forced into peace negotiations on German terms.

Convoys reduced German U-boat successes in the Mediterranean Sea as they had in the Atlantic. That was the situation that Doenitz and his fellow U-boat commanding officer were trying to deal with. Before convoy was instituted, they could stop, and search a merchant ship and either release or sink it depending upon its cargo, without any undue concern. However with convoy procedures in effect, surface gun or torpedo attacks were usually ruled out by the presence of armed escort ships. Submerged torpedo attacks were still possible but the rapid reaction of escorts armed with depth charges usually prevented a second attack. While the submerged U-boat was held down, the convoy proceeded over the horizon. Losses from convoys fell dramatically.

Prelude

Germany was precluded from having submarines in her Navy following WWI. That did not stop German leaders, both military and civilian, from pursuing rearmament secretly—well before Adolph Hitler came to power.[4] A cover engineering firm was set up in Holland to design and build submarines, its efforts funded by German shipbuilding firms. An advanced electric drive torpedo (G7e) was designed and tested successfully in Sweden during the 1920s. Once complete, its plans were set aside until political events would allow its production in Germany.[5]

U-boat development in Germany went through two distinct phases. The first was under the Weimar Republic from 1919 until 1933. This development was secret and conducted under cover. The second phase began with Adolph Hitler's election to power, and the German Reichstag's subsequent vote to allow him to exercise dictatorial powers. On 16 March 1934 Dr. Goebbels, head of the Nazi Propaganda Ministry, announced a new law authorizing universal military conscription—in violation of the Versailles Treaty. Full scale modernization of the German armed forces began and continued unchecked until 1 September 1939 when Germany attacked Poland and World War II began.

In 1932 the German Admiralty began preparations for U-boat construction in German shipyards, drawing on the experience gained through the efforts of its Netherlands-based "cover" engineering firm. In October 1934 the first class of officer training began at the *U-Bootabwerhrschule* (U-boat Defense School). The ASW title was a cover for training officers in U-boat operations.[6]

In July 1935 Capt. Doenitz, by this time the commanding officer of the cruiser *Emden*, was told by the chief of naval staff, Admiral Raeder, that he had been chosen to command the re-instituted U-boat Arm.

In early 1935 while Anglo-German negotiations over a treaty governing naval warship construction were in progress, Germany laid down the keels for several new submarines. They were Type II U-boats of only 250 tons displacement. By September 1935 the German U-boat Inventory totaled six boats, U-1 though U-6, all Type IIA. Their operators referred to them as "canoes" or "ducks" because of their small size, but they would serve to train a new generation of U-boat officers and crewmen who would be the equal of their WW I predecessors.

3

A total of 50 Type II U-boats were built in what today we would call four different "flights", by three separate German shipbuilding firms. Two were intended for sale to Yugoslavia, but were acquired by the German Navy instead. Six Type II A (U-1—U-6) were built *by Deutsche Werk* at Kiel. Twenty Type II B were built by *Germaniawerft* (18) at Kiel and *Flenderwerft* (2) at Lubeck. Eight Type II C were built by *Deutsche Werk* at Kiel, as well as another sixteen Type II D U-boats. The variations had additional bunkers (diesel oil tanks) to provide greater range and endurance. They ranged in length from 134' to 144', and in submerged displacement from 303 tons to 364 tons. Each had three torpedo tubes forward, a crew of 25 and speeds of 13 kts. surf./7 kts. submerged.

On 28 September 1935, U-I through U-9, became the *Weddigen* Flotilla with *Kapitan zur See* (Captain) Doenitz as Flotilla Commander. By the end of the year there were a total of 18 U-boats in the flotilla. Doenitz was given a free hand in the organization and training of the new U-boat officers and crews.[7] Doenitz's concept of future U-boat operations included the following points:[8]

Wolf pack vice solitary operations

Radio guidance from headquarters

Aircraft scouting and support

Primary target is UK ship tonnage

Night surface attacks to offset British Asdic capability

It is clear from these elements that Doenitz envisioned another unrestricted U-boat campaign as a method to defeat Great Britain. Intensive training began 1 October 1935. Doenitz's fundamental training principles included:[9]

U-boat is an offensive weapon

Training will be realistic to the extent possible

Torpedo attack range will be 600 yards, whether surfaced or submerged since this short range eliminates fire control errors and reduces the value of target evasive action

Concentration of a wolf pack against a convoy is key to success of the scheme

Recognition that U-boats were not suitable reconnaissance platforms, but that aircraft reconnaissance support would be required

Training would last six months before a U-boat and its commanding officer and crew were considered ready for combat

Type II boats were strictly "coastal" submarines which were capable of patrols in the Baltic Sea or close-in North Sea, but were not considered seaworthy for North Atlantic employment. Their principal purposes were two-fold: training a new generation of U-boat officers and crew; and working out convoy attack procedures. They were quite adequate for these purposes. Spreading construction around helped the recovering German industrial base and developed U-boat construction skills that had gone dormant in 1918.

A larger type U-boat was also built. It was Type IA with a displacement of 862/938 tons, 238 feet long, carried six torpedo tubes and a four-inch gun, plus a crew of 43. It could make 18/8 kts. The design was based on that of the Turkish submarine *Gur*, developed in Holland by the cover engineering firm IvS. *Gur* was laid down in Cadiz, Spain in 1930 at the *Echevarrieta y Larringa* yard, launched in 1932 and delivered to Turkey in January 1935. Two Type IA (U-25 and U-26) were built by *AG Weser* in Bremen, bringing a fourth German shipyard back into the U-boat building trade. However the type IA was found to be unsatisfactory.

A slightly smaller version, the Type VII emerged as the standard U-boat of early WW II days. It came in several variations, A though C. The Type VII C carried out much of the U-boat activity of the war. The Type VII C was 769/871 tons displacement, 220 feet long, had five torpedo tubes (four forward and one in the stern), and carried a total load of 14 torpedoes. It had a crew of 44 men, could make a maximum speed of 17 knots on the surface and about 8 knots submerged. With twin diesel engines it had fuel for a range of 6,500 nautical miles. The Type VII C was optimized for Doenitz's night surface attack tactic against convoys. It had a diving time of only 20 seconds.[10]

The Type VII U-boat was designed for combat and not comfort. It lacked a berth or bunk for each crewman, thus requiring "hot bunking" as a matter of course. It lacked air-conditioning and showers. It had no radar or ECM at the start of the war. It was almost a pure fighting machine, designed to sink the ships that Great Britain required to sustain its population and industry. It only required 500,000 man-hours of labor to construct. That compared quite favorably with the 300,000 MH required for building a Tiger tank.[11]

Finally a large Type IX was designed and built by *AG Weser* at Bremen during 1938 and 1939. A total of eight Type IX As were constructed. They displaced 1032/1153 tons, were 251' long, had two diesels, and could make 18.25/7.75 kts surfaced/submerged. They carried 154 tons of fuel which gave them a range of 8100 nm/65 nm at 12/4 kts surfaced/submerged. Their armament included six TT (4 forward and 2 aft). They could carry either 22 torpedoes or a combination of six torpedoes and 42 mines.[12] Their complement was 48 men. They were equipped with a significant gun armament: 1 x 4.1" gun, 1 x 37 mm AA, and 1 x 20 mm AA.

The Type VII C reflected Doenitz's ideas about how to deal with the convoy strategy that had defeated the German unrestricted submarine campaign of WW I and thus had, at least in German eyes', cost them the war. Doenitz went back to Admiral Tirpitz' vision of small fast torpedo boats conducting night torpedo attacks on enemy warships. Doenitz reasoned that coordinated night attacks by U-boats operating on the surface would be able to deal with convoy escorts. The U-boat superstructure was deliberately designed low to the water. That meant that a U-boat lookout's binoculars were the highest point on the U-boat, rendering U-boats very difficult to detect visually. Surface warships had masts and funnels that extended much higher and rendered them more visible even at night. Doenitz felt that the confusion generated by torpedo explosions at night would hinder escort activity. Night surfaced torpedo attacks would also offset the British Asdic capability, since Asdic (active sonar) was incapable of detecting a U-boat operating on the surface (one must remember that radar did not exist at this time). The concentration of a number of U-boats against a convoy would thus allow them to sink a large number of ships instead of only one or two.[13]

Doenitz did not gain popularity as strategic submarine thinker; as had General Gulio Douhet of Italy, and Lord Trenchard of Great Britain, and General Billy Mitchell of the United States with respect to strategic bombing. However none of the later gentlemen had an opportunity to put their conceptual ideas into practice in warfare. Doenitz did! He not only successfully conceptualized how to defeat the convoy system as it existed at that time, but prepared and trained his U-boat Commanders to carry out his ideas. The Type VII U-boat was optimized for coordinated night surface torpedo attacks against merchant ships in convoy.

By reducing the visual detectability of the U-boat, Doenitz was getting inside the OODA loop of his opponents. OODA stands for Observation-Orientation-Decision-Action. It is based upon sensor Observation of the situation, rapid Orientation of the observer to the situation, a Decision as to what to do about the situation, and finally—Action to exploit the situation.

Colonel John Boyd, USAF originated the OODA Loop theory in the 1950s-1960s, based upon his conclusions about the successes American F-86 Sabre jet fighters had against Soviet MiG 15s during the Korean War. The Sabre had a clear bubble canopy as opposed to the metal framed and reinforced MiG canopy. The bubble canopy gave American fighter pilots unequaled visibility as opposed to the less clear view that MiG pilots enjoyed. That better visibility gave the U.S. pilots additional time to observe their opponents in aerial combat, to decide on their next move, and to carry it out while the Soviet pilot was still trying to come to grips with the situation, but always lagging the problem.

By insisting on a low superstructure for the Type VII U-boat Doenitz was giving the U-boat Commander a distinct time advantage in sighting his target before the target could possibly sight the U-boat. That thought is included in the U-boat Commander's Handbook issued to all U-boat commanding officers, "the submarine must be guided by the motto "He who sees first has won.""[14]

Although Doenitz had never heard of OODA he grasped the essential principle back in 1918. Using low visibility, relatively high speed U-boats on the surface at night could penetrate escort screens and attack convoyed ships with relative impunity. Doenitz set about to train his new force in these tactics. Eventually he would be defeated but it would take the development and deployment of two new technologies that did not exist at that time: they were very long range aircraft, and airborne radar able to detect surfaced submarines at night.

Doenitz also understood that the U-boat by itself, or even as part of a long scouting line abreast on the surface at suitable intervals, was not an effective search platform. The U-boat superstructure was optimized for reducing its detectability by the convoy escorts' lookouts while maximizing the capability of the U-boat's lookouts to detect a convoy. However its visible horizon was quite limited. He knew that aircraft represented a much better search platform.

Another possibility existed—communications intelligence (comint). The German navy studied the lessons of WW I and became aware of the important role that Room 40 had played during the war. Room 40 of British Naval Intelligence was responsible for collecting communications intelligence on German naval operations. It did an outstanding job, and was able to provide British admirals with early warning on German warship sorties into the North Sea. It also collected all the radio information provided by U-boats and integrated them into an operational plot of U-boats at sea. After the convoy system was adopted in 1917 the submarine operational plot was able to provide early warning information to convoy commodores who could then move their convoys to evade U-boat concentrations. The German Navy established the *B-Dienst* service in the 1920s.[15] Its task was to break enemy communications and provide similar operational information to German naval units.

After Germany began construction of U-boats in 1934 in violation of the Versailles Treaty, the Royal Navy took note and back-fitted Acasta and Crusader class destroyers with Asdic. It also back-fitted Asdic into older V and W class destroyers. By September 1939 the Royal Navy had over one hundred destroyers with Asdic, as well as twenty trawlers. Additional Asdic sets were manufactured for installation as required. Royal Navy trials had shown that a fleet screen of Asdic-equipped destroyers had a 0.7 probability of detecting a submerged submarine as it tried to penetrate the screen, and a 0.5 probability of successful attack with depth charges. The Royal Navy considered that the U-boat "threat" was well in hand and was more concerned with the threat presented by surface raiders.[16] It had no idea that Doenitz had developed a U-boat tactic that would offset Asdic. In 1937 the Admiralty advised the Shipping Defense Advisory Committee that the U-boat would not be capable of confronting the Royal Navy with the problems it had faced in 1917.[17] It is significant that between 1918 and 1939 the Royal Navy ran no convoy protection exercises, a mark of how minor it considered the U-boat threat.[18]

In 1935 Adolph Hitler renounced the Versailles Treaty. Subsequently Great Britain and Germany concluded an Anglo-German Naval Agreement which allowed Germany to build up to 35% of British surface warship tonnage, and up to 45% of British submarine tonnage. There was a provision for Germany to build up to 100% of submarine tonnage should a future situation warrant it. In 1936 Germany signed the London Naval Agreement, which forbade sinking merchant ships without placing their crews in a place of safety—essentially ruling out unrestricted submarine warfare.[19]

In 1937 the Royal Navy established an Operational Intelligence Center. Radio bearings were plotted during the Spanish Civil War, and Italian submarines were tracked as they operated in support of Franco's forces. By 1939 there were six HF and four MF radio direction finding stations in the UK, three MF stations in the Med and two MF stations in the Far East.[20]

Admiral Hezlet argues that Great Britain knew that Germany had resumed U-boat construction but could not stop it short of war, which it was not prepared to undertake. Thus it agreed to release Germany from its former treaty obligations in the hope that Germany would abide by the new agreement. Hezlet also thinks that Adolph Hitler probably intended to do so—letting Great Britain control the seas while inferring that Great Britain would allow Hitler a "free hand" in Europe.[21]

The author would offer another thought: that the ruling classes in England were sympathetic with Germany and considered the Versailles Treaty too harsh and that feeling played into the equation. Perhaps the most striking example of this feeling was the unconstitutional interference of King Edward VIII in the re-occupation of the Rhineland by Germany in 1936 in violation of the Versailles Treaty. Edward let it be known to the German ambassador in London that Great Britain would not support any French military reaction, thereby undercutting the French government.[22] A short, sharp French military action to throw German forces out of the Rhineland, which Hitler's generals greatly feared, would probably have brought about Hitler's political downfall, changing the future of Europe.

In 1933 the *B-Dienst* section was strengthened, and again in 1935 during the Abyssinian crisis. The Royal Navy had been at peace for some 17 years and its radio traffic was largely unclassified, therefore few cipher messages were required. RN communications were incapable of dealing with the large volume of classified radio traffic generated by events involving the Italian venture into Abyssinia. A large RN force concentrated at Aden in the Gulf. Many messages flew back and forth in an administrative cipher and many encryption mistakes were made. By 1938 *B-Dienst* had reconstructed most of the RN administrative cipher without the British being aware. It also had broken the Merchant Marine code which would be used to control and route convoys.[23] It could not break re-ciphered messages used for operational traffic. However, by the time war broke out in late 1939 the *B-Dienst* service was well trained and ready for action.[24]

On 1 July 1936 a second U-boat flotilla was formed, "Flotilla *Hundius*", named for another notable WW I U-boat commanding officer. Doenitz took command of both flotillas under the title *Fuhrer der U-Boote*

(FdU). U-boat strength began to grow slowly. Doenitz was convinced that Germany and Great Britain would go to war eventually, and he had a target of 300 U-boats in mind to assure the success of his planned unrestricted submarine campaign. In January 1939 the German Navy adopted "Plan Z", calling for a number of large surface warships including an aircraft carrier. Plan Z included provisions for 250 U-boats, but it also assumed that there would be no war with the UK for a period of 5-10 years.[25]

During autumn of 1937 "wolf pack" tactics were first used in a large scale exercise. Doenitz controlled his U-boats from a submarine depot ship at Kiel, and directed their operations in the Baltic Sea by wireless.

The standard torpedoes that the new U-boat Arm would depend upon were the G7a (steam) (500 kg warhead) and G7e (electric) (380 kg warhead) torpedoes. Both warheads used torpex as the explosive charge. The G7a was propelled by a small steam turbine. It emitted a bubble wake that could be seen on the surface of the water in day time. The G7e was powered by rechargeable electric batteries and gave no sign of its passage through the water. A U-boat commanding officer would usually fire the G7e in daylight to avoid alerting a target ship or escorts, and use the G7a at night when it was much less likely to be spotted. Although both torpedoes were considered reliable, there were some signs of potential problems. Max Valentiner, a leading U-boat ace of WW I warned in 1937 of potential depth keeping problems dating back to the last war. Reports from the U-boats operating covertly off Spain also indicated possible problems. As a result the Torpedo Trials Command ran some tests. A fourteen day test from a torpedo boat indicated a serious depth problem. Destroyer trials followed. Her CO reported depth errors of up to 4 meters (13.2 feet).[26] There is no record that any torpedo modifications took place to correct the problems.

The U-boat Arm used an analogue fire control computer called a *Vorhaltrechner*, similar to a U.S. Torpedo Data Computer (TDC). It solved for gyro angle to insert into torpedoes in their tubes, based upon inputs of target bearing, range, course and speed.[27]

From 1933 to 1939 Adm. Raeder argued for an independent naval air service. However, *Luftwaffe* Commander Goering's attitude was unequivocal and to the point: "Anything that flies belongs to me." Goering was the number two man in the Nazi hierarchy and made full use of his position. Finally on 27 January 1939 there was a commanders in chief agreement. Aircraft would be detailed to the navy only when required for reconnaissance purposes or to participate in a tactical air battle in support of a fleet engagement. While it would seem that Raeder and Doenitz had made their point, the reality was that Goering controlled the number of aircraft that would be assigned for naval air reconnaissance—and they would never be enough to fill Doenitz's needs for adequate U-boat reconnaissance support.[28]

On April 26, 1939 Hitler repudiated the Anglo-German Naval Agreement, following the occupation of Czechoslovakia. As a result the British government issued a guarantee to Poland that Great Britain would come to Poland's defense if she were attacked by Germany.

In May 1939 a large scale German naval exercise took place at sea, in the Atlantic west of the Bay of Biscay and the Iberian Peninsula. The principal purpose of the cruise was to practice wolf pack tactics. Fifteen Type VII and IX U-boats were involved, along with an oiler, a freighter, a submarine tender and a command ship. The surface group of ships provided a "convoy" and "escorts". U-boats were strung out in five groups of three U-boats each over a patrol line of several hundred miles. Once a sighting was made, the wolf pack converged on the 'convoy". Attacks were conducted over a forty-eight hour period from May 12 to May 14.[29] Although everything did not go smoothly and many errors were noted, Doenitz was well pleased with the overall results. The exercise had validated his theory about how to deal with convoys.

He then tried unsuccessfully to get Adm. Raeder to increase the number of Type VII U-boats being constructed. However, the German Navy Admiralty (OKM) was focused on Plan Z to build up German surface forces, and dismissed the possible effectiveness of a submarine campaign in the face of British ASW defenses. Doenitz tried to end run the OKM by asking Raeder to place his views before Hitler. The reply he got back via Raeder was that in no case would there be war with Great Britain.

In July 1939 another large-scale exercise took place in the Baltic. This exercise was personally observed by Admiral Raeder, the German Navy Commander-in-Chief. The tactics developed were incorporated into "The Submarine Commander's Handbook", a secret publication. Curiously an unclassified German January 1939 publication *"Die U-bootwaffe"* discussed night surface attacks.[30]

Captain John F. O'Connell, USN (RET.)

World War Two begins
September 1939

The discussion about the German U-boat Arm during World War Two will basically follow Admiral Karl Doenitz's *Memoirs* in its look at various phases of the war and the corresponding U-boat campaigns. The first phase started in late August 1939 as Doenitz's U-boats deployed to their war patrol areas in anticipation of the attack on Poland scheduled for 1 September. It ended in March 1940 as Germany prepared for the invasion of Norway.

Having successfully occupied the Rhineland in 1936 in violation of the Versailles Treaty, swallowed Austria in the March 1938 *Anschluss*, and out maneuvered France and Great Britain later in 1938 to seize part of Czechoslovakia, Hitler was riding high.

However the 15 March 1939 seizure of the remainder of Czechoslovakia crossed a line. Both Great Britain and France then offered guarantees to Poland that they would come to her aid if Germany attacked her. As a diplomatic gesture it was dramatic, although the practical impact was very little. Great Britain had no common border with Germany, and France had given up the significant threat of inflicting a two-front war on Germany when she pusillanimously agreed to Germany dismembering her ally Czechoslovakia.

In any event Adolph Hitler was determined to invade Poland, and the guarantees by Great Britain and France figured very little in his calculus. He set the invasion date for late August 1939 but withheld his order at the last minute when Mussolini indicated that Italy would not enter the fray on Germany's side unless Germany was attacked. The late August secret pact between Germany and the USSR, agreeing to a mutual dismemberment of Poland, sealed Poland's fate. On 1 September 1939 German forces rolled across the border and the invasion began. World War Two was underway.

Doenitz was appalled by the turn of events. Earlier that year Adolph Hitler had assured him through Admiral Raeder that there would be no war with Great Britain. On 3 September 1939 in fulfillment of their guarantees to Poland, Great Britain and France declared war on Germany. Doenitz had calculated that about 300 U-boats would be required to wage a successful unrestricted submarine campaign against British shipping—and he had only 56. Of those 56 in commission some 46 were ready for action, a remarkably high percentage. However, of the 46 only 22 were suitable for service in the Atlantic Ocean. The rest were 250 ton boats, suitable only for North Sea operations. Using the tried and true one-third patrol ratio, that meant that only seven U-boats would be on patrol in the Atlantic at any one time, hardly enough to accomplish anything significant.[31]

As the story continues it will deal with actions by the U-boat Arm to attack British trade, and the counter-actions undertaken by the British to protect their ship-borne imports. The unrestricted U-boat campaign of 1917 had clearly demonstrated how vulnerable Great Britain was to submarine attack.

Phase One
Initial U-boat Operations

3 September 1939-28 February 1940

The "Phony War", at least on land and in the air. Terrible winter weather prevents a planned armored assault on France and the Low Countries during the fall and winter. At sea the RN discovers that Asdic is not quite what it was cracked up to be, with sinking of aircraft carrier HMS Courageous, and an unsuccessful attack on aircraft carrier Ark Royal. Gunther Prien, in U-47, penetrates the defenses of Scapa Flow and sinks battleship HMS Royal Oak. The British Admiralty institutes convoy operations. SS Athenia, a passenger liner, is attacked and sunk without warning by a U-boat.

At 1330 on 3 September 1939 German Naval Headquarters sent out the signal "Commence hostilities against Britain forthwith". The U-boat Arm began operations in accordance with the Prize Ordinance. That meant that suspect ships had to be stopped and inspected. They could be captured or sunk if carrying contraband—but only the later if the target ship's crew could be placed in a place of safety. These were the terms fixed during the 1936 London Submarine Agreement.

The Royal Navy had learned something about the usefulness of airpower in protecting shipping during WW I, and immediately assigned several aircraft carrier battle groups to ASW duties west of the British Isles. Their aircraft could undertake daytime patrols designed to force submarines off the surface where they were less likely to spot possible targets. Doenitz had assigned several U-boats to the same areas. On 17 September 1939 U-39 fired three torpedoes, equipped with magnetic exploders, at aircraft carrier HMS Ark Royal. The exploders malfunctioned and went off prematurely, startling but not harming Ark Royal. The explosion points marked the U-boat firing position and Ark Royal's destroyer escorts rapidly closed, picked up U-39 on Asdic, and depth charged her. She was forced to the surface and scuttled herself, with her crew being recovered by the destroyers.

Two days later U-29 fired three similar torpedoes at aircraft carrier HMS Courageous. These performed correctly, two hit her and exploded and sank her with a loss of 518 crewmen. Quite obviously Asdic was not performing up to RN expectations. As noted earlier RN fleet trials had predicted a 0.7 probability of detection of a submerged submarine attempting to penetrate an ASW screen. In practical terms that meant that seven out of every ten submarines attempting to penetrate a destroyer screen to get within torpedo firing range would be detected before they reached that point. Yet both U-boats had fired, undetected.[32] Either the ASW screens were not being properly used or actual Asdic detection probability was much lower than predicted. In any event the Royal Navy rapidly withdrew its aircraft carriers from ASW duties, having concluded that the aircraft carrier/U-boat exchange ratio to date was highly unsatisfactory.[33]

Actually, during the first year of the war, from 3 September 1939 through 3 September 1940, there were twenty-five Asdic detections of U-boats. Of these twenty-five detections, fifteen were prosecuted to the sinking or scuttling of the U-boat (60%). The other ten detections were prosecuted but the U-boats escaped albeit with occasional serious damage (40%). Royal Navy pre-war predictions of Asdic effectiveness were not too far off base. However, Doenitz's tactic of night surfaced attacks took the U-boats outside the Asdic "box", thus rendering it irrelevant in the case of convoys. It would take long range aircraft equipped with radar to expand the sensor detection "box" to drastically limit their effectiveness.

The Prize Ordinance (London Submarine Agreement of 1936) assumed that merchant ships would not be armed, and would not report submarines via radio if they were stopped, and in any case would not try to ram a submarine as it lay somewhat helpless on the surface while trying to ascertain whether the stopped merchant ship's cargo was contraband or not. From the German point of view several alarming incidents occurred not long after the war started. British-flagged merchant ships were signaling

"SSS" on the radio followed by their latitude and longitude when stopped by a U-boat. It turned out that a British Admiralty Instruction of 1938, Appendix 2 prescribed that action if a U-boat were encountered, thus alerting ASW forces to the incident and position. On 6 September 1939 a merchant ship fired on a U-boat when challenged. On 1 October 1939 the British Admiralty directed British merchant ships to ram U-boats that had stopped them.[34]

In German eyes, under International Law, these actions were not permitted to civilian ships. They automatically transformed the otherwise civilian merchant ship into a warship, and enemy warships could be sunk without warning under International Law. However at this early stage of hostilities Adolph Hitler was concerned over fine tuning his relationships with Great Britain and France. Yes, they had each declared war on Germany in line with their pledges to Poland, but how serious were they about pursuing the war? Great Britain had launched an air attack on German warships in harbor in Wilhelmshaven on 4 September but had accomplished little damage.[35] The French refrained from air attacks lest their own cities be bombed. The French Army sent nine divisions a few miles into German territory but then they basically sat there for a week or so and then withdrew back to the protection of the Maginot Line, giving Hitler an impression that their activities were cosmetic rather than serious. As a veteran of vicious trench warfare during WW I, Hitler was a capable judge of real ground fighting. Hitler hoped that Great Britain and France, having demonstrated their "support" for hapless Poland, would not seriously conduct warlike activities, and leave him free to pursue hegemony in Eastern Europe.

On September 3rd the German Admiralty advised that from 1700 hours that date France regards herself as at war with Germany, but that German forces would take no action except in self-defense. On September 6th U-boats were advised not to stop any French ship lest they generate an "incident".[36]

On September 4th there had been a serious "incident" involving a British passenger liner. U-30 sighted a darkened, high speed ship after sunset northwest of Ireland. She was running without navigation lights (mast head and side lights) and was zigzagging, not normal behavior for an innocent passenger liner. The U-boat commanding officer assumed that she was a former passenger liner converted to auxiliary cruiser duties, and thus a warship liable to be sunk on sight. He torpedoed her, and she sank the following morning. She was SS Athenia, and unfortunately was a real passenger liner carrying over 1,100 passengers enroute Canada including 311 Americans. One hundred and eighteen passengers perished. The U-boat commanding officer became aware of his target's identity when she began to broadcast distress signals. For some reason he chose not to advise U-boat headquarters of the situation. His actions were defensible up to that point. However he had inadvertently violated the Fuehrer's direct orders to leave passenger ships untouched.[37] Doenitz's headquarters suspected that U-30 was responsible since the sinking occurred in her assigned patrol area but apparently did not take action to query the CO or to advise higher authority. The Nazi propaganda machine went into its attack mode and accused the Royal Navy of having torpedoed Athenia to create an "incident". The British knew full well that Athenia had been torpedoed by a U-boat and concluded that this marked a return to the unrestricted submarine warfare of 1917-1918, exactly what Hitler was trying to avoid at this stage of events. For the British, the sinking of Athenia confirmed their worst fears of another unrestricted U-boat campaign.

From 26 August 1939 all British merchant ships came under the control of the Admiralty for routing. Routing was exercised through the Director of the Trade Division and subordinate Naval Control Service officers stationed around the world in ports frequented by British ships.[38] However, Great Britain was not the only player leading the problem. Several weeks before the German invasion of Poland on 1 September 1939, U-boats sailed from German ports enroute their assigned wartime patrol areas west of the British Isles. Both sides were prepared for the resumption of submarine warfare, although the U-boat Arm was initially constrained and not allowed to conduct unrestricted submarine warfare. On the 7th of September 1939 some 21 U-boats were deployed in the Atlantic from the north end of the Irish Sea down to Gibraltar. However, by the 18th only eleven were still on patrol, the remainder having departed for home and refit for further operations. The inexorable one-third patrol ratio was beginning to operate.[39]

Another constraint on the number of U-boats that could be at sea was a Doenitz-imposed requirement that four months must lapse between commissioning of a new U-boat until it embarked on its first operational patrol. The four month period allowed for intense training of the crew and necessary repair work that became apparent.[40]

At the outset of WW I U-boats had attempted a preemptive strike at the main Royal Navy anchorage at Scapa Flow in northern Scotland. The action proved futile. Several U-boats went missing and no damage was done to the Royal Navy. Admiral Doenitz had a similar venture in mind in 1939. He called in Gunther Prien, an up and coming U-boat Commander, and asked him to take a look at preliminary plans for a strike at Scapa Flow. After careful review, Prien deemed it possible and accepted the mission. On 12 October 1939 Prien, in U-47, penetrated the Scapa Flow anchorage and sank battleship HMS Royal Oak, much to the consternation of the Admiralty.[41] Slightly less than one month earlier a U-boat had sunk an aircraft carrier at sea, protected by ASW escorts equipped with Asdic. Now, another U-boat had penetrated a main harbor and sunk a battleship.

In November HMS Belfast, a cruiser, was mined in the Firth of Forth, victim to a U-boat-laid magnetic mine. The mine broke her back, and Belfast was out of service for a year. In early December battleship HMS Nelson was seriously damaged at Loch Ewe by a similar mine laid some five weeks earlier by a U-boat.[42] These events pointed to the vulnerability of Royal Navy fleet bases, as well as to the danger presented by U-boat mining operations.

Month	Number of ships sunk	Gross Register Tonnage sunk
September	41	153,879
October	27	134,879
November	21	51,589
December	25	80,881

In addition to sinking's and damage to major fleet units, U-boats had sunk some 114 ships of 421,228 gross register tons during the months from September through December. The table displays the toll by month. It should be noted that of the total 114 ships sunk; only twelve were sunk while in convoy. The remainder, 89 percent, were either sunk as independent sailers or as convoy stragglers. Convoy was not only in effect but was working as designed at this time. By the end of 1939 some 5,756 ships had sailed in convoy with only four lost to U-boats.[43]

As 1939 came to an end the U-boat Arm punctuated it with the torpedoing of battleship HMS Barham on 28 December. She was out of action for three months as a result.[44] She had been accompanied by five destroyers although it is not clear whether they were screening her at the time she was torpedoed near the Butt of Lewis. During 1939 fourteen U-boats were lost.

1940

In 1940 U-boat attacks on merchant ships continued. In January, 40 ships of 111,263 tons were lost. In February, 45 ships of 169,566 tons went down. Most of the ships sunk were independent sailers. In March the number fell to only 23 ships of 62,781 tons, and in April only 7 ships of 32,467 tons. There were two reasons; first the winter of 1939-1940 was very severe; and secondly U-boats were being repositioned for Hitler's invasion of Norway.[45]

By April 1940 some 28 U-boats were lurking from the vicinity of Narvik in northern Norway over westward to the Shetland Islands, and down in the Skagerrak and the eastern approaches to the English Channel. On 15 April HMS Fearless and HMS Brazen sank U-49 and recovered a plot of all the U-boat patrol stations.[46]

Phase Two
The Norwegian Campaign

March-May 1940

Germany invades Denmark and Norway in a surprise move. British and French forces move into Norway but suffer badly from Luftwaffe attacks. The threat of Italian moves to enter the war draws off RN resources. Finally the German panzer offensive against France and the Low Countries in May 1940 forces the withdrawal of Allied forces from Norway. The U-boat Arm is shown at its worst due to torpedo failures.

Much of the high quality iron ore used by Germany came from Sweden. It was mined in the north near Gallivare, moved by rail to the port of Lulea, and shipped down the Baltic Sea to northern Germany. However the Baltic Sea iced up in winter and sea transport from northern Sweden was no longer possible. During those months the ore traveled overland by rail into Norway, was loaded in ships there, and was carried down the Inner Leads of Norway, through the Skagerrak and Kattegat passages and on to Germany. Great Britain viewed the ore as war material contraband. In early 1940 Great Britain was intent on interfering with that trade. A number of schemes were postulated. One involved violating Norwegian neutrality by mining the Inner Leads. Another more complicated scenario involved landing troops at Narvik in northern Norway, and pressing on across northern Sweden to assist the Finns in their heroic and but doomed fight against the Soviet invasion, and incidentally seizing control of the iron ore mines while enroute. While the British Cabinet and the overall Defense Staff were debating the topic and analyzing each proposal, the Germans became aware of the threat to their vital raw material supply and decided to take preemptive action.

On 4 March 1940 the U-boat Headquarters Command received direction from the naval GHQ to prepare for action in support of a projected invasion of Norway and Denmark. The invasions were intended to counter projected Allied forces moving into northern Norway. German landings were planned for Narvik, Trondheim, Bergen, Egersund, Kristiansand, and Oslo.

A total of twelve ocean-going U-boats, thirteen "Ducks", and six U-boats from the Submarine School were alerted for operations. It was an all-out effort. U-boats were to be stationed off various ports: Narvik (4), Trondheim (2), Bergen (5), and Stavanger (2). In addition small groups of U-boats were stationed as follows: Northeast of the Shetland Islands (5), East of the Orkney Islands (3), off Stavanger (2), and west of the Naze (3). Sealed orders were provided to the U-boat commanding officers.

On 14 March radio interceptions indicated the presence of an unusually large number of British submarines in the North Sea. This was taken as confirmation of forthcoming Allied intervention in Norway. On 2 April the German Naval High Command notified Doenitz's headquarters that 9 April would mark the start of invasion operations. On 6 April all CO's were notified to open their sealed orders and to carry out their instructions.

On 9 April 1940 the German invasions of Denmark and Norway began. Denmark was easily overrun, Norway less so. The Norwegian invasion involved troops transported in innocent merchant ships, which sailed into Norwegian ports and disgorged their cargo to the surprise and dismay of Norwegian authorities. In addition, German surface warships forced their way past Norwegian port defenses, losing some of their number to stout Norwegian coastal defenses. Finally, German airborne forces descended and seized key airfields, so that additional troops could be brought in by succeeding waves of aircraft.[47] The Luftwaffe moved fighter and bomber aircraft into Norwegian airfields to support troop movements and activities. This put British ground forces at a severe disadvantage. The range from airfields in northern Scotland to Norway was such that it was very difficult for British aircraft to contest air superiority with the German air elements. In addition elements of the British fleet operating off Norway were subject to attack by German aircraft when they ventured within range.

The British government and Defense Staff were caught by surprise. Warships that had embarked troops for landings in the Narvik area had then been directed to offload them. As a result there was no ready reaction force available to move into northern Norway to take control of Narvik. German forces rapidly sent troops in destroyers into Vestfiord and on up to Narvik and seized control.

British air defense capability at sea was limited by several elements. There was no at sea ammunition replenishment capability such as the American fleet developed and used during its Pacific campaigns. Neither was there any at sea fuel replenishment capability. When a British aircraft carrier needed refueling it could not pull alongside a naval oiler and take on more fuel. It had to depart the operating area, proceed to a British port, refuel in port, and then transit back to its operating area. All that time its battle group was left without any air defense provided by fighters. Ships that ran low on anti-aircraft ammunition and many did so under sustained German air attack, had to get back to a British port to reload. Anti-aircraft cruisers had been expected to help defend the fleet against sustained shore based air attack and their temporary absence while rearming was sorely felt. Both elements were a distinct liability during the Norwegian campaign. German ground elements operating with strong Luftwaffe support were successful.

The overall British reaction to the German invasion of Norway was 'a day late and a dollar short'. There was a tremendous 'toing and froing' at the staff level, essentially all wasted motion. The British naval and ground operating forces were hampered even more than they might have been by such activity. Ground forces were dispatched to Norway without adequate cold weather clothing and equipment. Troops were put into ports some distance from their objective and ordered to move overland to take the objective. Heavy snows still lingered and they had no skis, snow shoes or tracked vehicles, and thus no way of moving through or over the intervening snow. No British Army AAA units were available so air defense depended entirely upon the Royal Navy.

The combined British-French effort to disrupt German invasion forces was ineffectual, and German forces gained control of Norway. In early May the German invasions of Holland, Belgium, and France put an end to any effort to save Norway. All Allied forces were withdrawn and redeployed to France to deal with the *Blitzkrieg*.

However all had not gone well on the German side. In particular, Doenitz's U-boats had performed very poorly. The Norwegian Campaign was a disaster for the U-boat Arm. The problem lay in torpedo performance. Several problems arose: magnetic pistols (exploders) malfunctioned; and torpedoes ran too deep. A large number of important naval targets were attacked at close range and torpedoes fired, without result. As daring a U-boat Commander as Gunther Prien, who had penetrated the harbor at Scapa Flow and sank battleship Royal Oak, told Doenitz bluntly on return to port that "he could not be expected to fight with a wooden rifle".

The really interested reader is referred to Doenitz's Memoirs. His Chapter 7, The Norwegian Operation and The Torpedo Crisis, provides many details. In summary, U-boats launched a large number of submerged attacks with torpedoes at British naval targets. Four attacks were made on battleship HMS Warspite, fourteen attacks on cruisers, ten attacks against destroyers, and ten attacks against transports. They sank only one transport.

Torpedoes ran too deep, they exploded prematurely—bringing down destroyer depth charge attacks on the attacker, some missed, and some were duds—hitting target hulls but not exploding. All in all it was a disaster of the first order. On 19 April after receiving reports from his U-boat commanding officers and assessing the situation, Doenitz issued orders for all U-boats to withdraw from the Norwegian theater of operations. Four U-boats were lost to enemy action during this period.

The real story is what was done to deal with the problem, and how German actions compared with American actions when similar problems were reported by American submarine commanders experiencing almost identical problems with torpedo attacks on Japanese forces in late 1941 and throughout 1942.

An early indication of potential torpedo problems was the attack on aircraft carrier Ark Royal on 17 September 1939. U-39 fired three torpedoes with magnetic exploders after having penetrated the destroyer screen around the carrier. The three torpedo warheads all exploded short of the carrier hull, doing no damage. The escort destroyers responded, picked up U-39 on active sonar (Asdic), depth charged her and brought her to the surface in sinking condition, where her CO ordered her scuttled. Whether details about this fiasco got back to U-boat headquarters is not clear. Presumably U-39 was busy with survival at the time, too busy to get off a message. Her sinking probably was reported in the British press and it is possible that the premature torpedo detonations were mentioned.

In mid-October three U-boats attacked a convoy and sank three ships and badly damaged a fourth, but reported torpedo problems.[48] At the end of the month U-56 fired three torpedoes at battleship HMS Nelson. The torpedoes ran true and struck Nelson's hull but failed to explode.[49] It is clear that by the end of October 1939 Doenitz was concerned over the G7a (steam) and G7e (electric) torpedoes.[50] His concerns dealt with the magnetic exploder, depth keeping, and the contact exploder (impact pistol). Neither torpedo could be considered reliable.

What had been suspicions earlier became certainties after the experiences off Norway. Doenitz, with the full support of the Commander-in-Chief focused on the torpedo test establishment for answers to the torpedo problems. This rapid headquarters response is in contrast to the very slow reaction in the U.S. Bureau of Ordnance in 1942 and 1943 to torpedo problems reported by submarine commanders.

It was discovered that mechanical oscillations could cause the German magnetic exploder to go off prematurely. It also turned out that some trials back in 1936 had given evidence that the torpedoes were running between six and nine feet deeper than set depth. The test establishment staff conducting the trials were not concerned because a magnetic exploder was also involved, and their erroneous thinking was that depth errors were therefore not relevant. They failed to realize that exact depth was important so that the maximum effect of the explosion would be underneath the keel, breaking it. If a magnetic exploder worked properly, only one "influence detonated" torpedo would be required to sink the average merchant ship instead of two or three contact torpedoes. The depth recorder used in those trials was also, later, determined to be unreliable.[51]

As soon as weather permitted torpedo trials were held in the Baltic. The results were "staggering and criminal" according to a report issued 1 May 1940. By 11 May the depth keeping problem was "solved", primarily by the addition of a depth keeping spring. However the basic cause of the depth problem was not actually determined until early 1942.

On 30 January 1942 torpedo men aboard U-94 were conducting an unauthorized inspection of a torpedo. They discovered that the rudder shaft went through the depth balance chamber and that the shaft seal was not tight. The basic design was flawed. The balance chamber had two different pressures: the first was atmospheric, that is what zero depth would be: 14.7 psi. The second pressure was desired running depth pressure, set into the torpedo before firing. The torpedo sensed what sea pressure was and tried to run at the set depth pressure over zero depth pressure. If all went well, and the torpedo were set to run at 16', the depth rudder would operate to cause the torpedo to run at 16', going through small oscillations as the depth smoothed out.

When a submarine submerges the pressure inside is the same as the air pressure at the surface, roughly 14.7 psi. However as time passes air pressure inside the submarine hull increases in response to air leaks from the submarine's installed air flasks. The leaky rudder shaft seal allowed the increased air pressure to build up on one side of the diaphragm in the balance chamber. Thereafter the torpedo would run that much deeper than set. Each pound of pressure in the U-boat over 14.7 psi would cause the torpedo to run two feet deeper than intended. If a U-boat submerged and fired its torpedoes within a fairly short period of time submerged, the depth problem would be small. However, the longer the U-boat was submerged the greater the depth problem potentially became. Off Norway where the nights were very short, forcing long submerged periods during daylight on the U-boats, the pressure inside each U-boat gradually built up and thus forced the torpedoes to run deeper.[52] Once this aspect was uncovered the torpedo was redesigned to eliminate that faulty element and torpedoes could be expected to run as set. However, it had taken some

22 months, from April 1940 to February 1942, to really solve the depth problem.

An examination of the contact (impact) pistol also showed room for improvement. Rather than the inertial movement of the firing pin when the torpedo warhead struck a solid object directly being used to set off a detonator, the action was reversed through 180 degrees, an entirely unnecessary mechanical complication. Occasionally it failed to detonate the warhead.

On 5 May 1940 HMS Seal, a British mine laying submarine was captured. It carried twelve steam torpedoes with contact pistols. The Germans examined the British contact pistols and found them simple and reliable. Shortly thereafter copies were made and introduced into German torpedoes.

Overall the Norwegian Campaign had proved a disaster for the U-boat Arm. They accomplished very little damage to British warships and transports. Their torpedoes exploded prematurely or not at all in many cases. Four boats were lost to enemy action. Admiral Doenitz had to order the withdrawal of all U-boats from Norwegian waters while the problems were sorted out.

Phase Three July—October 1940

Doenitz begins wolf pack operations after the fall of France. U-boats now have bases in coastal France and can extend their patrols by an extra week because of transit time saved. Construction on U-boat pens begins in France. Despite RN pleas, RAF Bomber Command refuses to attack them while they are vulnerable. On 17 September Adolph Hitler postponed Operation SEA LION, the invasion of England, indefinitely.

The French surrender gave the U-boat Arm a great advantage. No longer did their boats have to travel through the North Sea and around the north end of the British Isles to reach what British authorities called the Western Approaches where incoming ships bunched up. Their new French bases on the Atlantic saved them 450 nautical miles of transit, roughly equaling an additional week's time in their patrol areas. One day after the Armistice was signed in late June 1940 a special train carrying torpedoes and U-boat spare parts was in transit to the French Atlantic coast to help set up their new bases.[53]

Fairly rapidly the German Navy set about to build submarine pens or bunkers at various French ports.[54] The Todt Organization was employed to provide bomb-proof shelters for U-boats. The work was no secret and the Royal Navy realized the implications. It requested that RAF Bomber Command bomb the new structures while they were being built. Bomber Command, intent on its dogma of strategic bombardment of German industry, haughtily refused to have anything to do with such mundane operations. When the pens were completed, almost untouched by any RAF bombs, they were no longer capable of being penetrated by any size bomb in the RAF inventory at that time. Since the U-boats were targeting tankers bringing aviation gasoline to the British Isles, there was a very real battle between the RAF and the U-boat Arm, even if the RAF didn't realize it.

The British, fighting alone at this time, took great pride in the successful air defense of Great Britain against the best efforts of the Luftwaffe. Fighter Command had saved Great Britain from possible invasion, an achievement of which the RAF could well be proud. However, Bomber Command passed up an opportunity to achieve another significant victory by concentrating its efforts on preventing the Germans from building U-boats pens in the French ports of Bordeaux, Lorient, La Rochelle, and Saint-Nazaire. In the early stages of construction the pens were very vulnerable. Bomber Command could have hammered them night after night and perhaps have prevented them from being developed into the safe havens they became for U-boats in refit status. Despite the request and urging of Royal Navy headquarters, Bomber Command and the Air Staff would not be dislodged from their dogma of strategic bombing of German industry and cities. The "former naval person", Winston Churchill, showed no particular sensitivity to the potential submarine threat either at that time.

As a result the Todt organization, without interference, laid down heavy reinforced concrete pens that offered refuge to the U-boats when they were in port for rest and repairs. By the end of 1941 the pens at Lorient and La Pallice were completed. In mid 1942 those at Brest and Saint-Nazaire were done, and the pens at Bordeaux finished shortly thereafter. Some similar pens were built in Germany. Once the pens were completed it was futile to attempt to penetrate them with bombs. A splendid opportunity to affect the Battle of the Atlantic had been lost.

In 1940 after seizure of the French ports, the German Navy shipyard at Wilhelmshaven, *Kriegsmarine-Werft*, transferred 35% of its work force to the ports of Lorient, St. Nazaire and La Pallice to repair U-boats there. That action caused a delay in the delivery of new construction U-boats at that yard.[55] The civilian *Deschimag* shipyard at Bremen was the primary builder of the Type IX U-boat. In 1942 it took on responsibility for U-boat repair at Brest, transferring about 1,000 workers. That action caused the main yard to have about a 1.5 month delay in its deliveries of new construction U-boats.[56]

In his Memoirs Admiral Doenitz indicates that the Battle of the Atlantic began in July 1940. All of his boats had been withdrawn from the Atlantic for the unsuccessful Norwegian campaign described earlier. Actually U-37 was the first boat to begin the new campaign, sailing in May 1940. Her CO was Lieutenant-Commander Oehrn. She carried torpedoes with both contact and magnetic exploders. It was hoped that the magnetic exploders would perform satisfactorily away from the strong magnetic influences found in the Norway region. Alas, Oehrn reported firing five torpedoes with magnetic exploders, with two premature explosions and no explosions from two others. Doenitz then directed that only contact exploders would be used.[57]

Oehrn returned to Wilhelmshaven on 9 June, after a twenty-six day patrol, having sunk 43,000 tons of allied and neutral shipping. Doenitz was delighted that the Norwegian "jinx" had ended.

A formal investigation of the torpedo problems followed the end of the disastrous (for the U-boats) Norwegian Campaign. A six week trial in 1941, a State War Court, acquitted Vadm. Gotting, the former head of the Torpedo Inspectorate, but he never again had torpedo responsibilities. Radm. Wehr, head of the Torpedo Research Establishment, was found guilty and sentenced to a six-month prison term. Dr. Schreiber, involved with the faulty contact exploder, was found guilty and sentenced to a nine-month prison term. Dr. Rothermund, involved deeply in all aspects of the torpedo problems, was found guilty and sentenced to an eighteen-month prison term.[58]

During June 1940 U-boats sank 58 ships (300,000 tons). On 15 July the UK closed off their normal shipping approach route south of Ireland since it was too close to the new U-boat bases. Now the northern approach, north of Ireland would be used. Two days later Adolph Hitler declared a total blockade of the British Isles. The era of unrestricted submarine warfare had returned.

The use of French bases for U-boat repair and crew rest had the effect of increasing the size of the U-boat force by 25%. The shorter transit to U-boat operating areas allowed more U-boat time "on station". On 6 July 1940 the first U-boat, U-30 pulled in to Lorient for repairs, just a month after its capture by German forces.[59]

During the period August through October bad weather limited U-boat operations, but two convoys in October suffered grievous losses. SC 7 lost 17 ships between 18-20 October, and HX 71 lost 14 ships in the same period. The two convoy routes had overlapped and the wolf packs had a field day.[60]

Doenitz hoped that if he could put enough U-boats in to the North Atlantic he would be able to locate convoys and launch wolf pack attacks against them. He knew that it was a battle of attrition. One of his key figures of merit was the average sinking (in gross register tons) per U-boat per day for all U-boats at sea.[61] His principal problem was a lack of information about convoys. One can imagine Doenitz and the RN admiral in charge of the Western Approaches, as two blind but armed combatants in a room, listening for the slightest sound that would betray the other's presence so a blow could be struck. Comint was available to each side and sometimes provided useful information. U-boat sightings of convoys were very valuable.

Outbound convoys were initially escorted as far west as 12 degrees west longitude, and later as far west as 19 degrees west. Incoming convoys were met by escorts at those longitudes. On the other end westward across the Atlantic, outgoing convoys were escorted by Canadian destroyers to a point about 400 nm. eastward from their ports of origin. Incoming convoys were met at those points also. In between, in the broader stretches of the Atlantic, convoys usually proceeded with only a solitary naval auxiliary cruiser for protection against surface raiders. The central North Atlantic would be "a happy hunting ground" for wolf packs *if adequate information about convoy locations was available.*

Prior to October 1940 the principal area of U-boat operations in the Atlantic lay between 10 degrees west and 15 degrees west longitude. As time passed British air ASW efforts became stronger, and U-boats were hampered in daylight by longer range aerial patrols forcing them underwater to avoid detection and aerial attack.[62] After October 1940 the area eastern boundary was moved further westward to 15 degrees west, to ensure U-boat daytime surface mobility was not unduly hampered.[63] In May 1940 Great Britain occupied Iceland to provide bases there for destroyers and aircraft to extend ASW protection in the North Atlantic. She also swapped base leases to the United States in exchange for fifty old U.S. destroyers of WW I vintage to help fill her escort shortages.

Wolf pack procedures were in effect, and when possible Doenitz stationed a line of U-boats perpendicular to expected convoy travel routes. Those routes could be developed by B-Dienst deciphering section interception of convoy routing messages or by aerial reconnaissance reports, or by U-boat sightings. In the latter case, the sighting U-boat was directed to stay in contact with the convoy but not to attack until directed. It trailed and sent out frequent position reports to all the other "pack" boats, which were directed to close the target convoy as quickly as possible. Attacks normally commenced the first night after a U-boat concentration was achieved.

Doenitz also depended upon B-Dienst intercepts and breaking of convoy routing messages for vital information about convoy locations.[64] In June and again in August several concentration attempts based upon intercepts were made but failed to locate the convoys because of changes made by the routing authorities. There was an intercept war going on as well as a physical U-boat war. The Germans were intercepting and breaking convoy routing messages, and the British were intercepting and breaking messages trying to organize wolf pack concentrations against a convoy. Depending upon which side won the message battle, the convoy might escape attack entirely or be ravaged by a wolf pack.

Although the North Atlantic was the decisive theater of operations, Doenitz sent a few U-boats into the South Atlantic. On 3 August 1940 a U-boat sank a ship off the Cape Verde Islands. In November four ships were sunk off Freetown by U-boats. During the last ten days of December U-boats sank three more ships off Freetown.[65] Freetown is located in Sierra Leone along the Ivory Coast of West Africa, and was a convoy terminus for traffic from Capetown, South Africa. Convoys from Gibraltar and Capetown stopped there for fuel, and to change escorts for the next leg of their trip north or south. Although Freetown was an important base it lacked physical infrastructure, which was added only gradually. Coastal Command Sunderland flying boats, which could provide long range aerial search, only arrived at Freetown in March 1941.

In August 1940 a combined British-Free French naval expedition to seize the Vichy French controlled port of Dakar in Senegal was undertaken. The expedition was mounted, based upon fears that Dakar would become a base for U-boat operations against allied convoys in the South Atlantic. General de Gaulle proposed to seize Dakar and replace Vichy French control with Free French control. Churchill enthusiastically agreed and the expedition was undertaken based upon information from sources in Dakar that de Gaulle would be welcomed. Late information, proven correct, indicated that the "welcome" would be markedly less warm than predicted. Nevertheless the expedition proceeded. While the force was enroute, cruiser HMS Fiji was torpedoed by a U-boat and had to be replaced. On arrival at Dakar the local French authorities proved unwilling to accept the proposed change in regime. A subsequent bombardment of Dakar took place and Vichy French return gunfire from their ships damaged several RN ships. In addition a Vichy French submarine torpedoed and severely damaged battleship HMS Resolution. The Anglo-Free French expedition left with its tail between its legs.[66] Despite British fears Dakar never became a base for operations against allied convoys.

In September 1940 in the North Atlantic an eastbound 15-ship convoy was attacked by a five-boat wolf pack. Eleven ships were sunk or badly damaged. In mid-October convoy SC 7, from Sydney, Nova Scotia to the United Kingdom was attacked. Seventeen ships were sunk. On 19-20 October another convoy (HX 79) was attacked, losing fourteen ships. Convoy HX 79B lost seven ships. Within three days eight U-boats sank 38 ships, almost all in night surface wolf pack attacks on three convoys. No U-boats were lost.[67] It was clear that Doenitz's night-surface attack wolf pack tactics were proving successful against convoys.

It remained to be seen whether Doenitz could obtain enough U-boats to effectively blockade the British Isles. Although the aerial Battle of Britain had saved England from possible invasion, it was still possible that the U-boat campaign might force her to the negotiating table. In late 1917 England faced the same threat but the institution of convoy had saved her. Now, the German U-boat Arm seemed to have developed tactics that could defeat the convoy.

In his Memoirs, written after the war ended when he was in Spandau prison, Doenitz laid out his ideas about the only way that Britain might have been brought to the negotiating table. It depended upon U-boats sinking so much shipping that there was no other recourse. The results so far had been good but reflected the activities of only about a dozen U-boats on patrol. Doenitz felt that he needed a force of 100 boats on patrol, which required a total of 300 U-boats, a figure that he had repeatedly recommended to higher authority.[68] Granted that he had the advantage of hindsight when he wrote his memoirs, the ideas are consistent with all his actions. He bemoans the lack of focus on the part of the German high command and its inability to realize that Great Britain could only be defeated at sea by U-boats. He remarks favorably on the unified effort on the British side. The author will point out a few holes in that theory but compared to the Germans, the British side, or at least the Admiralty, was clearly focused on winning the Battle of the Atlantic. On the German side, Hitler and his generals were focused on land battles and ignored that which they did not understand—maritime warfare.[69]

During the period May through October 1940, U-boats sank 287 ships (1,450,878 tons). Most of those ships were sunk in convoy by night surface attacks. To add to the carnage, five auxiliary cruisers (armed merchant cruisers), HMS Andania, Carinthia, Dunvegan Castle, Scotstown and Transylvania were sunk, along with destroyer Whirlwind. Only six U-boats were lost during this period. The metric of tonnage sunk per U-boat per day at sea increased steadily from 514 tons in June, to 593 tons in July, to 664 tons in August, to 758 tons in September, and ending in 920 tons in October which was the month of large convoy battles.

The following table shows ship sinking's (and tonnage sunk) by month by U-boats and German aircraft during the latter part of 1940[70]:

Month	U-boat	Aircraft
August	56 (267,618 tons)	15 (53,283 tons)
September	59 (295,335 tons)	15 (56,328 tons)
October	63 (352,407 tons)	NA

Phase Four
November 1940-December 1941

This period offered Doenitz an opportunity to clearly demonstrate the damage his wolf packs could do to Allied convoys. However he was severely limited by the small numbers of U-boats available. Hitler's invasion of Russia in June 1941 diverted some U-boats to support operations in northern waters. Italy's failure to hold its own in the Mediterranean area meant that German resources had to be supplied to prevent British control of the Mediterranean. That included U-boats, further reducing the number Doenitz could employ in the North Atlantic—the decisive theater of U-boat operations.

The winter of 1940-1941 was notable for very bad weather in the North Atlantic which limited U-boat opportunities for sinking's. However, Doenitz resisted impulses to move his U-boats south to better weather, realizing that the center of gravity was in the North Atlantic area. Nevertheless, during the spring and summer of 1941 German naval command headquarters leveled requirements on U-boats for support operations including : weather reporting for the Luftwaffe; Arctic operations regarding the USSR; and escort of surface blockade runners, auxiliary cruisers and supply ships. In March 1941 some fourteen U-boats were tied up in these subsidiary operations leaving only 5-10 U-boats to concentrate on the Atlantic battle.[71]

In December 1940 convoy HX 90 was attacked by four U-boats which sank eleven ships, including armed merchant cruiser HMS Forfar. On 6 February 1941 Adolph Hitler directed attacks on Great Britain's overseas supply links. As a result U-boat and Luftwaffe air attacks on England's East Coast transportation routes increased markedly. This in turn led to Churchill's Battle of the Atlantic directive issued 6 March 1941.[72]

Bad weather during the months of January and February 1941 limited U-boat operations but in March they sank 41 ships (243,000 tons). However their successes were offset by the loss of three "U-boat Aces". On 17 March escorts for convoy OB 293 sank U-70 and U-47 (Prien). On 27 March escorts for convoy HX 112 sank U-99 (Kretschmer) and U-100 (Schepke). U-551 was also sunk at the end of March.[73] The loss of three distinguished U-boat commanders was a bitter blow to Admiral Doenitz.

There was only one, combined aircraft/U-boat/surface warship operation in the Atlantic during WW II. In mid-1941 U-37 sighted a convoy west of the Iberian Peninsula and per Doenitz's direction radiated signals that allowed Luftwaffe aircraft to home in from 150 miles distance. In addition battle cruiser Hipper joined the attack and sank one ship. U-37 sank four ships.[74]

By April 1941 some 100 U-boats were in commission. About one-third were operational, another one-third were "working up" in the Baltic, and the final one-third was being used to train officers and enlisted men needed to man the many new U-boats that were under construction. By this time about 230 new U-boats were on order.

U-boat sinking's for a number of months were as follow:[75]

Month	Ships sunk (tonnage)
April	43 (249,375 tons), but only ten in convoy
May	58 (325,492 tons), about 50% were sunk off Freetown by a group of six U-boats
June	61 (310,143 tons)
July	22 (94,209 tons)
August	23 (80,310 tons)
September	53 (202,820 tons)

On 9 May 1941 U-110 (Lemp) was captured intact, providing useful intelligence information. U-110 was taken under tow but sank enroute Scapa Flow.

On 23 May convoy HX 126 was hit by a wolf pack and lost heavily. This incident led the Admiralty to institute continuous escort for UK-bound convoys. A new base for RCN ships was established at St. Johns, Newfoundland. Convoy HX 129 sailed 29 May. It was the first convoy to have A/S escorts all the way across the Atlantic. In July continuous escort was extended to outbound convoys, and to Sierra Leone convoys.[76]

Beginning in early 1941 the Polish Intelligence Service working in occupied France, with the assistance of the re-instituted French Intelligence Service, began to provide "C", the head of the British Secret Service, with sailing data on German U-boats from first Bordeaux, and later Brest and Le Havre. Their insight was based upon U-boat crews picking up their clean clothes from French laundries.[77] The information was limited to the hull number and class of submarine. However human intelligence could not furnish information on assigned U-boat operating areas. That had to be divined from intercepts of radio messages from the U-boats as they reached station and reported to U-boat Command headquarters.

In May 1941 U-boats sank 58 ships (325,000 tons). June sinking's were only slightly more. On 23 June HX 133, south of Greenland, had its escort force beefed up to 13 ships. In a five day battle, five ships were sunk for the loss of two U boats. In July and August merchant ship sinking's in the North Atlantic fell as Luftwaffe aircraft were diverted to the invasion of Russia.[78]

During summer 1941 the *Kriegsmarine* first practiced refueling and resupply of submarines at sea. U-93 and U-557, both type VII boats, conducted the tests which were successful. U-boats had several sources of fuel and supplies once they left port. The first source was German surface ships, either in Spanish ports or at sea. The second source was other U-boats configured for resupply missions. A third was other combat U-boats. The resupply boats consisted of six converted Type XB minelayers and ten Type XIV *Milchkuh* (milk cow).From April 1942 to April 1944 they conducted 534 resupply operations at sea, usually in an area that ASW aircraft could not yet reach. During the period June 1941 through September 1944 other combat U-boats conducted 115 resupply operations for a total of 649.[79] These resupply operations allowed extra reach (range) to U-boats or extra time on patrol.

Starting in mid-July that year continuous escort was provided for convoys to Sierra Leone in West Africa. Escorts from Londonderry took the convoys to 19 degrees north latitude and there were relieved by escorts based on Freetown. Bathhurst in Gambia was used as a refueling base for the Londonderry escorts for their return voyage home.[80]

In June 1941 the Admiralty put together a full picture of the German secret re-supply ships that had been deployed to support raider *Bismarck* and U-boats. Within a twenty day period UK forces sank nine supply ships, including six tankers, in the North and South Atlantic oceans.[81] Although most of the information stemmed from comint, major efforts were made to disguise the source of locating information.

German supply ships operating from the Canary Islands regularly replenished U-boats as sea until diplomatic pressure on Spain brought those un-neutral shenanigans to a halt in July 1941. Special surface re-supply ships were then used as an alternative but the sinking of *Egerland* in the South Atlantic ended that gambit. Germany then broached using Dakar as a base for re-supply operations with Vichy France but got nowhere in the negotiations.

With surface raiders *Python, Kota Penang* and *Atlantis* all having been sunk, Doenitz went to the *"Milchkuh"* alternative, long range U-boats fitted out to replenish U-boats with fuel, provisions and even torpedoes. This type, Type XIV, had no torpedo tubes and its only armament was antiaircraft guns for self-protection. It carried 700 tons of fuel oil, and according to Gannon could extend the other operational U-boat endurance as follows: type VII—plus four weeks, type IX plus eight weeks.[82]-Ten were commissioned and all were lost in the Atlantic from 1942 to 1944. Bagnasco states that their fuel cargo capacity was only 423 tons of diesel fuel.[83] Doenitz indicates that they carried 700 tons of diesel oil, and could make available from 400 to 600 tons to other submarines depending upon their own operational orders.[84]

In July Doenitz had 65 operational U-boats. The number had increased to 80 by October.

In mid-August 1941 Doenitz reportedly placed escort ships as primary targets for his U-boats according to Roskill.[85] Doenitz's Memoirs do not confirm this surmise. Doenitz's main focus was on merchant tonnage sunk, not warships and particularly not escorts. Escorts were dangerous and usually to be avoided.

British convoys to Russia began in August 1941. The old aircraft carrier HMS Argus left the UK with 24 Hurricanes on board and an escort of seven destroyers. The first PQ convoy left Iceland for Archangel on 29 September. By the end of the year 55 merchant ships in eight convoys had sailed. QP convoys returned empty merchant ships to the UK.[86]

British intelligence credited Germany with a total of 184 U-boats at this time and estimated that it had suffered 44 losses. The actual numbers were 198 U-boats and 47 losses. By the end of 1941 the U-boat total reached about 229 units.[87]

During October some 32 ships (156,550 tons) were sunk. British operations analysis indicated the value of aerial ASW surveillance. None of the 32 was sunk within 400 miles of a Coastal Command base. Twelve (37.5%) were sunk in a range band of 400-600 nm from a Coastal Command air base. The remaining 20 (62.5%) were sunk in areas over 600 nm from a Coastal Command base, where no air coverage was possible.[88]

Doenitz attempted to use air reconnaissance by Luftwaffe long-range FW Condor aircraft to locate convoys and home in wolf packs on them.

He found that it was often unsuccessful because of poor navigation by the aircraft. They had the convoy in sight but the geographical position they reported was in serious error. Doenitz's staff developed a workaround to solve the problem. U-boats took bearings on the reporting aircraft signal and sent their own positions and the aircraft bearing to U-boat headquarters. There the bearings were plotted, producing a fairly accurate fix on the aircraft and hence on the convoy location, which was then rebroadcast to all available U-boats.[89] This procedure was developed during spring 1941.

During 1941 Italy had such significant problems in the Mediterranean area with the British that Hitler felt impelled to direct German forces to the area in aid of his somewhat hapless ally. They included *Luftflotte* 12 from Norway, which specialized in ship attack tactics; Field Marshall Rommel and his *Afrika Corps* armor and infantry formations; and a number of U-boats. At the end of September six U-boats were dispatched. In November another four U-boats were sent. They produced significant results there but sinking's in the North Atlantic declined. In October 32 ships (157,000 tons) were sunk, only one-half the sinking's in May and June.[90] The lull in sinking's during July and August resulted in pressure on the Admiralty to release LRA from Coastal Command back to Bomber Command to participate in Bomber Command's effort to destroy German cities.

On 13 November 1941 aircraft carrier Ark Royal was sunk by U-81 with one torpedo hit about 30 miles off Gibraltar. She sank slowly and only one man was lost. It was more a failure of ship design and damage control practices than a tribute to torpedo marksmanship.

On 24 November U-331 hit battleship HMS Barham with three torpedoes in the eastern Mediterranean. She capsized and sank due to a magazine explosion, with the loss of 55 officers and 806 men. RAN sloop Parramatta was also torpedoed in November. On 14 December cruiser HMS Galatea was sunk off Alexandria by two torpedoes from U-557.[91] These successes cast more doubt on Asdic capabilities to prevent submerged attacks. German U-boats proved as effective as German Stuka dive bombers and changed the complexion of the war in the Mediterranean to British disadvantage.

However, the diversion of U-boats to the Mediterranean Sea removed them from the center of gravity—the North Atlantic, where the main battle was being fought. The lack of a large number of U-boats as recommended by Doenitz was to limit German successes at a time when Allied ASW procedures were inadequate to deal with the U-boat threat. Terraine states that the diversion of U-boats from the North Atlantic to the Mediterranean Sea was ". . . most severe defeat so far sustained by the U-boats in the Battle of the Atlantic was inflicted by their own High Command."[92]

During the second half of 1941 the U-boat attack was suffering not only from a shortage of boats but also from the fact that Bletchley Park had penetrated the *Hydra* cipher. The Submarine Tracking Room rerouted a number of convoys saving an estimated 300 ships from being sunk.[93]

In June convoy HX 133 was attacked by 10 U-boats. Additional escorts were hastily sent, to increase the total escort numbers to 13. There was a five day and night battle. Five ships were sunk, along with U-556 and U-651. In July and August ship losses to U-boats again fell as U-boats were diverted to join in operations against the Soviet Union. Hitler launched an invasion of the USSR on 22 June 1941. By September about 200 U-boats were in commission.

In August 1941, because of a lull in sinking's during July and August, the Cabinet raised the question of diverting long range aircraft from Coastal Command to Bomber Command to increase the bombing efforts against German industry and cities. Roskill notes that the First Lord (of the Admiralty) defended the use of long range aircraft by Coastal Command, pointing out that the lull was seasonal. Indeed it was, and losses rose in September.[94]

During the autumn that year U.S. destroyers became entangled with U-boats because of their role in escorting convoys to the vicinity of Iceland. On 4 September USS Greer (DD-145) dropped depth charges on U-656 which got away unscathed. On 17 October USS Kearny (DD-432) was torpedoed and damaged. On 31 October USS Reuben James (DD-245) was sunk by a U-boat torpedo while escorting convoy HX 156.[95] On 21 November Navy Secretary Knox announced to the press that U.S. naval forces had probably sunk or damaged at least fourteen enemy submarines.[96] The actual score was zero. It would not be the last time that U.S. Navy officials made extravagant claims about U-boats destroyed.

Shipping losses in the Atlantic fell during the fall because of U-boat diversions to the Med and northern waters. In October 32 ships for 157,000 tons were sunk. However those figures were only 50% of the losses in May and June. In November 13 ships were sunk (60,000 tons). In December only ten ships were sunk. Convoy HG 76 set out for home waters with a total of 12 escorts and the first escort aircraft carrier (CVE) HMS Audacity. The convoy was attacked by a wolf pack but only two merchant ships were lost. Five U-boats were sunk by escorts. Unfortunately, HMS Audacity was sunk by a U-boat when her CO left the protective escort screen to operate aircraft in spite of contrary advice from the convoy commodore.[97]

Between October 1941 and January 1942 Coastal Command had to send 166 complete air crews overseas, mostly to the Far East as the Japanese threat increased. These diversions included complete squadrons, including those equipped with the Catalina long range aircraft, thus reducing the air resources available for the Battle of the Atlantic.[98]

Mediterranean Sea Excursion

On 22 November 1941 the German Naval High Command directed that the Mediterranean area be regarded as the primary theater of operations, with the outcome that the entire U-boat force was to be either in the Med itself or in the sea areas west of Gibraltar.[99] By 29 November some 15 U-boats were astride the Straits and another 10 were in the eastern Med. Doenitz protested unavailingly. He thought that the British would use the Cape Town route (around South Africa) to reinforce their ground forces in Egypt (as they did). Apparently the Fuehrer was concerned about Allied landings near Oran or Algiers, but Doenitz believed that was very unlikely considering the loss of aircraft carrier Ark Royal to a U-boat torpedo on 13 November. He also thought that it was a serious mistake to operate U-boats in the Mediterranean Sea where it was easily possible for the opposition to achieve heavy air coverage. One further problem existed with regard to the Med. It was easy to send a submarine in but difficult to get it back out again. The prevailing submerged currents ran from west to east, so a U-boat could submerge near the western entrance to the Strait and ride the current eastward into the Mediterranean Sea. Trying to get out was much more difficult since the submerged U-boat would be heading into the current.[100]

On 24 November Force K from Gibraltar sought to intercept an Axis convoy north of Benghazi. Another unit, Force B (7th and 17th cruiser squadrons) were also operating. Admiral Cunningham took the

Mediterranean Fleet, including battleships Queen Elizabeth, Barham and Valiant, to sea in support of Force K. Cunningham had eight destroyers to screen his battleships. About 60 nm north of Sollum, U-331 penetrated the destroyer screen and put three torpedoes into HMS Barham. She rolled over and blew up with the loss of 56 officers and 812 ratings. This loss, added to the loss of aircraft carrier Ark Royal off Gibraltar on 13 November, was shattering. It was clear that entirely too much faith had been placed on the ability of destroyer Asdic to detect submarines. At this time aircraft carriers Illustrious and Formidable were in U.S. shipyards having battle damage repaired, and HMS Indomitable had run aground off Kingston, Jamaica. The immediate effect in the Mediterranean Sea was that Force H at Gibraltar could no longer attempt to run a re-supply convoy to Malta—without an aircraft carrier to provide fighter interceptors against Italian and German aircraft.

In *Engage the Enemy More Closely*, author Correlli Barnett offers the opinion that Bletchley Park (BP) decryption successes were a key factor in forcing Doenitz to remove his U-boats from the North Atlantic and move them south to the Med.[101] However it looks as if other reasons were involved, rather than Bletchley Park successes. Hitler's "intuition" was to cause major problems for Admiral Doenitz now as it did at other times.

During 1941 a total of 496 ships (2,421,700 tons) were sunk by U-boats, surface warships or raiders, or Luftwaffe aircraft. Thirty-five U-boats were lost to all causes during the year.[102]

On 7 December 1941 Japan attacked U.S. bases on the island of Oahu in Hawaii. The U.S. declared war the following day. On 12 December Germany declared war on the United States and the favor was returned shortly. Doenitz launched an immediate attack on U.S. East Coast shipping where convoys were not in effect. During 1942 U-boats sank 6,266,215 tons of Allied and neutral shipping; overall losses from all causes were 7,790,697 tons. As a result, January 1943 imports to the United Kingdom were less than half the tonnage of January 1941 and down 40% from January 1942. During the period November 1942 through January 1943 about 50% of raw material for British industry had to be drawn from reserve stockpiles in the UK rather than from imports from overseas.*103*

Paukenschlag (Attack on the U.S.)

In December five Type IX U-boats sortied from their secure French submarine pens, enroute the East Coast of the United States. Doenitz had wanted to send twelve boats but could only get approval from German Naval Headquarters for six. This first U-boat attack on American East Coast shipping was named Operation *PAUKENSCHLAG* (Drumbeat). The first five U-boats sailed with only general charts of the U.S. coast. They lacked detailed charts and sailing directions, which is a little surprising since Admiral Doenitz had been thirsting to get at American targets for some time. When U-123 sailed again, on 2 March 1942, for its second American patrol, that deficiency had been made up. U-123 then carried detailed inshore charts and Sailing Directions that had been copied from British and U.S. publications and reprinted in German.[104]

Their initial patrol assignments were as follow:
Patrol Area I Off Cape Hatteras—*Zapp* in U-66
Patrol Area II—New York City to Atlantic City
(inshore)—*Hardegen* in U-123
Patrol Area III—NY and NJ off shore—*Follkers* in U-125
Patrol Area IV and V—SE of Halifax—*Bleichrodt* in U-109
Cabot Strait—*Kals* in U-130[105]

Happy times were in effect off the U.S. East Coast. There was good hunting there and in the Caribbean Sea area for U-boats in the absence of convoy. Later in the year three significant ASW developments take place that will significantly affect the battle in the future.

As U-123 approached the North American continent in late December 1942 her navigator was able to use Canadian-controlled radio signals from St. Johns and Cape Race radio beacons in Newfoundland to help correct his position plot. This is an interesting point since the United States has been severely criticized for leaving its light houses and other navigation beacons operating to the advantage of the U-boats.[106]

The overall U-boat situation for the week ending 12 January 1942 was as follows:
Six U-boats off Cape Race and St. Johns

> Group of five U-boats approaching the U.S. coast
> (*Paukenschlag*)
> Another five westbound (*Paukenschlag*)
> Plus another five enroute (*Paukenschlag*)

All this information was provided to the U.S. Navy by the British Submarine Tracking Room at the time.[107] *Hardegen* in U-123 began *Paukenschlag* one day early by sinking SS Cyclops, a large freighter on 12 January 1942.

In early 1942 the total number of U-boats was approaching 400 and operational U-boats were sinking an average of 450,000 tons of shipping per month. More tankers were being sunk than could be replaced by new construction. In May 1942 losses to U-boats were 585,451 tons of shipping. The U-boat Arm was beginning to have serious effects on the British economy, while Bomber Command was relatively ineffective in its efforts to destroy the German industrial base and hinder U-boat construction. U-boat depredations were threatening the petroleum supply which Bomber Command needed to carry out its attacks on German cities. In June 1942 U-boats sank 649,832 tons of shipping.[108]

In early 1942 Admiral Doenitz had a fourth wheel added to the Enigma encryption machines carried aboard U-boats. This was intended to make it harder to break the enciphered messages being exchanged between U-boat headquarters and U-boats on patrol. Doenitz had a lingering suspicion that somehow the British were reading German message traffic, but was unable to prove it.[109] His action caused great difficulty at Bletchley Park, which was busy at work doing exactly what he feared. There were too few "*bombes*" at Bletchley Park to handle all the Enigma traffic that was intercepted. A large number were dedicated to breaking Luftwaffe and German Army target messages. As a result the Admiralty began to fall behind in the contest to conceal convoy routings, and break messages dealing with U-boat search lines and locations.

During fall 1942 U-boat sinking's increased until they were beyond the capability of U.S. and British Empire shipyards to replace the lost ships.[110]

Month (1942)	Ships sunk in convoy	Independent sailers sunk	Total sunk
August	50	51	101
September	29	58	87
October	29	54	83
December	39	70	109
Total	147	233	380

On 1 February 1942 operational U-boat distribution was as follow:[111]

> 7 U-boats off Norway (per Hitler's "intuition" that the British had plans for an attack on Norway)
>
> 3 U-boats west of Gibraltar
>
> 6 U-boats off the east coast of the United States (instead of the 12 that Doenitz wanted)

The early days of the U-boat attacks against shipping off the east coast of the United States can best be crudely but accurately described as "amateur night" in which the U.S. forces involved, both Navy and Army, were overmatched and under prepared. Their German opponents were war-experienced operators who made the most of the situation.

The United States Navy had clear responsibility for protection of ocean shipping off the East Coast of the United States. However, despite the fact that it had the opportunity to profit from nearly two years of observation of British ASW operations against U-boats, it was almost completely unprepared. It appears there was no Navy master plan for merchant ship convoy operations or aerial patrols of offshore waters. The office of the Chief of Naval Operations had fallen down on the job. It is difficult to comprehend the state of affairs that existed, especially since U.S. Navy destroyers were already involved in ocean escort of British and Canadian merchant ship convoys as far east as Iceland. Destroyer USS Kearney had been damaged by a U-boat torpedo on 17 October 1941, and U.S. S. Ruben James sunk by a U-boat on 31 October 1941 during convoy escort operations prior to the Pearl Harbor attack by Japan.

The Chief of Naval Operations, Admiral Harold Rainsford Stark, USN had submitted a memorandum to President Roosevelt on November 12, 1940, dealing with recommendations for U.S. action if it should become involved in hostilities with the Axis powers. The memorandum became known as the Plan Dog Memorandum. It offered four possible courses of action, A through D. Recommendation D, or "Dog" in the phonetic military alphabet of that day, recommended that the United States go on the offensive in the Atlantic (against Germany and Italy) while remaining on the defensive in the Pacific (against Japan). This was in line with Rainbow Five, one of a current set of proposed war plans. The memorandum had been cleared with General Marshall, Chief of Staff of the United States Army.

President Roosevelt never formally endorsed Plan Dog, not surprising in view of the strong isolationist sentiment prevalent among the American voters of that period.[112] However it was clear to Marshall and Stark that he agreed with it. In January 1941 he ordered the Navy to prepare to assist in the escort of convoys.

The Naval War College exercised its students in a series of war games during the 1920s and 1930s. The usual scenario involved an older war plan, Plan Orange, dealing with war with Japan. Admiral Nimitz said later during WW II that there were few surprises during the Pacific phase of WW II, almost all the problems having been illuminated during Naval War College war games. It seems a shame that the problems of ASW against U-boats in the Atlantic were not the focus of a Naval War College war game during 1941. It might have helped.

Prior to the Pearl Harbor attack the North Atlantic Navy Coastal Frontier command (NANCF) had requested that the Army's Eastern Defense Command provide assistance with aerial patrols offshore due to a lack of an adequate number of naval aircraft[113]. On the afternoon of December 8, 1941 units of I Bomber Command commenced offshore flights. At that time there were no U-boats lurking in U.S. coastal waters, which was just as well. I Bomber Command aircraft crews had no training in identification of naval ships or submarines, no training in attacking submarines, and no depth charges with which to attack. These aircraft carried only high explosive bombs for use against land targets, and the crews were trained to attack land targets only.

About 100 aircraft were made available by I Bomber Command by the end of 1941. They began two flights a day in January 1942, from Westover Field, Massachusetts; Mitchell Field, Long Island in New York; and Langley Field in the Norfolk, Virginia area. Later they also flew from Bangor, Maine. The patrols consisted of three planes per flight and they ranged as far as 600 miles offshore. Initially their only sensors were eyes, augmented by binoculars. I Air Support Command, a subsidiary organization of I Bomber Command, provided single engine observation aircraft which could patrol out to about 40 miles offshore. They had fuel for 2-3 hours of flight but were unarmed. They operated from airfields from Portland, Maine south to Wilmington, North Carolina. By the end of January 1942 I Bomber Command had about 119 aircraft involved. Nine were B-17 heavy bombers, and the remainder B-18 and B-25 medium bombers.[114]

During the first two weeks of the U-boat campaign against the U.S. which officially began 13 January 1942, some 13 ships (100,000 tons) were sunk off the East Coast. In March, 28 ships (159,340 tons) were lost in the Eastern Sea Frontier area, while 15 ships (92,321 tons) were lost in the Gulf or Caribbean areas. Oil tankers were 57% of the tonnage lost.[115] After a very slow start convoy was finally instituted along the U.S. East Coast and in the Caribbean in May. The first convoys were assembled at Hampton Roads and Key West. The first south-bound convoy sailed 14 May, and the first north-bound convoy on 15 May. Convoys, plus greatly increased air cover, made life much more difficult for German U-boats along the East Coast. However, during May and June some 148 ships (752,009 tons) were sunk off U.S. coasts.[116]

During their early operations off the East Coast of the United States U-boat commanding officers could not believe their eyes. Ships were sailing with navigation lights on at night, navigation beacons, light houses, etc., were operating freely, and coastal cities were not blacked out. It was possible to operate on the surface at night and clearly see ships silhouetted against the background lighting ashore. During daytime U-boats would bottom in relatively shallow waters (150-200 feet) and rest their crews. After dark they would surface and go to work on the steady ship traffic moving north and south. U-123 sank 8 ships (53,360 tons), U-66 sank 5 ships (50,000 tons), and U-130 sank 4 ships (30,748 tons). The last total included three loaded tankers and one freighter.[117] The other two *Paukenschlag* boats had similar results.

Losses along the U.S. East Coast were as follow: March—42 ships, April—23 ships, May—4 ships. June—13 ships, July—only 3 ships, and none for the remainder of the year. Convoy procedures, once implemented, along with increasingly heavy air patrols, finally made East Coast waters unprofitable for the U-boats.[118] The British were appalled at the ship slaughter, particularly tankers, and the lack of American ASW preparedness after several years of observing the Battle of the Atlantic.

On 1 April 1942 the Navy Department announced that 28 U-boats had been sunk or presumably sunk off the U.S. East coast (four by Army aircraft, the remainder by naval forces). The actual score was no U-boats sunk by U.S. forces at that time.[119] The Navy was apparently winning the public affairs war while losing the real war. One can only imagine with what mirth that news was received at Admiral Doenitz's headquarters at Kernevel, near Lorient.

Admiral Doenitz had expected that U.S. forces would be unprepared for his initial U-boat strike in U.S. coastal waters. He was right. Responsibility for defense of east coast shipping rested with the Navy, which apparently had not thought the potential problems through despite over two years of observing events in Europe and the North Atlantic. Commander North Atlantic Naval Coastal Frontier, later renamed Eastern Sea Frontier, lacked adequate numbers of destroyers or other escort vessels and aircraft to protect shipping. Most destroyers and combat aircraft were attached to Commander, U.S. Fleet. There was no plan to implement convoys. On December 7, 1941, the afternoon after the Pearl Harbor attack, he requested aerial assistance from Commanding General Eastern Defense Command (Army).

Although Army aviators did their best, they were ill prepared. Most were untrained in navigating over water; they had almost no ship identification training, and no training at all in attacking U-boats. Their only weapons were machine guns and aerial bombs intended for use against land targets. They lacked depth charges, and tactics for attacking surfaced U-boats. They had no sensors other than eyes and binoculars. ASV radar was not yet available. I Bomber Command's responsibility still included land target attack so all of its training time could not be allocated to the U-boat target.

Naval surface ship patrols were similarly limited in effectiveness. U-boats could detect surface vessels at much greater ranges than the patrol vessel could spot the U-boat. The U-boat would submerge and wait for the patrol craft to continue on, not knowing that a U-boat was lurking nearby. It was fortunate that the escort vessels were not high on the target list, scarce U-boat torpedoes being reserved for laden merchant ships or tankers.

During January and February 1942 I Bomber Command aircraft flew some 8,000 operational hours. They made four attacks on suspected U-boats but inflicted no damage. In March they flew another 8,000 hours. By this time four aircraft were equipped with ASV radar.

On 19 February *Heyse* (U-128) went south into the Gulf Sea Frontier area and sank SS Pan Massachusetts (8,201 GRT) off Cape Canaveral. U-128 was one of five U-boats that made up the second *Paukenschlag* echelon (U-103, 106, 107, 108 and 128). They had sailed from France about 10 January.

Cdr. Roger Wynn, RNVR, went to Washington in May 1942 to try to get the Americans to take steps to reduce the huge shipping losses that were taking place in their home waters. He spoke first to Cdr. George Dyer, heading the ONI Information Room, and Dyer passed him on to Radm. Edwards. Edwards was somewhat cavalier, saying that we (Americans) had ships to lose in the learning process. Wynn reminded him forcefully that a large number of those ships being lost were in fact British and Great Britain could not afford their loss. Edwards then arranged for Wynn to talk to Admiral King. King was conciliatory and agreed to create a Submarine Tracking Room, mirroring the one in the UK; to institute coastal convoys; and to take steps to darken shore lighting that was illuminating merchant ships off the coastline. A recalled medically retired USN officer was immediately sent to the UK to spend several weeks intensively studying British ASW command and control procedures at the OIC Submarine Tracking Room. On return he organized OP-20-G, later F-21, as a clone of the UK Tracking Room.[120]

The Submarine Tracking Room employed a technique that used every available scrap of information about U-boat locations. It was called a "working fiction" which attempted to show their locations and prospective concentrations against convoys. Based on the best information available, convoys were re-routed based upon predictions of wolf pack moves. During 1942 while B-Dienst held the upper hand over BP and BP was trying desperately to solve the 4th rotor problem, the Submarine Tracking Room successfully routed 105 of 174 scheduled convoys entirely clear of U-boat wolf packs (60.3%).[121]

On 16 March Admiral King (COMINCH) called for a meeting with representatives of Eastern Sea Frontier, Gulf Sea Frontier, and Caribbean Sea Frontier to discuss the institution of convoys. On 27 March a conference report formally proposing convoys was approved by Admiral

King. On 1 April Admiral Andrews, commanding ESF, instituted a partial convoy system, in which merchant ships moved only in daylight hours within ESF waters, anchoring in roadsteads at night.[122] This was a partial solution since air patrols were keeping U-boats submerged in daylight.

As ASW measures increased in Eastern Sea Frontier, Doenitz started shifting his U-boats southward. In April 23 ships were sunk in Eastern Sea Frontier waters, but only two in the Gulf Sea Frontier. During May only five ships were sunk in ESF, but losses in GSF increased to 41 clearly marking the U-boat move southward.

On 15 May 1942 convoy procedures were placed into effect all along the East Coast. By the end of May the Navy began to employ long endurance Catalina PBY patrol aircraft (15 hours) in support of convoys. As ASW measures increased in a given area, particularly aerial patrols that drove U-boats underwater and limited their mobility, U-boat Command redeployed its forces to less well protected areas. In August-September a Galveston-Mississippi-Key West convoy leg was added to complete the convoy system.

In August there were 33 ships sunk in Caribbean Sea Frontier. By September 1942 U-boats had basically abandoned Eastern Sea Frontier and Gulf Sea Frontier, and were working the Cuba-Haiti-Puerto Rico areas. They then moved further south to Trinidad, where ships carrying oil and bauxite cargos were plentiful.

In early 1942 the United States committed itself to the escort carrier (CVE) building program, eventually turning out 128 CVEs by the end of the war. UK ship yards produced five CVEs. Many of the early U.S. produced CVEs went to the UK. HMS Biter and HMS Archer were in service during May 1943. The CVE provided air coverage for the convoys, when long range aircraft (LRA) were not available. A large percentage of LRA time was spent unprofitably in transit from the shore air base to the remote operational area around a convoy. CVE-based aircraft were much more economical. Their transit times were very short and a much higher percentage of their time was spent usefully in covering the area around a convoy searching for U-boats. A key point which applied to LRA and CVE aircraft alike—their mere presence prevented U-boats from transiting on the surface, seriously reducing their mobility and their capability to form wolf packs for attacks.[123] However, CVE's were not a factor during Operation *Paukenschlag* (Drumbeat), Doenitz's strike against what he thought would be an easy target—the unprepared East Coast shipping off the United States. He was entirely correct in his estimation.

There was another battle going on within the United States armed services about antisubmarine warfare which affected overall U.S. ability to respond to the U-boat offensive. In its simplest terms it might be stated as U.S. Navy—*protect convoys* versus U.S. Army Air Forces—*kill U-boats*. This was a fundamental and dogmatic difference. Adherents of the Army position held that convoy protection was a "defensive" strategy, one by definition incapable of winning wars. They opted for an "offensive" strategy of killing U-boats, which would end the U-boat threat. Their tactic was "search, strike and destroy". That stated tactic begged the question of how you found the U-boat in order to attack it.

It also focused on a lesser figure of merit regarding ASW—number of U-boats sunk. The better figure of merit was the number of ships that reached their destinations safely, carrying munitions, troops and fuel. Aviation fuel needed to reach Great Britain to support Bomber Command in its night bombing offensive and 8th U.S. Air Force in its strategic daylight bombing offensive. If enough ships carrying those vital cargoes reached the British Isles, it did not really matter how many U-boats were destroyed.

U.S. Navy strategy focused on convoy protection, first at close range with active sonar and radar equipped surface escorts, and secondly with long range aircraft that could drive approaching U-boats on the surface back under water where their limited submerged speed precluded them from concentrating for a wolf pack attack on a selected convoy.

Prior service arguments and agreements on long range aircraft had produced the situation where the U.S. Army controlled all land-based long range aircraft. The key aircraft whose employment was in question was the very long range B-24 "Liberator" bomber. The Army wanted it for the strategic bombing campaign against Germany; the Navy wanted some for ASW support operations.

As noted earlier, the U.S. Army controlled all land-based long range aviation (read bombers), while the U.S. Navy controlled all sea-based aviation (read patrol bombers). The rub came in when winter set in along the North Atlantic. Navy patrol bombers were strictly flying boats and needed clear water for takeoff and landing. Ice in harbors prevented their operations during the winter, whereas long range land-based bombers could take off and land freely from cleared air strips. Later patrol bombers would be amphibians, which had retractable landing gear in addition to boat-type hulls.

One of the problems with implementing the Army's doctrine was an inability to carry it out in an effective manner. In *The Battle of the Atlantic (September 1939-May 1943), Vol. I,* distinguished naval historian Morison noted that: few Army pilots' navigation skills were adequate to locate a convoy; their ship recognition skills were lacking and recognition training inadequate; they had no ship-to-air communications; and they were not trained to drop bombs on moving U-boats.[124]

On 24 March U-123 was approaching U.S. waters on its second *Paukenschlag* patrol. It spotted a Navy patrol aircraft well out at sea, probably a PBY. This was a change. No "bees" had been spotted during the previous patrol. "Bee" was U-boat slang for patrol aircraft. They called British Sunderland patrol bombers "tired bees" because they were so slow. The presence of patrol aircraft well out at sea was disturbing. They would force transiting U-boats to submerge in day time to avoid attack, thus interfering with their operations.

On 26 March 1942 an Army directive placed all AAF units allocated by defense commanders for operations over the sea to protect shipping and conduct ASW operations under the operational control of Navy Commander Eastern Sea Frontier.[125] This move satisfied a Navy objective: to concentrate on getting ship cargoes through threatened waters.

On 10 April U-123 was on the surface off St. Augustine, Florida and was attacked by an aircraft although no bombs were dropped. The emergency dive caused U-123 to hit bottom at 20 meters (about 66 feet). The aircraft may have been an unarmed observation plane doing inshore patrols. In any case *Hardegen* was risking his boat by operating so close to shore in very shallow water. He then headed on course 120 degrees towards deeper water (30 meters). Very shortly afterwards USS Dahlgren came on the scene and apparently picked U-123 up on sonar. She dropped six depth charges on U-123, and nearly destroyed her. U-123 sat on the bottom waiting for the inevitable return run which would seal its fate, but Dahlgren sailed away not knowing that victory was so close. *Hardegen* commented that a British destroyer would have stayed for as long as 36 hours to ensure destruction of a U-boat contact once made. However, U.S. destroyer commanding officers were not experienced in ASW and USN tactical doctrine was not fully developed so early in the war. U-123 crept away to nurse her wounds and fight another day.[126]

Not all such encounters were so fortunate for the U-boat. On 14 April USS Roper (DD-147) made radar contact at night on surfaced U-85 off Nags Head, North Carolina. Roper's lookouts then sighted U-85 and she attacked with gun fire. U-85 submerged and Roper dropped eleven depth charges in the swirl where she had submerged. U-85 was destroyed along with some 40 of her crew who had gone overboard during the gun battle and were in the water when the depth charges went off.[127]

On 16 April COMINCH halted all tanker traffic off the East Coast. No more tankers were allowed to transit during the month.

Finally, after a series of discussions between Army and Navy staffs, Army Chief of Staff General Marshall decided to pull the Army Air Forces out of its ASW role in the Western Atlantic. Later, on 1 September 1943 the Army Anti-Submarine Air Command was disestablished. Some 187 Liberator bombers outfitted for ASW operations were transferred to the Navy in return for a like number of standard Liberator bombers which had been consigned to the Navy.[128] However, the U-boat threat in the North Atlantic to British survival had been clearly defeated in April 1943.

On 30 March U-123 fired a G7e torpedo at SS Socony Vacuum, a 9,511 GRT tanker off Cape Hatteras. The torpedo ("eel" in U-boat slang) took a vertical dive and exploded against the sea bed at 30 meters (about 90 feet). The tanker's relatively high speed precluded U-123 from making a second attack.

U-123 rested on the bottom off Hatteras in 25 meters of water during daytime. Her captain, *Hardegen*, was surprised by the large number of picket ships patrolling off shore the Outer Banks, another change from his first patrol. He also was surprised by the frequent over flights of Army and Navy aircraft. While resting submerged on the bottom one day his passive sonar detected six ships passing by. However with so many surface and air patrols in the vicinity it was no longer safe to operate unless it was dark.

On 31 March U-123 attacked a heavily loaded freighter but missed its target when the G7e torpedo took a 20—30 degree course variation.

On 9 May Coast Guard Cutter Icarus made a sonar contact off Cape Lookout. It then heard an explosion, possibly caused by a torpedo from U-352. The torpedo had probably hit a shallow spot enroute Icarus. Icarus made a run on the torpedo explosion point and dropped five depth charges. U-352's commanding officer had chosen that exact spot to bottom and wait out the encounter. U-352 was mortally damaged, broached and was hit by Icarus' gunfire and sank. In addition, six other U-boats were destroyed off the East Coast between 14 January and 15 July 1942.

On 9 May 1942 U-110 was depth charged to the surface in the North Atlantic and captured. Her Enigma machine was captured intact along with settings good through the end of June. As a result between 25 May and 21 June BP was able to provide information resulting in the location and sinking of seven German supply ships which had assisted Bismarck, Prinz Eugen, and various U-boats.[129]

In June 1942 Atlantic escorts began the practice of refueling at sea from tankers accompanying the convoy. RN destroyers had older 300 psi steam plants and thus were less fuel efficient than contemporary U.S. destroyers with 600 psi steam plants, and consequently used more fuel. At sea refueling kept the escort groups intact, where before fuel shortages would have forced these escorts back to port to refuel thus breaking up the escort teams.

In June 1942 a German special submarine operation took place: Operation *PASTORIUS*, the landing of two teams of *saboteurs* on American soil. One team of four was put ashore at Amagansett, Long Island, New York on 13 June by U-202; and the second set of four at Ponte Vedra, Florida south of Jacksonville on 16 June by U-584. The operatives were equipped with U.S. currency, weapons, explosives, and civilian clothes, and had orders to target certain industrial facilities. One of the northern set turned informer and the FBI rapidly corralled them all before they could do any damage. All were court-martialed, and six were executed. The informer and another were imprisoned and returned to Germany after the end of the war.[130]

Phase Five

Back to the North Atlantic

On 19 July 1942 BdU withdrew the final two U-boats operating off Hatteras (U-754 and U-458). On 27 July BdU transferred almost all its U-boats back to the North Atlantic Theater of operations.[131]

From January through June 1942 U-boats sank 404 ships with 816 torpedoes, expending 2.02 torpedoes per ship sunk. All these torpedoes were equipped with contact exploders. Admiral Doenitz realized that an effective magnetic exploder would have meant the expenditure of only 404 torpedoes to accomplish the same number of sinking's.[132]It was fortunate for the allies that the German Navy did not have a workable magnetic exploder at that time. It could have almost doubled U-boat effectiveness. The magnetic exploder was not returned to service until 1944, too late to really matter. By that time the invasion of France had sealed Germany's doom.

In February 1942 Joubert of Coastal Command complained to the Under Secretary for Air that "Neither the Sunderland nor the Fortress (B-17) still less the Wellington or Whitley were long-range aircraft by Atlantic standards".

He suggested the reallocation of long range Lancaster bombers to Coastal Command for ASW purposes. Both Bomber Command and the Air Ministry stoutly opposed any such action.[133]

In April 1942 a copy of the new British Merchant Ship Code was captured by the Germans. British Naval Cipher No. 3 had also been penetrated by B-Dienst. Bletchley Park was unable to solve the 4th rotor problem at this time, so consequently B-Dienst was a step ahead in the cipher war.[134]

Toward mid-year the Admiralty decided that in order to win the ASW conflict Coastal Command would have to be strengthened at the expense of Bomber Command. Coastal Command was the air arm of the ASW battle which was the Admiralty's responsibility. The subject was delicate to say the least. The Admiralty was trying to advise the Royal Air Force about the proper distribution of long range and very long range aircraft between two major component forces of the RAF: Bomber Command and Coastal Command. In addition Bomber Command was embarked, with the full support of the RAF hierarchy and the Air Staff, on a city bombing campaign designed to win the war by destroying German industry. Bomber Command had started the war with a daylight strategic precision bombing campaign theory and had been blown out of the skies by German fighters and AAA. It then switched to night strategic precision bombing campaign until an investigation revealed that very few British bombers were finding the correct city let alone vital arms manufacturing facilities nearby. Finally Bomber Command shifted to a city bombing campaign to destroy the housing of German industrial workers. If they could not get adequate rest, war production would plummet, or so went the theory. To make matters even more delicate the Prime Minister, Winston Churchill, was a strong supporter of the bombing of Germany. It gave him an important talking point with Joseph Stalin who kept demanding a "Second Front" against the Germans. Churchill was determined that Great Britain would not attempt an invasion of France until it was much better prepared.

On 23 June the Admiralty sent a paper to the Chief of Air Staff and the Air Officer in Command, Coastal Command, noting that they had lost control over sea communications, and that ships alone were unable to control the seas. The paper pointed out that the loss of the "defensive" battle would hinder the ability of Allied forces to take the offensive (invade Europe).[135]

On 21 July Churchill issued a periodic review of the war, and discussed U-boat attacks, and the application of Allied air power.[136] At this time Doenitz was worried over the threat that Allied air power represented to his anti-convoy strategy, which depended upon the ability of U-boats to move freely on the surface to concentrate against convoys. He need not have worried.

Churchill was focused on Bomber Command's efforts to destroy German cities, ignoring the very real threat that U-boats would sink so much tanker tonnage that the bomber campaign would run short of fuel. There was a slight change in emphasis but no major action to beef-up Coastal Command with additional long range and very long range aircraft. It would be another year before the allocation of additional LRA to Coastal Command took place. During that year U-boats continued to sink ships and prevent vital cargoes from reaching the British Isles.

In 1942 only about six very long range (VLR) Liberator Mk I aircraft were available to Coastal Command. The "proper" use of long range aircraft was in dispute until late 1942 in Great Britain. Bomber Command thought that the proper use of long range aircraft (heavy bombers) was in destroying German industry and cities. Air Marshall Harris of Bomber Command was concentrating on area bombing of German cities, and looked on search time over the North Atlantic as lost motion, citing the infrequency of U-boat detections and attacks, let alone U-boat kills by LRA. He completely failed to recognize the devastating effect of long range air search on U-boat strategic mobility.

On 5 July the first ASV/Leigh Light U-boat kill took place in the Bay of Biscay. Doenitz immediately realized that aircraft had become a much more potent threat to his U-boats. About the same time, on 17 June

1942, Harris of Bomber Command was advising Churchill privately that Coastal Command was "merely an obstacle to victory."[137]

In August 1942 the Cabinet Anti-U-boat Warfare Committee was established to set priorities for the Battle of the Atlantic. It met weekly, and its membership included Ministers, Service Chiefs, their science advisors, and representatives of the U.S. government and U.S. Navy. The first meeting was held on 4 November 1942. At an early meeting the First Lord of the Admiralty noted the need to fill the "air gap" in the mid-Atlantic region. He recommended that some 40 long range radar-equipped aircraft be provided for this purpose, plus long range aircraft for the Bay of Biscay.[138]

On 17 July 1942 U-202 sighted a southbound convoy off the Canary Islands. The nearest Allied air base was just over 800 miles away but four-engine land based aircraft were screening the convoy. The report was received with shock by U-boat Command. Actually air escort at such long ranges would not be common for another nine months.[139]

During July 1942 Doenitz moved his main U-boat operating area back to the North Atlantic from American coastal waters. Increasingly heavy air cover and convoys had seriously reduced the vulnerability of shipping off the U.S. East Coast. Doenitz wanted to place his hunters in areas outside of Allied air cover where they could operate freely in wolf packs.[140] He did leave a few U-boats in Caribbean waters to ensure that AW forces could not be withdrawn completely and re-concentrated in new areas of U-boat activity.

In September 1942 Coastal Command still had only one Liberator squadron (6 Mk Is) in service. There were none based in Canada, Newfoundland, Gibraltar or West Africa. As late as February 1943 there was only one Coastal Command Liberator squadron, 120 Squadron at Aldergrove in Northern Ireland, and a detachment at Reykjavik.[141]

During 1942 Doenitz lost two of his *milchkuhs* to ASW forces, one type XB and one type XIV, limiting his operations in the South Atlantic.

In October 1942 Doenitz had 196 U-boats operational. OIC assessed their number at sea in the Atlantic as at least 100, which meant that Doenitz had at least two wolf packs available for operations against convoys. In mid-October convoy SC 104 lost 8 ships, for a toll of 3 U-boats by the escorts. SC 107 lost 15 ships at the end of October, with 3 more U-boats sunk. Convoy SL 125 (enr UK from Sierra Leone) was hit by a ten-strong wolf pack and lost 13 ships over a seven day period. However

SL 125 inadvertently distracted U-boat attention from a series of convoys converging on North Africa for the planned invasion in early November. The invasion was a strategic and tactical surprise to the Germans.[142]

In mid-November Admiral Max Horton took over command of Western Approaches from Admiral Percy Noble. Noble had built a very well structured command. Horton added a new wrinkle. In addition to the "Game", conducted in a school house environment to train escort ship commanders to work together, he took them to sea, using a converted yacht and RN submarines to simulate U-boats. This took their training to a new level.[143]

During the second half of 1942 U-boat Command came to the realization that the Allies were slowly gaining the upper hand with ASW countermeasures. Surfaced U-boats were being localized by both surface escorts and aircraft, depriving them of the vital element of surprise. U-boat Command thought that surface craft were using radar to detect the U-boats but did not realize that the main tool being used by surface escorts was HF/DF receivers which provided bearings to U-boat radio transmissions.[144] The frequent radio transmissions from U-boats were a key to their detection and localization.

During June 1942 U-boats transiting on the surface at night in the Bay of Biscay to and from their submarine pens began to be attacked by aircraft with searchlights. Three U-boats, outbound for patrols, were badly damaged and had to return to port for repairs. U-boat Command suspected a previously unknown electronic device was in use by British ASW aircraft. It looked to several possibilities to counter the new threat: new ESM receivers; radar on board the U-boats to detect the aircraft; and possible radar absorbing material to render the U-boat less detectable. The new device was the centimetric radar with a much shorter wave length than the more standard radars that were in use in Great Britain and Germany to detect enemy aircraft.[145]

Another possible countermeasure was to provide air escort for transiting U-boats until they reached the open ocean. Doenitz's request to Air Officer Commanding, Atlantic Command for air cover for his U-boats transiting the Bay of Biscay produced only one FW200 aircraft because no aircraft had been allotted for such duty by Air Force Headquarters.[146] Doenitz flew to Luftwaffe headquarters to see *Reichsmarschall* Goering, and was successful in having twenty-four JU88C6s, long range fighters, transferred to Atlantic Air Command.

Because of the danger from ASW aircraft Doenitz issued orders that transits of the Bay would be conducted submerged, day and night, with the U-boat surfacing only to charge batteries. He also allocated four 8 mm. machine guns to each boat for defense against air attack.

Doenitz realized that the use of ASW aircraft with a device that could locate surfaced U-boats at night threatened his whole scheme for night surfaced attacks by wolf packs against convoys. It led him to try to get higher priority for the *Walter* U-boat, which had been designed before the war started. The *Walter* boat was revolutionary in design and propulsion. It was highly streamlined for that time, designed for high underwater speed. It used steam turbines for propulsion with stored hydrogen peroxide (H_2O_2) called Perhydrol. Perhydrol mixed with oil was burned to produce steam. An experimental submarine of Professor *Hellmuth Walter's* design, V-80, was built at *Germaniawerft* in Kiel in 1940. It reached 23 knots submerged.

U-boat Command had three U-tankers (*milchkuhs*) in commission, and between the end of April and mid-June 1942 used them to refuel 20 of the 37 U-boats that were deployed to the Caribbean area.[147]

During fall 1942 there were three significant developments on the ASW side of the ledger that promised to bear fruit in the future. They were: dedicated ASW Support Groups (escort ship teams), trained and maintained as a unit, that went to sea to provide convoy support; the first escort carriers (CVE) equipped with ASW aircraft went to sea to operate in support of convoys; and finally, 10 cm. radar went to sea aboard escorts. U-boats did not have a radar intercept receiver capable of detecting the 10 cm. radar emissions so had no idea when they had been detected by an escort's radar.

About six months lapsed before the Support Groups and CVEs joined forces in convoy protection. When they did, along with a larger number of LRA, it spelled the end of the wolf pack reign of terror in the North Atlantic. Included in their tools were shallow set depth charges (25 foot setting) and with larger explosive charges, and the new 10 centimeter radar installed in LRA.

On 13 December 1942 BP finally penetrated the U-boat *Triton* (Shark) cipher, and could again read the instructions going out from *BdU* to U-boats in the Atlantic.[148]

The U-boat score for 1942 was 1,664 ships sunk (about 8 million tons). During 1942 some 108 German and Italian submarines were lost. U-boat depredations had reduced commercial fuel oil stocks in the United Kingdom to only two months supply. Imports to the British Isles during the year were only about one-third those of 1939. During the second half of 1942 some 121 U-boats were built but only 58 were sunk.

Mediterranean Operations 1942

In the Mediterranean Sea destroyer HMS Gurkha was torpedoed and sunk by U-133 on 17 January. On 16 June cruiser HMS Hermione was sunk by U-205 while escorting the VIGOROUS convoy to Malta. Also in June Submarine Tender HMS Medway was sunk by a U-boat while underway from Alexandria to Haifa, an unfortunate outcome of the temporary, partial abandonment of Alexandria as a base area because of the threat of Rommel's forces advancing eastward. The loss of torpedoes and repair parts would hinder British submarine operations. In August U-73 put four torpedoes into HMS Eagle, an older aircraft carrier completed in 1923. She sank in only eight minutes.

Important British oil convoys ran from the Levant ports to Egypt to fuel 8th Army vehicles.[149] They were a target for U-boats, but the U-boats themselves were targets in return. In the period January-March escorts sank three U-boats, with another five U-boats sunk during April-June. U-boat strength went down from 21 at the start of the year to only 16. During the June-July period another five were lost.[150]

During November the Allies invaded French North Africa. The invasion involved thousands of ships in a number of large convoys from the United Kingdom to the Mediterranean Sea area, and directly from the United States to the landing beaches on the North African Atlantic coastline. On 27 October U-boats operating west of Morocco sighted a north-bound merchant convoy from Sierra Leone and attacked it, sinking 13 ships. Fortunately the convoy distracted them and no U-boats detected the massive invasion convoys moving toward their targets.[151]

TORCH, the name given to the North African landings by British and American forces, had an associated deception plan that served to mask the real target. Dakar, on the coast of West Africa which had been attacked earlier and unsuccessfully by British-Free French forces, was indicated as the target for such forces as the German intelligence network became aware. Another deception element was information about a planned resupply effort to move needed supplies to Malta. The deceptions were successful in causing German intelligence analysts' attention to be diverted from the real objectives.

As soon as word of the North African invasions reached German authorities a U-boat concentration was ordered to try to disrupt the operations. Four days after the invasion began U-boats operating in the Med sank Viceroy of India (19,600 tons), Nieuw Amsterdam (11,600 tons), destroyer HMS Martin, and Dutch destroyer HNLMS Isaac Sweers. However the invasions of Algeria and Morocco proceeded without major difficulty. Admiral Doenitz notes somewhat bitterly that the German Intelligence Service under Admiral Canaris had failed to determine anything about the invasion in advance.[152]

On 16 November German Naval Command Headquarters issued orders to make up U-boat losses in the Med, and to maintain 20 U-boats west of Gibraltar and Morocco. On 18 November Doenitz challenged the order, pointing out that the real battle was a tonnage war best fought in the North Atlantic outside of allied air cover where the returns were greatest. On 23 December the Naval Command Headquarters canceled their previous orders and directed Doenitz to concentrate on the battle in the North Atlantic.

1943—Defeat in the North Atlantic

On 23 January 1943 Admiral Doenitz relieved Admiral Raeder as Commander-in-Chief of the German Navy. He retained his role as commander of all U-boats. The daily average of U-boats in the Atlantic at this time was 116, of which some 60 were in the North Atlantic. The latter number was still 40 U-boats short of the 100-average in the North Atlantic that Doenitz calculated would suffice to attrite shipping sufficiently to force Great Britain to negotiate.

B-Dienst was ahead of the GC & CS at this time in its decryption activities. Each supporting group was doing its best to provide accurate data about the enemy: B-Dienst about Allied convoy locations and movements; and GC & CS about U-boats.

In December 1942 a dispute over allocation of the new centimetric radar device to Coastal Command (for ASW) or to Bomber Command (for bombing accuracy against German targets) was resolved by Churchill—in favor of Bomber Command. Predictably a Stirling bomber equipped with the new radar device was shot down near Rotterdam on 2 February 1943. German investigators who examined the aircraft wreckage were astonished at the advanced radar capability. The centimetric radar device was thus compromised almost immediately.[153]

Terraine notes that ". . . more lip service than sincerity in responsible quarters . . ." was to be noted regarding the failure of British authorities to divert long range aircraft to fill the mid-Atlantic gap.[154] He remarks on Slessors' attempt to shift blame over to the American side—"King's obsession with the Pacific and the Battle of Washington cost us dear in the Battle of the Atlantic." The stark reality was that British authorities, starting with Harris at Bomber Command, Slessor the Chief of Air Staff, the Air Ministry, and Winston Churchill were all focused on punishing Germany by bombing her cities into dust on the false premise that such air attacks would seriously damage her defense industry and force her to surrender without an invasion. Terraine states that "A far smaller number of long range aircraft transferred in good time to Coastal Command would have been infinitely more useful—but the mere thought of such a thing would put Harris at the risk of apoplexy".[155]

In January convoy TM 1 (Trinidad to the UK) was almost destroyed. U-boats sank seven of nine tankers in the convoy.

During January 1943 Allied leaders met at Casablanca, Morocco to continue long range planning of the war effort. The continuing major U-boat threat led to a directive to RAF Bomber Command to focus on attacking German U-boat pens and submarine building yards. From January through May 1943 some 11,000 tons of high explosive and about 8,000 tons of incendiaries were dropped on those targets. However no U-boats were sunk or destroyed.[156] Finally on 23 July 1943 the first U-boat was finally destroyed in a RAF bombing raid.

Other major outcomes of the conference were that the U.S. would withdraw from North Atlantic convoy protection. Canada and the UK would share that responsibility. Canada then established a North West Atlantic Command at Halifax. The new CHOP line for shift of escorts was set at 47 degrees West longitude. In return the U.S. took on sole responsibility for the tanker convoys between Trinidad and the United Kingdom.

At this time Coastal Command had only 18 Liberator long range bombers assigned. Pressure was put on Admiral King, the U.S. Chief of Naval Operations, to divert some of the U.S. Navy's Liberators from the Pacific Theater to the North Atlantic. By July 1943 Coastal Command's Liberator inventory had climbed to 37 aircraft. However one squadron, 120 Squadron, carried most of the ASW load in the North Atlantic.

In February 1943 slightly more than 100 U-boats were on patrol, with 37 in the Greenland "air gap" where LRA did not yet cover. Out of nine convoys totaling 242 ships, 34 were lost, a 14% loss rate. On 4 February convoy SC 118 (63 ships) ran into a wolf pack of 21 U-boats which harassed them over a track of one thousand miles. Thirteen ships were lost (20.6%). Three U-boats were sunk and two more badly damaged by escorts. Only one squadron of Very Long Range aircraft was available in Coastal Command to cover the entire Atlantic area at this time.[157] These losses led to Churchill halting convoys to Russia in order to increase surface ship escorts for the North Atlantic convoys.[158]

In 1943 BdU had 212 operational U-boats of 393 in service, the remainder being in various phases of training and workup for operational patrols. This compared quite favorably with 1942 when only 91 U-boats were operational of 249 in service. In March U-boats sank 97 ships in 20 days, while losing only seven U-boats, and gaining another 14 from new construction. In mid-March (17-20 March) 40 U-boats engaged convoys SC 122, HX 229 and HX 229A. They sank 22 ships for the loss of only one U-boat.

During March 1943 U-boat attacks on convoys intensified. During the first ten days they sank 41 ships, and during the following ten days—another 56 ships, totaling 97 ships for more than half a million tons of shipping. The Admiralty was concerned that the wolf pack tactic had overcome the convoy system. They had lost some 500,000 tons in 20 days, and two-thirds of the lost ships had been sunk in convoy. If the convoy system failed, what could they do? No one knew the answer, although it was about to creep up on them. It consisted of the number of elements that finally came together that spring. They included:

Escort aircraft carriers that extended air cover into the regions not covered by LRA

Surface warship "Support Groups", formations of four to six antisubmarine warfare escorts commanded by RN Captains, organized and trained to pursue U-boats and hunt them to destruction.

Increased number of LRA to reduce the "air gap" which allowed U-boats to use their surface speed to concentrate for wolf pack attacks

In a series of coordinated U-boat attacks on convoys during March, April and May the collective effect of these ASW elements became clear. No longer could U-boats use their high surface speed at night to close on convoys. LRA with 10 cm radar detected them and attacked without any warning. CVE aircraft helped fill in gaps that LRA could not reach. Convoy escorts with HF/DF could detect U-boat radio transmissions at ranges of 20—25 miles, and anticipate their approach. High frequency radar aboard the escorts detected the surfaced U-boat at a range of about five miles and allowed them to take action before the U-boat could get into torpedo firing range. Support Groups tenaciously hung on to each U-boat contact and hunted it to destruction, leaving the protected convoy to proceed on its way.

However in March 1943 the U-boat toll was still high. SC 121 lost 13 ships from 7-11 March. SC 122/HX 229 lost a total of 21 ships (141,000 tons) that month to a 40-U-boat wolf pack.[159]

A number of convoys in April and May escaped loss at all while their escorts took a toll of the wolf packs. Convoy SC 130 (19-20 May) lost no ships and sank 5 U-boats. HX 239 and ON 184 were attacked by 21 U-boats. No ships were lost but 2 U-boats were sunk. From 6 April to 19 May, 912 ships sailed in convoy but only 17 were sunk plus 6 more stragglers lost. However 27 U-boats were sunk by escorts.

By 22 May 1943 U-boat losses for the month reached 31 sunk, with others damaged by depth charges and bombs. Admiral Doenitz and his staff had to accept the fact that Allied ASW counter-measures had reached such a stage that the strategic U-boat campaign was lost. There was no way that it could continue in the face of the attrition figures. On 24 May 1943 Admiral Doenitz issued an order to his U-boats to withdraw from the North Atlantic, acknowledging that the Allies had gained the upper hand for good. Wolf pack operations on the surface at night were no longer feasible due to the heavy losses of U-boats being inflicted by improved Allied ASW measures.[160] During that month some 41 U-boats were lost in all theaters for the gain of only 50 ships sunk (265,000 tons).

German scientists had believed that it was not possible to resolve weight and size problems with HF/DF equipment to make it feasible to install aboard ships. However, in early 1940 British scientists solved the problem, and a prototype FH 1 set was installed aboard destroyer HMS Hesperus that March. Improved FH 3 sets were installed in destroyers Gurkha and Lance in July 1941. By spring 1943 at least two escorts for each North Atlantic convoy carried either a FH 3 or FH 4 set. The HF/DF sets provided about 25 nm detection on German U-boat radio signals, furnishing accurate bearings to the signals. It was a relatively simple matter for the escort group commander to maintain a plot of reported U-boat signals to provide a rough fix on U-boats closing the convoy at night. The Type 271 radar set (2997 Mhz) only provided a range of 3-5 km on a trimmed down U-boat superstructure, so HF/DF provided a real tactical advantage. U-boat Command and U-boat COs were unaware of this development and ascribed their detections to British radar capability.[161] Consequently they did not reduce their radio transmissions.

Early radar sets had begun to be installed in British escorts in fall 1940. The British labeled them Radio Direction Finder (RDF) sets. The Type 286 set operated in the 1.5 meter frequency band (214 Mhz) and could detect a surfaced U-boat superstructure at about 1,000 meters. By March 1941 some 90 escorts were fitted with this set.

The Western Approaches Tactical Unit (WATU) was established on the top floor of the Tate & Lyle Exchange Building in Liverpool. Commander Gilbert Howland Roberts, RN (later Captain) directed tactical courses using floor plots forming a "tactical table". Models of ships, escorts, and U-boats represented the theoretical scene at sea. The entire floor could be used for 24 participants, or it could be cordoned off to provide three separate sets for 8 participants each. A staff of WRNS moved the models as directed by the exercise staff or the exercise participants. The participants were Escort Group Commanders and watch officers. Their task was to solve the tactical problem presented to them.

Cdr. Roberts conducted extensive interviews of returning Escort Group Commanders to determine the latest German tactics, and which

Escort Group tactics had worked well. The results were continuously fed into the current tactical courses, which lasted about six days.

A number of escort plans: Raspberry, Pineapple, and Gooseberry, among others, were introduced as simulations, tried out on the tactical table and then taken to sea where they proved effective. Sea training in these procedures, using tame submarines as U-boat attackers, was carried out at: Londonderry; Greenock; Birkenhead; Freetown; Bombay; St. Johns, Newfoundland; and Sydney, Nova Scotia. The escort groups practiced under their own senior officers, gaining experience and confidence at sea.[162]

An improved radar set, Type 271, operated in the 10 centimeter band and could detect a U-boat superstructure at 3,000-5,000 meters. By May 1942 some 236 RN ships had Type 271 installations. No German electronic search receiver installed in U-boats was capable of detecting its electronic signal.[163]

Convoy ONS 5, from the UK to North America was a turning point in the Battle of the Atlantic according to Admiral Doenitz. It was one of the last examples of an attempted coordinated wolf pack attack. ONS 5 consisted of 43 ships in ballast, escorted by B7 Escort Flotilla, consisting of seven warships. In late April—early May 1943 Doenitz concentrated 30 U-boats to take on ONS 5. No ships were sunk, and four U-boats were destroyed, with four more very probably destroyed and two probably destroyed according to the Escort Group Commander's report.[164]

The U-boat arm introduced *Bold,* a chemical solution giving off bubbles that could be mistaken for a submerged U-boat, as an evasion device to be used when escorts had a U-Boat cornered with their Asdic transmissions. *Bold* was also called *Pillenwerfer.* The device produced bubbles for a period from 25 to 30 minutes. The key to distinguishing an actual U-boat from the bubble simulation was the lack of Doppler Effect when the target consisted of gas bubbles. Inexperienced Asdic operators might fail to detect the lack of Doppler and conclude that they had a U-boat trapped.[165]

BdU and German Naval Intelligence firmly believed that British and American HF/DF coverage was only provided by shore stations. The Germans knew from their own experience the navigational uncertainty introduced by long range bearings and the consequent very large area of probable location of a contact. They did not realize that Allied ships and aircraft were equipped with efficient HF/DF equipment that could quickly and accurately localize U-boats from their radio transmissions at close range.[166]

By and large German scientific advances related to submarine warfare lagged those of the Allies. The United States had been working on a deadly U-boat counter-measure, an acoustic homing torpedo, nicknamed "Fido". It was originally intended for use against IJN submarines in the Pacific. However, the UK delegates to a Washington, D.C. Convoy Conference in March 1943 talked Admiral King into allowing its simultaneous deployment in the Atlantic. May 1943 was the month set for initial use. Strict rules were in effect to preserve secrecy and forestall German counter-measures. Fido could only be used in deep water, never in view of surface escorts (it was dropped by ASW aircraft), and only on diving U-boats. The tight security measures imposed ensured that the Germans only learned about Fido after the end of the war. The initial order was for 10,000 Mk 24 Mines, a designation intended to hide the fact that it was an acoustic ASW torpedo. Its effectiveness was so great that the production order was later reduced to 4,000 units.

On 12 May 1943 three Fido were dropped, one hit U-456 and forced it to surface. As a surface escort came up the U-boat dove again and never came up.[167] This was the first recorded kill. A total of 37 submarines (German and Japanese) are credited to Fido beginning in 1943. Another 18 were damaged by Fido attacks. Fido was modified for use by U.S. submarines in the Pacific. It was officially designated the Mk 24 torpedo, but called the "Cutie". It was successful in damaging or sinking a number of Japanese ASW vessels.

In May 1943 Admiral Doenitz realized that the U-boat wolf pack campaign against the convoy system had been defeated by a combination of Allied countermeasures. The question for him was to continue U-boat attacks or not? He decided to continue attacks while trying to minimize U-boat losses in order to keep pressure on the Allies so that their ASW forces could not be freed up for other activities. He was trying to hold on until the *Walter* boats, which were very advanced submarines, could become available.[168]

As conditions for U-boats in the North Atlantic were steadily worsening in April 1943 Doenitz decided to send several Type IXC and IXD U-boats to the Indian Ocean. The Japanese had earlier expressed a desire to have German U-boat pressure in the Indian Ocean. A number of U-boats sailed in June, and conducted patrols in the Indian Ocean, before proceeding to Penang in Malaya for upkeep and crew rest. They sank 57 ships (365,807 tons). Twenty-two U-boats were dispatched, but sixteen were sunk by Allied ASW forces in the Atlantic while in transit.[169]

During 1943 Doenitz lost eleven resupply U-boats in the Atlantic (4 x XB and 7 x XIV). Many were lost to the increasing number of CVEs which were operating in the Atlantic.[170]

In June 1943 no North Atlantic convoy was attacked by U-boats. Doenitz diverted 16 U-boats to the area north of the Azores where there might be better hunting and fewer hounds. Unfortunately it was an area saturated with U.S. CVEs and their aircraft.[171]

Only one ship was lost in a convoy between 6/01/43 and 9/18/43. Only 15 ships were lost in the North Atlantic during this time frame.[172]

In earlier years one U-boat had been sunk for about 100,000 tons of target shipping sunk. By May 1943 one U-boat was being sunk for only each 10,000 tons of shipping sunk. Doenitz decided that the new exchange ratio was unacceptable and unsustainable. Action was taken to withdraw U-boats from the North Atlantic and redirect them to West Africa and Brazilian coasts, the Caribbean basin, and to oppose U.S.—Gibraltar traffic in the Central Atlantic region.[173]

The U.S. escort carrier production lines had swung into full action earlier. CVEs were being produced for both the USN and the RN By mid-1943 a number of the USN CVEs were worked up and at sea with their escorts. They operated mostly in the mid-Atlantic region. During a 98-day period ending in August 1943 Admiral Ingersoll's escort carrier groups sank 16 U-boats and *8 milchkuhs*. The *milchkuhs* were probably the more valuable targets since their operations allowed regular U-boats to extend their operational patrols.[174]

In July 1943 conversion of Type VII and IX U-boats to include a *snorkel* capability began. By June 1944 some thirty U-boats would have *snorkels*. Their existence was confirmed by the Allies in February 1944. Enigma decrypts had revealed Baltic Sea trials of the *snorkel* in December 1943.[175]

Mediterranean Defeat

As the chances of successful U-boat operations in the North Atlantic dimmed, Admiral Doenitz, ever the opportunist, shifted his boats to areas that either promised better tonnage scores or were dictated by higher authority. The Mediterranean Sea fell into the latter category. The German and Italian high commands split the Med as follows:

Germans	Straits of Gibraltar to 3 degrees West (12 U-boats)
	Aegean Sea and south of Crete (U-boats)
Italians	Central Mediterranean

In July 1943 the Axis concentrated 16 submarines south of Sicily. Between September 1943 and May 1944 some 27 U-boats attempted to pass eastward through the Strait of Gibraltar. Fourteen were successful, seven were detected and sunk, and six turned back in the face of operational difficulties.

During the period January through May 1943 nine Italian submarines and eleven U-boats were sunk in the Med. Between June and December 1943 another twenty (this time nine U-boats and eleven Italian) submarines were sunk in the Med. The U-boat/submarine sinking's totaled 40 for the year. The victory over Axis submarines in the Med lagged that in the North Atlantic by about four months, but was just as decisive.[176]

On 18 February cruiser HMS Penelope was sunk by a U-boat while operating off the Anzio beachhead.

From January through May 1944 U-boats and German bombers sank ten merchant ships. Twelve U-boats were destroyed in air attacks on their base at Toulon, France, or at sea using "swamp" tactics. By the end of May there were only eleven U-boats left in the Mediterranean. After May 1944 no further Allied or neutral merchant ships were sunk in the Mediterranean by U-boats.[177]

The defeat of U-boats and Italian submarines in the Mediterranean meant that major British warships could be sent to the Eastern Fleet in the Indian Ocean for operations against the Japanese, or to Home Fleet in preparation for the coming invasion of France.

In the Bay of Biscay a major ASW campaign was waged by the RAF Coastal Command and the USAAF, with Royal Navy assistance. An early effort in February was defeated by the German *Metox*, an ESM receiver installed in U-boats that detected the standard high frequency airborne radar. On 20 March 1943 Coastal Command first began to employ a higher frequency radar (10 centimeter wave length) that could not be detected by the *Metox* receiver. The new radar, teamed with the high intensity

Leigh (search) light, allowed the patrolling aircraft to electronically detect, close, illuminate and attack a surfaced U-boat without the U-boat watch having any idea of the aircraft's proximity until their bridge was suddenly illuminated. The bright light was followed by a string of depth bombs.

May 1943 marked the end of the Coastal Command Bay of Biscay offensive against U-boats. There had been 2,425 transits. Fifty U-boats were sunk and another fifty-six damaged. Three hundred fifty aircraft were lost.

Between May and December 1943 some 32 transiting U-boats were sunk by these forces, mostly by aircraft. The air ASW offensive largely succeeded because the Luftwaffe chose not to adequately contest air superiority over the Bay of Biscay. Goering and Doenitz did not get along well, and Luftwaffe support, in the form of long range reconnaissance for U-boat operations was sadly lacking. This particular failure in the Bay of Biscay highlights the lack of focus among the German higher command elements upon which parts of their war effort were most important. The buildup of Allied forces in the British Isles for the eventual invasion of France could only be stopped or delayed by U-boat operations. And yet U-boat transits across the Bay of Biscay were rendered hazardous to an extreme by Allied ASW aircraft while the Luftwaffe headquarters essentially stood by looking on with its hands in its pockets, whistling idly.[178]

During 1943 some 263 German and Italian submarines were lost, more than twice the number lost during the previous year.

Despite attempts by Bomber Command of the RAF and the United States 8th Air Force to attack German U-boats at their source: the shipbuilding yards in Germany; U-boat production continued without much interruption. U-boat production figures for the years 1939 through 1945 are shown in the following table:[179]

1939	18
1940	50
1941	199
1942	237
1943	284
1944	229
1945 (through 4 May 1945 when U-boats were directed to surrender)	91
Total	1108

In September 1943 Doenitz sent 28 U-boats back into the North Atlantic struggle, equipped with a new anti-radar ESM receiver and a new T5 acoustic torpedo (*Zaunkonig*). The new ESM receiver undoubtedly saved some U-boats from destruction by LRA equipped with the 10-centimeter radar, but since they dived to avoid attack the result was to lose their surface mobility—a key requirement of the wolf pack tactic. U-boats sank six merchant ships, a destroyer, a frigate and a corvette—all with acoustic torpedoes that homed on their propellers. They also seriously damaged a destroyer and a frigate. The UK was aware of the new threat and devised a noisemaker, called "Foxer", designed to be towed behind escorts to attract the acoustic torpedo. Despite the new acoustic torpedo Doenitz lost nine U-boats that month for slightly less than 44,000 tons of shipping sunk. "Foxer" effectively decoyed the German acoustic torpedo and rapidly reduced its threat.

Convoy ONS 18 consisting of 28 ships departed Milford Haven on 12 September, and ON 202 of 40 ships departed Liverpool three days later, both convoys headed westward. Nineteen U-boats engaged the two convoys. Six ships and three escorts were lost for the sinking of three U-boats.

In October Escort Group B7 escorted convoys ON 206 and ONS 20. They engaged in a five day battle with U-boats. Only one ship was sunk but six U-boats succumbed to air and surface escort attack.

That month negotiations between Portugal and Great Britain finally resulted in the Portuguese government granting rights to establish air and naval bases in the Azores. That greatly assisted in extending surface and air escort coverage in the middle Atlantic.

In September and October some 2,468 ships sailed in 64 North Atlantic convoys and only nine were sunk by U-boats. In October 26 U-boats were sunk, six of them by USN CVE group aircraft. On 16 November 1943 Doenitz again withdrew his U-boats from the North Atlantic, this time for good.[180]

Eight Japanese submarines were busy working the trade routes off the coast of East Africa during 1943. They and seven German U-boats sank 57 ships (337,000 tons) during the period June-December 1943.[181]

1944

On 1 January 1944 in a 'state of the Reich' speech at the *Reichstag*, Adolph Hitler attributed the "decline in U-boat successes" to "only one invention" referring to ASV (airborne radar).[182] He was only partially correct. ASV played a significant role in the search for U-boats. But a greater role was played by HF/DF installed in escort ships. In fact it was a combination of well equipped escorts, LRA, and cryptographic intelligence that allowed Allied ASW forces to prevail over sophisticated U-boat attacks against convoys.

In mid-January Doenitz concentrated his U-boats in the Western Approaches. The British Submarine Tracking Room was forewarned by intelligence. The WA Commander concentrated several Support Groups plus Coastal Command aircraft. On 28 January CC aircraft sank 2 U-boats. On 31 January HMS Stanley sank U-592. On 8 February U-762 was sunk by HMS Woodpecker. On 9 February U-238 finally succumbed to eight hours of "creeping attacks" and 266 depth charges. On 10 February aircraft from CVE HMS Fencer sank U-666, and a Leigh-Light equipped Wellington bomber damaged U-283 to the point that her crew scuttled her. On 11 February U-424 was lost. On 18 February U-406 went down for the last time. On 19 February U-264 and U-386 were sunk. During a 27-day period 2nd Escort Group, which included five sloops, sank six U-boats. Other Escort Groups and aircraft sank five more. Twelve convoys passed unattacked during this period.[183]

During the spring of 1944 Capt. Daniel Gallery, USN commanded a HUK (hunter-killer) Group. He was looking for an opportunity to capture a U-boat and seize its cryptographic material. He had not been briefed on the Allies' success in cracking the German Enigma machine traffic. He trained special boarding teams to go aboard any U-boat that was forced to the surface, and to seize cryptographic material and capture the boat if possible. On 4 June 1944 U-505 was forced to the surface. Gallery's teams went into action and captured it with all cryptographic material and Enigma machine intact. Admiral King was furious. If the German Navy learned of her capture they would assume that the current cryptographic material was compromised, and would change their ciphers. King ordered that the U-505 be towed to Norfolk and the entire HUK Group personnel sworn to secrecy. Admiral Doenitz thought U-505 had been sunk and no cipher changes took place—fortunately for the Allies.[184]

In May 1944 Admiral Doenitz cancelled all attacks against convoys and advised Adolph Hitler that they would not be restarted until the new types of U-boats became available, referring to the Types XXI and XXIII. In January through March some 3,360 ships had sailed in 105 convoys and only three ships were sunk by U-boats. During this period 29 U-boats were sunk. Six more U-boats were lost in April.

By early 1944 U-boats had a new ESM receiver designed to detect the 10-centimeter radar that had been recovered from the shot-down Stirling bomber. During January and February some 116 U-boat transits of the Bay of Biscay took place, but Coastal Command aircraft sank only two of the transiting U-boats.

In early May ice in the Baltic Sea finally thawed and U-boats could move out of the Baltic. From 16 May through 3 June, seven U-boats were detected, attacked and sunk. Another four had to turn back. However all but one of the *snorkel* equipped U-boats got through safely to their new bases in Norway.

During the period June through September 1944 U.S. CVEs and their aircraft sank seven U-boats and one Japanese submarine in the mid-Atlantic.[185] They were greatly assisted by locating information provided by Ultra information. Their victims included one U-cruiser (long range U-boat) and one *milchkuh*, the latter loss further reducing U-boat reach and endurance.

U-boats in the Indian Ocean

During World War II some 66 U-boats deployed to the Indian Ocean. Thirty-nine of those boats were sunk, either in the Indian Ocean or in transit. Two U-boats returned to their occupied French base with cargos from the Far East. They sank 150 allied or neutral merchant ships (about 1.5 million gross register tons).[186]

In November 1942 a group of U-boats using U-tankers to refuel them, went around Cape Horn into the Indian Ocean. They operated in the Mozambique Channel, sinking thirty ships before returning to their bases in occupied France.

In December 1942 Japan proposed that Germany base some U-boats at Penang in captured Malaya. In April 1943 a large U-cruiser was sent to Penang to check out base facilities. In May 1943 Doenitz realized the wolf pack operations in the Atlantic were becoming marginal. At the end of June eleven large U-boats sailed for the Far East. They planned to refuel in mid-Atlantic from U-tankers and near Mauritius from a tanker. Only four of them reached Penang. They sank 40 ships in the Indian Ocean. Later another seven U-cruisers attempted to proceed to the Indian Ocean. None reached Penang.

Through 1944 Germany maintained a level of about four U-boats in the Indian Ocean. In the fall of 1944 Great Britain finally instituted convoys for all merchant traffic in the Indian Ocean

In the Indian Ocean during the period January to March 1944 six German U-boats and 3-4 Japanese submarines sank 29 ships (188,000 tons). During June-August 1944 some 4—5 U-boats and 2 IJN submarines sank 17 merchant ships (over 100,000 tons), for the loss of only two of their number, one German and one Japanese. The lack of an adequate number of surface escorts precluded convoying all merchant traffic in the Indian Ocean. In May all U-boats returned to their advanced base at Penang, in Malaya.

In October 1944 Germany ordered all those U-boats operating in the Indian Ocean, which could make the journey, back to Germany. Four were sunk enroute and three arrived safely. Four others were turned over to the IJN.[187]

The Imperial Japanese Navy wrapped up their Indian Ocean submarine operations in August 1944. During a three year period Japanese submarines sank 70 ships. U-boats sank 118 ships in a two-year period.[188]

A total of nineteen U-boats were lost in transit in the Atlantic.

Too Little, Too Late

By May 1944 U-boat Command had worked out technical and operational problems with the new *snorkel* and sent its first *snorkel*-equipped U-boats to sea. The *snorkel* was a Dutch-originated device that allowed submarines to raise a breathing tube just above the surface to replenish the atmosphere within the submarine. The Germans modified and adapted the device to allow the U-boat to run its diesel engines while submerged. *Snorkel* speed was slow, about a maximum of six knots, as compared to the 17 knots the U-boat could make on the surface. However, the radar signature of the *snorkel* head valve was very small and thus difficult to detect.[189] The *snorkel* equipped Type VII U-boat was an interim step before new high speed U-boats (Types XXI and XXIII *Electroboote*) could be introduced. The ultimate U-boat was to be the *Walter* boat, a hydrogen peroxide fueled submarine whose propulsion was independent of atmospheric air and could make very high speed submerged, faster than any surface escort.

The invasion of Normandy took place on 6 June 1944. The exact location was a surprise to German commanders who expected a crossing at the *Pas de Calais,* the narrowest stretch of the English Channel, near Dover. Admiral Doenitz immediately ordered all available U-boats into the area fully realizing that the non-*snorkel* boats were almost sure to be lost to Allied ASW forces. Nine *snorkel* boats went to the vicinity of the Isle of Wight, and seven without *snorkels* to the Scilly Isles. Another 18 operated in the Bay of Biscay. In all, U-boats only sank two frigates and one corvette. Twenty-five U-boats were sunk in the Channel or its approaches, and seven more were sunk in the Bay of Biscay. The U-boat arm was as ineffective in preventing the invasion and its resupply operations as it had been in preventing BOLERO, the buildup of forces and material in Great Britain in the years preceding.

New manufacturing techniques were introduced to reduce production time for the Type XXI (1600 ton) submarine. They involved section production at dispersed factories located inland and shipment of the pre-fabricated sections by barge along canals to assembly shipyards for final assembly. These techniques reduced production man hours (MH) required from 460,000 to a range of 260,000-300,000 MH. Plans called for the first XXI to be ready by spring 1944 and a number more that fall, and 140 Type XXIII (230 tons) also to be ready for operations. In line

71

with these changes, no conventional U-boats were laid down after July 1943.

For once Allied bombing campaigns began to play a large role in ASW even if not directly. They managed to seriously damage a number of the canals needed to move the pre-fab U-boat sections to their assembly yards and thus seriously delay production.[190] The end result was that only a handful of Type XXIII and only one Type XXI U-boat became operational before the end of the European War in May 1945.

During 1944 the North Atlantic convoy campaign exposed 266 convoys consisting of a total of 12,907 ships to U-boat attack. Only 16 ships were sunk in convoy, with another three convoy stragglers sunk[191] The decisive defeat of the U-boat during 1943 continued into 1944. Admiral Doenitz had counted on new development U-boats restoring chances of victory. The type XXI and XXIII were advanced in design and performance but they were very slow in coming out of the shipyards and getting into service. Similarly, the revolutionary *Walter* boat, powered by a hydrogen peroxide engine, and thus not needing atmospheric air for propulsion was very slow in development. Allied air attacks on U-boat building yards were finally beginning to have an effect. Several *Walter* boats entered service in 1945 but none made an operational patrol.

During August-October 1944 Germany transferred all its French-based U-boats to Norway. This marked the end of U-boat opposition to the invasion forces. From Norway they embarked on patrols off the United Kingdom. U-boats equipped with *snorkels* were usually able to make the trip to their patrol areas without being detected by radar-equipped Allied ASW aircraft. In late August—early September U-482 (*snorkel*) sank a corvette and four merchant ships off Northern Ireland, without being attacked itself.

In October 1944 some 49 U-boats transited the northern route from Norway to UK coastal areas and only one was attacked and damaged. In December 50 U-boats were on passage and none were detected by aircraft. However, during the last four months of 1944, U-boats only sank 14 merchant ships and over 12,000 ships were safely convoyed. The entire massive ASW effort only accounted for 20 U-boats. Although the fact that it had gotten harder to kill a U-boat was frustrating to ASW Forces, the reality was that U-boats had lost their strategic mobility after being forced off the surface. They were still dangerous tactically but no longer a strategic threat.

In March 1945 U-boat Command successfully employed several *snorkel* equipped U-boats against a convoy to Russia. Convoy JW-65 (North-bound) was attacked off the Kola Inlet of North Russia. Sloop HMS Lapwing, an escort, was sunk by a U-boat homing torpedo along with a Liberty ship. Although the convoy was supported by two Royal Navy CVEs, their aircraft had no luck in detecting the *snorkel* boats.[192] Admittedly the attacks took place close inshore which could have made it more difficult for aircraft radar to detect a *snorkel*.

The first two Type XXIIIs became operational in January and February 1945. They only carried two torpedoes apiece. U-2324 used both its torpedoes to sink a merchant ship in February and then returned to port in Bergen, Norway. Later five more Type XXIIIs arrived in Home Waters off the UK, and sank seven ships without loss to themselves. U-2326 sank two ships the last night of the European War, 4 May 1945.

By the end of April, 12 Type XXI boats had completed their workups, and another 99 were in their acceptance trials. On 30 April, the first Type XXI (U-2511) became operational. On 4 May Admiral Doenitz directed all U-boats to surrender.[193]

The last U-boat campaign against the continental United States took place during April and May 1945. It was Operation SEA WOLF, and involved six *snorkel* equipped U-boats sent towards the U.S. East Coast to attack shipping. It had no real strategic purpose since the war was already lost by Germany. Faulty Allied intelligence indicated that the U-boats involved might be equipped to launch rocket attacks on American coastal cities, mirroring the V-1 and V-2 missile attacks on England and London. As a result Operation TEARDROP, a major ASW operation involving two escort carrier ASW groups, was set in motion. Five of the *snorkel* boats were sunk by U.S. surface escorts, with one DE lost to a U-boat. Aircraft had serious problems detecting the *snorkel* boats, which were finally run to ground by the active sonar equipped surface escorts also equipped with radar.[194]

On 4 May 1945 Admiral Doenitz ordered his U-boats to surface and fly a black flag signifying their surrender. 156 did so. Another 221 were scuttled by their crews in defiance of orders to surrender. Two stayed at sea, using their *snorkels* and reached Argentine waters safely in late July and early August respectively. There the crews were interned.

The final score for the German U-boat campaign of 1939-1945 was as follows:[195]

2,828 Allied or neutral ships sunk[196]

14,687,231 gross register tons of shipping lost

158 British Commonwealth warships sunk

29 American warships sunk

781 German U-boats lost

32,000 U-boat crew men killed or captured

Morison had this to say about the Battle of the Atlantic, ". . . in all probability the British Isles would have been blockaded and starved into submission.", referring to a possible final success by the German U-boats.[197]

The table below shows the total score of sinking's and U-boat sinking's by year.

Year	Total Ships Sunk	Sunk By Submarine
1939	222	114
1940	1059	471
1941	1299	432
1942	1664	1160
1943	597	377
1944	205	132
1945	105	56

Doenitz's U-boat Arm had proven to be a deadly threat to British survival, with its innovative wolf pack tactics and night surfaced attacks that bypassed British Asdic capability. The wolf packs almost destroyed the British convoy system. Only a massive ASW effort, with the contribution of long range aircraft and radar, enabled the British to defeat the wolf packs. Consequently, one must rate the U-boat Arm as highly effective.

The following two charts display million gross register tons of shipping sunk in the Atlantic from 1939 through 1945, and the number of U-boats sunk during those same years:

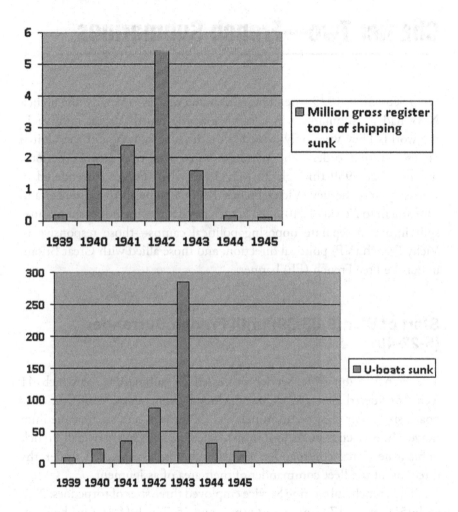

Chapter Two—French Submarines

On 3 September 1939 when France declared war on Germany, the French Navy had 77 submarines in commission, the fourth largest number in the world. They were only exceeded by the USSR, Italy and the United States—in that order. The narrative will cover two distinct periods; 3 September 1939 through 22 May 1940 when France surrendered to Germany and the new Vichy French Regime came in to existence; and subsequent to 22 May 1940 when French naval forces including submarines split into two separate opposing political camps—those responsive to Vichy French (VF) political direction, and those allied with Great Britain under the Free French (FF) banner.

Start of War (9-03-39) until French Surrender (5-22-40)

The French Submarine Service possessed 77 submarines of which 41 were considered first rate. These included twenty-nine 1500 ton class boats, six Saphir class ocean minelayers (925 tons), and six new medium range Minerve class boats (856 tons). There was no single overall French Submarine Force commander. French submarines operated under the direction of the fleet commander of their area of assignment.

The French Submarine Service employed three sizes of torpedoes: 21.7 inch (550 mm), 17.7 inch (450 mm.), and 15.7 inch (400 mm) between WW I and WW II. The older boats carried only 450 mm. torpedoes, while newer submarines employed 550 mm. and 400 mm. torpedoes.[198] All the classes built from 1930-on had a mix of torpedo tube sizes, with most their tubes 21.7 inch (550 mm.), and at least two or three tubes 15.7 inch (400 mm.)

The largest size torpedoes were reportedly incapable of being set for less than ten foot depth and thus unusable against shallow draft targets like escorts. They were reserved for major warship targets. The smallest torpedo had a smaller warhead, but was capable of sinking an escort, or a merchant ship that lacked the internal compartmentation of a large warship.

At the end of 1938 French submarines *Le Phenix* and *L'Espoir* were temporarily detached from the 5th Submarine Squadron at Toulon and sent out to Saigon via the Suez Canal. Lack of air conditioning machinery meant that their stay in the tropical area of the Far East would be relatively short.

On 15 June 1939 *Le Phenix* was lost just off Cam Ranh Bay at French Indo-China, reportedly due to a battery explosion. The French Navy was concerned about information about submarine problems getting around at a time when events in Europe foretold war, and put out a story that *Le Phenix* had dived with a hatch open, thus slandering her crew rather than admitting to a possible problem with French submarine material.[199]

L'Espoir conducted limited surveillance patrols off the coast of Indo-China after the war began. On 2 November 1939 she departed Saigon and transited through the Indian Ocean stopping at Djibouti, French Somaliland, before passing through the Suez Canal enroute Toulon.

According to Blair, there was no apparent coordination between the Royal Navy of Great Britain and the French Navy regarding submarine operations during the period 9-03-39 and the date of the armistice signed between France and Germany on 5-22-40.[200] However it seems more than likely that the Royal Navy and the French Navy exchanged some information about assigned submarine patrol areas during the short-lived Norwegian Campaign. Both countries had experienced submarine fratricide in submarine operations during World War I when they were strong allies, and the French had a naval liaison office in London headed by a Vice Admiral.

In the Far East it appears there was some cooperative initiative between the British and French area commanders. *L'Espoir* arrived at Singapore in mid-August 1939. There apparently was a plan for her to work with British submarines in the event of war. However she returned to Saigon on 1 September. Subsequently she sailed for surveillance patrols off Indo-China.[201]

At the beginning of the war on 3 September 1939 French submarines were deployed as follows:[202]

Mediterranean Sea	53
Morocco	4
Indo-China	1

A brief review of major military activities from the start of the war until the French surrender may help the reader follow the submarine narrative more easily.

Germany invaded Poland on September 1, 1939 and France and Great Britain declared war on Germany on September 3rd in keeping with the political guarantees they had extended to Poland when the Nazi threat became clear. The German regime was only able to launch its attack on Poland without undue concern because Germany and the Soviet Union had signed a secret treaty in late August 1939, giving Germany a free hand in western Poland. In return the USSR was accorded a free hand in eastern Poland and the Baltic States of Estonia, Latvia, and Lithuania.

Germany, using its new *blitzkrieg* tactics, made short work of the Polish army and air force. To add insult to injury the USSR attacked from Poland's eastern border on 17 September and sealed her fate. On 27 September Poland surrendered. The French General Staff had promised the Polish General Staff that it would launch a major ground offensive on Germany's western front in the event that Germany invaded Poland. The attack was to include 35 to 38 divisions and was intended to force the German army to look over its shoulder and thus hinder its attack on Poland. Four days after the start of the war, only nine French divisions moved forward into German territory, occupied some rapidly deserted villages, sat on their haunches for a few days and then returned to their original positions. The French had also promised to send a number of bomber squadrons to operate from Polish air bases against German forces. When a French air force general and his small staff arrived in Poland they found that German armor and infantry forces had moved so rapidly that the air bases intended for their use had already been captured.[203]

France, fearing an air attack on its major cities, particularly Paris, forbore from launching any bombing raids on German targets. Great Britain had no common border with Germany and so could not use its ground forces. The Royal Navy immediately established a distant blockade of Germany in the North Sea and commenced operations against German naval targets and merchant ships. The Royal Air Force was tasked to conduct air attacks on German naval targets but with paralyzing restrictions. Bombs were not allowed to fall on German soil. Attacks on German warships in their harbors were severely limited by that factor. They were also limited by the rapid realization that the German air force possessed radar and an effective air defense fighter arm. The RAF at this time only dropped leaflets on German cities at night, deploring the warlike measures that Germany was employing. No explosive bombs fell on German industry at this time.

After the Polish Campaign ended in late September, events on the ground and in the air slowed to a crawl-like pace. The British Expeditionary Force had moved over to France soon after the war started and took up positions in northern France along the Belgian border. Major French forces were tied up in Maginot Line fortifications, intended to protect France from German invasion. The Maginot Line had originally been intended to cover northern France all the way to the North Sea, but financial concerns limited it, leaving an unfortified and thus vulnerable area along the Belgian-French border.

The so called "Phony War" began, a period of waiting on the Allied side. On the German side Adolph Hitler had planned to attack Belgium and France during the fall of 1939. His plans were deterred and delayed by a series of occurrences. A German officer carrying plans for the coming attack hitched a ride in an aircraft which got lost in bad weather and came down in neutral Belgium. He tried to destroy the plans but they were retrieved and handed over to the French and British. They were not sure what to make of the event, thinking it might be a provocation trying to lead them astray. However the immediate result was to delay the German attack. Subsequently weather that late fall and winter was very severe, thwarting modified attack plans.

Both the Allies and Germany had their eyes on Norway. In the early spring of 1940 Churchill focused on plans to invade neutral Norway or to mine its territorial waters to interfere with iron ore shipments from mines in northern Sweden that moved across northern Norway in winter by rail and then were loaded aboard ship to sail south to Germany. The Germans became aware of possible British intentions and set into operation a plan to invade Norway suddenly and secure their iron ore supplies. They struck on April 9th, 1940 with ship loads of troops and airborne landings in Norway. That was the start of the Norwegian Campaign. Great Britain and France immediately responded with air, naval, and ground forces. Naval forces included submarines.

In late March 1940 French Submarine Tender (depot ship) *Jules Verne* relocated from France. It brought with it the French 10th Flotilla of eight submarines.[204]

In April 1940 the French 10th Submarine Flotilla was established at Harwich in southeastern England. Four French boats operated off the Dutch coast at this time.[205] They were primarily looking for blockade runners. In early May the 10th Flotilla was transferred north to Blythe. The French depot ship *Jules Verne* and UK depot ship Cyclops were sent north to get them out of air attack range. On 9 May French submarine *Doris* was torpedoed and sunk by U-9 off the Dutch coast[206]. After the French surrender in May the flotilla was disestablished. All French submarines except *Rubis* returned to France.

On 10 May 1940 the long planned German *blitzkrieg* attack on the western front into Belgium, Holland and France finally began. Shortly thereafter all British and French forces were withdrawn from Norway, hurrying south to try to stem the German advance. The BEF had to be evacuated from Dunkirk in northern France after German armored forces cut them off from the main formations to the south. On 22 May, the French government signed surrender documents and the war was officially over for the French. Germany occupied the northern part of France but left the southern zone unoccupied under the control of the new French government in the town of Vichy. The new French Regime, under Marshall Petain, a hero of the First World War, governed the unoccupied portion of mainland France along with French colonies overseas, particularly those in North Africa. All French military forces at home and overseas now owed their allegiance to the new government in Vichy.

In mid-May 1940 as defeat loomed most French warships departed their ports in France and sailed to French North Africa. However, two old battleships, four destroyers, seven submarines, and a few mine sweepers sailed to England instead.[207] In June 1940 four French submarines were destroyed in Brest (*Achille, Agosta, Ouessant and Pasteur*) lest they be seized by the Germans.

A young French Cabinet Minister, General Charles DeGaulle, escaped to England and broadcast a manifesto declaring that the "Free French" would fight on, calling for patriotic Frenchmen to join his cause. The Vichy Government tried him in absentia and condemned him to death as a traitor to France. Nevertheless the Free French movement was established, and was supported by Great Britain.

Vichy French Submarine Operations

Despite Vichy French assurances to the British government that the French Fleet would not be used against British interests, Churchill was not convinced. As a result he instituted action (Operation CATAPULT) on 3 July 1940 to forcibly seize control of those French warships that had taken refuge in ports in the United Kingdom after the fall of France. Some seizures were accomplished peacefully, but in others blood was shed on both sides.

Churchill sent a Royal Navy Task Force to Mers-el-Kebir in North Africa to demand that the French Admiral in command there direct his forces to either: join RN forces; sail to British ports or the French West Indies with reduced crews; or scuttle themselves within six hours. The alternative was to come under immediate attack by the RN Force. The French Admiral refused to comply and the RN began a bombardment that sank a number of French ships and inflicted heavy casualties on French seamen. Battleship *Bretagne* blew up, and *Provence* and other ships were seriously damaged. Some 1,297 French sailors and officers were killed and others wounded. Battle cruiser *Strasbourg* and five destroyers escaped and made their way to Toulon despite an attack by torpedo-carrying aircraft from aircraft carrier HMS Ark Royal.

On 8 July another attack was made, at Dakar. Vichy French battleship *Richelieu* was attacked by a motor boat from aircraft carrier HMS Hermes. It dropped explosive charges under the stern of the target, but they failed to explode. Torpedo planes then attacked but failed to put *Richelieu* out of action.

Later that year in September Churchill sent another naval expedition to Africa, this one a joint Free French-British expedition to seize the Vichy French port of Dakar on the coast of West Africa. De Gaulle's intelligence organization had convinced him that the colony was ready to foreswear allegiance to the Vichy government and turn to De Gaulle and the Free French movement. Late intelligence from Dakar indicated otherwise but the expedition was about to sail and the last minute contrary information was ignored. The expedition's leaders were somewhat surprised to find the local government officials not ready to welcome the Free French contingent with open arms.

Hostilities ensued. On 23 September two British destroyers sank Vichy French submarine *Persee*. On 24 September destroyer HMS

Fortune sank Vichy French submarine *Ajax* which was about to attack British ships. While bombarding the port and shore batteries, battleship HMS Resolution was hit by a torpedo from Vichy French submarine *Beveziers* and seriously damaged on 25 September.[208] The hit on her portside inflicted major structural damage. Thirty feet of her double bottom was destroyed. Extensive flooding ensued including a boiler room and she took a 15 degree list that put her main armament out of action. She was taken in tow by battleship HMS Barham and towed to Freetown, arriving 30 September. She remained under repair there from October through December. She had to be sent to Philadelphia Naval Shipyard in the United States for permanent repairs during the period April though August 1941.

In summary the Dakar operation, Operation MENACE, was a disaster. Cruiser HMS Fiji was torpedoed by a U-boat while enroute Dakar and had to be replaced. Nineteen aircraft were lost during the operation. The end result was that Dakar remained under Vichy French rule until the end of the war. Fears that German U-boats would use Dakar as a base of operations against British ships off the west coast of Africa turned out to be groundless. Despite German entreaties, the Vichy French government did not allow U-boats to call there.

In June 1940 there were no French submarines in the Indian Ocean. After the surrender the French Admiralty petitioned the German-Italian Armistice Commission to allow them to move some submarines into the Indian Ocean. The French had colonies at Madagascar Island, and in French Somaliland at the Horn of Africa. Permission was granted and *L'Espoir* and *Le Vengeur* departed Toulon on 11 October 1940. They rendezvoused with *Monge* and *Pegase* from Bizerta, and sailed past Gibraltar down to Dakar on the African West Coast. On 17 December they sailed in company with tanker *Lot* via the Cape of Good Hope, arriving at the port of Tamatave, Madagascar on 15 January 1941, and then continued on to the main French naval port of Diego Suarez at the north end of Madagascar. After a short stay at Diego Suarez, *Lot* and *Monge* and *Pegase* continued across the Indian Ocean to Indo-China.[209]

In May 1941 the British moved to take control of Syria, a League of Nations Mandate under Vichy French control. There were fears of German influence and a move towards the Iraqi oil fields which were crucial to Great Britain. During fighting UK submarine HMS Parthian torpedoed and sank Vichy French submarine *Souffleur*.[210]

The British had declared a blockade of French Somaliland, although it was somewhat porous. On 30 July 1941 *Le Vengeur* reached Djibouti on a resupply run from Diego Suarez. On the 29th she encountered a Free French Sloop *Savorgnan de Brazza* which was towing a captured dhow, which had tried to run the blockade. *Le Vengeur* fired two torpedoes that missed the sloop, which promptly cut her tow line and departed the scene.[211]

The British were concerned over French commercial trade between un-occupied France and Indo-China, fearing that strategic materials would make their way to German war industry. They therefore directed that French merchant traffic in the Indian Ocean be stopped and examined for contraband. In October 1941 Operation BELLRINGER involved stopping a large French convoy about 500 nm from South Africa. The superior British forces included two cruisers. The French merchant ships were sent to South African ports for examination, despite sabotage attempts by their crews. The accompanying French sloop was allowed to proceed to Madagascar.

Vichy French submarines *Heros* and *Glorieux* were enroute to Madagascar from France when BELLRINGER took place. The French Admiralty ordered them to attack British ships off South Africa in retaliation. On 15 June, *Glorieux* fired two torpedoes at a ship target about 100 nm south of South Africa but missed. Finally two days later fuel limits forced *Glorieux* to proceed to Diego Suarez. On 17 June, *Heros* 60 nm east of Port London, fired one torpedo which hit and sank a 5,700 ton Norwegian tanker. *Heros* then headed for Diego Suarez.[212]

On 25 October 1941 *Monge*, having returned from Indo-China to Madagascar, arrive in Djibouti on a resupply trip. She sailed for Diego Suarez on 15 November. That same day *Heros* sailed for Djibouti. In January 1942 *Le Vengeur* made a final resupply run to Djibouti before sailing for France in company with *L'Espoir*. *Beveziers*, recently arrived form Dakar, made a final resupply run to Djibouti. She arrived back in Diego Suarez in early May just before a British invasion of the port.[213]

In late November 1941 the War Cabinet in London had discussed seizing Madagascar to eliminate the possibility that it might be used by hostile forces to interdict the trade route between India and Suez. But the Dakar operation had ended badly and there were inadequate forces to mount another operation. However in December 1941 after Japan entered the war, planning began anew. The operation was called IRONSIDE.

Troopships sailed from the Clyde in March 1942 and the landings at Diego Suarez took place 4 May.[214] French submarine *Beveziers*, alongside in Diego Suarez, was sunk by Fleet Air Arm aircraft during the initial attack.

Heros and *Monge* were at sea, and *Glorieux* was at Majunga 300 nm south on the west coast of Madagascar. *Heros* was 500 nm north escorting a merchant ship to Djibouti. She reversed course and headed for Diego Suarez at 17 knots, her top speed. As she neared Diego Suarez, a Swordfish aircraft from HMS Illustrious depth-charged and sank her with all hands. *Monge*, broke off from escorting a convoy to La Reunion, headed for Diego Suarez and made an unsuccessful attack on aircraft carrier HMS Indomitable. Escorting destroyers sank her. *Glorieux* arrived at the Diego Suarez area but was unable to attack a British task group because of their speed and course changes. Vichy then ordered her back to Majunga, and then to Dakar.[215]

On 8 November 1942 British and American invasion forces landed in North Africa. The Allies hoped that resistance by Vichy French forces would be restrained if not entirely absent, especially against the American forces which did not have the taint the British carried from Mers-el-Kebir. Although local French authorities did not prolong their resistance, at first it was quite sharp. At Casablanca, an American landing site, there were 11 Vichy French subs present. USS Ranger dive bombers sank three at anchor in the harbor (*Amphitrite*, *Psyche*, and *Oreade*).[216] The other eight sortied to attack the U.S. invasion fleet. *Amazone* fired five torpedoes at cruiser USS Brooklyn (CL-40), but all missed. *Tonnant* fired at aircraft carrier USS Ranger (CV-4)but also missed. *Meduse* and *Antiope* attacked transports at Fedala but missed. Four of the eight sortieing Vichy French submarines were sunk by Allied forces. Aircraft from escort carrier USS Suwannee (CVE-27) sank *Sidi-Ferruch*. Two Catalina flying boats attacked *Conquerant* on the surface and sank her with depth charges. *Tonnant* scuttled herself while under fire from a British aircraft. Vichy French submarine *Sibylle* disappeared without a trace.[217] At Oran three Vichy French submarines were scuttled during the attack (*Ceres, Pallen and Danae*).[218]

Vichy French submarines *Amazone*, *Antiope*, and *Meduse* sailed to Dakar and joined Vichy French forces there. *Orphee* re-entered Casablanca without serious damage, and later joined Allied forces under Free French colors.

After Adolph Hitler learned of Admiral Darlan's dealings with General Eisenhower, he ordered the seizure of unoccupied France. The French Navy carried out Admiral Darlan's instructions and scuttled a battleship, two battle cruisers, four heavy cruisers, three light cruisers, 24 destroyers and 16 submarines at Toulon—before German forces could seize them.[219] Five Vichy French subs risked a German-laid mine field to flee Toulon. Of these—three joined the Allies, one was interned in Spain and the other one was scuttled.[220]

The French government promise to the British that the French Fleet would not be used against them was kept. The only time they fought was when the British attacked, as at Dakar and Mers-el-Kebir and Diego Suarez.

Free French Submarine Operations

Surcouf was seized at Plymouth, England on 3 July 1940 by British forces. Several French personnel resisted, and two British subjects and one Frenchman died. The *Surcouf* crew was offered an opportunity to return to France or stay and operate the submarine under Free French colors. One officer chose to stay and he was later confirmed in command.

Narval was lost on patrol in the Med during 1941 while under Royal Navy opcon.[221]

In early 1942 *Surcouf* was enroute from Portsmouth, New Hampshire to Tahiti via the Panama Canal. On 18 February she radioed that she planned to reach Colon on the 19th. She never arrived. The SS Thompson Lykes later reported that during the night of the 18th she had struck an unidentified low lying object about 80 nm north east of the canal. Lykes was sailing under wartime restrictions with no running lights. Presumably *Surcouf* was blacked out also. The Lykes' bow later showed damage. One hundred twenty-nine men were lost with *Surcouf*.

A few French submarines agreed to operate under British submarine operational control. They will be dealt with in the sections dealing with British submarine operations in various theaters.

Chapter Three—British Submarines

The story of British submarine operations includes activities of nations whose homelands were overrun by Germany, but whose governments continued to function in exile and whose submarines then operated under Royal Navy operational control. These include Poland (after September 1939 when she was overrun), Norway (after April-May 1940 when she was occupied), The Netherlands (invaded and surrendered in May 1940), France (after June 1940 some French submarines chose to switch allegiance to the Free French cause); and Greece (invaded in 1941), and finally Italy (after her surrender to the Allies in 1943).

In 1939 the British Submarine Service was spread across four geographic areas: the Far East (China Station) based on Hong Kong and Singapore; the Indian Ocean; Home Waters, around the British Isles including the North Sea; and the Mediterranean Sea. A total of 44 submarines were operational (ready for patrol duty). Five more were considered obsolete or in poor mechanical/electrical shape.

Far East (China Station)

British submarines in the Far East numbered 15, of which 13 were operational with two in refit (overhaul). They were of the older long range "O", "P" and "R" classes. These classes had a large number of torpedo tubes forward and power reloading gear. They could reload six torpedoes in seven minutes. A submarine minelayer, Seal, was in Aden enroute the Far East. The large number of submarines in the Far East reflected British concerns over Japanese intentions. There were two minelayers, Grampus and Rorqual, in addition to the thirteen "O", "P" and "R" classes.

British war plans for the Far East accepted the early fall of Hong Kong. It was expected to hold out only a few weeks in the event of a Japanese attack. Its water supply was very vulnerable, and once cutoff surrender was inevitable. Hence only a small ground force garrison was in place, adequate to deal with rampaging Chinese warlords but not a Japanese division. Tentative arrangements were in effect to establish advanced fleet bases at Labuan in North Borneo, and at Cam Ranh Bay in French Indo-China. Royal Navy reinforcements were expected to arrive at Singapore about three months after commencement of hostilities with Japan.[222] The role of British submarines was to prevent the invasion of Malaya until reinforcements arrived from Home Waters or the Mediterranean Sea. This scenario assumed no war in Europe.[223]

Some very advanced training took place in the Far East 4th Submarine Flotilla based at Hong Kong as early as 1938. HMS Regulus made a 28-day patrol, twice the normal peacetime period at sea, starting 5 January 1938. During a major submarine exercise a force of ten submarines intercepted depot ship HMS Medway, enroute from Manila to Labuan, simulating a Japanese force. Regulus steamed 3,940 miles (391 miles dived) during the exercise, making 14 submerged attacks.[224]

Submarines of the 4th Flotilla exercised in coordinated operations, keeping station through VHF radio, and submerged sound CW communications to a maximum distance of seven miles. Messages from the submarine operational commander went to Singapore, thence to Rugby, England and then out on a VLF broadcast to the submarines on patrol. The time interval could be as short as 30 minutes and up to four hours. The Rugby VLF signal could be received as deep as 50 feet in the Sea of Japan.

1939

In July 1939 the 4th Flotilla was up in Wei Hai Wei, China, its normal summer station, conducting exercises. Events in Europe began to heat up as the British government became aware of German moves of troops to the Polish border. In August 1939 the situation in Europe was serious enough that Admiral Sir Geoffrey Layton, Commander in Chief, China Fleet, began considering whether to send UK submarines to patrol areas or stations ("billets" in RN submarine lingo) off Japan against the possibility that war came and Japan allied herself actively with Germany. [225]

Some 4th Flotilla subs sailed to Hong Kong and were at two hours notice to go to sea and war. On 3 September word arrived of the start of war between Great Britain and Germany. The Foreign Office predicted correctly that Japan would remain neutral. Submarine patrol goals were to sink German ships specified by the Admiralty, and intercept enemy merchant ships headed for neutral ports in Japan or the USSR. Patrol areas included the Sundra Strait, Sabang Strait, Malacca Strait, and Formosa Strait. There were some 40 German merchant ships in the Far East at that time, some suitable for conversion to raiders. German raiders had raised havoc on the high seas during WW I. HMS Regulus sailed for a fourteen day patrol in the Bashi Channel, on alert for German raiders.

Later, submarine patrol areas were shifted north to Japanese waters. Japan and Germany were allied in the Axis Pact and it was feared that German raiders might begin operating from Japanese ports. Information about possible raiders in Japanese ports was expected to be forthcoming from the British Embassy in Tokyo. Patrols took place off the *Kii* and *Bungo* Channels as well as the *Shimonoseki* Strait. These areas would later, in 1942, become a hunting round for American submarines, operating against the Japanese merchant marine.

In later 1939 Regulus was again off Japan, and then was assigned to a patrol area off Vladivostok, USSR. The USSR and Germany had allied themselves and it was feared that raider Graf Spee might come out to the Far East. Regulus inadvertently got "involved" in a Soviet ASW exercise, was not detected, and took careful notes. Her CO came to the conclusion that Soviet ASW tactics were at least a decade out of date.

Regulus moved up in the Gulf of Tartary above Vladivostok to check Soviet ports for any relevant activity. She found none. She was relieved by HMS Rainbow in that area. In March 1940 HMS Proteus was the last 4th Flotilla submarine assigned to patrol Soviet areas.[226]

In late 1939 British submarines operating from Singapore conducted patrols around the Netherlands East Indies (NEI) looking for German raiders or merchant ships. By the end of October four large "O" class subs had been sent west into the Indian Ocean and were now based at Ceylon.

1940

In May 1940 due to the threat of Italy entering the war against Great Britain and France, British submarines were withdrawn from the Far East and the Indian Ocean and moved to the Mediterranean. For the remainder of 1940 and all of 1941 there were no British submarines on the "China

Station". They would not return until 1944, and then they would operate under American submarine commander opcon from the allied submarine base at Fremantle in Western Australia.

1941-Early 1942

With no British submarines in the Far East, local British authorities at Singapore signed an agreement with Dutch authorities at Batavia, the Dutch capital of the Netherlands East Indies, to the effect that in the event the threat of war with Japan escalated, some Dutch submarines would operate out of Singapore under British naval opcon.[227]

There were fifteen Royal Netherlands Navy (RNN) (Dutch) submarines based at Surabaya in Java. In early December 1941 seven of them were placed under Royal Navy opcon by Dutch authorities. They were patrolling in the Gulf of Siam when Japanese amphibious invasion forces landed troops on 8 December in northern Malaya. It was the beginning of a long planned effort to take over Malaya and the NEI. Dutch submarines sank a total of three Japanese transports and damaged another four transports for the loss of three of their number. K-XIV sank two transports off North Borneo.[228] The waters in the Gulf of Siam are shallow and treacherous in which to operate.[229] Dutch submarine O-16 attacked four loaded transports off Patni but achieved no sinking's. She was lost in that area to a British mine.[230] On 24 December K-XVI sank IJN destroyer *Sagiri* with two torpedo hits and damaged three transports.

Other Dutch submarines, operating under RNN opcon, were on patrol in the Makassar Straits and off North Borneo. They sank a Japanese destroyer and two transports, and damaged two more transports. Two Dutch boats were lost. For the sinking's of five Japanese transports and one destroyer, plus damage to four more transports, the Dutch had lost five of their scarce submarines, a 33.3% loss of their submarine strength in the area.

British authorities at Singapore called for RN submarine reinforcements and two sailed (Trusty and Truant), but only HMS Trusty arrived in the Far East before the fall of Singapore on 15 February 1942. Both then joined the British flotilla in Ceylon.

After the loss of Singapore K-VII was bombed and sunk in port in the NEI and K-XVI was sunk off Borneo by Japanese submarine I-66. As the Japanese closed in on Java, three Dutch submarines (K-X, K-XIII and K-XVIII), all unfit for sea, were destroyed lest they fall into Japanese hands.

The remaining Dutch submarines fit for sea headed in two different directions:[231]

Ceylon (British opcon): K-XI, K-XIII, K-XV and O-19

Fremantle (U.S. opcon): K-VIII, K-IX and K-XII

British submarines returned to the Far East in 1944. However this time they operated under American operational control from the port of Fremantle in Western Australia. One of their commanding officers, Edward Young, described them as "poor cousins" to the American fleet submarines.[232] The American boats were bigger and had much greater range, having been designed with long range operations against the Japanese in the western Pacific in mind.

U.S. fleet boat crew accommodations were vastly better and they were all equipped with showers and air conditioning, a requisite for operations in the tropical area around the Dutch East Indies. They carried air search radar and surface search radar, the latter key to their night surfaced attacks against Japanese convoys, while British subs had only air search radar to detect enemy aircraft. Young comments ironically that the British had led in radar development but were now lagging behind in its application.[233] He notes correctly that British emphasis on radar focused on its use by ASW ships and aircraft, neglecting its submarine applications as less important. Given the German wolf pack threat that emphasis is quite understandable.

From Fremantle the British T-class could reach Singapore and the north shore of Borneo, while the S-class could only go as far as just north of the Makassar Strait and the west end of the Java Sea. Those ranges severely limited the number of worthwhile ship targets that they could attack.

In October 1944 HMS Storm set off on its first Pacific patrol. It topped off fuel at Exmouth Gulf and then headed north to the Gulf of Bovi, to the south of the Celebes Islands. When the patrol was completed Storm had sailed 6,200 miles.

Indian Ocean

1939

By the end of October 1939 four "O" class were sent west from the China Station to join the 8th Submarine Flotilla at Colombo, Ceylon (now Sri Lanka) in the Indian Ocean. The former *Spreewald*, renamed HMS Lucia, served as a depot ship. They conducted patrols in the Chagos Archipelago, the Seychelles Islands, and the Maldives. A number of German raiders, disguised merchant ships, were active during these early years and a great deal of effort was spent trying to track them down and sink them.

HMS Olympus began a "long patrol", departing Columbo 17 November 1939 enroute the Seychelles. On 15 November 1939 warship raider *Graf Spee* sank the tanker Africa Shell in the Mozambique Channel off East Africa. *Graf Spee* then returned to the South Atlantic. Her excursion into the Indian Ocean was merely an attempt to confuse British forces searching for her. Olympus was diverted to the Mozambique Channel to search. Olympus put in to French-controlled Diego Suarez in North Madagascar for fuel and food. Later she went after a reported raider near Prince Edward Island, some 2,000 nm south, based upon DF transmissions. She checked Prince Edward Island and the Crozet Islands but found nothing but heavy weather and lack of shelter. Force 11 seas and 33 degree temperatures made her task almost intolerable. Her crew had only "tropical rig", not suitable for operating in the latitude of 47 degrees south.[234] Olympus finally reached Durban, South Africa on 29 December after 12,000 nm steaming.

In early November HMS Otus and HMS Odin departed Columbo for "short patrols" to investigate the Chagos Archipelago. On 5 December Otus returned having seen no sign of German raiders. Odin reported similar results. Her CO noted that the only suitable anchorages for a raider and resupply ships were at Peros Banhos and Diego Garcia. The Chagos Bank would be unsuitable until March because of prevailing weather.[235]

The first ANZAC convoy was being assembled to carry Australian and New Zealand troops to reinforce the Army of the Nile for operations in North Africa. It consisted of 12 liners. Submarines Odin and Olympus checked the Chagos Archipelago, Addu Atoll, and the Maldives for enemy raiders, and then protected the liners as they transited the Nine Degree Channel between the Lacadive Islands and Minicoy.

By March 1940 events in the Mediterranean were heating up. A decision was made to send all submarines in 4th (Far East) and 8th (Colombo) Submarine Flotillas to the Med. HMS Medway arrived in Alexandria in May 1940. The newly arrived submarines and depot ships joined 1st Submarine Flotilla there.

The last five submarines in Singapore departed as they finished their refits. HMS Rover was the last to sail, on 22 August 1940. The Far East and Indian Ocean were now bare of any British submarines. [236] This situation reflected a lack of an adequate number of ships and submarines in the Royal Navy to cover all Empire requirements, which included Home Waters, the Mediterranean Sea, the Indian Ocean and the Far East. The Admiralty had "to rob Peter to pay Paul". It could not cover all these widely separated areas at the same time. The coupling of Germany, Italy and Japan in an alliance presented the worst nightmare the British Admiralty could imagine.

Much later, in March 1942 the British Eastern Fleet was reformed. It consisted of two aircraft carriers, one light carrier, five battleships including four old and slow "R" class BBs, seven cruisers, sixteen destroyers and some submarines. The main bases were at Colombo and Trincomalee in Ceylon (current Sri Lanka) but there was also a secret base at Addu Atoll in the Maldive Islands.[237]

In late March-early April 1942 IJN planners sent a five-aircraft carrier battle force in to the Indian Ocean to remove any RN threat to Japanese forces in Burma. UK submarines were on patrol at the western end of the Straits of Malacca but the Japanese TF went south of the NEI and into the Indian Ocean by an uncovered route. Admiral Nagumo, the victor at Pearl Harbor, in addition to five CVs, had four battleships and three cruisers, along with escort destroyers in his TF. Admiral Ozawa took one CVL and six cruisers to attack UK shipping in the Bay of Bengal while Nagumo sought out Eastern Fleet.

No pitched battle akin to Coral Sea or Midway took place, which probably saved Great Britain's Eastern Fleet from annihilation. Nagumo's carrier strikes at Ceylon sank a large number of ships and damaged shore facilities. Ozawa's raiders in the Bay of Bengal sank 25 merchant ships (112,000 tons). IJN submarines went to the west coast of India and there sank five ships (32,400 tons).[238] Eastern Fleet fell back on East African bases for the time being.

Eastern Fleet's submarines continued to conduct patrols from Ceylon off Malaya, particularly the port of Penang, which was a main Japanese base. Nagumo's goal to preclude active operations against Japanese forces in Burma was achieved. Much later, after the surrender of the Italian Fleet in the Med in mid-1943 the Eastern Fleet moved its headquarters back to Ceylon.[239]

The Special Operations Executive (SOE) was set up at Churchill's instigation after the fall of France "to set Europe ablaze" by staging frequent small scale incursions from the sea and air against the German occupiers. After Japan entered the war in late 1941 the SOE set up Force 136 in India and Ceylon to pursue its goals in the Far East. Prior to late 1943 only Dutch submarines were available in the Indian Ocean to transport SOE-sponsored personnel to the Andaman Islands and Malaya.

On 14 January 1943 Dutch O-24 departed Colombo enroute the Andaman Islands to put an SOE party ashore. The Andaman Islands had been occupied by the Japanese. It provided them a forward air base on the Indian Ocean. She also patrolled for Japanese ship traffic between Singapore and Rangoon. On 21 February she gunned a 4,000 ton ship which escaped. On 21 March she successfully extracted the SOE party from the Andaman Islands.

O-24 sailed again on 11 May to land a party at Perak in Malaya. The operation was successful and she was back in Colombo by 31 May. O-23 was assigned to extract that party, and did so on 4 August.

On 12 September O-24 departed for another insertion operation and was back in Colombo 3 October. After one more special operation O-24 sailed to the United States for a refit.[240]

HMS Trident arrived in August 1943 and on patrol fired eight torpedoes at long range at an IJN cruiser. They missed. Trident had severe engine problems and was sent back to the UK for refit.[241]

UK submarines returned to the Indian Ocean after Italy's surrender in September 1943 left the Med virtually uncontested from a naval standpoint. HMS Templar made her first patrol in late October, followed by HMS Tactician. Both patrols were unproductive.

HMS Tally Ho was third, departing Colombo 26 October. On 6 November she sighted a U-boat departing the harbor at Penang in the Malacca Strait and fired five torpedoes at just fewer than 2,000 yards range. All missed and one ran circular and nearly hit Tally Ho. On 8 November she fired two torpedoes at a merchant ship, departing Penang and had two misses with another circular torpedo run. On 12 November she fired at *Kisogana Maru* and sank her with five torpedoes, but incurred a third circular running torpedo. On 12 November she encountered yet another U-boat but a Japanese escort destroyer forced Tally Ho to dive preventing an attack. That afternoon another U-boat was sighted but a turn away by the U-boat precluded an attack.[242]

On 14 November HMS Taurus was on patrol off Penang and sighted a Japanese submarine on the surface coming north up the strait towards Penang. Taurus fired six torpedoes at a range of about 2,000 yards. One hit and sank I-34 which was loaded with supplies of rubber, tin, tungsten and quinine intended for Germany. On her way home to Colombo, about 250 miles out Taurus had a narrow escape. She was bombed by a Japanese seaplane that came in from astern.[243]

At the end of 1943 depot ship HMS Adamant and 4th Submarine Flotilla shifted from Colombo on the west coast to Trincomalee on the east coast of Ceylon. More UK submarines continued to arrive to beef up the flotilla. In March 1944 another depot ship, HMS Maidstone, arrived. 4th Submarine Flotilla then split into 4th and 8th Flotillas, but operational control continued to be vested in 4th Flotilla. A number of the new submarine arrivals were fitted with air conditioning machinery which allowed them to make longer patrols. Some also had main ballast tanks converted to fuel ballast tanks, increasing their range substantially.[244]

Later a third depot ship, HMS Wolfe, arrived. HMS Maidstone took her brood and moved down to Fremantle, Western Australia to operate there under U.S. Navy opcon. Their history at Fremantle is covered in the chapter on U.S. submarines.

In January 1944 Tally Ho was again on patrol off Penang. She sighted IJN cruiser *Kuma*. The target zigged away and thus no attack was possible. Two days later *Kuma* came into view again. This time Tally Ho was able to fire a seven torpedo salvo from her forward tubes. Three hit and *Kuma* went down. Tally Ho was worked over by Japanese destroyers but escaped. On 14 January Tally Ho sank merchant ship *Ryuko Maru* off the Nicobar Islands in a surface attack at night firing six torpedoes. Sometime later during the night of 14/15 February Tally ho sighted a surfaced submarine at about 0515. Tally Ho fired and sank U-IT-23, a former Italian submarine that had been taken over by the Germans after Italy's surrender. U-IT-23 was the former *Reinaldo Giuliani*, enroute from Singapore to Penang and then on to France with a cargo of tin.[245]

HMS Stonehenge departed Trincomalee on 25 February for a patrol off the north coast of Sumatra. She failed to return.

This seems an appropriate place to talk, albeit somewhat disparagingly, about Japanese area ASW. The waters around Malaya are very constricted and well within range of land based aircraft. British or Dutch submarines of that era had to conduct surfaced battery charges at night, every night. Aircraft equipped with radar could have made that practice deadly for the submarines involved. Although the Japanese lagged in radar development they used magnetic airborne detection (MAD) as an area search sensor. Although not optimal for large area search, it could have been effective over the confined waters of the Malacca Straits. Yet despite the clear evidence that Allied submarines were hunting targets in the area, there seemed to be no consistent ASW aerial patrols of the area. One wonders if there was a Japanese area ASW command at all. The Imperial Japanese Navy was narrowly focused upon a climactic battle between fleets and appeared to place ASW concerns at the bottom of their list of things to do.

In early 1944 HMS Templar damaged Japanese cruiser *Kitagami* with two hits out of eight fired at long range. *Kitagami* was steaming with three DD escorts at the time of the night attack. The "T" class boats had eight tubes forward, six internal and two external topside.

In March 1944 a long term mine laying campaign was begun in the Malacca Strait and waters north to force Japanese shipping away from the coastline so submarines could better attack. By the end of the war some twenty-four minefields had been laid along with two more in the Andaman Islands vicinity.[246]

In July HMS Telemachus sank I-166 off the One Fathom Bank. In September Trenchant sank U-859 with one hit from a three-torpedo stern salvo as the target was preparing to enter Penang.[247]

HMS Tradewind landed agents on Sumatra in September 1944, and then went to the Sunda Strait to make contact with an agent there, unsuccessfully. On 18 September she sank an escorted merchant ship, *Junyo Maru*, with two hits. Later it was learned that the ship was carrying nearly 6,000 American, British and Dutch POWS, most of who perished in the sinking.[248]

By August 1944 it was clear that there were too many British submarines in the Indian Ocean for the limited number of worthwhile ship targets. HMS Maidstone and Submarine Flotilla 8 (three T-class boats, six S-class boats and Dutch sub 0-9) were transferred to Fremantle to operate under the operational control of Commander Submarines South West Pacific, an American submarine operational control authority. Their areas were the South China Sea from north of the Netherlands East Indies.

On 19 November HMS Stratagem was conducting its fourth patrol near the One Fathom Bank. She attacked a five-ship convoy and sank *Nichinan Maru*. However, the following day she was attacked by an aircraft and a destroyer and sunk. Some survivors were taken prisoner and three survived the war.

On 9 January 1945 HMS Porpoise, a dedicated mine layer, reported that she had laid two fields off Penang. She became overdue on 16 January. There were no Japanese reports of her destruction. She was the 75th British submarine lost during the war, and the third in the Far East.

HMS Rorqual, the last of six dedicated mine layers of the class, continued to lay mines. She laid a total of 1,350 mines in 38 different mine plants during the war. She was the only dedicated British mine laying submarine to survive the war.[249]

That year as Eastern Fleet aircraft carriers conducted air raids on oil facilities in Sumatra, British submarines supported the carrier task groups by providing plane guard duties, rescuing downed pilots who ditched at sea.

British and Dutch submarines conducted 182 patrols in the Indian Ocean. Forty-eight (26.3%) included special operations, usually involving the insertion or extraction of agents in Sumatra or Malaya. To some extent these special operations limited the submarines' ability to attack ship targets. There was usually a several day window before and after an insertion/extraction during which shipping attacks were prohibited, in order to not draw attention to the special operations.

Home Waters

1939

On 3 September 1939 when war started there were 18 operational submarines in Home Waters, four of them obsolete. The 2nd Submarine Flotilla based at Dundee in Scotland, had 8 "S" class and 3 "T" class boats plus older Oxley and was supported by depot ship HMS Medway. 6th Flotilla was at Blyth, with 3 "U' class, 2 old "L" class and very old H 32, and was supported by depot ship HMS Titania.

Radm. B. C. Watson, RN was Radm. Submarines, responsible for general submarine administration, liaison and submarine training. Submarine operational control belonged to flag officers commanding fleets or areas. The 1938 Home Fleet War Orders stated that Radm. Submarines would command submarine flotillas operating in the North Sea, under the overall command of Commander-in-Chief, Home Fleet. Watson set up shop in Aberdour, near Rosyth in Scotland, after having moved his headquarters from Gosport in southern England. His administrative staff remained at Gosport. In addition there were seven training submarines at Gosport, plus four more in refit and twelve under construction in various shipyards.

On 30 August 1939 five submarines from 2nd Flotilla were on patrol along a line from Obrestal near Stavanger, Norway leading west-southwest. As the immediate threat of war increased they were looking for sortieing German warships or raiders. On 31 August another six subs from 6th Flotilla sailed for patrol stations in the Heligoland Bight. Unfortunately German surface raiders and U-boats had already sailed before the British submarines took up their patrol stations. The *Graf Spee* and *Deutschland* had already gotten out, and the first warning of their unwelcome presence in the wide Atlantic was raider reports from ships they stopped and sank.

On 3 September HMS Spearfish's watch officer spotted torpedo tracks and dove, avoiding a very bad start to her war. On 9 September HMS Ursula attacked U 35 whose alert lookouts saw the torpedo discharge splash (Ursula was on the surface at night) and avoided the torpedoes. On 10 September HMS Triton spotted HMS Oxley which was out of assigned position. Triton challenged her three times and fired a recognition grenade, without response. Triton then fired torpedoes and sank Oxley, the first friendly fire victim of the war.[250]

On 23 December HMS Triumph hit a mine and was badly damaged. She got home safely after radioing for help and being escorted by Hudsons of Coastal Command of the RAF. HMS Triad fractured her after hydroplane shaft and was towed into Stavanger, Norway where repairs were made on a slipway. That same month HMS Salmon sank U-36, and torpedoed cruisers *Leipzig* and *Nuremberg* in the North Sea.[251]

The 9th British Submarine Flotilla was established at Dundee, Scotland.[252] It was a "Foreign Legion" of submariners, including British, Free French, Dutch, Norwegian and Polish submarine officers and men and their submarines. The first commander, Captain James G. Roger, RN apparently was a very flexible individual, dealing successfully with a variety of national temperaments and predilections as well as with mechanical matters including "English" and "Metric" measurements involved in different types of submarines.

Polish submarines *Orzel* and *Wilk* escaped to England after the fall of Poland in late September 1939. After events of May-June 1940, Norwegian, Free French and Dutch submarines relocated to the British Isles. Severe losses in the British submarine flotillas in "Home Waters" made the newcomers welcome additions.[253]

The Dutch, Norwegian, and Polish naval attaches in London provided key points of coordination with the allied submarine crews. There was a large French Liaison Office already in London, headed by a Vice Admiral. In addition there were strong links between Great Britain and Greece dating back to 1911 when a British Naval mission to Greece was established. British officers had a hand in guiding the development and training of Royal Hellenic Navy officers and men until 1955. No Greek submarines operated from the UK, but after the occupation of Greece by German forces in 1941, Greek submarines relocated to various British bases in the Mediterranean Sea, including Alexandria, Beirut and Malta, and operated under British opcon. All the governments-in-exile were in London, except for the Greek which set itself up in Alexandria, Egypt.

Each foreign submarine was assigned a British liaison team consisting of a junior officer, frequently RNVR, and several communications' ratings. Their task was to ensure that communications from and to the British submarine operational commander were handled correctly.

1940

During early 1940 submarine patrols continued. On 21 March HMS Ursula sank iron ore carrier *Heddernheim* (6,000 tons) in the Skagerrak. She was enroute Germany. On 23 March HMS Truant chased *Edmund Hugo Stiles* into Norwegian waters where her crew scuttled her.

On 8 April Polish submarine *Orzel*, operating under RN operational control since the loss of Poland, sank troopship *Rio de Janeiro* (6,000 tons) off Kristiansand (S). This was the first solid indication of the German invasion of Norway. At this time there were two UK subs and two French subs in the southwest part of the North Sea, and ten UK subs off Norway with six more enroute.

On 9 April German warships, troopships and aircraft landed troops in southern Norway and rapidly took over. The British and French governments responded, landing troops in Northern and Central Norway, but were at a severe disadvantage from lack of air power.[254] The German *Luftwaffe* rapidly established itself in airfields captured by airborne troops. The Royal Navy and French Navy attempted to assist but came under very heavy air attack by the *Luftwaffe*.

2nd Flotilla at Rosyth included ten "T" class subs and two submarine minelayers plus Polish *Orzel*. 6th Flotilla at Blyth had three "S" class, 1 "U" class, one submarine minelayer and two River class boats—Clyde and Severn. South at Harwich were seven "S" class. By this time Admiral Max Horton of WW I submarine fame, had relieved Admiral Watson. He exercised operational control of all UK and allied subs in Norwegian waters and the North Sea, keeping the flotilla commanders cut in on operational orders issued.

On 9 April the British Cabinet approved orders to sink German ships in the Heligoland Bight, the Skagerrak (sea passage between Norway and Denmark) and the Kattegat (sea passage between Sweden and Denmark)—on sight, thus eliminating any pretense of following pre-war rules. Most of Norway's key ports were now under German control.

HMS Sunfish was making a practice approach on a 7,000 ton ship on 9 April and received the authorizing message in time to convert the practice run into a real torpedo approach and sank *Anasis*. She also sank *Antares* (2,500 tons), *Florida* (6,000 tons) and another 3,000 ton ship.

That day HMS Truant doomed light cruiser *Karlsruhe* with a ten torpedo salvo. *Karlsruhe* was hit in the stern knocking out her engines and steering. She had to be sunk later by German torpedoes. Truant got away despite a heavy depth charge attack by the escorts.

On 10 April HMS Triton attacked a large convoy with a spread of six torpedoes. She sank three ships of 5,000 tons, 4,000 tons and 300 tons. The escorts went after Triton with hammer and tongs and dropped some 80 depth charges. HMS Spearfish, operating nearby, was also detected by German active sonar, and had another 60 depth charges dropped in her vicinity. Both Triton and Spearfish finally escaped.

This may be a good time to discuss British torpedo firing techniques. The standard Mk VIII torpedo used by British submarines was limited to a zero gyro shot or a left or right 90 degree shot.[255] The approach officer mentally solved the firing angle problem for a zero gyro shot, determined the angle off at which to fire the torpedo, and then gave the order to shoot. He could fire a spread of torpedoes by firing in sequence separated by a few seconds. Lacking a torpedo data computer (TDC) installed in U.S. fleet submarines, which automatically generated a gyro angle to hit the target, transmitted it to the tube and inserted it automatically into the torpedo—the British submarine CO needed to engage in serious mental gymnastics to solve the problem.

He did have a plastic "Is-Was" device, roughly similar to ones used in the U.S. Submarine Service, to visualize the firing setup. In addition he had a 'Torpedo Control Calculator, commonly referred to as the "Fruit Machine". The Fruit Machine, unlike the American TDC, did not track continuously, and had to be reset at each observation. However as Compton-Hall reports, the British scored 1,363 hits in 3,220 attacks (42.3%). They sank 1,040 ships with 5,121 torpedoes fired (4.92 torpedoes per ship sunk). By comparison, the American Submarine Service sank 1,314 ships with 14,748 torpedoes (11.22 torpedoes per ship sunk).[256] US submariners with their marvelous semi-automated fire control system took over twice as many torpedoes to sink each ship.

After Spearfish surfaced that evening she sighted pocket-battleship *Lutzow* which was returning from Oslo and her part in the initial attack. Spearfish fired six torpedoes. At least one struck *Lutzow* aft, blowing off both screws and jamming her steering gear. She had to be towed to Kiel and was under repair for a full year as a result.[257]

On 11 April HMS Triad sank 3,000 ton *Ionia* off Oslo Fjord. HMS Sea Lion sank a 2,500 ton ore ship south of Anholt Island in the Kattegat. That day the British Cabinet extended its "sink on sight" order as far north as Bergen to a distance of ten miles offshore.[258]

On 15 April German gunnery ship *Brummer* (2,400 tons) was sunk by HMS Sterelet near The Skaw (northernmost tip of Denmark, marking the boundary between the Skagerrak and Kattegat passages). Sterelet was then lost, presumably to ASW attack by escorts. The water in that vicinity is shallow.

Back on 9 April HMS Thistle had a shot at U 4 but missed. U 4 then dove, but remained in the area to see if she might get a crack at her attacker in turn. The following day during the early morning hours of 10 April Thistle was torpedoed and sunk by U 4.

HMS Tarpon was lost while on patrol off Heligoland sometime in April, whether to ASW efforts or a mine is unknown. A number of early British submarines losses were attributable to ASW trawlers which they had attacked. This tactic reflected the COs' inexperience and poor operational orders from submarine operational commanders. As a rule of thumb, shallow draft ASW vessels are not acceptable targets for submarine torpedoes. They are hard to hit, are dangerous, and are not vital targets under most circumstances.

British submarine efforts to seriously impede the German invasion of Norway were too little and too late, but they had an effect. Admiral Raeder, the German Navy commander, issued orders that barred western Norwegian ports to German supply ships. They were restricted to Oslo and Larvik. Plans to send a large number of troops to Trondheim on liners *Europa* and *Bremen* were canceled because of the British submarine threat.[259] British torpedoes with contact exploders were running at set depth and exploding as programmed, unlike German torpedoes with magnetic exploders that were running deeper than set and going off prematurely or not at all. Admiral Doenitz had to recall his boats from Norwegian because of these failures that were discussed in detail in Chapter One.

In April HMS Tetrach's torpedoes missed in an attack on a merchant ship and she was set upon by three destroyer escorts. She was forced down to 400 feet, 100 feet deeper than her normal operational depth. After 43 hours submergence she finally was able to surface and get away, a narrow escape indeed and clear evidence of German ASW determination. On 24 April she was mined near Sogne Fjord and damaged but returned safely, two of her nine lives used up.

At the end of April HMS Unity was sunk in a collision with a Norwegian ship at the port of Blythe, a victim of a marine accident. Four of her crew were lost. By the end of April there were only four UK subs in the Kattegat and eastern part of the Skagerrak including minelayers HMS Narwhal and Seal. Narwhal laid mines near the island of Laeso, and then sank a 6,000 ton ship and damaged another of 8,500 tons.

HMS Seal was not as fortunate as Tetrach. She laid a mine field southwest of Goteborg, and not long after was harassed by German aircraft and E-boats. She entered a German minefield without realizing it and exploded a mine. She sank by the stern in 130 feet of water, and bottomed. She was able to regain the surface but had to surrender. German forces towed her into a Danish port. Her torpedoes were examined with interest since German torpedoes were performing poorly at this time. Her simple contact exploder was copied and used by the Germans.

During the latter part of April and early May 1940 several older and experienced submarine COs in 4th Submarine Flotilla realized that the stress and strain of wartime operations was getting to be too much for them, and requested relief. The same phenomena took place in other Home Waters' submarine flotillas. Higher authorities, upon reflection, realized it took great moral courage for them to do so, and moved them to less stressful positions.[260] Incidentally, several older American COs in the Pacific did likewise in the early days of the Pacific War.

When Holland fell to the Germans, four brand new "O" class submarines sailed to the UK. None of the four had yet conducted their initial sea trials. They were joined there by O-14 and O-15, which had been assigned to the Dutch West Indies in the Caribbean.

In late May Polish submarine *Orzel* was lost in the North Sea. Dutch submarine O-13 was lost in June. The Dutch entertained suspicions about Polish submarine *Wilk*, which had reported a collision with a U-boat in the vicinity of O-13's patrol area. HMS Thames was lost in July 1940, possibly to a mine in the North Sea. Dutch O-22 failed to return from a patrol off Norway in November (her wreckage was finally located in 1993 about 40 nm off Egersund, Norway).

The northern Norwegian port of Narvik was captured by a combined British-French ground force on 28 May, but it was clear that Norway could not be held. The British Cabinet directed an evacuation of the 25,000 troops in Norway. By 8 June the final increment of British and French forces withdrew from Norway, defeated in their efforts to block German ground and air forces from conquering Norway. On 10 May *Wehrmacht panzer* divisions had struck in a *blitzkrieg* attack into Holland, Belgium and France. Holland and Belgium were rapidly overrun and surrendered.

On 10 June Mussolini declared war on Great Britain and France, adding immensely to Allied problems. France signed an armistice on 22 June that took effect on the 25th. German forces occupied northern France including Paris, leaving the southern unoccupied portion under the control of the new Vichy French government. The Dutch government removed itself to England and constituted itself a government-in-exile. Those Dutch submarines that could do so moved to British ports, and operated under Royal Navy operational control.

Norwegian submarine B-1 sailed to the UK after Norway's surrender. However she was considered not fit for war patrols. Therefore she served to train Norwegian submarine personnel and to serve as a submarine target vessel at Rothesay under Submarine Training Flotilla 7. Dutch subs O-9 and O-10 also served there.

The French were in a more difficult circumstance. The French government had surrendered. All French forces that had not been captured or surrendered came under the lawful authority of the French government at Vichy and were out of the war. However General Charles DeGaulle, a French Cabinet Minister of the former government, escaped to England and set himself up as the head of the "Free French" forces which would continue the struggle against Germany. DeGaulle was tried for treason "in absentia" by the Vichy government. See Chapter 2 for a description of the events of those days.

Some French submarines continued to operate under Royal Navy operational control, although coming under the provisional Free French government for political purposes. French mine laying submarine *Rubis* was active in Norwegian and North Sea waters in May and June. She operated from the Lofoten islands in the north down to La Rochelle, laying mines that sank some 22 ships of 30,000 tons. She also sank a 4,500 ton ship with torpedoes.

In May HMS Truant sank *Preusse* (8,000 tons). Unfortunately Polish submarine *Orzel* was lost, probably to German aircraft at the end of May in the western Skagerrak.

On 20 June HMS Clyde hit battle cruiser *Gneisenau* with a torpedo near Trondheim, and put her out of commission for six months. Seas were rough at the time and Clyde was not detected by German escorts prior to firing. Also in June HMS Tetrach sank oiler *Sanland* (8,000 tons) off Egersund, and HMS Snapper sank *Cygnus* (1,400 tons).

German cruiser raider *Hipper* returned to the port of Brest on 27 December. Thereafter strong British submarine patrols were maintained off Brest to attempt an ambush if she sailed again on a raiding mission.[261]

Twenty-five British submarines were lost during the year.

1941

During 1941 Home Fleet submarines patrolled off Norway and the Bay of Biscay. In March some 22 submarines were sent to establish patrol areas off the port of Brest, France in the hopes that they might get torpedo shots in at German warship raiders *Gneisenau* and *Scharnhorst*. Their patrol areas were at a radius of about 220 nm from Brest. However, both ships arrived safely at Brest before the planned submarine ambush could be established.

The submarines involved included five "H" class boats left over from WW I, and three Dutch submarines.[262] The inclusion of "H" class submarines, seriously obsolete, reflected a note of desperation on the part of the Admiralty.

In June Germany attacked the Soviet Union, in what turned out to be Hitler's first fatal mistake. Although Great Britain and the USSR were ideological foes, the need to support the USSR overcame other issues. Convoys of war materials were sent on their way to northern Russian ports. At times UK submarines were called upon to escort those convoys. In addition some submarines were sent to operate from the Kola Inlet.[263] Their operations are discussed in Chapter Seven.

On 8 December Japan attacked British possessions at Hong Kong and Malaya. The UK now had a third adversary in its world war.

There were a number of troubles with submarines operating in Home Waters including increasing mechanical/electrical problems in Allied submarines.[264] Given that they were removed from their normal submarine shipyards, operating bases and depot ships it was only to be expected that their condition would slowly deteriorate. The fact that British submarines were built using the English system of weights and measures—pounds and feet, and most Allied submarines used the metric scale only added to the problems.

Lacking an assigned depot ship, Flotilla 9 submarines were repaired and refitted at Dundee-Caledon Shipbuilding and Engineering Company at Dundee. Grangemouth port, south west of Dundee on the Fifth of Forth, was also used to moor Flotilla 9 boats.

French subs *Ondine* and *Orion* were cannibalized to provide parts to repair *Junon* and *Minerve*. *Junon's* diesel engines were a constant problem. *Rubis* had her own problems although some were self-induced. She attacked a ship target with torpedoes but was too close to the target when it exploded, damaging many of her battery cells. Damaged cells were later replaced with cells from other French subs in the UK. In September 1942 Polish sub *Wilk* gave up her battery to replace *Rubis'*. *Wilk* had been built in a French shipyard and had a standard French submarine battery.

There were problems with foreign torpedoes and mines. When they were expended, British torpedoes and mines had to be substituted. Torpedo tubes and mine wells had to be modified to accept slightly different ones.

Rubis' mine wells were modified in December 1940 after she ran out of French-produced mines and had to reload with British mines.

In December H 31 failed to return from patrol, probably lost to a floating mine.[265]

1942

In February the so-called "Channel Dash" took place in which several major German warships which were holed up in Brest, France, made a dash up the English Channel and made their way to relative safety in northern German waters. There was great embarrassment on the British side and a major inquiry into the particulars was launched.

Prinz Eugen was one of the ships that escaped from Brest. Later she and *Scheer* moved to Norway where they represented a continuing threat to convoys to Russia. In February 1942 a PQ convoy, headed for northern Russia, was threatened by possible sorties by heavy naval units from Trondheim. There were two main entrances, Fro Havet (north) and Ytra Fjord (south). Free French sub *Minerve* and HMS Unbending were moved to the south to cover that entrance, and HMS Tuna and Trident were also dispatched to the locality. Trident spotted *Prinz Eugen*, and fired a salvo of seven torpedoes. *Prinz Eugen* was hit aft and seriously damaged.[266]

During 1942, 18 British subs were lost, 15 of them in the Med.

1943

In February 1943 *Uredd*, a Norwegian submarine was mined and sank off Bodo. Her wreck was discovered in 1985. She was one of three "U" class submarines transferred from the Royal Navy to the Royal Norwegian Navy.

1944

On `19 April 1944 Norwegian sub *Ula* sank U-974 near Stavanger. On 11 November 1944 HMS Venturer, from Flotilla 9, sank U-771 west of Tromso, Norway

1945

In February 1945 HMS Venturer was on patrol northwest of Bergen, Norway. She had dived at dawn, and during the forenoon heard propeller noises on her passive hydrophones. About twenty minutes later she sighted a periscope confirming that her sound contact was a submerged submarine, obviously a U-boat. Venturer's CO set out to track the other submarine, using his active sonar for an occasional range, with bearing being provided by the passive side of his set. At least one more sighting of the target's periscope was made. Venturer's fire control plot established the target's course and speed. Venturer maneuvered to get ahead of the target and fired a salvo of torpedoes set to run at 40 feet. At least one hit and sank U-864. As far as is known, this was the first fully submerged attack made by one submarine on another submerged submarine. Royal Navy submarines did not have homing torpedoes at this time. The only possible criticism must be aimed at U-864, whose sound operator failed to detect the Asdic signals from Venturer. HMS Venturer's CO and his fire control party invented procedures that had not previously existed.[267]

From 1942 through the end of hostilities in May 1945 Flotilla 9 submarines sank six—U-boats. Boats from the flotilla also conducted special operations, landing and extracting SOE agents in occupied Norway.

Mediterranean Sea

When war began in September 1939 Great Britain was concerned about potential Italian threats to the sea lanes in the Mediterranean Sea, the principal and most direct route to India and Singapore. Although the Med was closed to through British shipping temporarily, it was soon reopened. For the time being that route was safe. German U-boat attacks on British shipping only took place in the Atlantic.

1940

In June 1940 the British Mediterranean Fleet was based at Alexandria, Egypt. Italy entered the war on 10 June against Great Britain and France. The British had expected that France would carry a major part of the fighting in the Mediterranean against Italy in the event of war but, as of 25 June 1940, France was out of the war. The burden now fell solely on the UK.

The geographic position of Italy reaching down into the center of the Mediterranean Sea split that body of water in two connected by a relatively narrow passageway. Italy was in a position to control the center except for the island of Malta, a British base. The eastern and western Mediterranean basins had British bases at each end: Gibraltar in the west and Alexandria in Egypt to the east. Prior to the war the Royal Air Force and Royal Army had considered that Malta was not defensible in the event of war because of the threat offered by the Italian Air Force. When war came its defenses were very weak.

The naval war in the Mediterranean was basically one of sea borne logistics. The Italians were busy moving supplies to their ground and air forces in North Africa, primarily to Libya from Italy. After Germany sent the Afrika Corps there in 1941, the battles in the desert between the British 8th Army and the Afrika Corps took center stage and Italian logistics communications were a major target for British naval and air forces. The introduction of Luftwaffe units, especially dive bombers, into the theater in late 1940 made life very difficult for British surface naval forces and merchant convoys attempting to bolster Malta.

British logistic traffic in the Med was limited to keeping Malta viable as a base for naval and air forces that could hinder Axis traffic to North Africa. British forces in North Africa had to be supplied by sea traffic that went by way of Cape Horn and the Suez Canal.

Both sides recognized the value of Malta as a base for British air, surface and submarine operations against the Italian supply lines to Libya. Malta came under increasingly severe air attack. Finally surface forces could not operate from there, and submarines only with great difficulty. Submarines had to submerge at their berths during daylight hours, interfering with repair work. Italian and German forces, primarily air forces, struck at any British convoy bound for Malta, trying to starve the island of the means of continuing its role as an effective operating base.

These two threads intertwined for several years as the battles continued in North Africa, and in the central Mediterranean Sea to control the sea. This is the basic setting in which British submarines operated until Italy finally fell in 1943.

At Alexandria was 1ˢᵗ Submarine Flotilla with HMS Medway as depot ship. The flotilla included submarines Olympus, Odin, Orpheus, Otus, Phoenix, Pandora, and Partian plus submarine minelayers Grampus and Rorqual, a total of nine submarines. Enroute from the Far East were five more: Regulus, Regent, Rainbow, Rover and Perseus. Odin and Otus were at Malta for refit.

By the time HMS Perseus arrived at Alexandria about 8 August 1940, five UK submarines had already been lost: Grampus, Odin, Orpheus, Phoenix, and Oswald. The details are as follow:[268]

Grampus:	Depth charged by an Italian torpedo boat off Syracuse after laying mines in June.
Odin:	Sunk by Italian DD *Strale* in the Gulf of Taranto in mid-June
Orpheus:	Sunk off Tobruk by Italian DD *Tribune* in mid-June
Phoenix:	Sunk with depth charges by sub chaser *Albatross* after missing a torpedo attack on her
Oswald:	Rammed and sunk by Italian DD *Vivaldi* at night near the Strait of Messina

In October 1940 Italy invaded Greece from Albania. Great Britain and Greece were now allied against Italy, a common foe. The Royal Hellenic Navy possessed six submarines. The first two were *Katsonis* (Y1) and *Papanikolis* (Y2), both built in France between 1925 and 1927. They were 205 feet in length, displaced 787 tons submerged, had a crew of 30 and six torpedo tubes, four forward and two aft. They carried a 100 mm gun (3.9 inch). *Proteus* (Y3) was also a French shipyard product, very similar in design to *Papanikolis*.

Proteus was the only Greek submarine which did not operate under Royal Navy operational control during the war, having been lost during the winter of 1940 while Greece was conducting an independent submarine campaign against Italy. On 29 December 1940 *Proteus* was on patrol in the Strait of Otranto east of Brindisi. She located an Italian convoy and sank 11,452 ton cargo ship *Sardegna*. Destroyer Escort *Antares* spotted her and dropped eleven depth charges, forcing *Proteus* to the surface where *Antares* rammed and sank her with all hands. It was not until 10 January 1941 that the Greek Navy learned the details of *Proteus'* demise. Another Greek ship had copied *Sardegna's* SOS signal from *Proteus'* assigned patrol area. On 10 January Italian radio announced the sinking of a Greek submarine in late December.

Papanikolis and *Katsonis* were also active during late 1940, operating in the Adriatic Sea against Italian shipping. *Papanikolis* conducted six war patrols in the Adriatic. On 22 December *Papanikolis* sank small Italian motor ship *Antonietta* by ramming, and larger vessel *San Giorgio* with gun fire. The following day she sank 3,952 ton troop carrier *Firenze* near Sazan Island with torpedoes. After Greece fell in May 1941 she relocated to the Middle East and operated under RN opcon, conducting three more war patrols.

During the first six months of war UK submarines in the Mediterranean Sea sank only twelve merchant ships (45,000 tons). Ten British submarines failed to return from their patrols by the end of the year. Most were the older and larger submarines attached to 1st Submarine Flotilla at Alexandria.

The older "P" and "R" class submarines and the Triton class were normally employed off Italy. They were considered too large to be able to operate effectively in the shallow waters off the Tunisian and Libyan coastlines. Three of the much smaller "U" class (630 tons) arrived at Malta in December 1940. They operated against the inshore Italian convoy route from Cape Bon to Tripoli along the North African coast.

1941

On 9 December 1940 the British Army of the Nile began an offensive that captured Tobruk and Derna in January 1941. On 6 February 1941 advance troops entered Benghazi. It appeared that the British Army and Air Force would capture the entire Italian foothold in North Africa. However Germany had decided to assist Italy and sent forces into Greece. The British Cabinet decided to send troops to Greece to assist despite concerns about loss of momentum in North Africa.

The German push into Greece was in overwhelming strength, particularly air power as applied by Luftwaffe units. First, British troops had to be evacuated from Greece; and later after a German airborne assault on Crete, from that island. The entire affair was very costly to the British Mediterranean Fleet. German dive bombers displayed a high degree of accuracy, much greater than the Italian air Force had demonstrated with its level bombing efforts from high altitude. A large number of British surface warships were sunk or badly damaged. It rapidly became apparent that the interdiction of Italian shipping would be the main role for British submarines as well as for aircraft based on Malta.

Environmental conditions in the Mediterranean Sea varied with seasons. From June through October Asdic (active sonar) conditions were poor, which was good for submarines. They could hide beneath different density layers of sea water that formed. During summer there was a high rate of evaporation of surface sea water in the Med, and it was replaced by lesser density water from the Black Sea and the Atlantic. From November through May conditions changed and Asdic conditions became good for ASW vessels and hence bad for submarines. The smart submarine CO took these factors into account in planning attacks and evasion tactics.

Captain 8th Submarines at Gibraltar was relieved of Atlantic responsibilities and could now concentrate on the western Mediterranean area. UK and Dutch subs operated from Gibraltar in the Gulf of Genoa, off the west coast of Italy and the north coast of Sicily, and in the Tyrrhenian Sea west of Italy. Some subs from Malta also operated in the south part of the Tyrrhenian Sea but there was close coordination between the two British submarine operational commanders to avoid friendly fire encounters. Large submarine Clyde was converted to carry supplies to Malta and made a number of these trips at a time when surface convoys could not get through. However the Italians were constantly laying mines in the Sicily Channel, making each journey hazardous.

By February 1941 there were a number of "U" class submarines stationed at Malta. Five were sent off to attack a convoy but there were many misses. HMS Upright, off Sfax, made a night surface attack on two Italian cruisers and sank *Armando Diaz*.

In March 1941 the German Afrika Corps, a highly mobile panzer-type formation, was transported to Libya. Its commander was Erwin Rommel, who soon acquired the nickname "the Desert Fox". Although Adolph Hitler sent Rommel and the Afrika Corps to North Africa as a defensive move to prevent the expulsion of Italian forces, Rommel had his own ideas and they had little to do with defense.

From time to time boats were sent off on special operations, presumably landing agents behind enemy lines. HMS Utmost accomplished one of those missions, and subsequently the CO was awarded the Distinguished Service Order (DSO), an award usually reserved for sinking a major warship or similar target. The details of the mission were not published.

In March HMS Unique sank *Fenecia* (2,500 tons) off Tunisia. Utmost sank 6,000 ton troopship *Kapo Vita* in the Gulf of Hammanet, and the 2,500 ton German ship *Herakleo* off Kerhennah. HMS Rover sank 6,000 ton tanker *Cosco* off Calabria.

Also in March, Greek submarine HHMS *Triton* sank the 5,000 ton ship *Carnia* about 30 nm east of Cape Gallo in the southern Tyrrhenian Sea off Sicily.[269] Through April since the first of the year UK subs had sunk ten ships (27, 168 tons).[270]

In April 1941 Germany invaded Greece to assist Italy, and rapidly overran it. Great Britain moved ground and air forces into Greece to assist in its defense at the expense of her position in North Africa. However, German forces, particularly the Luftwaffe, were too strong and British forces had to be evacuated from Greece. Greece was conquered in about a month. Greek naval forces still afloat went to Alexandria and continued operations there under Royal Navy operational control.

In April HMS Tetrach sank tanker *Persiano* off Tripoli. On 21 April HMS Upholder sank transport *Antonietta Laura* in the Lampedusa Channel. Upholder than went alongside German transport *Arta*, which was beached and abandoned on the Kerhennah Bank and set her a fire to destroy her cargo before it could be salvaged. In late April Upholder torpedoed two ships; *Arcturus* (sunk) and *Leverkusen* (damaged). After evading depth charge attacks Upholder finished off *Leverkusen* with two more torpedoes.[271]

Greek Submarine HHMS *Nereus* (Y4), a *Proteus* class boat, commissioned in March 1930, escaped to Alexandria and operated under British operational control with pendant number N 56. Greek submarine *Glavkos* (Y6), another *Proteus* class boat also escaped to Alexandria. Unfortunately she was lost to German bombs on 4 April 1942 while at Malta. During July 1941 while under British opcon she sank several small sailers with gunfire in the vicinity of Rhodos, In November she torpedoed and damaged German steamship *Norburg* (2,392 GRT) near Suda Bay, Crete.

On 20 May HMS Urge was submerged east of Tunisia and detected the distant sound of depth charges exploding. It was Italian practice to drop depth charges randomly in order to discourage submarines from attacking, or so British COs surmised. In any case Urge was attracted in the direction of the noise and a convoy of ships escorted by five destroyers came into periscope view. Urge sank 5,000 ton *Zeffiro* and damaged 5,000 ton *Perseo* with torpedoes.

Also in May Upholder conducted a daring attack and sank 18,000 ton troopship *Conte Rosso*, an exploit that earned her CO the Victoria Cross. Upholder's Asdic set was out of commission and she had only two torpedoes left when she commenced that attack. Asdic had both active and passive elements, and once Upholder left periscope depth she had no way of knowing what the enemy ships above were doing.

During May 1941 a U.S. naval officer, Commander J. Fife, USN visited with British submariners in the Med, gathering first hand information about their war time activities. He was a submariner and later exercised command of American submarines operating from Australia. He was impressed with the short diving times that British submarines had: U class—20 seconds, and T class—30 seconds. He was also advised that with the air threat in the Med there was no time for the watch officer to consult with the captain—when he discerned a threat he initiated a dive immediately. U.S. fleet boats of that time had an average diving time of about 35—45 seconds.

French submarine *Narval* was lost while on patrol in the Med during the first half of 1941. From April through August five UK subs were lost: Usk, Undaunted, Unison, P-32 and P-33.[272]

In September 1941, 10th Submarine Flotilla was established at Malta. It exercised operational control of British and allied submarines in the Central Med area. 8th Submarine Flotilla was at Gibraltar, handling operations in the western Med. Malta lacked a great amount of submarine material. As a consequence each sub that transited from Gibraltar to Malta was heavily loaded with extra torpedoes and submarine repair parts. There was a dearth of submarine torpedoes, so converted destroyer torpedoes were put to use. They had the limitation that their running depth could not be reset once loaded in a submarine torpedo tube. They were usually set to run at 18 feet for use against deep draft ships.[273]

In September 1941 intelligence indicated an important Italian troop convoy would proceed from Italy to Cape Bon in North Africa and then by a coastal route to Tripoli. A four submarine ambush was set up by 10th Flotilla at Malta. Unbeaten was stationed at the North African landfall, Upholder and Upright along the coast enroute to Tripoli, and Ursula at the entrance to the swept channel to Tripoli. The convoy consisted of troopships *Oceania, Neptunia* and *Vulcania* with five destroyer escorts.

They departed late on 16 September. At 0330 on 17 September Unbeaten sighted the convoy but was too far off the track to make an attack. However it reported the sighting and convoy position. Upholder intercepted the convoy and torpedoed *Oceania* aft, wrecking her propellers and stopping her. She also hit *Neptunia* with two torpedoes and sank her. She then finished off *Oceania*. Ursula's torpedoes missed *Vulcania* at Tripoli.[274]

From June through September 1941 British submarines sank 49 troopships/supply ships, putting a severe crimp in Axis operations in North Africa. As a consequence Italian ASW operations intensified, with some German technical assistance. By late 1941 it was clear to all British submarine COs that Italian ASW tactics and techniques were getting very dangerous for them.[275]

In addition to furnishing technical assistance and advice to the Italian Navy, Adolph Hitler ordered the dispatch of six U-boats to the Mediterranean Theater, over the objections of the German General Staff.

In late September an Italian convoy was ambushed by Force "K" from Malta. Force "K" consisted of cruisers HMS Aurora and Penelope, and two destroyers borrowed from Force "H" at Gibraltar. The Italian convoy consisted of seven freighters with a close escort of six destroyers, and two heavy cruisers and four destroyers in support. In addition the Italians had stationed submarines off Valetta, Malta to warn of any surface force sortie. However Force "K" got out undetected and in conjunction with HMS Upholder, sank a number of ships and escorts.[276]

On 20 November a convoy of four ships left from Naples. It had a very heavy escort group; three heavy cruisers, two light cruisers and seven destroyers plus aircraft. An RAF Sunderland flying boat sighted the convoy as it transited the Straits of Messina on 21 November and reported. RAF and FAA air attacks damaged a cruiser which had to return to Messina. HMS Utmost torpedoed cruiser *Trieste* which also had to return to port. The convoy was recalled.[277]

In December HMS Upright sank two supply ships, and battleship *Vittorio Veneto* enroute Messina was torpedoed and severely damaged by HMS Urge. It took several months to restore her to service.

December 7, 1941 marked the Japanese attack on Pearl Harbor that brought the United States into war with Japan the following day. December 8 marked the Japanese attacks on British possessions in the Far East and thus the start of Great Britain's war with Japan. She was now fully engaged against the three Axis nations: Germany, Italy and Japan.

1942

In early 1942, 1ˢᵗ Submarine Flotilla at Alexandria was reduced to only four submarines by the need to dispatch submarines back to the Pacific in light of the Japanese attacks. HMS Trusty and Truant left, as did Dutch submarines O. 23 and O. 24.

Count Ciano's diary for 26 January indicated concerns over food shortages in Greece and possible disorders as a result. It also notes that the Italian merchant marine has hardly any ships to spare because of losses in Libyan convoys. Ciano muses about checking to see if the Italian Red Cross can secure some ships for that purpose.[278]

In late February Italian cruisers *Banda Nere* and *Armando Diaz* and two destroyers were dispatched to support an Italian convoy to North Africa. Near the Kerhennah Bank off Tunisia the Italian Admiral slowed his force to 13.5 kts. at about 0200 on 25 February. HMS Upholder was in the vicinity and attacked. She hit *Armando Diaz* with two torpedoes forward and the target blew up.

HMS Clyde, Olympus and Pandora were all busy making supply runs to Malta. All were older and less capable than the newer, smaller "T" and "U" class submarines that made most operational patrols.

March was a busy month for UK submarines. On 9 March Utmost sank transport *Capo Vita* on the Tripoli route. On 10 March Unique sank *Fenicia*.[279] On 19 March Utmost's torpedoes hit two ships: *Heraklia* sank but *Ruhr* made it to port. Later *Gaililea* was severely damaged by a torpedo from Upright. Sinking the target was the primary goal of each submarine commanding officer. However, severely damaged ships took up scarce dockyard space and manpower.

In early March heavy Axis bombing raids on Malta began and continued. Submarines in port had to spend all day submerged with relief crews aboard to attempt to avoid damage or sinking. P.39 was sunk and two other boats damaged. On 1 April Pandora was hit twice and sunk. P.36 was damaged beyond repair. Unbeaten was badly damaged and had to sail to Gibraltar for repairs. On 4 April Greek sub *Glaucos* was sunk by bombs and Polish sub *Sokol* badly damaged. She sailed for Gibraltar on 13 April with over 200 holes in her upper casing above the pressure hull.

In March the 2ⁿᵈ Battle of Sirte took place. After the battle, cruiser *Banda Nere* was damaged in a storm and sailed to Spezia for dockyard repairs. HMS Urge torpedoed and sank her. In the same storm battleship

Littoro was also damaged and shipped thousands of tons of water. Two destroyers reportedly foundered in the storm.[280] These losses point to poor seamanship on the part of Italian senior naval officers.

On 25-26 March HMS Rorqual laid mines off Palermo. One sank tanker *Verde*. Rorqual then used torpedoes to sink tanker *Ticino*. After that she torpedoed and damaged *Laura Cornulo*, and then sank her with gunfire on 30 March. On 31 March Rorqual sighted Italian submarine *Capponi* on the surface in daylight and torpedoed and sank her.[281]

In April, 10th Submarine Flotilla shifted to Alexandria to avoid its submarines being penned in by minefields. Constant air attacks had sunk most of the available minesweepers. From 24-27 April the German 3rd E-boat Flotilla laid 124 mines. By 10 May all submarines had departed Malta. HMS Urge was lost to a mine on 27 April. She had been just behind HMS Upholder in order of enemy ship tonnage sunk.

At the end of April 1942 the Germans moved most of their aircraft away from Sicily, believing that Malta was neutralized as a base for air and submarine operations against Axis traffic from Italy to North Africa. They were mistaken, but perhaps understandably so. The Luftwaffe was short of aircraft for the several theaters of operations in which it was engaged.

The British pushed fighter aircraft back into Malta and regained control of the air overhead, and never lost it again. Minesweepers returned to Malta and cleared out the channels. By the end of June—early July, 10th Submarine Flotilla returned to Malta.

During 1942 HHMS *Papanikolis* conducted two war patrols in the Aegean Sea. In June she sank six small sailing vessels, put SOE agents ashore in Greece, and recovered a team of New Zealand commandos. During her following patrol from the end of August to 15 September, she missed an 8,000 ton oil carrier, and landed two mixed British-Greek commando teams on Rhodes where they attacked the island's two airfields and destroyed a large number of aircraft.

In April 1942 HMS Upholder sailed for her first operational patrol. She had previously made a practice patrol off Spanish Morocco. By this time three "U" class boats had been lost during the year. They were P.38, P.36 and P.39. The last two were lost in bombing attacks while in harbor at Malta. The Admiralty ceased to assign names to new construction submarines for a while. This feature caught the eye of the Prime Minister and he demanded that they be named feeling that their crews needed to be part of a named vessel rather than a numbered one.

On 12 May Count Ciano noted in his diary about plans for war in the Med that Rommel will attack about the end of May, and then forces will be concentrated for the attack on Malta. Ciano notes "If we take Malta, Libya will be safe".[282] Unfortunately for Italy and Germany, Malta was not taken and that ultimately led to the loss of Libya and the Axis position in North Africa.

In June 1942 another large convoy departed for Malta to replenish the island. The operation was named VIGOROUS. Nine UK-controlled submarines screened the north of the convoy route from Gibraltar to Malta. The convoy came under very heavy air attack. Of 17 ships in the convoy, only two arrived at Malta with 15,000 tons of supplies. Beaufort aircraft torpedoes had crippled Italian cruiser *Trento* during the convoy battles. HMS Umbra sank *Trento* before she could seek refuge in port.

From January through June 1942 British forces sank eight enemy submarines: 5 German U-boats and 3 Italian submarines. Seven of the eight were sunk by British submarines.[283] As in WW I the submarine was proving to be an effective ASW weapons system.

In July 1942 HHMS *Katsonis*, now operating with British pendant number N 16, was damaged while exiting a dry dock at Port Said. Later, after overhaul she went on to conduct three patrols in the Aegean Sea.

Upholder was lost off Tripoli while attacking a convoy. With her went her CO, a Victoria Cross holder. Pandora was sunk by bombs at Malta. Urge was lost on passage from Malta to Alexandria, probably to a mine east of Malta.

In June the threat of Rommel's Afrika Corps advances led to a temporary evacuation of some units from Alexandria. Depot ship HMS Medway departed for Haifa in Palestine to be further from harm's way. On 30 June U 372 penetrated her protective destroyer screen and put two torpedoes into her. She sank in twenty minutes, taking with her 90 submarine torpedoes and essential submarine repair parts. Her loss was seriously felt.

HHMS *Nereus* was at sea on patrol during June, July, August and September 1942. On 15 June she sank a sailer with gunfire off Scarpanto. On 15 July she sank three sailers with gunfire off Karpathos. On 19 July she fortunately missed 9,646 ton *Sicilia* off Karpathos with four torpedoes. *Sicilia* was an Italian hospital ship. In August *Nereus* sank a small Greek sailer with gunfire off Rhodes. On 5 August *Nereus* attempted to torpedo German steamship *Wachtfels* but missed. *Wachtfels* was sunk two days later by HMS Proteus. In late September *Nereus* sank Italian vessel *Fiume* (662 GRT) off Rhodes.

In August another large convoy effort was prepared (Operation PEDESTAL) to relieve Malta. On 13 August HMS Unbroken torpedoed and damaged Italian cruisers *Bolzano* and *Attendolo* south of Sicily.[284] Unbroken was subjected to an eight hour depth charge attack (103 depth charges), but escaped. *Bolzano* was beached and burned out, *Attendolo* had its bow blown off but managed to reach Messsina and safety.

By August 1942 UK submarines had made 31 supply trips to Malta to bring in vital materials since January 1941. In that same period 82 merchant ships had sailed, in convoy. But only 49 arrived, the remainder being sunk by Axis air, surface or submarine elements.[285] From June through December 1941 there were 16 submarine supply missions. A typical load included: 24 personnel, 147 mail bags, 2 tons of medical stores, 62 tons of aviation gasoline and 45 tons of kerosene.[286]

In August *Rosolino Pilo* (8,325 tons) had been bombed and damaged south of Pantelleria by RAF aircraft. HMS United was sent in to sink her. United went in at night and fired a torpedo while on the surface. It hit *Pilo* and she blew up. A twelve foot section of iron frame from *Pilo* hit and partially wrecked United's bridge. That same month HMS Porpoise sank *Ogaden* (4,553 tons) and *Lerici* (6,070 tons).

On 27 September HMS Umbra hit *Barbaro* and disabled her off Greece. She was taken in tow but then sunk by Umbra in another attack after nightfall. Umbra also torpedoed and damaged *Unione* but enemy forces managed to tow her into Navarino.

On 29 September Count Ciano noted in his diary that there is great concern over the loss of merchant ships, whose replacement is slow and inadequate. He thinks the 'African problem' will end in six months because there will be no more ships to supply Libya.[287]

On 8 November 1942 Allied amphibious forces landed at Casablanca, Oran and Algiers. Despite initial resistance a deal was soon struck with Admiral Darlan, who was visiting in Algiers at the time, for a cease fire. Darlan commanded the respect of many French senior officers in North Africa, and his orders to cease resistance were rapidly carried out.

In November HHMS *Papanikolis* set out on another patrol in the eastern Med. She inserted men and equipment into Crete. On 30 November she sank an 8,000 ton ship at Alimnia Islet, near Rhodes.

"S" class submarine P 222 was sunk by depth charges off Capri by Italian torpedo boat *Fortuna* in December 1942. On 5 December a captured Italian submarine (former *Perla*) was transferred to the Greek Navy. She had been captured off Beirut and commissioned in the Royal Navy as HMS P 712. On transfer to the Greek Navy she was renamed *Matrozos*.

1943

As the new year of 1943 opened, the fierce battle to disrupt Axis logistic traffic to North Africa continued. In January some 51 Axis ships sailed for North Africa: 11 were sunk by submarines, 4 by surface ships, 2 by mines, and 7 by aircraft—a 47% sinking rate.[288]

The UK submarine command setup in the Mediterranean at the beginning of 1943 was a trio of submarine flotillas as follows: 8th at Gibraltar covering the western Mediterranean; 10th at Malta covering the center; and 1st at Alexandria.

Papanikolis was again at sea carrying agents and equipment to Hydra. She captured a 200-ton sailing vessel, put a prize crew aboard, and sailed her back to Alexandria, a modern day take on 18th Century sailing ship tactics. The day following that capture, she sank another 150 ton sailer. During March and May she sank four more sailers, totaling 450 tons. By this time the Axis forces in the eastern Med were reduced to using small vessels to resupply their island bases. *Papanikolis* survived the war and was decommissioned in 1945.

On 9 February Dutch submarine HNMS *Dolfijn* torpedoed and sank Italian submarine *Malachite* near Cape Spartivento.[289]

On 2 April 1943 HHMS *Katsonis* sank a German minelayer in the port of *Gytheio*, and the Spanish 1,500 ton *San Isidoro* three days later. On 29 May she sank freighter *Rigel* near Skiathos. On 14 September while pursuing a German troop transport she was sunk by German submarine chaser UJ-2101. Fifteen of her crew survived the sinking and were captured.

From January through May 1943 at least 500 Axis merchant ships were sunk in the Mediterranean, isolating the Afrika Corps and the surviving Italian armies. During that same period 11 U-boats were sunk, along with 9 Italian submarines.

On May 13, 1943 German and Italian troops in North Africa surrendered. The Allied battle to interdict Axis supplies to their forces in North Africa was finally over. British submarines had played a major role in the fight. On July 9 Operation HUSKY, the Allied invasion of Sicily began. By August 17 all of Sicily had been conquered, and negotiations were underway to seek an Italian surrender.

The Mediterranean Sea was now open to Allied and neutral merchant traffic. Ships bound for India and Australia could use the Suez Canal rather than making the long voyage around the Cape of Good Hope, saving thousands of miles. That represented a huge savings in merchant tonnage, an important factor in a war that still raged in two oceans.

During the period June-December 1943 some 20 Axis submarines were destroyed (9 German and 11 Italian). Many were sunk during "swamp" operations, in which continuous air coverage was maintained in an area in which a submarine had been detected and surface forces were then brought in to search and prosecute with Asdic. Aircraft equipped with radar could detect surfaced submarines and force them down again. The *snorkel* had not yet made its way into the German Med U-boat flotilla. Before long the submarine had to seek the surface to attempt to recharge its batteries and renew its air supply, leading to its destruction. German U-boats in the Med had numbered 25 in November 1942. By December 1943 they were down to 13. However September 1943 can be viewed as the date of defeat of U-boats in the Med just as April 1943 marked their defeat in the North Atlantic[290].

The center of British submarine operations shifted into the Tyrrhenian Sea, under the control of 8th Flotilla at Algiers. T-class boats were sent from Alexandria and U-class boats from Malta to reinforce 8th Flotilla.[291]

On September 8 1943 General Eisenhower announced the unconditional surrender of Italy. That did not mean the end of fighting in the Italian Peninsula. German forces continued to resist strongly and expertly. However naval operations were now strictly in support of the ground fighting ashore as the Allied armies gradually worked their way north against the German armies.

On September 9 Allied forces landed at Salerno on the Italian mainland. On September 30 the U.S. Fifth Army captured Naples. On October 13 the new Italian government declared war on Germany.

On 1 November 1943 HMS Veldt (P 71), a "V" class submarine, launched 19 July at Vickers Armstrong (Barrow-in-Furness, U.K.), was commissioned and turned over to the Royal Hellenic Navy of Greece. She was renamed HHMS *Pipinos* (Y8). The V class was an offshoot of the U class with roughly the same characteristics. They were 203 feet 5 inches in length, with a submerged displacement of 740 tons, single hull, welded construction with an operating depth of 300 feet. They had four TT forward and 8 torpedoes, plus a 3-inch (76 mm.) gun, and a complement of 37. Their surfaced/submerged speeds were 12.5/9 kts.

From the fall of 1943 until November 1944 much of UK submarine activity shifted from the Mediterranean Sea into the Aegean Sea. Prime Minister Churchill focused on that area and tried to inveigle his American allies into supporting a drive into Yugoslavia. They were intent on opening a second front by invading France and would have nothing to do with another Mediterranean Sea adventure. The British were left to muck about in the Dodecanese Islands and Aegean by themselves.

After the Italian surrender, HMS Severn and HMS Rorqual and four Italian submarines were engaged in running supplies to Leros in the Dodecanese islands.

Toward the end of 1943 10th Submarine Flotilla moved from Malta to Maddalena, Sardinia. 1st Submarine Flotilla moved from Beirut to Malta.

The war in the Mediterranean with Italy ended with the Armistice signed by Italy on 8 September, and her subsequent declaration of war on Germany on 13 October 1943. German forces immediately occupied northern and central Italy. There was subsequent naval fighting along the coasts of Italy in support of Allied ground forces, and in the Aegean and Adriatic seas but the major campaign for control of the seas in the Med was over.

During the period 1940-1943 Italy sent 883 major convoys to North Africa. About 50% experienced at least one allied attack. 220 Italian convoys were attacked by Allied, mostly British, submarines. Another 294 were attacked by Allied aircraft. The Italians lost 342 ships (1,229,777 tons), about 60% of Italian merchant shipping available at the beginning of the war.[292]

The first six months of 1943 marked what The Italians termed "The Third Battle of the African Convoys". Some 119 convoys departed Italy: 69 were subject to submarine attack (33 ships hit); there were 164 air attacks (73 ships hit). In addition to the convoys there were 578 voyages by smaller ships.[293]

1944

On January 12 American troops landed at Anzio, Italy attempting to bypass German positions and move on Rome. On June 4 Rome finally fell to Allied forces.

In June 1944 HMS Sickle was lost to a mine, the last UK submarine lost in the Mediterranean Sea. A total of 45 UK submarines had been lost in the Mediterranean since the war began. Twenty-one of them were mined or presumed mined.

On June 6, 1944 Allied troops landed in Normandy marking the long awaited "Second Front". On August 15 Allied forces landed in southern France in Operation DRAGOON.

On 9 August 1944 HHMS *Pipinos* sank a German torpedo boat (former Italian *Calatafimi*) with torpedoes.

1945

During early 1945 a second V class submarine, HMS Vengeful (P 86) was turned over to the Royal Hellenic Navy as HHMS Delphin (Y9)

British Midget Submarines and Manned Torpedoes

Midget Submarines

The German battleship Tirpitz, resting in a Norwegian Fjord, was a constant threat to the British convoys to northern Russia. With her eight 15-inch main battery, she could destroy an entire convoys and its escorts. In September 1941 the first Wellman X-craft, midget submarines, were laid down to try to deal with the Tirpitz threat. Unlike Japanese midget submarines, they did not carry torpedoes.

They were small, about 60 feet by six foot diameter, with an operational crew of four men, one a diver. Their weapons were two cargo sections that could be released. They each carried either a supply of limpet mines to be placed on ships' hulls or a two-ton explosive charge to be released under the keel of the target.

The operational plan was to tow each X-craft behind a standard submarine to the vicinity of the target. A passage crew of three men was embarked and a telephone wire connection between towing sub and towed X-craft allowed communications. Most of the tow was submerged. The passage crew was responsible to keep the X-craft ready for its attack, including battery charging. The X-craft had a small diesel engine plus its battery. On arrival near the target area, the operational crew would take over, the passage crew would transfer to the towing sub, and the tow would be released.

The diver had a Wet-Dry compartment to use to lock out and back in to the X-craft. His main task was to use a hydraulic gun to cut through anti-submarine nets surrounding the target.

In September 1943 six X-craft and their towing subs departed Scotland. One was lost enroute with its passage crew. One had to jettison its explosive charges. One reached the outer target fjord but had mechanical problems and had to abort.

That left X-5, X-6 and X-7 to carry on the attack. X-5 was sunk by gunfire in the inner fjord. X-6 and X-7 reached Tirpitz after various adventures and released their four-two ton explosive charges under her hull. On 22 September 1943 they all exploded and Tirpitz was out of action until March 1944.

Half a world away in July 1945 midget submarine XE-3 damaged IJN cruiser *Takao* beyond repair at Singapore in a very daring attack. In that theater midget submarines also cut Japanese undersea communication cables, forcing them to send traffic by radio where it could be intercepted and decrypted.

Manned Torpedoes

The Italian successes with manned torpedoes in the Mediterranean Sea led the British to emulate them. The British Chariot, Mark I, was based roughly on an Italian machine used against British targets at Gibraltar. Like the Italian "pig" it was a two man machine. The driver/commander sat in front and navigated and steered. The second man assisted in net penetration and in fixing the detachable warhead to the target. Both wore an oxygen cylinder, a re-breather, with a carbon dioxide absorbent device. Below 30 feet, pure oxygen becomes dangerous to the breather but that was not well known at that time.

The chariots were carried in containers on board T-class submarines and transported with their crews to the target area, where they were launched. On 2 January 1943 HMS Trooper and HMS Thunderbolt, with chariots, attacked Palermo, Sicily. They launched five chariots. Three broke down, but two penetrated into the harbor. They badly damaged liner *Viminale* (8,500 tons) and sank new cruiser *Ulpio Traiano*. Their chariot crews also attached limpet mines to three destroyers, but they were discovered and removed before they could explode.

Chapter Four—Dutch Submarines

In 1939 The Netherlands had some 28 submarines in commission, split between The Netherlands (Holland), and the Netherlands East Indies (NEI) (current day Indonesia). The Netherlands was neutral during initial WW II fighting that started on 1 September 1939 with the German invasion of Poland. The sudden German *blitzkrieg* assault on Western Europe that struck Luxembourg, Belgium, France and The Netherlands on 10 May 1940 ended Dutch hopes that it could remain neutral during the conflict as it had during the First World War. Holland was rapidly overrun and occupied. Her government relocated to the British Isles and continued as a "government in exile".

Those Dutch submarines that could get underway sailed to England. There they operated under Royal Navy operational control during the war. The colonial portion of the Dutch Submarine Service based in the NEI, remained under Dutch political and operational control. Both the British and the Dutch governments kept a wary eye on Japan, concerned that its adherence to the "Axis Pact" would bring it into war on the side of Germany. Japanese focus on obtaining an unrestricted supply of raw materials to support its unending war in China made the NEI a tempting target since it was a primary source of oil. Similarly the availability of tin and rubber in Malaya made it a target also.

Later during the war, the British government loaned four submarines to the Dutch: one S-class, two T-class and one U-class. One of the T-class, HMS Talent became *Zwaardvisch* in the Dutch Navy. Dutch submarine personnel were top notch and made good use of their new boats.[294]

Dutch submarine operations in "Home Waters", the Mediterranean Sea, and the Indian Ocean are covered in Chapter Three, dealing with British submarines, since Dutch submarines operated under RN operational control in those theaters.

Dutch Submarines in the Far East

When the war began in Europe in 1939 The Netherlands remained neutral. Some 18 German merchant ships sought refuge in NEI ports lest they be captured by British forces, and Dutch authorities interned them. There was no formal cooperation between Great Britain and the Netherlands, both cautious about offending Japan, which was a lurking threat in the Far East. However informal talks began between British, Dutch, and Australian military officials sounding each other out about military cooperation in the event that Japan came south. Americans attended these discussions, but only as observers.

The British indicated that they would assist the NEI if the NEI would support the British Far Eastern Strategy, which depended upon Singapore as the linchpin of their position. The NEI agreed. Australia agreed to furnish the NEI with arms and troops. Agreements were concluded for the use of Australian-controlled ports like Rabaul and Port Moresby by NEI ships.[295]

In April 1941 a Singapore-Batavia (later Jakarta) Agreement was concluded between British and Dutch authorities in the Far East. By this time all 18 British submarines had left the China Station. The agreement indicated that some of the 15 Royal Netherlands Navy (RNN) submarines based at Surabaya in Java would operate under British Royal Navy (RN) opcon if Japanese military actions became threatening. Other items included the dispatch of three NEI Glen Martin B-12 bomber squadrons and one Buffalo fighter squadron to Singapore. RAAF Hudsons visited Ambon and Timor in the NEI. Some Dutch ammunition and bombs were relocated to Singapore. NEI B-12s visited Jolo in the Philippines in May 1941 and Singapore in September 1941.[296] However, the informal agreement between the U.S. and Great Britain that in the event of war the new allies would concentrate first on the defeat of Germany while holding Japan off defensively, left the NEI in a weak position. Australia agreed to furnish the NEI with rifles, machine guns, mortars, and anti-aircraft weapons and ammunition but her industrial capacity was somewhat limited.

Hurst points out in *The Fourth Ally* that the forthcoming loss of the NEI can be traced to "a principled allied stance against Japan that lacked the military power to back it up."[297] That applied to all the allied positions in the Far East including Great Britain, the Netherlands and the United

States. With the principal allies, Great Britain and the United States, focused on Europe the stage was set for Japan to run wild.

Of the 15 Dutch submarines in the NEI at that time, four were over eighteen years old and thus not expected to be of great value if fighting erupted. The remaining first line boats were intended to be used in three boat mini-wolf packs against an invasion force. Long range patrol flying boats would provide early warning and allow the Dutch submarines time to reach an ambush position. The RNN had 59 flying boats available: 34 German Dorniers and 25 American Catalinas. Five more Catalinas arrived in late 1941-early 1942.[298]

On 1 December the Dutch commander in chief ordered O 16 and K-XVII to Singapore to operate under RN opcon in the southern Gulf of Siam (now Thailand).[299] Intelligence was available to British and Dutch authorities through interception and decryption of Japanese naval radio traffic indicating the formation and movement of large amphibious forces towards Malaya and the NEI. Dutch submarines K-XI, K-XII and K-XIII were also sent to intercept the Japanese invasion forces heading into the Gulf of Siam. Unfortunately they arrived after the initial landings on 8 December. O-19 and O-20 were also diverted to operate under RN opcon. A total of seven Dutch submarines were involved in opposing the Japanese invasion of British Malaya.[300]

The Royal Navy operational commander assigned Dutch submarines to individual patrol stations, instead of using their practiced wolf pack technique. They lacked any long range air reconnaissance assistance. They sank three transports, damaged another four transports, and lost three of their number.

On 8 December Japanese invasion forces landed in Malaya and Thailand. The remaining Dutch subs under RNN opcon were on patrol in the Makassar Straits and off North Borneo. They operated as planned using RNN doctrine. They sank a destroyer, 2 transports and damaged another two transports.[301] The British naval commander called for return of British submarines to the Far East. Two sailed but only HMS Trusty arrived before Singapore surrendered.[302]

On 10 December HMS Prince of Wales and HMS Repulse were sunk by IJN torpedo bombers operating from Indo-China. In late December K-XIV was credited with sinking two Japanese transports off North Borneo.[303]

On 16 December Miri in North Borneo was seized by a Japanese force. By Christmas four Dutch subs had been lost. O-16, O-20 and K-XVII were destroyed in action by Imperial Japanese Navy forces. K-XII was badly damaged by an internal battery explosion while at Singapore and was out of action. As the British surrender at Singapore loomed, all the remaining Dutch boats seconded temporarily to Royal Navy opcon, returned to Surabaya to take part in the defense of the Malay Barrier, under Dutch opcon. The term Malay Barrier was used to refer to the string of islands that composed the Netherlands East Indies, now Indonesia. They formed a barrier to a Japanese advance towards Australia.

The new combined Allied Command ABDA (American-British-Dutch-Australian) had roughly forty submarines available. There were Dutch (12 K-class and 4 O-class) and American (4 S-class (old) and 22 modern fleet boats)[304] However; the Japanese controlled the skies in the area. The NEI fighter force consisted of 20 Curtiss CW-22s, 16 Curtiss Hawk 75As and 66 Brewster Buffalos.[305] They were all good fighter aircraft but not adequate to take on IJN Zero fighters. The Dutch lacked a radar-based air defense system in the NEI. Repeated air raids whittled down the NEI fighter force to the point that they could not protect the major naval port at Surabaya from repeated bombing attacks.

1942

On 23 January 1942 K-XVIII sank the transport *Tsuruga Maru* which was involved in landings at Balikpapan.[306]

On 4 February an IJN destroyer was torpedoed and damaged by a submarine torpedo. On 8 February U.S. submarine S-37 torpedoed and badly damaged IJN destroyer *Natsushio*. She was taken in tow but sank 9 February.[307]

The "fortress" of Singapore fell to Japanese ground forces on 15 February 1942. Following the surrender of Singapore, five more Dutch submarines were lost. K-VII was bombed and sunk in harbor. K-XVI was reportedly torpedoed and sunk by Japanese submarine I-66 off Borneo while on patrol.[308] Three (K-X, K-XIII and K-XVIII) were all unfit for sea, and were destroyed by their own forces at Surabaya as the Japanese closed in.

On 19 February Bali and Lombok fell to Japanese forces. The airfield at Bali was used by Japanese aircraft beginning on 20 February, allowing them to cover all of the island of Java. That same day an IJN carrier strike hit Darwin in northern Australia and put it out of business as a staging point for reinforcements from Australia to the NEI. On 25 February, the ABDA commander, General Wavell dissolved the ABDA command. Responsibility for the defense of the NEI fell back on the Dutch, namely Admiral Helfrich.[309]

On 7 March 1942 the capital of Batavia fell to Japanese troops. On 10 March the main naval port of Surabaya was captured. The remaining seven seaworthy Dutch submarines scattered in two directions. Four boats (K-XI, K-XIV, K-XV and O-19) headed for Colombo, Ceylon and there operated under RN opcon. Three K-class (K-VIII, K-IX and K-XII) sailed to Fremantle in Western Australia and operated under USN opcon.[310]

The further operations of Dutch submarines are covered under the British and American submarine chapters.

Chapter Five—Italian Submarines

The Battle of the Atlantic dealt with German U-boats and Allied or neutral shipping in convoys. The Battle of the Mediterranean also dealt in convoys: British convoys to Malta; and Italian convoys to North Africa. Italian submarines were mainly involved in the Mediterranean Sea although at the beginning of fighting with the British they also operated in the Red Sea area. Italian submarines later joined their German ally in the Battle of the Atlantic but they were a relatively minor player in that theater.

The Italian Navy suffered under a number of serious impediments during WW II. First and most limiting to fleet operations was a lack of fuel oil. Second was the lack of a naval air arm, or a cooperative Italian Air Force (IAF) which would furnish aerial reconnaissance for naval operations and provide effective air attack against enemy navy ships, and defensive air cover for Italian navy ships. Third was the lack of radar aboard Italian ships. They were essentially blind at night whereas British aircraft and warships could use radar to engage them.[311] Another major impediment was British penetration of Italian military cipher systems.

The lack of radar aboard ships was a distinctly Italian Navy failure. Experimental radar was developed in 1935 and 1936 by Italian scientists, but the Italian Navy staff stifled the development. Until mid-1941 each successful radar prototype was sent to storage. In February 1941 the Navy Ordnance Chief rejected radar as "futuristic". The Battle Fleet Commander, Admiral Iachino, refused an offer of three prototype radars to mount on his flagship.[312]

There was another material issue that affected Italian submarines assigned to the Red Sea area. Italian submarines had air conditioning machinery but apparently it was not well maintained because it frequently leaked a by-product of the working fluid. That fluid was methyl chloride, an inherently dangerous substance.[313] The Red Sea area was particularly hot and humid during the worst season and the submarine crew desperately needed air conditioning to operate effectively. Instead they frequently suffered poisoning from the fluid leakage.

In late September 1939 the Italian Naval Attaché in Berlin returned to Rome and met with Mussolini to convey German requests for naval cooperation. They included providing port support for U-boats, information about British-French convoys, and the transfer of some U-boats into the Mediterranean Sea. Mussolini was receptive at first. However Count Ciano, his Foreign Minister and Admiral Cavagnari, Chief of Naval Staff, eventually dissuaded him from granting what was asked.[314] Both were very hesitant at the time about involving Italy in the war on the side of Germany.

The Italian Navy was given little warning of Benito Mussolini's intention to enter the war in 1940. Mussolini indicated that the war would be short—perhaps three months in duration. Therefore the Italian Navy did not plan to escort ships to Libya from Italy. Italian forces in Libya were expected to survive on prepositioned stocks for six months. In 1939 the senior Italian naval command *Supermarina*, had reviewed war plans. These plans assumed that Italy would be opposed in the Mediterranean Sea by Great Britain and France. Other assumptions were a short war, and a cooperative Italian Air Force capable of neutralizing Malta as a base for British air and naval operations. The Italian Navy planned an occupation of Malta as a prerequisite for successful operations in the central Mediterranean.[315]

Perhaps the first clue that the assumptions were suspect was an indication that the IAF could only spare about one hundred more or less obsolete aircraft for the task of neutralizing Malta. Bragadin goes on to say ". . . (the) Italian Air Force fought with great energy but with little or no coordination with the Navy's activities . . ." He remarks favorably about the apparently smooth coordination between British surface naval units and air units, in comparing the two opposing sides.

The missions laid out for the Italian Submarine Service in the Med were as follow:

Offensive missions

Reconnaissance missions covering Alexandria, the Otranto Straits, Malta, and convoy routes

Resupply of the Dodecanese Islands (between Greece and Turkey) and Libya

Training at the Submarine School at Pola[316]

In addition to the Italian Submarine Service, the Italian Navy included "special warfare" units, which will be mentioned from time to time. They include:

"Pocket" submarines, of 30 and 12 tons displacement, with crews of 4 and 2 men respectively, each with two torpedo tubes. These were used in the Black Sea against the USSR.

Explosive motor boats (operator jumped overboard just before hitting target)

Guided torpedoes ("pigs"), carrying a detachable warhead, and two operators. Two submarines were equipped to transport three pigs apiece.

Limpet mines placed by swimmers with breathing apparatus[317]

1940

On 10 May 1940 Germany invaded France, Belgium, The Netherlands and Luxemburg. On 10 June Italy declared war on France and Great Britain. Mussolini, seeing the blitzkrieg attack on France about to force her surrender, declared war in order to realize some territorial gains from France's fall.[318]

Reference has been made elsewhere about the role of comint in submarine warfare. The submarine is a very inefficient search platform. Either aerial reconnaissance or communications intelligence can provide target locating information essential to placing slow moving submarines into positions where prey may be found.

The Italian Navy's most secret cipher and its General Naval Code Book was being largely read by the British as early as 1937. In addition high-grade ciphers used by the Italian Air Force in East Africa and the Med, the Italian Army in Libya, and Italian diplomats in Spain, were also being read by the British.[319]

When war began the submarine roster in the Mediterranean was:[320]

France	55
Great Britain	10
Italy	105[321]

On 2 June 1940 there were discussions about operations of Italian submarines in the Atlantic between Radm. Kurt Friche, Chief of the Operations Department of the German Navy and Adm. Maraghini, Italian Naval Attaché in Berlin. On 13 and 24 July *Supermarina* sent letters to the German Naval Staff about proposed Italian submarine operations. Italy indicated that it could send up to 40 submarines into the Atlantic and asked for a base in German-occupied France since any Spanish base option was too difficult politically to obtain.

The Italian offer was immediately accepted in view of the shortage of German U-boats and Doenitz's keen understanding that the war he was waging was a war of attrition against Allied and neutral shipping. Numbers were everything. Doenitz planned to send Italian COs on war patrols with experienced U-boat commanders and to train their crews in German schools. Each country's senior submarine staff sent a senior officer (Commander rank or higher) to serve on the other's staff. [322]

On 25 July Admiral Raeder and Adolph Hitler formally accepted the Italian proposals and agreed that Italian submarines in the Atlantic would operate under an Italian admiral. This concession precluded the Italian government asking for tactical control of any Luftwaffe squadrons that might be sent to operate in the Mediterranean theater.[323]

Although happy to have additional numbers, Admiral Doenitz was somewhat skeptical about potential Italian submarine effectiveness against convoys, because they had no experience in Atlantic operations or in convoy tracking and attack.[324]

Vadm. Hezlet reports that per pre-war agreements with Germany, Italy planned to operate about 30 submarines in the Atlantic south of the latitude of Lisbon. Eight submarines were deployed in the Red Sea. The remainder was attached to the 3rd squadron of the Italian Fleet, operating from seven bases in the Mediterranean: from Cagliari in the west to Leros and Tobruk in the east. They were used for reconnaissance to make up for the shortage of naval air reconnaissance. They were trained for daylight submerged attacks only. Of some 70 Italian subs in the Med at the start of the war, 49 were available and deployed at the war's beginning. They were in three groups by area: Gibraltar to Sicily, Gulf of Genoa, and between Greece and Alexandria.

During the first three days of war 28 Italian submarines aborted their missions, *Fieramosca* had a battery explosion, and two, *Guglielmotti* and *Macalle*, ran aground with *Macalle* scuttled by its crew and *Guglielmotti* salvaged. *Ferraris* had major engine failures.[325] It was not a promising start.

British forces promptly sank seven Italian submarines: *Diamante*, *Liuzzi*, *Uebi Scebeli*, *Rubino*, *Argonauta*, *Torricelli*, and *Galvani*. They captured *Galilei*. A French sloop sank *Provanna*. On 29 June the Royal Navy recovered the naval code book for the Italian equivalent of Enigma (a four rotor machine without a plug board) from *Uebi Scebeli* west of Crete.[326]

Blair argues that the losses were due to a combination of poor design and quality of Italian submarines, to unrealistic peacetime training, and to reckless bravado on the part of their COs. He also notes that these losses during the first twenty days of operations led to a high degree of caution in future Italian submarine operations. Another outcome of these losses was that Rome changed all Italian naval codes, leaving Bletchley Park in the dark.

After mid-July 1940 British intelligence regarding the Italian Navy went "down hill". On 5 July the Italian Navy introduced a separate cipher system for submarines, where before they had been using a general naval code book that was being read by British intelligence. On 17 July they issued new cipher tables for surface ships, and in October new tables for the most secret naval cipher.[327]

On 12 June *Bagnolini* sank light cruiser HMS Calypso south of Crete. On 29 June *Beilul* reported the British Mediterranean Fleet departing Alexandria before the Battle of Calabria. After the initial surge effort the Italian submarine presence was reduced to about ten boats on patrol at each end of the Med for the remainder of 1940.[328]

On 11 June 1940, one day after the declaration of war, *Finzi* departed La Spezia and passed Gibraltar while surfaced and entered the Atlantic. *Veniero* and *Calvi* conducted the next transits of the Gibraltar Straits, submerged. *Cappellini* had to turn back. Most of the Italian submarines that transited the straits did so submerged.

On 17 June Italian submarine *Provana* was sunk off Oran by the French destroyer *La Curieuse*.

After the fall of France in June 1940 an Italian submarine base was set up at Bordeaux. Italian submarines in the Atlantic operated from there after September 1940. At the end of 1941 ten Italian submarines returned into the Mediterranean Sea. Some 48 passages of the Straits of Gibraltar were made by Italian submarines without suffering any losses. Bragadin points out, in comparison, that five U-boats were lost trying to enter the Med in the fall of 1941.[329]

Three days after hostilities began, Marshal Badoglio, Chief of the Italian General Staff, called on the Navy to begin escort of supplies to Libya. On 16 June *Zoea* began loading ammunition, and sailed for Tobruk on 19 June. On 25 June submarine *Bragadin* sailed with a cargo of airport supplies for Tobruk.[330]

During August 1940 a number of Italian submarines sank or damaged ships in the Atlantic as shown in the following table:

Date	Submarine	Target	Results
12 August	Malaspina	Motor tanker British Fame (8,406 tons)	Sunk at 32N/23W
19 August	Malaspina	Unknown, Est. 8,000 tons	Torpedo missed at 39N/21W
19 August	Barbarigo	Steam freighter Aquila (3,255 tons)	Damaged in a gun action
21 August	Dandolo	Motor freighter Hermes (3,768 tons)	Damaged at 37N/14W
26 August	Dandolo	Steam freighter Ilvington Court (5,187 tons)	Sunk at 37N/22W

On 1 September 1940 the new Italian Navy Submarine Base at Bordeaux was commissioned. It was named *"Betasom"* and commanded by Adm. Parone. The base was mainly equipped and defended by Germans. Two passenger ships were converted into floating accommodations for Italian submarine officers and crews. Initially Italian submarines in the Atlantic operated south of 42 degrees north latitude. *Barbarigo, Malaspina* and *Dandolo* were the first boats assigned to Betasom. They sank only two ships (British Fame and Ilvington Court) during their August transits.[331]

Italy asked for assignment of the Atlantic area below 45 degrees north, but Admiral Raeder rejected their request in order to avoid interference with German surface commerce raiders.

Italian submarines operating in the Atlantic were technically inferior to their German rivals. The bridge-conning tower arrangement was too long and too high.[332] They lacked a main induction valve to deliver air directly to the engine room, with the result that there was a constant noisy flow of air through the conning tower and control room during night surface operations. The arrangement led to flooding in the control room when heavy seas were present, with unfortunate results for auxiliary machinery and electrical switchboards. They had lengthy diving times and poor maneuverability, as well as slow surface speeds. In addition their commanding officers were far too old by German standards.[333]

Knox's remarks about Italian submarines in *Hitler's Italian Allies* are interesting. He notes that submarines had a high priority in the Italian Navy but then states that they were backward technogically and doctrinally. He goes on to list some problem areas:[334]

Submerged speed about 1/3 that of German U-boats
Surface speed of only 11-12 knots
Inadequate torpedo capability
Too short periscopes

With German advice and oversight some of these problems were remedied. Bridge structures were lowered and shortened. Some Italian COs attended the U-boat training center in the Baltic Sea for instruction. Technical cooperation between the German U-boat Arm and the Italian Submarine Service was improved.

During October and November 1940 Italian submarines were unable to bring U-boats into contact with targets. Their reports were too late or inaccurate. They failed to attack on their own and failed to maintain contact with the enemy. The reader will recognize that these failings were a violation of all Admiral Doenitz's rules for his U-boat commanders, as recounted in Chapter One. When U-boats sighted convoys, Italian submarines in the same area failed to join the attacks.

From 10 October to 30 November 1940 there were some 243 Italian submarine days at sea. They sank only one ship of 4,866 tons. During the same period there were 378 U-boat days at sea. The U-boats involved sank 80 ships, totaling 435,189 tons. Expressed as ratios the Italian and German scores are startlingly different and very revealing about relative effectiveness:[335]

Italian submarines: 20 tons sunk/per submarine/per day at sea
German U-boats: 1,115 tons sunk/per U-boat/per day at sea

Doenitz's evaluation of Italian submarine operations is interesting. He considered them well trained in routine submarine operations, that is independent patrol operations and submerged attacks. He thought their gun installation excellent. It was designed for bombarding enemy bases. He realized that they were not trained for the mobile submarine warfare that he had developed. Their submarine superstructure was too high and easily detectable. Their lack of an independent main induction valve might have been all right for Mediterranean operations but was hazardous in the Atlantic where heavy seas tended to break on the submarine bridge and flood into the control room. With Adm. Parone's consent Doenitz assigned Italian submarines to patrol areas west and south of those assigned to U-boats, where the Italians could operate against independent sailers.[336] Effectively he wrote them off as participants in Axis wolf pack operations against convoys.

It is interesting to compare the Italian Submarine Service and the American Submarine Service (Chapter Eight), and see how each reacted to the stress of war. The Italians outnumbered the Americans slightly in numbers of submarines: 115 to 98. Both trained prior to entry into the war using similar tactics: submerged patrols against naval targets with no effort to destroy merchant shipping. The Italians fought as they had trained, but not very well. The American Submarine Service had to deal with a terrible set of problems of its own making, in torpedoes that ran too deep, magnetic exploders that detonated prematurely or failed to detonate at all, and a contact exploder that reacted to a perfect attack (90 degree hit) by failing to detonate.

They cut down their pre-war "covered wagon" superstructures to reduce their detectability. They changed their prewar tactics to operate on the surface at night using radar against Japanese convoys. They solved the torpedo problem, and went on to destroy the Japanese Merchant Marine by mid-1944—bringing the Empire of Japan to a point at which a rational regime would have begun surrender negotiations. They did to Japan what the Germans tried to do to Great Britain, completely isolating the main islands of their enemy from its overseas resources.

On 28 October 1940 Italy declared war on Greece, with little notice to *Supermarina*. This situation left the Italian-controlled Dodecanese Islands near Turkey isolated and forced the Italian Navy to commit several submarines to making resupply trips to the islands. Later some small ships of about 1200 tons were pressed into service to run the British blockade and resupply the islands.

On 15 October a decision meeting regarding war with Greece was held by Mussolini. Representatives from *Supermarina* were not invited although the invasion of Greek islands and ports and landings on the Greek coast were discussed. *Supermarina* learned of the decisions on 16 October. Attacks began on 31 October.[337] Bragadin, a Italian Navy Reserve Commander during the war, notes repeatedly that Mussolini and the Italian High Command were ignorant of naval matters, and strongly biased in favor of the Italian Army and Air Force.

At the end of October *Supermarina* asked *BdU* to extend the Atlantic operating areas assigned to *Betasom*. *BdU* agreed to let Italian submarines operate in the Western Approaches. The newly assigned area was 51 degrees north to 58-20 north latitude, and 17 degrees west to 27 degrees west longitude. On 9 November *Marconi* sank a ship, and on 18 November *Barocca* sank another. The other six Italian submarines sank nothing. In December six Italian submarines sank six ships.

From October through December *Betasom* employed 19 SS in its assigned areas. They encountered ten convoys and 38 independent sailers. No convoy was attacked and only 19 of the 38 independent sailers. Thirteen independent sailers were sunk. A Canadian DD was badly damaged on 1 December. Two Italian submarines were lost during this period.[338]

Red Sea operations

There were eight submarines stationed in the Red Sea, at Masawa. Operating conditions in that latitude and climate were very difficult. Heat stroke and skin rashes were common, as was frequent gas poisoning according to Bragadin. In addition to the submarines, there were nine Italian destroyers and a surface raider, *Ramb I*, in the Red Sea when hostilities broke out.

The Italian base at Masawa, near the Horn of Africa, was in a position to provide Italian surface and submarine forces a marvelous location from which to interdict British sea commerce from India to Suez. It speaks volumes for Mussolini's slap dash approach to war that they were not in larger numbers and better prepared when he declared war on Great Britain. Although the Red Sea was a difficult operating area with many shoals,

Italian forces could have isolated Aden and controlled the approaches to the strait that led into the Red Sea from the Indian Ocean.

War began on 10 May 1940. Submarines *Ferraris, Galvani, Galilei* and *Maccale* sailed from Masawa to attack British and French shipping. *Ferraris* had engine problems after only three days off the French port of Djibouti and had to return to Masawa. Her replacement was *Torricelli*.

Maccale's crew was suffering from poisoning from leakage of her air conditioning machinery fluid. At 0200 on 15 June she ran hard aground and could not free herself. Her crew evacuated to a small island, Barra Musa, where they spent a few anxious days waiting for rescue. Eventually submarine *Guglielmotti* showed up and took them back to Masawa. *Maccale* was lost.[339]

On 10 June *Galilei* sailed to patrol off Aden at the southwest corner of the Arabian Peninsula, a major British port in the area. On 16 June she stopped and sank Norwegian tanker *James Stove* about ten miles south of Aden. This was the first Italian submarine sinking of the war. On the 18th she stopped neutral Yugoslavian steamer *Drava* with shots across the bow, and then released it after identifying it. However her gun fire had been heard ashore and a Gloster Gladiator fighter responded and spotted *Gaililei*. A bomber also came to the scene and attacked but missed. That was only the beginning. British destroyer HMS Kandahar and sloop HMS Shoreham intercepted a radio signal from *Gaililei*. Shoreham attacked with depth charges but *Gaililei* escaped. The following day ASW trawler HMS Moonstone gained Asdic contact on *Gaililei*. Depth charges brought her to the surface and a gun battle ensued. *Galilei* was captured and towed into Aden. It was a *coup* to celebrate, but the real victory was finding charts and information aboard *Gaililei* that indicated the positions of other Italian submarine patrol areas.[340]

Torricelli had been sent to patrol Djibouti in place of *Ferraris*. She arrived 19 June. Seas were rough, and heat (45 degrees C (113 degrees Fahrenheit)) and humidity (100 percent) made operations very difficult. Soon after arrival she was diverted to operations off the Somali coast. As soon as she reached her new area on 21 June she was detected and attacked by three RN destroyers, first with gun fire and then with depth charges. The DDs lost contact but *Torricelli's* crew were suffering from poisoning from leaking AC machinery fluid. Early on 23 June she was sighted on the surface in the Straits of Perim by sloop HMS Shoreham. *Torricelli* dove and escaped. She watched through her periscope and observed

Shoreham heading away toward Perim Island. *Torricelli* then surfaced and headed in the opposite direction. She had not been on the surface long before Shoreham came around and closed her. Unfortunately Shoreham was joined by sloop Indus and three destroyers—Khartoum, Kandahar and Kingston. There was a gun and torpedo duel in which *Torricelli's* torpedoes missed. Her commanding officer put up a good fight against overwhelming odds in spite of being wounded. Finally he had *Torricelli* scuttled. An ironic footnote to the battle was the loss of HMS Khartoum about six hours later due to an accidental torpedo air flask explosion and subsequent fire.[341]

On 23 June *Galvani*, on patrol in the Gulf of Oman, torpedoed Indian Navy sloop Pathan, damaging it. Sloop HMS Falmouth and destroyer HMS Kimberley were immediately diverted to the Oman area. About 2300 on 23 June Falmouth gained visual contact on a surfaced submarine, closed to 600 yards and opened fire after the other ship did not respond to a signal light challenge. One of Falmouth's shells penetrated *Galvani's* pressure hull. *Galvani* dove, and Falmouth dropped three depth charges into the swirl. *Galvani* was literally blown to the surface. Her crew abandoned her and she sank. A number of survivors were picked up by Kimberley.[342]

Perla departed Masawa on 19 June to patrol off Berbera and Djibouti. On the evening of 26 June she was attacked by HMS Khartoum but not seriously damaged. After Khartoum left the scene *Perla* surfaced and then ran aground. Two days late cruiser HMS Leander gunned her but failed to destroy her. A Walrus aircraft from Leander also attacked her. However she survived and two days later was refloated and towed back to Masawa.[343]

On 6 September 1940 convoy BN 4 was headed for Suez escorted by cruiser HMS Leander with no ASW escorts. Greek tanker *Atlas* straggled and was spotted and sunk by *Guglielmotti*. This was the second sinking by an Italian submarine in three months.[344]

Perla had been towed back to Masawa in July 1940 after running aground. Repairs took the rest of the year. She was again damaged in a British air raid on Masawa harbor in January 1941.

By 1 April 1941 one Italian destroyer and four subs had been sunk in the Red Sea. Ten days later eight more destroyers were sunk, mostly by Swordfish torpedo planes operating from the Royal Naval Air Station at Port Sudan.[345]

During the next eight months until the end of February 1941 the remaining three long range Italian submarines made 21 patrols, however targets were in short supply. They only fired torpedoes twice. In August *Ferraris* attacked a convoy enroute Egypt with no luck. British convoys basically were undisturbed by Italian submarine activity. During the following periods, convoys passed in each direction without loss. A total of 86 north-bound and 72 south-bound ships were in these convoys:

August	4 convoys each way
September	5 convoys each way
October	7 convoys each way

The Italian naval command in East Africa decided to send the remaining three long range submarines to Japan, and send short—range *Perla* to Bushir in Iran to be interned. However *Supermarina*, the high naval command in Rome, contacted the German naval high command, and made arrangements for German resupply ships to support a long voyage back to Bordeaux in western occupied France.

Back in the Med on 7 July *Beilul* sighted and attacked a British force from Alexandria, consisting of three BB, one CV, five cruisers and sixteen DDs. However no hits were obtained. This was the classic task for submarines, to attrite the enemy fleet by torpedoing major units. Three days later another Italian submarine, *Marconi*, was more successful. It attacked a British force which was enroute Gibraltar. A destroyer, HMS Escort, was hit on the starboard side between two boiler rooms, blowing a 20 foot hole in the hull. At 0610 on 11 July Escort developed a list of 34 degrees and sank about five hours later.[346]

From 10 June through 5 July some ten Italian submarines had been located, and sunk or captured, primarily due to comint information. The Royal Navy had been reading high grade Italian naval ciphers since 1937.

In October 1940 British submarine HMS Rainbow was sunk in a gun/torpedo duel with Italian submarine *Toti* south of Calabria.[347]

On 27 November a British convoy was enroute Malta. Italian submarines *Tembien* and *Dessie* reported attacking British ships near Malta and scoring hits with two torpedoes.

Through November 1940, 13 Italian submarines were lost in the Mediterranean and four in the Red Sea. These losses, measured against ships sunk, were not a good indicator. The Submarine School at Pola was provided new equipment and assigned training submarines and auxiliary units for training at sea as the Italian Submarine Service realized that it must replace its losses.[348]

During December UK units attacked the main Italian naval port at Naples. The Italian fleet then relocated its units to Sardinia: Maddalena in the north and Cagliari in the south. The UK seized the opportunity to run a resupply convoy to Malta from Alexandria. Only Italian submarine and air units were able to respond. *Serpente* torpedoed and sank destroyer HMS Hyperion SE of Malta.

In December British submarine HMS Thunderbolt torpedoed and sank *Taranatini* off Bordeaux.[349]

By December 1940 Admiral Doenitz had written off the Italian submarine contribution in the Atlantic completely. He indicated that he would deploy his U-boats without reference to the Italian effort. By May 1941 there were only ten Italian submarines still operating in the Atlantic.[350]

During 1940 a total of 20 Italian submarines were lost: 14 in the Med, 2 in the Atlantic, and 4 in the Red Sea.

1941

The British went on the offensive in North Africa and pushed the Italians back, taking large numbers of prisoners. In February General Rommel arrived in Tripoli to take charge of the Afrika Korps. In May German airborne forces seized the island of Crete. Heavy losses were inflicted on Royal Navy surface forces by German dive bombers. In June Germany invaded the Soviet Union, thus spreading the Luftwaffe thinly between the Eastern Front and the Mediterranean Theater. In December Japan attacked the United States. Germany declared war on the United States and was followed by Italy.

On 11 January a group of British ships enroute Malta was attacked at night by *Settimo*, but no hits were recorded. On 31 March *Ambra* sank cruiser HMS Bonaventure in a night surface attack. *Dagabur* launched several torpedoes at targets that same night but scored no hits.

The Greek campaign which started in late October 1940 required a great deal of maritime traffic across the lower Adriatic Sea. Lacking adequate aerial reconnaissance assets, the Italian Navy was forced to substitute submarine patrols south of the Otranto Straits.

In January in the Red Sea British forces were closing in on remaining Italian bases. Supermarina ordered the last four surviving submarines: *Guglielmotti, Ferraris, Archimede,* and *Perla*—to break out and sail to Bordeaux. That entailed a 14,000 nautical mile journey down the east coast of Africa, around the Cape of Good Hope, and up the west coast of Africa to southern France. For SS *Perla*, a short-legged coastal submarine, with only one functioning motor, the odds were particularly poor. *Perla* set sail on 1 March 1941, and the other three SS sailed on the 3rd. Guglielmotti was the first to arrive at Bordeaux after 64 days at sea. *Perla* arrived last on 20 May, after 80 days at sea.[351] *Perla* was a 700 ton (surf. displacement) submarine with a range of 5,200 nm at 8 knots. She was replenished twice at sea during her epic voyage, the other submarines only once by German ships.[352]

In February the independent successes of Italian submarines and progress in their training led Doenitz to try joint operations with them. As of 18 February Italian submarines were sent north to extend the German U-boat picket line south of Greenland. This practice continued through May 1941. Italian submarines sank a few stragglers, but proved to be no help in locating and attacking convoys.

On 5 May Doenitz came to the conclusion that joint operations were of little use. He met with Admiral Parone and laid down independent operational areas for Italian submarines. They were: West of Gibraltar; the north Atlantic south of German areas; and an area off Freetown in the south Atlantic. Italian submarines had some successes in these areas, and off Brazil their sinking's of independent sailers matched those of U-boats.

Some of the more successful Italian submarine commanding officers included:

> Lt. Grazzone, who sank 11 ships (90, 601 tons) and was awarded the German Knight's Cross of the Iron Cross (the "Blue Max")
> Cdr. Longobardo
> Lcdr. Carlo Fecia di Corsato, 16 ships (86, 438 tons), also awarded the Knight's Cross
> Lcdr. Giovanini
> Lcdr. Longanesi Cattari

Doenitz attributed Italian CO successes and failures to national traits. He thought that Italian COs displayed great dash and daring in battle, often exceeding that of Germans. He also felt that his German U-boat COs had greater toughness and endurance that allowed them to persevere in the very difficult North Atlantic conditions and the tenacity to hang on until a wolf pack could form.[353]

In the Med the Germans increased pressure on the Italians to interdict British supplies to Greece, where British Army forces were assisting the Greek Army. As a result the number of Italian submarines on patrol in the area of Crete was increased. In addition a highly successful attack by Special Attack Forces against British ships in the port at Suda Bay on the northern coast of Crete was carried out. Italian surface forces were also alerted for offensive strikes.[354]

On 20 May German airborne forces assaulted British positions on Crete, and after fierce fighting were successful in battle, forcing the British evacuation of their own and Greek troops beginning on 27 May. A large number of Italian submarines were in the area, ten between Crete, Alexandria and Sollum; and one north of Crete. None were successful. A large number of British warships were sunk, and many others seriously damaged but the attacks were largely those of German Stuka dive bombers. During the afternoon of 21 May *Platino* and *Onice* were successful in sighting and reporting the presence of cruiser HMS Cleopatra and escorts which were operating in support of a relief convoy for Malta. Italian Air Force air reconnaissance had not sighted the group.

On 23 May *Scire*, with three human torpedoes ("pigs" as referred to by their operators) aboard, put in to the Spanish port of Cadiz at night, moored alongside interned Italian tanker *Fulgor* and embarked the "pigs" crews.[355] They had entered Spain using false passports. *Scire* departed just before dawn on 25 May and entered the port area of Gibraltar in order to launch her "pigs" against British fleet units. However she found that no fleet units were present and so launched attacks against merchant ships. As planned, *Scire* departed the area after launching the three "pigs". However, the mission was almost a complete failure. The "pigs" problems were as follow:

Pig # 1—Broke down, had to be sunk
Pig # 2—Crewman became ill, had to scuttle the pig
Pig # 3—Sank

The only saving grace was that all pig crew members reached the neutral Spanish coast safely, made contact with Italian agents there, and were successfully extracted and returned to their base at La Spezia in Italy. British authorities had no indication that a special operation using manned torpedoes had been attempted.[356]

The "pigs" and their daring crewmen belonged to *Decima Flottiglia MAS*, which translates to Tenth Assault Vehicle Flotilla. *Decima MAS* utilized surface boats, manned torpedoes, and *Gamma* frogmen, in a series of attacks in the Mediterranean during the war.

A shortage of fuel oil was mentioned earlier. The shortage was in the area of "black oil", that is the variety used in the boilers of steam-propelled ships. As far as I can determine diesel oil, which was used by Italian submarines, never became an issue. However by the summer of 1941 Italian Navy black oil reserves were almost entirely expended. Italian Navy surface warship operations became almost entirely dependent upon the arrival of supplies of black oil, and its distribution to various ports.

In May 1941 four subs finally arrived back from the Red Sea. In June Mussolini withdrew ten of the 27 *Betasom* boats back to the eastern Med. *Glauco* was lost off Gibraltar while enroute from Bordeaux. In September Captain Romolo Palocchini took command at *Betasom*.[357]

The sinking score for Italian submarines for a four month period was as follows:

June	6 ships sunk
July	7 ships sunk
August	2 ships sunk
September	0 ships sunk

From June 1940 through September 1941 some 80 Italian submarines sank only 11 Allied supply ships, all unescorted in the eastern Med. They also sank two cruisers and one destroyer. However 21 Italian submarines were lost in return, a terrible exchange ratio.[358]

In July British submarine HMS Torbay sank *Jantina* with a salvo of six torpedoes near Mikonos Island (in the Cyclades Islands south east of Athens).

On 21 July *Supermarina* learned of a British force from Gibraltar that was headed eastward. On the night of 23 July *Diaspro* sighted the group which was east of Bougie, North Africa. *Diaspro* attacked and just missed destroyer HMS Nestor. In early August British submarine HMS Severn sank *Bianci* west of the Strait of Gibraltar.

In September Admiral Doenitz noted that the situation in the Mediterranean Sea Theater was getting worse. He stated that there was no overall joint German-Italian war plan of any kind, and none for operations in the Mediterranean.[359]

Italian Foreign Minister Ciano noted in his diary entry of 25 September that losses of Italian merchant ships in the Mediterranean are getting "very serious". His diary entry of 1 October indicates that where merchant ships losses in convoy had amounted to about 5 % earlier, in September they jumped to 18 %.[360]

On 29 September three Italian submarines were operating off French Algeria. They attacked ships but *Diaspro* and *Serpente* missed their targets, and *Adua* was sunk by British escorts.[361]

In fall 1941 two convoys were attacked by Italian submarines and U-boats respectively. The results are indicative of the relative ineffectiveness of Italian submarines compared to U-boats. HG 72 departed Gibraltar on 10 September and was attacked by a group of four Italian submarines. The escorts, six destroyers and a sloop, successfully fought off the submarines and no convoyed ships were lost. By comparison, convoy SL 87 from Sierra Leone, consisting of 11 ships and four escorts, was attacked by four U-boats. Seven ships (33,000 tons) were sunk.[362]

During the latter half of 1941 Italian submarines were pressed into service to carry cargoes to support Italian ground forces in Libya. They carried out 46 resupply missions. *Caracciolo* and *Saint-Bon* were lost during these missions. *Atropo* was seriously damaged by fire when its gasoline cargo exploded. Gasoline was being transported aboard the submarines in tins.[363] Italian troop replacements were transported almost exclusively aboard destroyers when troop ships and ordinary merchant ships became too vulnerable to enemy air and submarine attack.

On 24 November a British cruiser division departed Malta to intercept Italian ships in convoy to North Africa. *Settembrini*, on patrol, sighted them and reported. As a result all Italian convoys were directed to return to port. At Churchill's insistence Admiral Cunningham had taken the Mediterranean Fleet to sea from Alexandria in general support of anti-convoy operations. There were three Italian submarines and three German U-boats operating in their general area. A U-boat penetrated the destroyer screen and fired four torpedoes at battleship HMS Barham. Three "eels" hit and Barham capsized and exploded on 25 November.[364]

On 11 December 1941 Italy, following Germany's lead, declared war on the United States. *Betasom* moved Italian submarines westward to operate from the Bahamas to Brazil. Five submarines were in this group. From 20 February through 23 March 1942 they sank 16 merchant ships, mostly independent sailers. From 29 March through 12 April they sank five merchant ships off the coast of Brazil.[365]

On 19 December *Scire* conducted another and successful special operation—against major British units at Alexandria. About a mile off the harbor entrance at 2047 she launched three pigs. The results were as follow, listing by target:

Battleship HMS Valiant—Pig crew had to drag their pig underneath Valiant and then took refuge on as buoy where they were spotted and captured. They were placed in a lower compartment of Valiant. The pig warhead exploded on schedule and damaged Valiant alongside the pier. The pig crew survived.

Battleship HMS Queen Elizabeth—A perfect attack. The pig warhead exploded and sank Queen Elizabeth alongside the pier. The pig crew was later captured.

Large tanker—Another perfect attack. The tanker sank and a destroyer alongside was badly damaged. Pig crew later captured.

This attack was perfectly planned and executed. It changed the balance of naval power in the Mediterranean Sea in favor of Italy, measured in terms of battleships. Valiant was still barely afloat but had a heavy trim forward. Queen Elizabeth sank into the mud at her berth, but her main decks were still above water. It took several weeks for the Italian aerial reconnaissance to confirm that the attacks had been successful.[366] The two British battleships were out of action for a considerable period. Valiant, the less seriously damaged, was repaired in Durban, South Africa and returned to the Med in time to participate in the invasion of Sicily in 1943. Queen Elizabeth, more seriously damaged, had to go to an American naval shipyard where she was in repair status from September 1942 until June 1943.

Toward the end of December 1941 *Dandolo, Cagni* and *Settimio* managed to reach Bardia in North Africa with supplies. *Emo* made the last supply run, but found British units in the port area and had to fight its way out of the harbor.[367]

During 1941 the Italian Navy developed and deployed a magnetic fuse for torpedoes, which it considered superior to both German and British models. Another factor entered into the naval situation in the Mediterranean Sea—German "E" boats began to arrive in the theater. They were large, sturdy motor torpedo boats built for rugged North Sea conditions, and would join Italian MTB operating in the Sicilian Channel east of Malta against British convoys.

Italian submarines were making forty day patrols by the end of 1941. There were only eleven of them left in the North Atlantic. During 1941 a total of 19 Italian submarines were lost: 12 in the Med and 7 in the Atlantic.

In June Rommel captured Tobruk. In July the British stopped Rommel at El Alamein. In October at the second Battle of El Alamein Rommel was defeated and began a fighting retreat back to Tunisia. On 8 November the Allies landed in French North Africa.

During April 1942 a momentous decision was made by the Italian and German high commands—not to invade Malta.[368] Both the Italian Navy and Field Marshal Rommel had earlier believed that Malta would have to be seized in order to ensure a steady flow of supplies to North Africa. Rommel evidently lost track of the basic issue, the vulnerability of an Axis ground campaign in North Africa without a secure logistic route back to Italy. He had clearly recognized it earlier. Count Ciano noted in his diary that Rommel was intent on the capture of Malta to secure the supply lines to Libya. However, seeing an opportunity to push on into Egypt and seize Cairo, he took a shortsighted viewpoint, one that would cost him, the Afrika Corps, Italy and Germany the war. The severe losses to German airborne forces suffered in early 1941 during the airborne landing at Crete may have had an influence on subsequent events. The German paratroops (*Fallschirmjager*) never made another air assault.

During March five Italian submarines were operating in the western North Atlantic east of the Windward Islands. They ran up a good score:

Tazzoli	6 ships (29,200 tons)
Morosini	3 ships (22,000 tons)
Finzi	3 ships (21,500 tons)
Torelli	2 ships (16,500 tons)
Da Vinci	1 ship (3,644 tons)

Their total was 15 ships sunk including six tankers for an overall tonnage of 93,000 tons. *Torelli* was caught on the surface and attacked by aircraft, losing two men as a result. However she and the others returned safely to Bordeaux.[369]

In April 1942 plans were made to transfer HMS Queen Elizabeth from Alexandria to a shipyard to conduct repairs to make her operational again. *Supermarina* became aware of the plans and sent *Ambra*, equipped with three "pigs" to attack and finish her off. All three were launched off Alexandria harbor but two could not locate the harbor entrance and failed to attack. The third pig entered the harbor but by the time it got in, it was daylight. The pig crew sought concealment in a ship wreck. However they were spotted. One crew member was captured. The other crew member got ashore and made contact with Italian agents in Alexandria. They provided a hiding place in the city. He escaped capture for a month, but then was picked up by the police who were looking for him.[370]

Later that year *Scire* was enroute to attack ship targets at the port of Haifa with assault swimmers and "pigs". She was detected and destroyed by ASW units.

In April 1942 10th MAS sent six pocket subs to Costanza, Romania by rail to work against Soviet naval forces in the Black Sea. They conducted a large number of missions, including sinking two Soviet submarines. One pocket sub was lost to a Soviet bombing raid in port. After the Italian armistice, the remaining pocket subs were donated to the Romanian Navy.[371]

In early May aircraft carrier USS Wasp entered the Mediterranean on its second trip to carry Spitfire fighters for Malta in order to build up its air defense capability. On 9 May west of Malta she launched her deck load of Spitfire fighters. On a previous trip in April the Spitfires she delivered were caught on the ground and shot up by German fighters soon after arrival. This time proper revetments had been prepared and as soon as the Spitfires landed they were protected and refueled. It was the beginning of a major shift in Malta's air defense status.

In connection with the Wasp trip, HMS Welshman, a high speed minelayer was making one of its periodic resupply voyages from Gibraltar to Malta. The Italian Navy tracked Welshman carefully but had been unsuccessful in catching her. This time she was sighted at night by *Onice*. However a group of British night fighters forced *Onice* off the surface and

Welshman passed unharmed. *Onice* was one of two Italian submarines conducting operations in the Sicilian Channel.[372]

On 8 June Italian submarine *Alagi* sank Italian destroyer *Antoniotto Usodinare* by mistake.[373]

On 12 June a major British convoy was enroute Malta from Gibraltar. During the night of 14 June *Usarsciek* and *Giada*, operating south of Sardinia, attacked the formation. *Usarsciek's* CO reported that two of his torpedoes exploded. At 0450 *Giada* fired at several stopped ships and may have hit merchant ship Brown Ranger.[374]

During the summer of 1942 the Italian Navy fuel situation had deteriorated to the point that convoy ships for Libya had to draw their fuel from the tanks of battleships *Doria* and *Dulio*, leaving those two ships unable to get underway. They were transferred to a reserve status until the end of the year and their crews were transferred to other duty. Only two battleships were left in an active status: *Littorio* and *Vittorio Veneto*. New construction battleship *Roma* finally joined them in May 1943.

During July 1942 a major British convoy from Gibraltar to Malta sailed. There were twenty Italian submarines active in the western and central Mediterranean at that time, as well as ten U-boats in the eastern Mediterranean. U-boats sank destroyers HMS Hasty and HMS Hermione. Several other submarines were successful. Italian cruiser *Trento*, disabled by a British aerial torpedo, was sunk by a British submarine. Italian battleship *Littorio* was hit forward by a British submarine torpedo and damaged.[375]

On 15 July HMS Welshman made another high speed run to Malta. Welshman and her sister ships (Abdiel class) were designed as very high speed minelayers for work in European waters where land-based aircraft could cover sea areas in daylight very quickly. These ships were capable of speeds up to 38 knots at full power. They would sail after dark, dash to their objective area, lay mines and scoot back to port before dawn broke. At the time they were built and until late during WW II there were few military aircraft capable of operating at night, let alone detecting and attacking them.

The Italian Navy laid an ambush for Welshman. *Axum* was off Bizerte, and 28 Italian bombers and 16 Stukas were on call. In addition seven Italian SS were north of Tunis, a number of Italian MTB were lying in wait off Cape Bon, and the 7th Cruiser Division was at sea south of Sardinia. The stage was set for an execution.

Unfortunately the scheduled Malta-Tunis reconnaissance flights did not take place. Welshman left Malta and reached the vicinity of Cape Bon undetected on her way back to Gibraltar. In that vicinity severe storms had forced the MTB back into port, and she was not sighted by any submarines. Eventually she was spotted by a reconnaissance airplane and eleven Italian torpedo bombers and five Stukas attacked but scored no hits, probably due to her high speed and expert evasive maneuvers.

In August 1942 a large heavily escorted British convoy (Operation PEDESTAL) set out for Malta (62 ships including 14 merchant ships carrying supplies). Sixteen Italian submarines and five U-boats were deployed to intercept the convoy in the western Mediterranean. Submarines/U-boats were stationed from the Balearics to Tunis, and off Cape Bon. New minefields were laid off Cape Bon. MTB were stationed from Cape Bon to Pantelleria. Three Italian cruisers and eleven destroyers were operating south of Pantelleria. The scheme was for the submarines, MTB and mine fields to disperse the convoy and its escorts, then for the cruiser-destroyer task group to destroy the merchant ships forming the heart of the convoy.

On 11 August *Usarsciek* fired three torpedoes at an aircraft carrier (possibly HMS Furious), and observed two explosions. *Usarsciek* then suffered a long hunt by British ASW escorts but finally escaped. That afternoon Furious turned back for Gibraltar after launching 37 Spitfires for Malta. Furious was attacked enroute by *Dagabur* which missed and was then sunk by ramming by HMS Wolverine. Upon arrival at Gibraltar HMS Furious entered dry-dock.

Emo and *Cobalto* launched torpedo attacks against the convoy NW of Cape Bon. *Cobalto* was rammed and sunk by HMS Ithuriel after being depth-charged to the surface. *Dessie* and *Axum* each fired four torpedoes at the convoy at about 1945. Cruisers Nigeria and Cairo, and merchant ships SS Ohio and Brisbane Star were hit. Anti-aircraft cruiser Cairo sank. About 2110 *Alagi* fired four torpedoes and hit cruiser Kenya (flagship), and merchant ship Clan Ferguson which sank. About 2300 *Bronzo* blew the bow off a disabled merchant ship similar to Empire Hope, which then sank.[376]

The Italian-German air assets scheduled for this effort could have been used in either of two ways: to attack by themselves; or to provide air support for the cruiser-destroyer task group which then could have finished off the remaining merchant ships. The issue went up to Mussolini himself. He finally ruled in favor of an air attack, and *Supermarina* then canceled the planned surface action. The unfortunate result for the Axis was that Ohio and several other ships limped in to Malta, sustaining it for the immediate future.[377]

In November some 22 Italian submarines sortied in reaction to Operation TORCH, the Allied invasion of French North Africa. They sank four ships near or at Bougie Bay: Narkunda, a 16,600 ton troopship; Awatea, a 13,482 ton troopship; HMS Tynwald, a CLAA; and minesweeper HMS Algerine. The later three had been previously damaged by *Luftwaffe* air attacks.[378]

In early December *Ambra* set off from La Spezia on another special assault mission aimed at targets in the port of Algiers. She carried three pigs plus ten frogmen with limpet mines. On 11 December *Ambra* successfully entered the roadstead and settled on the bottom in shallow water at 2100. An officer equipped with a telephone was locked out and reached the surface, where he described the situation there to special assault personnel in the submarine. It took three hours to launch the three pigs, and the frogmen. One pig got near a large ship, then broke down and had to be abandoned. A second pig reached its target successfully. The third pig was also successful, its operators attaching warheads to two ships. At about 0230 *Ambra* departed the area as planned. Three ships were sunk and two more seriously damaged.[379]

About 13 December cruiser HMS Argonaut was torpedoed by Italian submarine *Mocenigo*. It was hit forward and aft, blowing off its bow and its bridge, and aft—its rudder assembly and two of four screws. Argonaut managed to make port but had to be moved to the United States for repairs at Philadelphia Naval Shipyard from April 30 through 13 November 1943.[380]

During 1942 a total of 22 Italian submarines were lost, 20 in the Med and 2 in the Atlantic.

1943

In January the British 8th Army captured Tripoli. In April British and American forces linked up in Tunisia. On 15 May Axis forces in North Africa surrendered. On 9 July the Allied invasion of Sicily began. On 22 July Palermo fell, and on 25 July Mussolini was ousted as head of the Italian government. On 17 August Sicily was conquered. On 8 September

Italy surrendered to the Allies. On 13 October Italy declared war on Germany.

In late 1942 and early 1943 Axis forces were being withdrawn into Tunisia. Italian submarines were pressed into service to carry supplies. They accomplished some 47 transportation missions.

In late 1942 and early 1943 *Platino* conducted three attacks on targets in the roadstead at Bougie in North Africa. On the night of 29-30 January *Platino,* operating on the surface, sighted a 16 ship convoy with escorts. The CO attacked and fired four torpedoes at close range, hitting two DDs and a supply ship. Both DDs sank. *Platino* then fired two torpedoes from her aft tubes, and hit a cargo ship which caught fire. Escorts charged in. *Palatino's* CO took her down and went under the convoy and out astern of it eluding the escorts.[381]

In 1943 a turning point was reached because of Italian submarine losses. *Betasom* reduced its operational areas and directed that Italian submarines only make attacks on independently sailing ships. *Da Vinci* sank two ships in March and four in April. *Barbarigo* sank three in Feb-Mar. *Finzi* sank two in March.

Supermarina and *BdU* then agreed on a new employment of the ten remaining Italian submarines at Bordeaux. All except *Cagni* became cargo carriers to bring badly needed rubber and tin from Japanese controlled areas to Bordeaux. To replace them, BdU turned over nine Type VIIC U-boats to the Italian Navy. They were delivered in August 1943 and redesignated S-1 through S-9 in Italian service.

Archimedes and *Da Vinci* were sunk in April and May, so there were only seven conversions. The conversions stripped them of all armament in favor of cargo space. They could cruise from Bordeaux to Singapore without refueling.[382]

During the period May through June five transport submarines departed for Singapore (*Cappellini, Giuliani, Torelli, Tazzoli and Barbariga*). *Tazzoli* and *Barbariga* were lost at sea, possibly to mines since no Allied attacks were recorded. In July and August the remaining three arrived at Singapore. Several had been attacked by aircraft in the Atlantic but escaped. Two more designated transport submarines (*Bagnolina* and *Finzi*) were at Bordeaux at the time of the Italian Armistice on 8 August 1943. They were seized by the Germans and then turned over to the new Italian Social-Fascist Republic (RSI), established by the Germans with

Benito Mussolini at its head. *Betasom,* with Capt. Grossi as its commander, was now under the RSI.

The three transport submarines that arrived at Singapore were seized by the Japanese, and then turned over to Germany. *Giuliani* was recommissioned as U-IT-23, and later sunk off Sumatra in the Netherlands East Indies by HMS Tally Ho on 14 February 1944. *Cappellini* (U-IT-24) and *Torelli* (U-IT-25) were seized again by the Japanese after the German surrender in May 1945, reclassified as I-503 and I-504, captured in turn by the United States and scuttled off Kobe, Japan on 16 April 1946.[383]

In May the island of Pantelleria was isolated and came under heavy Allied air attacks. Limited resupply to the garrison and residents was carried out by LCM-type craft and three submarines. *Fanno* was lost during these operations.[384]

On 23 May *Da Vinci*, an 1100 ton boat commissioned in April 1940, was lost about 300 nm. west of Cape Finisterre. *Da Vinci* had reached Bordeaux on 31 October 1940. Her total was 17 sinking's (120,243 tons). It was the best record of all Italian submarines during WW II. *Tazzoli* sank 96,650 tons from 1941 to 1943. She was lost in March 1943 while enroute to Singapore.[385]

In June two large Italian submarines planned to transit the Straits of Messina enroute the Tyrrhenian Sea. They were each capable of carrying 220 tons of cargo. *Remo* was torpedoed by a British submarine south of the strait on 15 June. *Romolo* was lost on 18 June to Allied bombers in the same area.

On 9 July Operation HUSKY, the Allied invasion of Sicily, began. Only 40 Italian submarines, excluding two told off for special assault missions, were left active. About 50% were in port for repairs. Fewer than 12 were available in the Sicily area, the others being either in the northern Tyrrhenian Sea or Aegean Sea. Six Italian submarines were lost to very strong Allied ASW forces during the invasion. It was estimated that an Italian submarine that reached an attack position had a 90% chance of being detected, and once detected only a 1% chance of escaping destruction. The later very low figure was probably due to "swamp" tactics which involved flooding the contact area with radar-equipped aircraft—denying the submarine an opportunity to surface and recharge its battery and renew its air supply.

On 25 July *Ambra* set out to attack Allied shipping at Syracuse. After surfacing for a navigational fix it was sighted and attacked by aircraft. The exit doors to the pig storage containers were buckled by the explosions. *Ambra* had to cancel its mission and return to base.[386]

After the capture of Sicily on 17 August Italian Navy forces were split between the Tyrrhenian Sea and the Ionian Sea sector. There were 15 submarines in the Tyrrhenian Sea, and 9 in the Ionian Sea. During August one submarine in the Tyrrhenian Sea was sunk.

On 7 September *Velella* was sunk by a British submarine. *Velella* was the last Italian submarine sunk before Italy signed an armistice on 8 September 1943. The armistice concluded Italy's participation in World War II as part of the Axis Powers. Italian submarines had sunk 135 Allied or neutral ships totaling 842,000 tons. For comparison, German U-boats sank 2,828 ships of 14,687,231 gross register tons.

During 1943 a total of 31 Italian submarines were lost, 28 in the Med and 3 in the Atlantic.

Italian Submarine Operations post-Armistice

Upon conclusion of the Armistice Italian submarines were deployed as follows:

> Central and Western Mediterranean—16
> Eastern Mediterranean and Red Sea—14
> Atlantic (Bermuda)—8
> Indian Ocean (Columbo)—2

Most were involved in helping train Allied ASW forces. Some carried out wartime missions assisting the Allies. Italy declared war on Germany on 13 October 1943. On 28 December *Axum* was lost off the coast of Morea while waiting to pick up saboteurs returning from a mission.[387] On 15 November 1944 *Settembrini* was lost in a collision with U.S. destroyer Fremont in the Atlantic during training operations.[388]

In the *Submarine and Sea Power* Vice Admiral Hezlet notes that the Italians operated about 136 submarines in the Med during the war. His judgment is that they were not a major factor, being used primarily as scouts for the Italian Navy and offensively against resupply convoys to Malta. He also notes their use to resupply outposts like Tobruk and Leros. He credits them with sinking three British cruisers and damaging three more, noting that they sank more British warships than the Italian Air

Force did or the Italian surface fleet. This was at the cost of 66 Italian submarines.[389] One bright spot for the Italian Submarine Service was torpedo performance. They did not have the problems that plagued the Germans and the Americans.

Chapter Six—Japanese Submarines

The Imperial Japanese Navy Submarine Service was reorganized during 1940. A separate Submarine Fleet (6th Fleet) was established, containing three of seven submarine flotillas. The other flotillas were distributed among Combined Fleet, Third Fleet and Fourth Fleet. The training varied with the missions assigned. There were no submarines bases as such. The Navy Yard Submarine Department handled repairs and overhauls at the navy yards at Yokosuka, Kure, Maizuru and Sasebo. In addition, Submarine Base Support units were organized. There was one at Ominato in northern Honshu. During the war, others were established at Kwajalein, Rabaul, Penang, Surabaya, Palau, Cebu and Truk as the need arose. The IJN also had submarine tenders, fitted out to repair and support alongside submarines. They would usually operate at an advance base like Kwajalein, Rabaul or Truk.[390]

During the 1920s Admiral Nobumasa Suetsugu had laid out proposed missions for submarines as part of a long range offensive system. Their tasks included surveillance of enemy bases, pursuit when the enemy fleet sortied, and ambush of the enemy fleet prior to the planned decisive surface warship encounter.[391] As described in Part One of this series, development of Japanese submarines followed this general theme. The I-class submarine was a long range scout, capable of lengthy voyages, and carrying a first class long range wake-less torpedo (Type 95) to deal with enemy warships.

In 1940 Japanese military leaders extended their desired defensive perimeter. They shifted it from the Mariana Islands to the Marshall Islands, some 2,000 nautical miles further eastward.[392] Japanese submarines were tasked with conducting reconnaissance of enemy fleet units as they approached the perimeter boundary, and attacking them.

From February to August 1941, 6th Fleet submarines conducted extensive exercises from Honshu down to Micronesia, practicing their assigned role of long range scouts to locate the "enemy" fleet, track it and ambush it. There were a number of problems encountered. The submarines had difficulties maintaining contact with the enemy fleet, and making attacks. The results clearly showed that Japanese submarine doctrine of attrition of the enemy fleet might not work out as well as described in training manuals. Nevertheless no changes were made to doctrine. The Japanese Submarine Service as well as the rest of the Japanese fleet remained focused on the "decisive" battle. There was little attention paid to interdicting enemy supply lines. Submarine tactical doctrine favored passive acoustic search. No radar was installed in Japanese submarines at this time.[393]

The Navy General Staff thought it necessary to include submarines in the Pearl Harbor attack, and to interdict supplies and reinforcements coming from the U.S. West Coast. Twenty-seven submarines were earmarked for the operation "Advance Force". On 17-18 November 1941 Advance Force submarines sortied from Yokosuka and Kure, twenty-five of them enroute Kwajalein in the Marianas Islands. Two headed in different directions, one to the Aleutians and the other to Samoa and the Fiji Islands. After topping off on fuel at Kwajalein the bulk headed for Oahu via a southern route. Radio silence was in effect. On 2 December they heard the signal "Climb Mount Niitaka" indicating that the attack date of 8 December (Tokyo time) was in effect.

Although there was cooperation between Japan and Nazi Germany from time to time, the "alliance" was rather shapeless. There was no parallel structure to the formal American-British Combined Chiefs of Staff organization. There was no overall strategy, i.e., a pincer's move on the Middle East, although such was suspected from time to time. At best there were vague talks about strategy.[394] Japan did not notify Adolph Hitler of the decision to attack the United States.

After Japan entered the war, the Japanese ambassador in Berlin became a key source of information about German plans. A Japanese general, he was well thought of in the upper levels of the Nazi Party, and was fully briefed on German operations and plans. His encrypted message traffic back to the Foreign Office in Tokyo was being intercepted and read by the Americans and shared with the British.

Pearl Harbor Attack and Immediate Aftermath

Twenty-five Japanese submarines were included in the Pearl Harbor striking force.[395] They took station off Oahu, prepared to attack U.S. fleet units that might sortie from Pearl Harbor as a result of the air strikes. They also reconnoitered the U.S. fleet anchorage at Lahaina Roads near Maui to try to locate alternative targets for the coming air strike, particularly aircraft carriers. At 1725 on December 6th, I-72 reported by radio that the "American fleet is not in Lahaina anchorage". [396]

Five I-class (I-16, I-18, I-20, I-22 and I-24) submarines carried a midget submarine apiece on their after decks. These were launched close to the entrance to Pearl Harbor in advance of the air strike with the goal of getting into the harbor and torpedoing major enemy ships. Each midget sub had two torpedoes. After the attack, the midgets were to be recovered at Lahaina Roads near Maui.[397]

Midget submarines were a new weapons system for the IJN. The first launch of a midget submarine took place from the tender *Chitose* in spring 1941. They displaced about 50 tons, were 25 meters long and 2 meters in diameter, and had a crew of one officer and one petty officer, had two torpedo tubes and two torpedoes, and a submerged speed of up to 19 knots. After 50 minutes at 19 knots, they had an endurance of about 8 hours at low speed. They did not carry a diesel engine capable of recharging the battery. They were not necessarily a "throwaway weapon" but did require support.[398]

The midget submarine attack failed. All five were lost. None of the large submarines sank any ships in the immediate aftermath of the surprise attack, and one was sunk by an American aircraft carrier aircraft. After the attack most of the Japanese submarines returned to their bases in the Mariana Islands. All of the midget submarine crew except for the one captive were enshrined at the Japanese Naval Academy at Eta Jima, and promoted two ranks posthumously. They were erroneously given credit for sinking's and damage actually accomplished by Japanese naval aviators, who were a bit chapped by the outcome[399].

On 8 December I-12 sank a small cargo ship 250 miles south of Oahu. On 14 December I-26 sank the C. Olsen (2,340 tons) some 900 miles northeast of Hawaii. On 17 December I-75 claimed another cargo ship south of Kauai. That day I-7 launched its seaplane for a successful aerial reconnaissance of Pearl Harbor, confirming the after action reports of Japanese naval aviators Further south I-10 had conducted an aerial reconnaissance of Suva in the Fijis on 30 November and then went on to patrol off American Samoa, arriving 4 December.[400]

On 9 December I-9 reported spotting a U.S. CVBG east of Oahu on course 060 and speed 20 knots, apparently headed back to the U.S. west coast. As a result Commander 6th Fleet ordered his picket lines of submarines to shift eastward. He also directed the 1st Submarine Group plus two subs of the Reconnaissance Unit to proceed east and establish patrols off the west coast. That put nine IJN subs off the west coast, stretching from Cape Flattery near the U. S—Canada border all the way south down to San Diego and the Mexican border.

The carrier spotted by I-9 was USS Enterprise (CV-6), actually out on ASW patrol. On 10 December three scout bombers from Enterprise sank I-70. The three U.S. aircraft carriers which had survived the Japanese surprise attack, because they were not in Pearl Harbor, lived to fight another day.

The surprise attack on Pearl Harbor was a stunning tactical victory for Japan, but operationally less so. It was designed to protect the Japanese flank which was exposed by its move into Southeast Asia. The Japanese were well aware of an American war plan which called for a naval force from Pearl Harbor to steam west to the relief of American forces in the Philippine Islands. What Japanese intelligence officers failed to convey to their leaders was the fact that the American "fleet train", the large number of naval oilers and supply ships required for a fleet move westward, were not available. They did not exist yet. The U.S. Pacific Fleet could not have moved west to the Philippines even if the Japanese attack on Pearl Harbor had not happened.

Strategically and psychologically the surprise attack was a monumental blunder. It took place while Japanese envoys were in Washington supposedly negotiating in good faith with the U.S. State Department. The attack on a Sunday morning at a time when most Americans were at church services outraged both cultural and religious mores. It took place before a declaration of war was made, in violation of the laws of war. The attack acted to motivate most Americans, a significant number of who had isolationist views, to wholeheartedly support the war effort. The greatest mistake of all was to take on a nation which had ten times the industrial capacity of Japan.

On 7 December three IJN submarines attempted to bombard Midway Island. They were driven off by fighters from the island air base without doing any damage.[401]

During 1941 twenty-four IJN submarines had been on patrol. They sank a total of eight ships (40,700 tons) and damaged seven (47,500 tons). One SS was lost along with five midget submarines.[402]

1942

On 11 January 1942 I-6 was operating 500 miles south of Oahu. She spotted USS Saratoga (CV-3). I-6 fired a salvo of three Type 89 torpedoes at her. One struck her hull, and Saratoga had to return to the U.S. west coast for repairs. I-6 had four torpedo tubes in her bow and two in her stern. As valuable a target as an aircraft carrier comes along once in a submarine commanding officer's wartime career—if he is fortunate. Not to have fired a full four tube salvo at Saratoga was a serious error in judgment. She was one of only four U.S. aircraft carriers in the Pacific.

Three boats of Submarine Division 27 (RO-65, RO-66 and RO—67) were assigned to participate in the attack on Wake Island. The attack failed with the loss of two Japanese destroyers to Marine aircraft and shore batteries. Aircraft carriers *Soryu* and *Hiryu* were then tasked to soften up the defenses for the second assault. Submarines RO-60, RO-61, RO-62 and RO-66 departed Kwajalein on 12 December for the second attack. RO-66 sank after colliding with RO-62 some 25 nm. SW of Wake during the night of 17 December. After its return from Wake to Kwajalein Atoll, RO-60 ran on a reef at the north end and sank.[403]

On 23 January I-172 sank fleet oiler USS Neches (AO-5) enroute to join Task Force 11 (USS Lexington). That loss led to abandonment of the relief mission to save Wake Island.[404] This incident serves as punctuation to the earlier remark about the "fleet train" and its importance.

The nine Japanese submarines operating off the west coast of the United States sank only five ships (30,370 tons) and damaged five more (34,299 tons). It was a shock to the American nervous system but not nearly as deadly as German U-boat operations off the U.S. east coast. I-17 shelled an oil derrick off Santa Barbara further alarming the locals.[405]

Southeast Asia (Late 1941-early 1942)

Simultaneous with the Pearl Harbor attack, Japanese naval and air forces attacked Hong Kong, the Philippine Islands and Malaya. IJN submarines were assigned to watch for a British naval response from Singapore to their invasion convoys. Force "Z" had recently taken up residency there. It consisted of battle ship HMS Prince of Wales and battle cruiser HMS Repulse. An aircraft carrier had been earmarked to join the two large surface combatants, but had run aground in the Caribbean Sea. Force "Z" had four destroyer escorts but no air cover.

On 9 December Force "Z" was sighted and reported at 1340 by a Japanese submarine. On 10 December at 0210 another Japanese submarine fired five torpedoes at Force "Z" but got no hits. However it reported Force "Z"s position, course and speed to headquarters.[406] 22nd Air Fleet in Indo-China was alerted. 22nd Air Fleet dispatched a large force of long range G3M bombers, most equipped with torpedoes but some with bombs. Later that day they located Force "Z" and attacked. HMS Prince of Wales and HMS Repulse were sunk by air attack. With them died the faint hope that naval reinforcements from the British Isles could hold back the Japanese advance.

Netherlands East Indies (NEI)

The NEI was a principal target of the Japanese move into Southeast Asia, particularly its oil fields. Air attacks on NEI airfields and the Dutch naval base at Surabaya on the island of Java began very shortly after the initial attacks on Malaya and the Philippines. On 26 December the Philippines Islands invasion force was reorganized into a Netherlands East Indies invasion force. Submarines I-1 and I-7 were brought back from Hawaiian waters to join the effort.

IJN submarines were organized into three groups for operations in SEAsia: A (*Ko*) CSS 4 and CSS 6 (six I-class, two RO-class, and four mine layers); B (*Otsu*) CSS 5 (six older fleet class); and C (*Hei*) CSS 2 (seven older fleet class subs), a total of 25 submarines.

IJN submarines were formed into several picket lines off Malaya just in advance of the start of hostilities. They were successful in sighting and reporting the location and movements of Force "Z", although their torpedo attacks missed. I-56 sank a small cargo ship and I-66 sank a Dutch submarine. I-21 and I-22 laid mines at the east end of the Johore Strait.[407]

Philippine Islands Invasion

The invasion of the Philippines was designed to secure Japanese flanks from attack by American air and naval power based in the Philippine Islands. The Japanese submarine force involvement in the invasion of the Philippines was minor. Two mine laying submarines, I-23 and I-24 of Submarine Squadron 6 were assigned. I-23 laid 40 mines at the east end of Manila Bay. I-24 laid 39 mines in Balabac Strait, between Borneo and Palawan. I-24 sank a small cargo ship on 10 December.[408]

The main activity in the invasion involved Imperial Japanese Navy and Army air forces, and IJA troops which landed on the island of Luzon and rapidly forced General MacArthur's combined U.S. and Philippine Army troops back into the Bataan Peninsula, where they held out for several months before surrendering.

Indian Ocean Excursions

In April 1942 Admiral Nagumo led a five carrier task force into the Indian Ocean towards Ceylon. His mission was to ensure that Royal Navy surface forces in the Indian Ocean (Eastern Fleet) could not interfere with ongoing Japanese ground and naval operations in Burma. Admiral Ozawa led a smaller force northwestward into the Bay of Bengal.

In late March six long range Japanese submarines from 2nd Submarine Squadron operated from Penang to provide reconnaissance of the area near Ceylon, and to occupy patrol stations in the Laccadive and Maldive Islands in order to protect the western flank of the Japanese task force.[409]

I-1 was to conduct an aerial reconnaissance of Ceylon but enemy patrols precluded her launching her seaplane. She sank one vessel. I-2 reported the weather off Trincomalee and sank one ship. I-3 was also assigned weather reporting duties in advance of the Japanese carrier attacks. She damaged a 4,972 ton ship in a gun action, and sank another. I-4, I-5, and I-6 operated off India's west coast. I-4 sank one ship off the

Maldive Islands, I-5 sank two ships, and I-6, off Bombay (now Mumbai) sank two ships also.[410]

British submarines based at Ceylon were stationed in the Malacca Straits to give early warning of Japanese movements, but Nagumo took his forces south through one of the other straits in the NEI and entered the Indian Ocean undetected. Finally his forces were sighted by long range patrol aircraft from Ceylon. The Japanese force was too powerful for the forces the British had in place. Basically the Royal Navy scurried for cover, and those forces that could not find shelter were sunk by Japanese air attack. British surface forces withdrew to East Africa. Although there were British fears that Ceylon might be invaded, that was not on the Japanese agenda. While Nagumo's carriers were running wild near Ceylon, another Japanese Task Force under Admiral Ozawa (one CVL and six cruisers) ran up a large score of British shipping sunk in the Bay of Bengal. Between 3 and 6 April his forces sank 21 ships for 93,247 gross register tons (GRT), and damaged four more. IJN submarines sank five ships (32,404 GRT), and damaged a transport.

In May 1942 five Japanese submarines operated as far west as the Mozambique Channel near East Africa. They sank 20 ships (94,000 tons). Later that month the British seized the northern Madagascar port of Diego Suarez from Vichy French control. Thereafter fairly strong ASW patrols were placed in effect. However the IJN submarines had returned to their base at Penang.[411]

Submarine Group A sortied from Penang, in Malaya, on 30 April 1942. There were five subs in the group. Three carried midget submarines, designated here by (M) after the submarine number: They were I-10, I-16 (M), I-18 (M), I-20 (M), and I-30. I-10 and I-30 each embarked one seaplane for aerial reconnaissance.

I-10 conducted aerial reconnaissance of Diego Suarez, a naval port at the north end of Madagascar, on 30 May and 1 June. Her pilot reported the presence of a British battleship, HMS Ramillies, in port. A coordinated midget submarine attack was planned and executed. However I-18 (M) had problems and could not launch. I-16 (M) and I-20 (M), each launched one midget submarine on the evening of 30 May.

Ramillies was badly damaged by a torpedo fired by I-20's midget sub. She was out of service for a year as a result. The other torpedo from I-20's midget sub hit and sank British Loyalty, a 6,993 ton tanker. The two crew member from I-20's midget sub grounded it on a reef. They left it and attempted to escape overland. They refused to surrender to an English patrol which tracked them down, and were shot and killed on 2 June.

I-10 sank eight cargo ships in the Mozambique Channel and off Madagascar's east coast. I-16 sank 4 ships. I-18 sank three and I-20 sank seven.

Between August and November 1942 Submarine Group 8, based at Penang, carried out a commerce destruction campaign in the Indian Ocean. I-27 sank one ship in the Arabian Sea. I-29 sank four ships on the African side of the Indian Ocean. I-162 sank two ships and damaged another in the Bay of Bengal. Between them I-165 and I-166 sank three ships and damaged another, also in the Bay of Bengal.[412]

It was a good score but it was the wrong ocean and the wrong enemy. Loss of British shipping in the Indian Ocean hurt Great Britain, but Japan's far deadlier enemy was the United States. The British were heavily involved in the Battle of the Atlantic and in no position to threaten Japan. The United States on the other hand was pursuing an aggressive posture of attacking Japanese conquests with the intent of destroying the Imperial Japanese Navy. Japan and the IJN would have been better served by employing its submarines in the Pacific against American shipping rather than in the Indian Ocean.

Australian Excursion

Four IJN mine laying submarines were sent down to lay mines in the Torres and Clarence Straits. Torres Strait separates the Cape York Peninsula from Papua New Guinea, and Clarence Strait is northeast of Darwin. Darwin was serving as a resupply site for Australian and American forces in the NEI. HMAS Deloraine detected a submarine in Beagle Gulf, just north of Darwin. She and two RAN corvettes and two USN destroyers combined to sink IJN submarine I-124.[413]

The IJN sent a carrier strike group into the Timor Sea in February 1942 to take a crack at Darwin. On 12 February a large force of IJN carrier aircraft attacked, finding the harbor loaded with ships and seaplanes. When they left eight ships had been sunk including destroyer USS Peary (DD-226) and fifteen others damaged, along with twenty-three aircraft destroyed. RAAF fighters did not stand a chance against the experienced IJN carrier pilots. Deaths numbered 243 with 302 injured.[414]

In March 1942 Broome and Wyndham in Western Australia were attacked by air, as were Darwin and Katherine in the Northern Territory. Intermittent bombing raids on Darwin continued until late 1943.

I-25 sent a reconnaissance seaplane over Sydney, Melbourne and Hobart during the period 17 February through 1 March 1942. I-2 and I-3 operated off Australia's west coast from northwest of North Cape down to Fremantle in early March 1942.

In May-June 1942 an "Eastern Unit" of five IJN submarines was formed to operate off New South Wales on the east coast of Australia. I-21 sank three ships and shelled Newcastle on 8 June. I-24 and I-27 sank one ship apiece, and I-29 damaged a ship. I-22 conducted a successful aerial reconnaissance of Wellington and Auckland, New Zealand. Between 16 May and 3 August eight more ships were damaged by IJN subs.[415]

On 31 May some escorts with a convoy that had just left Sydney harbor reported sonar contact. They were told to remain with the convoy.[416] They may have had valid contact on one of several Japanese submarines which were preparing to launch a midget submarine raid on Sydney harbor. On 29 May a seaplane from I-21 carried out a successful aerial reconnaissance of Sydney. During the afternoon of 31 May three midget-carrying mother submarines (I-22, I-24, and I-27) launched their attack craft off Sydney harbor. Two of the midgets penetrated the harbor and fired torpedoes. One torpedo narrowly missed USS Chicago (CA-29) and passed underneath Dutch submarine K-IX. Another struck a converted ferry being used for berthing at Garden Island, killing a number of people. Those two midget submarines were lost. The third midget got caught in an anti-torpedo net and finally was destroyed by its crew. They went up with the explosive charges also.[417] On 5 June a Dutch B-25 of 18 Squadron was credited with sinking a Japanese submarine, which was thought to be associated with the attack at Sydney. There is nothing in Japanese records to corroborate the reported sinking.[418]

Midway Invasion Attempt (June 1942)

In April 1942 the U.S. launched a carrier-based air strike against Tokyo and other cities on the main island of Honshu. It was a morale boosting gesture, one that was sorely needed at that time. Japanese naval forces had sunk a number of the battleships of the U.S. Pacific Fleet at Pearl Harbor.

They and Japanese Army forces had invaded the Philippines, Malaya and the Dutch East Indies and conquered all of them. For a while it seemed that nothing could stop the Japanese juggernaut.

The Doolittle air raid was conceived by a submarine officer on Admiral King's staff who had watched carrier aircraft practicing at an air base near Norfolk, landing and taking off from a small marked-off portion of the runway, similar to the short space that would be afforded them aboard an aircraft carrier. While an aircraft carrier raid on Tokyo was feasible, the relatively short range of carrier aircraft meant that the carrier would have to get close to land to launch, thus placing it in grave danger from land-based bombers. However the Army had a B-25 bomber that might be able to take off from a carrier and had a much greater range.

The details were worked out and USAAF Lieutenant Colonel Jimmy Doolittle led the historic attack from the carrier USS Hornet (CV-12). The physical damage was small but the psychological damage to the Japanese was enormous. Senior officers had promised the Emperor that Japan itself would not be attacked. One of the results of the raid was a decision to invade Midway Island, a gambit that was sure to bring the remainder of the American Pacific Fleet into action where it could be destroyed in a climactic battle.

The planned invasion of Midway involved a proliferation of Japanese forces, including a four-aircraft carrier attack group, a battleship group, and an invasion force with troop transports.

Besides those forces, two squadrons of IJN submarines (sixteen submarines) were involved. They were to establish two cordon lines; A (SubRon 3) west of Hawaii; and B (SubRon 5) north of Hawaii. Their job was to detect and report the sortie of major U.S. surface units, particularly aircraft carriers to the Japanese fleet commander. However, none of the assigned submarines arrived on station until 4 June, the day the battle began. Subs of SubRon 5 had been delayed leaving Japan because of refit problems, while SubRon 3 subs were involved in Operation "K".

Operation "K" involved placing submarines at French Frigate Shoal, about halfway between Oahu and Midway Island. The Japanese submarines were intended to refuel a long range flying boat that would carry out a reconnaissance of the Pearl Harbor base area. However, an earlier aerial reconnaissance of Oahu had been detected, and suspicions fell on French Frigate Shoal as a likely refueling area. The U.S. Pacific Fleet sent units to French Frigate Shoal to preclude it being used in that fashion. The end result was that the early sortie of three U.S. aircraft carriers from Pearl Harbor was not detected and reported. The Combined Fleet Commander, Admiral Yamamoto, was thus unaware that there were any U. S. carriers lying in ambush in the vicinity of Midway.[419] Comint had identified Midway as the target and allowed Admiral Nimitz to position his forces in advance.

In addition to the submarine cordon, Vadm. Kamatsu, commanding 6th fleet (IJN submarines), placed a submarine between French Frigate Shoal and Wotje, another one off Keahole Point, Hawaii for search and rescue (SAR), and a last one about 80 miles south of Oahu for weather observation and reporting purposes.[420]

The Battle of Midway unfolded on 4 and 5 May 1942 without any significant activity by Japanese submarines. The battle consisted of a series of air strikes: Japanese carrier air against Midway Island; Midway-based panes including a squadron of B-17s against the IJN carrier strike force; and U.S. carrier strikes against the IJN carrier task force. When it was over, four Japanese fleet carriers had been sunk and about 250 Japanese naval aircraft were lost. It was a turning point in the war.

IJN CV *Kaga* was dead in the water some three hours after the air strike that had disabled her. About 1410 her damage control officer saw three torpedo tracks coming at *Kaga*. Two missed but the third torpedo struck the ship. Fortunately or unfortunately depending on your viewpoint, it was a dud. The warhead broke off and sank. The after body floated and some of the *Kaga* crew used it for flotation. The torpedoes had been fired by USS Nautilus (SS-168). *Kaga* eventually sank.[421]

One U. S. carrier was badly damaged but the damage was being brought back under control. Just when it seemed that USS Yorktown (CV-10) could be saved, Japanese submarine I-168 slipped through a four destroyer protective screen and torpedoed her and destroyer USS Hammann (DD-412) which was moored alongside to help fight fires. Both sank and I-168 got away unscathed. The damage to Yorktown had been accomplished by Japanese naval aircraft but the Japanese submarine force could take due credit for finishing her off. It was the only bright spot during a very bad day for the IJN.

U.S. code breakers had tracked IJN submarines, and ComSubPac informed his COs of their reported positions. Admiral Nimitz, knowing Japanese submarine positions, sent submarine tender USS Fulton (AS-11) to bring back the Yorktown survivors, thus freeing combat units for fighting. Fulton brought back 2,025 men from Yorktown and others ships.[422]

Aleutians Campaign

Operation *MI* (Midway) had a diversion. It was Operation *AL* designating the Aleutian Islands as a target. Apparently the attack on the Aleutians was supposed to draw U.S. aircraft carriers north from Pearl Harbor although the intended timing doesn't make complete sense. If the Aleutian attack started the U.S. aircraft carrier battle groups moving north, they would be that much nearer to Midway. Historian Dull indicates that the *AL* operation was added as a "distraction tactic."[423]—

There were eight IJN submarines involved as well as two light aircraft carriers and escorts. A carrier air strike against naval installations at Dutch Harbor was conducted the night of 2-3 June, and another raid the following night. The Japanese took possession of Kiska and Attu Islands.

RO-61 later damaged seaplane tender USS Casio (AVP-12) on 30 August. She was lost in an ASW action the following day. RO-65 dove in harbor during an air raid and flooded, causing her loss.

In June and July 1942 a number of Japanese submarines conducted patrols off the U.S. west coast. Five SS of the 1st Submarine Group went there from the Aleutians. They were relieved in mid-June by seven submarines of the 2nd Submarine Group. In mid-June I-25 damaged a Canadian ship, and shelled Astoria, Oregon at the mouth of the Columbia River on 21 June. I-26 sank a cargo ship on 7 June, and shelled a radio station in British Columbia on 20 June. I-7 also sank a cargo ship. 2nd Submarine Group boats departed in mid-July. [424] This effort, similar to the one earlier in the year, was feeble by comparison with the number of ships sunk off the U.S. east coast by German U-boats during the same time frame.

In late August I-25 operated off Cape Blanco, Oregon in direct response to the Doolittle attack on the Japanese home islands in April. On 9 September, and again on 27 September, her seaplane dropped 170 lb. incendiary bombs into Oregon forests, vainly hoping to start a major conflagration.

I-25 sank two oil tankers in early October. Enroute home she spotted two submarines transiting on the surface. She fired her last torpedo and hit one of them, sinking it. It turned out that she had sunk Soviet submarine L-16 by accident, having misidentified the submarines as American. On 24 October she reached Yokosuka after 70 days at sea and 12,000 nautical miles.[425]

Solomon Islands Campaign

Japanese strategy became more expansive in the wake of so many early successes. Fairly early in 1942 it was clear that with General MacArthur in Australia, that continent would be built up to form a huge supply and training base for American moves northward to retake the NEI and the Philippines. In order to preclude that, the IJN decided that it should move its land-based air components further south in order to interdict allied shipping from the United States to Australia.

The first step was to put Special Naval Landing Force troops (Japanese Marines) ashore on Tulagi Island in the Solomons and then to develop an air base on neighboring Guadalcanal. Once strongly established at Guadalcanal they would then have used their air power to move further south island by island until their long range aircraft could interdict the ship supply routes.[426]

What the Japanese were up to was fairly obvious and Admiral King determined that it was time to step in and upset their scheme. He has been criticized for being too Navy-biased in his actions during WW II, but his idea of a spoiling offensive landing at Guadalcanal stood to help General MacArthur and the Army. The Navy's main thrust against Japan would go through the central Pacific as laid out in War Plan Orange and succeeding Rainbow war plans. MacArthur's chosen axis of attack went north through New Guinea and on to the Philippines.

The Marines landed on Guadalcanal on 7 August 1942. The Japanese response was swift and deadly. That afternoon Japanese bombers attacked the landing force. During the night of 8-9 August, a Japanese surface force wreaked havoc on U.S. and Australian cruisers at the Battle of Savo Island, described as the worst defeat the U.S. Navy had suffered in 130 years.

Initially no IJN submarines were assigned to the area. But Admiral Yamamoto moved his flagship, battleship Yamato, to Truk to be nearer the scene of action. About two weeks later Commander 6th Fleet was ready to send his submarines into action. He sent Squadron 3 and Squadron 7 plus those Squadron 8 boats not already in the Indian Ocean, to contest the area with the Americans.

I-169 and I-171 were off Guadalcanal, while I-174 and I-175 were off New Caledonia. I-121, I-122, I-123, RO-33 and RO-34 were stationed east of Guadalcanal and in the vicinity of Indispensable Strait forming several picket lines.[427]

The Japanese command fed ground forces into Guadalcanal in penny packets, badly underestimating the number of U.S. Marines who had been landed. The first group, the *Ichiki* Detachment, made a frontal assault on Marine positions and was chewed up by Marine Corps machine gunners. A battalion size force was then landed and attempted to seize Henderson field from the entrenched Marines. Two Japanese carrier battle groups were sent to support them. The U.S. commander was aware of this move and sent three CVBGs to counter them.

The Battle of the Eastern Solomons ensued, beginning 24 August 1942. Picket line "A" failed to detect U.S. forces. Air strikes sank Japanese light aircraft carrier *Ryujo*. USS Enterprise was damaged in return.

About midnight I-15 and I-17 sighted a U.S. aircraft carrier but were unable to attack. Com6thFlt reoriented his picket lines in response. During the three weeks since the initial landings Japanese submarines made little attempt to interdict the lightly defended supply shipping to Guadalcanal. Their focus was almost purely on major warship targets, particularly aircraft carriers. On 29 August RO-33 was sunk off Port Moresby by a RAN destroyer. One day earlier I-123 was sunk off Savo Island by USS Gamble (DM-15). Two other IJN subs were detected, attacked and damaged enough so that they had to return to port for urgent repairs.

A new IJN sub picket line was set up between Santa Cruz Island and San Christobal Island. At dawn on 31 August I-26 sighted a CV and launched six torpedoes, a full bow salvo, at a range of 3,800 yards, a long range shot. The angle on the bow (AOB) was 120 degrees. One torpedo hit, damaging USS Saratoga (CV-3), although not as badly as the attack in January. Nevertheless Saratoga had to retire to Tongatapu for temporary repairs to her hull breach before heading for Pearl Harbor Naval Shipyard for permanent repairs. I-26 underwent a four hour depth charge attack but finally escaped.[428] I-26's CO could congratulate himself on a job well done.

On 13 September IJN reconnaissance aircraft spotted a U.S. CVBG southeast of San Cristobal Island. Japanese submarines were alerted. There were nine in a picket line between San Cristobal and Santa Cruz. About noon I-19 detected propeller noise on her passive sonar, and about fifty minutes later sighted an aircraft carrier, cruiser and destroyers about eight miles away. Gradually the CVBG wandered towards I-19's position.

At 1345 I-19 fired six Type 95 (oxygen fueled) torpedoes at the carrier at a range of 1,000 yards AOB 50 degrees. Three hit USS Wasp (CV-7) and she later had to be sunk by U.S. forces. Of the remaining three long range torpedoes which kept running, one struck battleship USS North Carolina (BB-55), some 12 miles away, lightly damaging her. Another blew the bow off destroyer USS O'Brien (DD-415). She was provided a temporary bow and then headed for Pearl Harbor Naval Shipyard for permanent repairs. However she foundered off American Samoa. The sixth torpedo came to the end of its run and sank into the depths of the Pacific. I-19's salvo was among the most effective fired by any submarine during WW II.[429]

The following months saw a series of bitter engagements ashore and at sea as the Japanese tried to wrest control of the air field, Henderson Field, from the Marines. If the Japanese could neutralize Henderson Field, they could throw the Americans out. A series of vicious surface engagements took place just off Guadalcanal, giving the sound there the nickname "Iron Bottom Sound" for all the sunken warships that littered the ocean floor. Several carrier battles also took place to the east of the Solomon Islands. This was the general state of affairs from August 1942 until the end of January 1943 when the Japanese evacuated their defeated forces from Guadalcanal.

In October 1942 SubDiv 8 was ordered into the Guadalcanal area. That month battleships *Hiei* and *Kirishima* were lost to American surface forces and aircraft. A Japanese troop convoy was savaged by American aircraft with 9,000 of 14,000 troops drowned. Midget submarine attacks were initiated from I-16, I-20 and I-24.

Three submarines were positioned south of San Cristobal Island to intercept American reinforcements. I-15 of this group was lost to ASW activity. Another group of four SS were positioned northeast of San Cristobal for the same purpose. I-172 of this group was sunk. Three more IJN subs were off Noumea.

Midget submarines were brought down to Truk aboard *Chiyoda* and then to an advance base at Shortland Island where they were hoisted aboard their mother submarines. A total of eight midgets were carried down to the Guadalcanal area. One midget, from I-20, damaged a transport. The other seven were lost without scoring any hits on target ships.

On 13 November I-26 torpedoed USS Juneau (CL-52) and sank her. I-7 was involved in reconnaissance of Vanikoro, I-9 likewise at Espiritu Santo, and I-31 at Pago Pago. I-17 and I-22 refueled long range flying boats for aerial reconnaissance purposes.

There were four major fleet engagements during the Pacific War: Coral Sea (April 1942); Midway (June 1942); the Battle of the Philippine Sea (June 1944); and the Battle of Leyte Gulf (October 1944). In none of these battles did Japanese submarines play the major role envisioned for them in pre-war games.[430]

However, during the ongoing battle for the Solomon Islands, Japanese submarines for the first time did play a major role in sinking and damaging U.S. aircraft carriers, which were the key chess pieces in the war. Although events had not played out quite as predicted, the idea that submarines could be used to attrite the enemy fleet held true.

The targets that IJN subs were generally not used against were the softer variety, the supply ships and oilers that allowed the war ships to carry out their missions. The term "softer" is used in the sense that they were generally not as well protected as an aircraft carrier or a battleship. U.S. aircraft carriers and battleships generally cruised in circular ASW formations, with a ring of destroyers around them at a range calculated to put the main targets out of torpedo range, using active sonar to probe the depths for enemy submarines. It takes a steady nerve to penetrate an active destroyer screen

In late August 1942 the Battle of the Eastern Solomons was fought, known as Operation *KA* to Japanese forces. Twelve IJN submarines were involved. Japanese carrier *Ryujo* was sunk and USS Enterprise (CV-6) was damaged by air attacks. USS Saratoga was torpedoed and seriously damaged by Japanese submarine I-26. Her repairs took her out of action for three months.

During 1942 IJN submarines had been effective against major U.S. warship targets. They sank aircraft carriers Yorktown and Wasp and damaged Saratoga twice, this at a time when aircraft carriers were worth their weight in gold to the harassed U.S. commanders. However they never successfully attacked another major U.S. warship (aircraft carrier or battleship) after that.

They were drawn into resupply missions in the Solomons as American air cover made it very difficult for surface vessels to resupply Japanese ground forces on Guadalcanal. In November Admiral Yamamoto directed the use of submarines as transports. Thirteen were employed. They moved 1,115 tons of cargo and evacuated some 2,000 troops.

However, a number of the transport submarines were sunk by allied escorts using radar to detect them on the surface at night. I-3 was lost 9 December to a PT boat. I-4 was lost 20 December. I-1 was captured 23 January, with the loss of code books. I-18 was lost in early February 1943. In mid-February the use of submarines for transport missions ended.[431]

This usage precluded them from being employed against the steady stream of cargo ships necessary to support allied forces on Guadalcanal. In the open ocean they were much more likely to be successful against soft targets. It was a misuse of a vital resource by the IJN.

In March 1943 the Japanese attempted to reinforce their garrisons in New Guinea which were coming under increasing pressure from Australian and American ground forces. A convoy of eight transports and eight destroyers left Rabaul enroute New Guinea to assist the threatened locations. General Kenny, General MacArthur's air commander, launched a devastating air attack on the convoy. It was called the Battle of the Bismarck Sea and took place on 3 March. All eight transports were lost and along with them many of the Japanese Army troops they had carried. In addition four destroyers went under. Submarines I-17 and I-26 were dispatched on search and rescue duties. I-17 rescued 156 soldiers, and I-26 saved 54 more. Later I-26 sank two ships off Australia's east coast.[432]

In April 1943 a new commander of Squadron 1 directed an anti-commerce campaign off Fiji and Samoa by I-17, I-19, I-25 and I-32. They sank ships as follow:

I-17	Sank 1 ship
I-19	Sank 2 ships
I-25	Sank 1 ship

Commander Squadron 3 sent his boats on a similar mission near the Solomons and Eastern New Guinea. Their toll was:

I-174	Sank 1 ship/damaged 1 ship
I-177	Sank 2 ships

I-178   Sank 1 ship

I-180   Sank 2 ships/damaged 1 ship

Earlier I criticized IJN authorities for using their submarines against British commerce in the Indian Ocean, pointing out that victories there were not relevant to Japan's situation. The initial Marine toehold on Guadalcanal was very tenuous and a strong submarine attack on U.S. supply shipping coming north from Noumea and New Caledonia to Guadalcanal during the fall of 1942 might have allowed the Japanese to neutralize Henderson Field. The specific anti-shipping effort described above was pertinent to the defense of the Japanese position in the Solomon Islands, although it was a bit late.

The United States and its allies lost 24 warships of destroyer size and larger (126,000 tons) including two aircraft carriers during the battles in and around the Solomons. The Japanese lost 24 warships (135,000 tons) including two battleships and six submarines. The U.S. and allies employed 60,000 troops and had 1,600 KIA. The Japanese employed 36,000 troops. Their losses were 15,000 KIA, another 10,000 dead from disease and starvation, and 1,000 POWs.[433]

After stopping off at Truk in early June, I-178 disappeared. She was probably torpedoed by a U.S. submarine patrolling in the Truk area.

Squadron 7 at Rabaul sent a number of boats out on assorted missions. RO-101 rescued 45 IJA troops from the Bismarck Sea disaster. RO-103 struck a reef and was damaged enough that she had to abort her SAR mission, but later she sank three ships. RO-34 and RO-102 were lost near Guadalcanal, RO-34 to destroyer O'Bannon (DD-450), and RO-102 to PT 150 and PT-152.[434]

In continuing fighting in June 1943 the island of New Georgia had become the next target for allied invasion, on the way to seize the stronghold of Rabaul. On 30 June Japanese submarine RO-103 sighted and reported Vadm. Turner's amphibious task force which was approaching New Georgia. Other IJN submarines sank two of Turner's cargo ships off New Georgia.[435]

The New Guinea area also required submarine resupply operations due to the effectiveness of Allied air power. Squadron 7 provided 48 sorties, lifting 1,000 men and 1,400 tons of material. No IJN subs were lost during these missions. However the Lae garrison was overwhelmed by MacArthur's forces by the end of September 1943.[436]

Indian Ocean (1943)

In January 1943 the Navy General Staff issued a publication titled "Strategic Reference for the Destruction of Marine Traffic by Submarine". There is little evidence to indicate that it had much influence on IJN submarine operations. However many submarines were in refit and only a few were available to carry out a war on commerce in the Indian Ocean. I-27, I-29 and I-37 sank a total of eight ships. Between July and December of the year six subs sank 16 ships and damaged 5 more. In addition I-26 carried out a special operation, landing agents in India. One other special operation took place during 1943. U-180 came around from the Atlantic, carrying Chandra Bose and an assistant. Bose was a noted Indian nationalist leader. The Japanese had hopes that he could stir up trouble in India for the British. U-180 and I-29 rendezvoused southeast of Madagascar on 23 April. I-29 retuned to Penang with Bose and his assistant. U-180 went back to occupied France with three *Kaiten* and a supply of gold for delivery to the Japanese embassy in Berlin.[437]

End of the Aleutians Campaign

In March 1943 a surface warship clash between the IJN and the USN ended Japanese efforts to resupply their garrisons on Attu and Kiska Islands using surface ships. Japanese submarines were once again chosen to carry the load. They included I-2, I-7, I-31, I-34, I-35, I-168, I-169 and I-171. It was difficult and dangerous work because of fogs and bad weather. None of the Japanese subs involved had radar while radar was in use by many of the U.S. forces. The first radar was finally installed in an IJN submarine in mid-1944.

On 12 May U.S. and Canadian forces invaded Attu Island. The overpowered Japanese fought fiercely and ended their resistance with a futile *banzai* charge on 29 May into American guns. By that time I-35 had been damaged and I-31 sunk.

The Japanese area commander decided to evacuate Kiska Island rather than disputing it with superior American and Canadian forces. He chose to use submarines. Thirteen submarines of 1st Submarine Group were tasked for the mission. It did not go well. The evacuation began on 27 May. I-24 was sunk by a submarine chaser on 11 June. I-9 was lost to a destroyer one week later. On 20 June I-7 was forced to beach herself on Kiska Island, with the loss of a large number of her crew. After that loss the submarine evacuation effort was ended. Some 900 troops had been lifted off Kiska by that time.

On 28 July all remaining Japanese troops on Kiska were taken off by surface ships which had successfully navigated through thick fog without benefit of radar, and evaded U.S. patrolling aircraft and submarines.[438] In mid-August American and Canadian amphibious forces stormed ashore, prepared for a tough fight. They found the island deserted.

The Aleutians campaign had employed a number of Japanese submarines, but not necessarily profitably. Although the Aleutian Island route was the shortest route between the United States and Japan, being on the Great Circle line between the two countries, the weather was equally abominable for all ships including submarines, and aircraft. Neither Japan nor the United States faced a serious attempt to use the Aleutians as an invasion route against the other country.

Japanese losses during the campaign included 2,400 troops, three destroyers, nine supply ships, and six submarines.[439]

Solomon Islands

On 30 June 1943 the Allies invaded Rendova in the central Solomons. Japanese submarines were committed to the area. RO-108 sank an escort on 5 July and RO-106 sank an LST on 18 July. However seven Japanese submarines were sunk by Allied ASW forces during this period (RO-107 on 12 July, RO-103 on 28 July, RO-101 on 15 September, RO-100 on 25 November, I-11 on 11 January 1944, and I-181 on 16 January). RO-37 sank a tanker on 25 January, but was lost that same day.[440]

In July I-177 and I-180 patrolled in the central Solomons but had no contacts. In early August four boats were off Santa Cruz, Espiritu Santo, Fiji and New Caledonia. I-11 badly damaged HMAS Hobart on 20 July. I-19 sank a cargo ship. I-17 was sunk by a RNZ corvette on 19 August. Five days later I-25 was lost.

In late August another four boats started patrols. I-20 damaged a cargo ship, and I-39 sank a cargo ship. Three of the four submarines were lost: RO-35 just after 25 August, I-20 at the end of August, and I-182 on 3 September. The toll was five IJN subs sunk in a two week period.

In October 1943 only seven subs were on patrol. I-176 was sunk by a U.S. sub near Truk on 17 October. I-21 sank a cargo ship near Fiji, and I-32 conducted reconnaissance operations at Pago Pago.[441]

Central Pacific Operations

During the first week of October 1943 the U.S. conducted a carrier strike at Wake Island. Five IJN subs responded but had no contact with U.S. forces. Carrier raids were usually quick moving affairs. The CVBG moved quickly into position, launched, recovered and moved away at high speed to preclude becoming a target for Japanese submarines or land based aircraft.

During October and November the IJN sent two subs to conduct a reconnaissance of Pearl Harbor. On 17 October I-36 had to launch its seaplane about 150 nm south of Oahu because of ASW patrols. The pilot reported that there were four carriers and 4 battleships at Pearl Harbor, but did not return for recovery.

On 16 November I-19 made a successful aerial reconnaissance of Pearl Harbor, its plane reporting one aircraft carrier and one battleship at Pearl. It was clear to the Japanese commanders that U.S. forces in the Pacific were steadily increasing.[442]

Gilberts Operations (November 1943)

In November 1943 U.S. forces under Admiral Nimitz's control launched an invasion of Tarawa and Makin Atolls in the Gilbert Islands. Japanese land-based air and submarines responded. Nine submarines were immediately available, and they dashed around setting up picket lines east of Tarawa, and then east and west of Makin.

I-175 was successful, sinking escort carrier USS Liscome Bay (CVE-56) on 24 November. However American ASW forces sank six submarines, and IJN sub operations were discontinued as of 4 December.

Marshall Islands Assault (February 1944)

The next target for the U.S. Central Pacific amphibious forces were the Marshall Islands. But first the major Japanese naval base at Truk had to be neutralized. Apparently the IJN had some intelligence information about a pending strike at Truk. However it failed, either deliberately or through negligence, to notify Imperial Japanese Army headquarters about the strike. A U.S. carrier battle force consisting of six fleet and six light carriers launched air strikes on 17 and 18 February 1944. They found the harbor loaded with Japanese shipping, much of it belonging to the Japanese Army. Most of it was sunk. In addition Commander 6th Fleet's flagship *Katori* went down, along with an auxiliary submarine tender *Heian Maru* (11, 614 tons).[443] There were seven IJN subs in the area at the time but there was no contact with U.S. forces.

I-131 was sunk near Rabaul on 16 January. I-41 was ambushed and sunk on 15 February by USS Aspro (SS-309) while evacuating troops to Truk. RO-40 was sunk by surface forces off Kwajalein on 16 February.

Eight IJN subs were sent to the Marshalls to attack U.S. forces. All eight were lost. US Tunny (SS-282) ambushed one on the surface on 23 March (I-42). I-32 was sunk on 24 March. I-2 was lost on 2 April, and I-7 on 7 April. I-174 and RO-45 were lost at the end of April.[444]

Philippine Sea Battle (June 1944)

The Battle of the Philippine Sea took place in June 1944. It focused on the invasion of islands in the Mariana Island chain. The battle is frequently referred to as the "Marianas Turkey Shoot" because of the large number of Japanese naval aircraft destroyed by American fighter aircraft and by surface ship anti-aircraft fire, with very few U.S. aircraft having been lost.

The Japanese response to the American drive into the Marianas was named Operation *A-Go*. Japanese 6th Fleet deployed two dozen submarines to try to defend the Marianas. Seventeen of them were sunk by U.S. destroyers, destroyer escorts and naval aircraft.[445] Japanese submarines were unsuccessful in blocking the invasions. Three IJN aircraft carriers were also lost during the battle, two to American submarines and one to carrier air attack. The seizure of the Marianas gave the United States air bases within range of mainland Japan. Soon the Marianas became the center of B-29 bomber activity.

Indian Ocean (1944)

IJN subs continued anti-shipping operations during the first six months of 1944. On 11 February RO-110 damaged a cargo ship but was sunk the same day. I-27 sank British troopship *Khedive Ismail* but was sunk in turn off the Maldive Islands on 12 February.

Six other IJN subs sank a total of 13 ships without loss to themselves. Earlier comments about misdirected IJN efforts apply here also. I-166 was sunk in the Straits of Malacca by a British submarine.[446]

Peleliu (September 1944)

Five IJN subs were deployed to contest the invasion of Peleliu, an invasion that Admiral Halsey recommended be skipped as unnecessary. The Marines found the Japanese dug into caves and suffered very severe casualties before the island was secured. IJN subs sank one U.S. destroyer escort but two of them were lost (RO-47 and I-177)

Leyte Gulf (October 1944)

The planned invasion of the Philippines in 1944 was advanced to October. In preparation for that battle Japanese 6th Fleet deployed 17 submarines in four different groups.

The Battle of Leyte Gulf was the final "decisive" battle for which the IJN had prepared during pre-war years. Rather than an open sea encounter between two great fleets, it consisted of three major actions, two of them in close proximity to land. Two major IJN fleet components sailed from Lingga Roads southeast of Singapore when word came of the landings at Leyte Island. The northern component, under Admiral Kurita aimed to penetrate the San Bernardino Strait in the Central Philippines and fall on the American invasion forces at Leyte from the north. Simultaneously another major force, under Admiral Nishimura, sailed through the southern Surigao Strait. Its intent was to scissor the Americans from the south.

A third force under Admiral Ozawa, sailed south from Japan. It contained several aircraft carriers and was intended as bait for Admiral Halsey. Japanese planners believed that he could not resist the impulse to go for a final kill of the remaining Japanese aircraft carriers. There were very few aircraft embarked in those carriers, most of Japanese naval aircraft having been lost in the Battle of the Philippine Sea. While Halsey was occupied with the sacrificial forces, the other two Japanese forces would destroy the American invasion force—or so the Japanese script for the battle predicted.

American naval forces were a divided command during this operation, and that division led to a near disaster. Admiral Kincaid, under General MacArthur, led 7th Fleet which included amphibious shipping and supporting battleships and escort carriers. The fleet carriers were all under Admiral Halsey's command, 3rd Fleet, subordinate to Admiral Nimitz, Commander in Chief Pacific Ocean Area.

A large number of U.S. submarines were stationed in and around the Philippines in anticipation of a major Japanese effort to oppose the Leyte landings. They reported on Admiral Kurita's force location, course and speed, and sank two of his heavy cruisers and damaged two more to boot. U.S. naval air strikes from Admiral Halsey's fleet carriers then savaged Kurita's force before it could pass through the San Bernardino Strait, sinking battleship *Musashi*. Kurita turned west and it was thought that the northern force was defeated and out of action.

The southern force was also being tracked and an ambush prepared. The Surigao Strait was infested with PT boats with instructions to report and attack. Further on in the narrow passage were several squadrons of destroyers ready to engage Nishimura's surface units. Finally, a line of Admiral Kincaid's older battleships, some resurrected from the mud of Pearl Harbor, lay ready to "cross the T" of the southern force when it came into range.

To some extent the IJN script played out as it was written. The "bait force" was detected and Halsey took his 3rd Fleet north to destroy it. He failed to leave his battleships behind to guard the San Bernardino Strait, or to tell Admiral Kincaid that it was unguarded.

While Halsey went north to destroy the remaining Japanese aircraft carriers at the battle of Cape Engano, Admiral Kurita turned his force around and came back through the San Bernardino Strait. He fell on Taffy Five, an escort carrier task group that was operating in support of the landing forces. A head long, "death or glory" charge by the destroyers and destroyer escorts of Taffy Five, and an all out attack by all available escort carrier aircraft with whatever ordnance they could rapidly load, managed to convince Admiral Kurita that he was in contact with a major aircraft carrier task force. Given the damage such a force had already inflicted on his force, he hesitated and then turned away. His surface ships sank an escort carrier, two destroyers and one destroyer escort, but the damage could have been much greater.

During the Leyte Gulf battles the IJN lost one fleet aircraft carrier, three light carriers, three battleships, six heavy cruisers, four light cruisers, eleven destroyers, and four submarines. In addition they lost 116 naval aircraft. It was the final decisive battle of the Pacific War. IJN submarines contributed not a whit.[447]

Last Gasps

In late 1944 the I-12 was sent to the U.S. west coast. She sank only one cargo ship between Hawaii and San Francisco on 29 October. On 13 December 1944 she was sunk.[448]

On 29 July 1945 I-58 was on patrol in the Philippine Sea. It sighted USS Indianapolis (CA-35) which was enroute from Tinian to Leyte Gulf, after delivering the nuclear core of the first atomic bomb to Tinian. Indianapolis was not zigzagging at the time and had no destroyer escorts. I-58 hit her with three torpedoes out of six fired and she sank without being able to get off a message report of the attack. What followed was a tragic error in the Navy ship arrival reporting system. When Indianapolis did not arrive on schedule at Leyte Gulf, her failure to arrive should have triggered a search. Her non-arrival was not noticed and no search was launched. 3.5 days later a Navy patrol plane was overflying that part of the Philippines Sea and saw a large number of survivors in the water. It landed and learned of the sinking. Only 316 men of the entire crew of 1,199 men were rescued. Many died in the water subsequent to the sinking.

In mid-July 1945 two very large (5,000 ton) I-400 class submarines set sail from Honshu for an aerial attack on the U.S. fleet anchorage at Ulithi Atoll. Each submarine was equipped with a very long hangar that carried three *Seiran* foldable wing seaplanes (*Aichi* type M6A1). After surfacing, the planes were withdrawn from the hangar, their wings unfolded and pontoons attached. They were then launched over the submarine bow by a catapult. Each could carry a 850 kg weapon load. The original concept had been to use them to attack the Gatun locks in the Panama Canal and shut down the Canal, forcing a long voyage around Cape Horn rather than the much shorter passage through the canal into the Pacific.

By the time they were ready for action it was obvious that an attack on the Panama Canal would be fruitless. A nearer and more urgent target was selected—the U.S. Navy fleet anchorage at Ulithi Atoll, where ships were preparing for the invasion of the Japanese home islands. They were enroute when the Emperor accepted the Allied demand of an unconditional surrender. The submarine-aircraft carriers turned their bows toward Japan and headed hone to surrender. Before arriving they launched all six aircraft into the sea.

Japanese Midget Submarines

High hopes were entertained for the tactical use of midget submarines. They were employed during the Pearl Harbor attack on December 7, 1941 without successful results. They were used in a successful attack on British naval units at the port of Diego Suarez on Madagascar on 31 May 1942. One of the midgets severely damaged battleship HMS Ramillies, putting it out of action for a year. The same midget submarine sank 6,993 ton tanker British Loyalty. The crew then abandoned their craft after running aground on a reef. They set out on foot to make their escape. A British patrol shot them to death when they refused to surrender. One day later, midget submarines were used to attack ships in Sydney Harbor, Australia with poor results. In the Solomons, one sank a ship but the rest were lost.

The first launch of a midget submarine was in the spring of 1941.[449] Five midget submarines were carried to the Pearl Harbor attack on board I-class submarines. All five were launched by their mother submarines but lost without inflicting any known damage. Their task was to penetrate into Pearl Harbor and torpedo major units in the harbor. One was detected just outside the harbor entrance by USS Ward (DD-139) at 0630, when its periscope was spotted. Ward was on antisubmarine patrol at the time.

The area just seaward of Pearl Harbor had been declared a "defensive sea area" by Presidential Directive and no submarines were allowed to operate submerged within its boundaries. Ward's CO directed an immediate attack with guns and depth charges, and reported his attack to the 14th Naval District operations office ashore. Reported submarine sightings were not uncommon and as the report and its implications were being mused by the weekend duty officer, the Japanese naval air strike was approaching Oahu.

There is one aerial photograph of the torpedo attacks on battleships at Ford Island, taken during the attack showing various torpedo tracks, that has led to speculation that at least one midget submarine did successfully penetrate the harbor and launch its torpedoes at a target on battleship row. Another incident involved USS Monaghan (DD-354) ramming a midget submarine, and then depth charging it and destroying it just North West of Ford Island inside the harbor.

One of the midget submarines had gyroscope problems, grounded on a reef outside Pearl Harbor and eventually wound up on the northeast side of the island of Oahu at Bellows Beach. It ran aground there and was abandoned by its crew members. The petty officer drowned in the surf but its CO, Ensign *Sakamaki*, got ashore and was captured—the first Japanese POW of WW II.

The five midget submarines were supposed to rally at Lahaina Roads anchorage just off the island of Maui to be recovered by their parent submarines. None reached Lahaina.

Kaiten (Submarine *kamikaze*)

The *kaiten* mirrored the use of airplanes in *kamikaze* tactics. As the war went on and it became apparent that only desperate measures could stave off defeat, the old legend of a "divine wind" (*kamikaze*) that had defeated the Mongol attempt to invade Japan during the 13th century was updated. Rather than an airplane attempting to hit its ship target with bombs, the airplane itself was the bomb. Guided by its pilot, it would dive into a large ship target and hopefully inflict serious damage if it didn't cause the loss of the ship. The pilot willingly sacrificed his life for the good of the Empire.

During the Okinawa invasion, *kamikazes* inflicted a great deal of damage on the allied fleet offshore supporting the ground fighting.

Kamikazes sank 34 ships and damaged 368 more off Okinawa. About 4,800 men died and another 4,900 were wounded.

Kaitens were nowhere nearly so effective. The first *GEN* operation, attacking with *kaitens*, was carried out at Ulithi Atoll in November 1944. Three IJN submarines, I-36, I-37 and I-47, each transported four *kaitens*. On 20 November I-36 launched one *kaiten* and I-47 launched four. One destroyed a fleet oiler, USS Mississinewa (AO-39), which went up in a fiery explosion inside the lagoon. Both submarines returned safely. However I-37, which headed for Palau, was sunk by U.S. ASW forces.[450]

IJN authorities, desperate for any hope of stopping the American juggernaut, sent out six more parent submarines with *kaitens* around the end of the year. None sank any ships.

The *kaiten* was a manned torpedo, several usually being carried on the after deck of a large I-class submarine to the scene of action. Once launched, the pilot's job was to guide the *kaiten* into the side of the target, ensuring its destruction.

Overall Evaluation of IJN submarine effectiveness

When the war ended there were 59 undamaged submarines remaining in the IJN. They sank 170 merchant ships (1 million tons), as well as a number of warships.

The following table compares the statistics of German U-boats and Japanese submarines:[451]

	German U-boats	IJN submarines
Number of units	1,000	187
Number of ships sunk	2,000	170
Tonnage sunk	14.5 million tons	1 million tons
Ships sunk per unit	2.0	0.9
Tonnage sunk per unit	14,500	5,348

In addition to the merchant ships sunk, IJN submarines sank two aircraft carriers, two cruisers, ten destroyer escorts and a number of smaller ships including submarines.

One hundred twenty-nine of 187 IJN submarines were lost in combat to the following causes:[452]

70	Surface ships
22	Other causes
19	U.S. submarines
18	Aircraft

The Imperial Japanese Navy was intently focused on a climactic battle, one like the famous battle of Tsushima Straits, which would lead to a negotiated peace in Japan's favor. IJN submarines attempted to play their assigned role in the script. During 1942 their successes in sinking and damaging U.S. aircraft carriers and a battleship were commendable. However they were largely irrelevant otherwise.

IJN planners seemed to entirely overlook the pivotal role of submarines against maritime commerce, although the history of WW I and the more current story of the Atlantic Battle were there to be explored. That pivotal role was both a threat and an opportunity. The threat was to Japan's vital trade with SEAsia. The answer to the threat was to concentrate on ASW concepts, escort force levels, and tactics, an area in which IJN submarines would have little place.

However, there was an opportunity to use IJN submarines to attack the American enemy's soft targets, supply ships and tankers that allowed him to operate overseas. With the exception of some operations in the Solomons area late in 1942 and early in 1943 that role was generally ignored. The IJN had the best torpedoes in the world, but failed to use their submarine service effectively.

In the Indian Ocean IJN submarines did operate against commerce and were reasonably successful. However, those successes had nothing to do with the main threat to Japan—the U.S. Navy with its growing number of CVBGs and its amphibious task forces. Thus they were a waste of vital resources, a waste that Japan could not afford in a struggle with an industrial giant like the United States.

Chapter Seven—Soviet Submarines

On 23 August 1939 Joseph Stalin, head of the Soviet Union (USSR), chose to hedge his political bets by signing a non-aggression pact with Adolph Hitler. It freed Germany to undertake its invasion of Poland on 1 September 1939 without fear of adverse Soviet reaction. In accordance with a secret provision, on 17 September the USSR's armies rolled across Poland's eastern borders and occupied half of the country. The USSR went on to occupy Estonia, Latvia and Lithuania, all independent Baltic states that had emerged after the end of WW I and the Czarist Empire's dissolution.

Communist Party news organs in the West had to do an abrupt "about face". Where a week earlier they had been railing against "fascist Germany", they now spoke well of Hitler and Nazi Germany. That move cost the Communist movement in Western Europe and the United States many supporters who could not stomach such naked aggression and the embrace of a hated fascist leader.

In November 1939 the USSR attacked Finland, a former part of the Russian Empire. The USSR, concerned over protection of the Leningrad area, wanted to obtain a naval base on the northern side of the Gulf of Finland, the port of Hango. When the Finns refused the Soviet request, the USSR attacked. Fighting did not go well for the Soviets. They bogged down in severe snows. Both the Red Army and Red Air Force displayed a high degree of ineptitude and lack of competent leadership. Some of that stemmed from a severe and bloody purge of senior Soviet military men starting in 1937. However, despite some aid from Great Britain, France and the United States, Finland was forced to sign an accommodation with the USSR in March 1940.

In June 1941 the "chickens came home to roost" with a vengeance. On 22 June a massive German air and ground assault struck the USSR. Soviet intelligence organizations had been warning Stalin for months about German intentions. He had also been warned by President Roosevelt and by Prime Minister Winston Churchill. Stalin shrugged off the warnings, and left his aerial borders open to German reconnaissance aircraft, busily taking photographs of key installations for the attack. Finland not unexpectedly joined Germany in the war on the USSR.

At the start of the Russo-German War, the Soviet Submarine Service had a total of 215 submarines, distributed as follows: Baltic Fleet-69; Northern Fleet-15; Black Sea Fleet-44; and Pacific Fleet-87.

Interestingly some Soviet submarines were already on patrol stations when the war started. Stalin had specifically forbidden Army and Air Force leaders from taking protective measures along the USSR's western border prior to the German attack. However some Baltic Fleet subs and Northern Fleet subs had been sent out to sea as fears mounted.

The role of Soviet submarines in defense of the "Motherland" will be broken into sections by fleets, starting with the Baltic Fleet, followed by the Northern, Black and Pacific Fleets in that order. There was a limited ability to move small submarines by rail or barge between the Baltic Fleet and the Northern Fleet and the Black Sea Fleet. However large submarines could not be moved between fleets except by sea.

Baltic Fleet Submarines

In mid-October 1939 after the seizure of the three formerly independent states, the Soviet Navy based submarines at Revel (now Tallinn), Libau (now Liepaya) and Baltiski Port (now Paldiski), as well as at Leningrad There were some 25 Soviet subs and three submarine tenders scattered among the three advance locations.

Winter War

There was little Soviet submarine activity during the Winter War against Finland that started in November 1939 and ended in March 1940. Stalin was interested in a close blockade of the Finnish coastline by submarines, but the head of the Soviet Navy was able to dissuade him. However, the Soviet Navy gained the use of Finnish naval bases on the north side of the Gulf of Finland. Submarines and their tenders were stationed there.

There were now 69 submarines in the Baltic Fleet, most built between 1930 and 1941. Four submarines had been seized from the recently acquired Baltic states, two from Estonia and two from Latvia. In addition there were several much older submarines: the former British L-55, one Bars class sub, and five AG class. These seven all dated back to the First World War time frame. They could be used for training but were not up to combat patrols. About 37 submarines were combat-ready on 21 June 1941.

Operation BARBAROSSA (June 1941)

On 22 June 1941 just before dawn German forces staged a surprise massed air-ground attack against the Soviet western frontier. They inflicted very heavy casualties, particularly on air squadrons, whose planes were lined up neatly on their runways. Stalin had forbidden local commanders from intercepting German reconnaissance aircraft which were overflying border positions and taking photographs of Soviet installations. Apparently he was concerned about creating an "incident" that would give Hitler an excuse to attack. In a late night hastily called session at the Kremlin on the night of 21-22 June Stalin finally began to give some direction to his commanders, but it was far too late. German attack aircraft found Soviet squadrons lined up as if on parade when they reached their targets. Literally thousands of Soviet aircraft were destroyed, most on the ground.

Ten submarines of the 1st Submarine Brigade were already at sea when the Germans attacked. Two were off the Danzig Bight, another two off Gotland in the middle Baltic Sea, and the remaining six strung off the coastline from Libau to the Irben Strait. Of the ten subs on station, four were lost to enemy action during the first week: two to U-boat torpedoes, another to MTB torpedoes, and the fourth lost to A/S surface craft off the Danzig Bight.[453]

The problem with the Baltic Sea from a submarine point of view is that it is relatively small and shallow and easily mineable. Being small puts submarines at sea even in the middle of the Baltic at risk from fast flying aircraft. Shallow waters provide little room for depth maneuvers, or for acoustic layers that can make it harder to detect submarines. During WW I both Germans and Russians had heavily mined various areas of the Baltic and inflicted a number of submarine casualties.

One key German objective for their ground forces was Leningrad. On the south side of the Gulf of Finland they closed in to a range of about 50 miles from their target. On the north side, the Finns did likewise.

Leningrad was hemmed in and surrounded and subjected to a lengthy siege. The movement of German and Finnish ground forces forced the USSR to withdraw its submarines and sub tenders back into the Kronshtadt-Leningrad area. By September Leningrad was under siege, an ordeal that did not end until January 1944.

Soviet naval forces withdrew from Libau on 27-28 June, destroying six submarines there rather than letting them be captured. By the end of June they were forced out of Hango in Finland. The submarines and sub tender stationed there fled to Kronshtadt. Submarines M-81 and M-99 were lost while transiting mine fields.[454]

During the July-August time frame four Soviet subs laid mines: *Kalev*, L-3, K-3 and *Lembit*. Both *Kalev* and *Lembit* were former Estonian submarines. On 28 July SHCH-307 sank U-144 near Dago, an appropriate reprisal for U-144 having sunk M-78 earlier.[455] U-144 was a small Type IID U-boat well suited to work in shallow waters as were the slightly smaller Soviet M-class boats. SHCH is an abbreviation of *Shchuka* (Pike), the name assigned to a large class of Soviet submarines.

In August 1941 the Germans attacked Revel and the Soviets withdrew to the Kronshtadt—Leningrad area. Some 200 ships fled there. Three boats were lost to German mines or aircraft attack: SHCH-301, S-5 and S-6.

In mid-September a number of Soviet boats were active laying mines near Helsinki and Hango. They also operated against German shipping along the coast of Sweden. On 28 September SHCH-317 attacked and missed light cruiser *Leipsig*. That month four boats were tapped for transport duties to move personnel from Hango to Kronshtadt: L-1, L-2, P-1 and P-3.

P-1 was lost in a mine field in September, and L-2 in November. On 21—23 September severe air attacks hit Kronshtadt, damaging P-2, SHCH-302 and SHCH-306. Hango was finally evacuated in November 1941.

On 16 October, near Oland, SHCH-323 torpedoed and sank German cargo ship *Baltenland*.(3,724 tons) with three torpedoes. On 24 October steamer *Hohenhorn* was missed by a torpedo. Polmar and Noot attribute the attack to S-4, but Jurgen Rohwer states that only M-97 was in the area at that time.[456] In any case *Hohenhorn* got away without damage. L-3 was busy laying mines. S-7 landed agents in Varna Bay. S-8 was lost to a mine. In late October ice formation forced a stop to submarine operations.

Obvious limitations on submarine operations in the Baltic led the Soviets to transfer six active and ten more (not yet completed) to the Northern Fleet via the Stalin (White Sea) river—canal system. Six others were sent to the Caspian Sea which removed them from any possible wartime operations. So few subs were left, that they were consolidated into a single brigade under a Soviet Navy Captain First Rank.

1942

On 19 March 1942 German aerial reconnaissance showed 48 submarines in the Kronshtadt-Leningrad area. On 1 May 1942 there were 57 Soviet subs there, of which 33 were available for operations. The Germans and Finns decided to lay enough mines to make it very difficult for Soviet submarines to get out of the eastern portion of the Gulf of Finland to operate against German shipping off Sweden. The Finns began a laying a mine barrier on 9-10 May 1942. The two countries laid slightly over 12,000 mines.[457]

In April 1942 the Military Council of the Soviet Baltic Fleet planned a three-echelon submarine penetration of the German-Finnish mine barriers. From Lavansaari to the mouth of the Gulf of Finland is about 200 nm. On 25 May M-97 began its initial reconnaissance. She was lost later during her second reconnaissance effort, on 14 August. M-89 and M-95 also attempted reconnaissance of the mine barrier. M-95 was lost on 15 June. The entire exploration process lasted from early June until early November of 1942.

The three echelons are shown here with results:

Date began	Echelon number	Number of SS	SS lost
3 June	1	11	3
9 August	2	11	2
Mid-September	3	15	7
Totals		37	12

When U.S. subs penetrated into the Sea of Japan in June 1945, their second excursion, they were equipped and trained in the use of the frequency modulated (FM) active sonar, that had the capability of detecting mines using active acoustic energy. Even so it was a very hazardous operation. At best the Soviet submarines had to rely on passive sonar to hope to hear a sound from the mine anchor cables as they worked their way through the mine barrier. That could provide a rough bearing but no range. Usually the first indication they had that a mine was close by was the sound of a mine cable scraping against the hull.[458] It is not surprising that nearly 33% were lost. The toughness and determination shown by Soviet submariners was admirable, even though the results were not.

Red Star Under the Baltic by *Viktor Korzh* is an outstanding account of life in Baltic Submarine Brigade submarines, as they undertook to clear the mine fields, and later the A/S net barriers in order to attack German shipping. *Korzh* was an engineering specialist. The Soviet submarine service, like several other European submarine services, used professional engineers rather than rotating line officers through that function.

German records indicate 31 attempts by Soviet submarines to penetrate the mine barrier. Twenty-two were successful. Those Soviet subs sank 20 ships (about 40,000 GRT) and damaged 8 ships (34,000 GRT).

The real figure of merit (or demerit) for Soviet submarine operations during 1942 is the fact that 1,900 ships (5.6 million GRT) and 400,000 troops were transported safely in the Baltic Sea by the Germans despite the Soviet submarine threat.[459]

1943

When the ice cleared away in spring 1943 Germany and Finland reinforced their mine barriers. Germany added 7,293 mines to its Porkkala Barrier, and Finland added 1,965 mines to its Hogland system, both in the Gulf of Finland.

In addition construction of an anti-submarine net barrier was begun. It was west of the Porkkala mine barrier. The new system, called "Walrus", consisted of two net lines, parallel to each other and separated by about 100 meters (109 feet). The nets were heavily anchored on the bottom and buoyed on top. The nets extended down to 60 meters (197 feet). The greatest depth of water in the area was 92 meters (302 feet). There were narrow passages through the net barriers to allow A/S trawlers to operate within the new barrier system. Shore monitoring stations communicated with the trawlers by UHF radio.

Around 1 April the first Soviet submarine began its transit from Leningrad to Kronshtadt. SHCH-303 was the first to attempt to penetrate the net system on 18 May. It failed and returned eastward to base. SHCH-323 was sunk by a mine in the Leningrad-Kronshtadt ship channel while enroute westward. SHCH-406 and 408 were destroyed while attempting to penetrate the nets.

The Soviets turned to air attacks on the net system to destroy it, or damage it enough that Soviet submarines could get through. During June, July and August there were massive air attacks on the net barriers. They all failed. S-12 was lost on 16 August, and S-9 was lost on 5 September. After that Soviet submarine ops in the Gulf of Finland were limited to landing or extracting agents behind Finnish lines. The German-Finnish net barrier plus mine barriers were highly effective in keeping Soviet submarines out of the Baltic Sea during 1943.

1944

The ice cleared in April-May 1944. The Germans and Finns planned to increase their minefields and force of patrol vessels to beef up the mine barriers and the A/S barrier. By mid-April, the nets were refurbished. The Finns added 1,971 mines to the Hogland mine barrier. By mid-April the Soviet submarine brigade had 21 submarines combat ready. Two older units, B-2 and L-55, were being used as battery charging stations.

On 10 July the Soviets attacked the Finnish front on the Karelian Isthmus and rapidly pushed the Finns back. On 4 September the Finns signed an armistice with the USSR. On the south side of the Gulf of Finland, Soviet armies pushed forward also. By mid-August they seized Riga. The German strategic position was now untenable. From 4-21 September the Germans evacuated their personnel from Finland. On 23 September they evacuated Revel.

The Germans employed 19 U-boats against Soviet naval forces from June on. Six were lost. U-250 was salvaged by the Soviet Navy. It had two T-5 acoustic torpedoes aboard. These were the first T-5s to be recovered by the Allies. Great Britain, Canada and the United States were very interested and obtained access to the German technology. They had already developed a counter-measure, "Foxer gear", that was trailed aft by ships and attracted acoustic torpedoes, but no one had actually examined a T-5.

The Soviets could now use the Finnish skerrries to move their submarines from Kronshtadt out to the mouth of the Gulf of Finland. Therefore they left the Porkkala mine barrage in place until after the end of the war. Clearing it of thousands of mines would have used up many resources, unnecessarily at this stage.[460]

The Soviet submarine offensive resumed in early September 1944. M-96 was mined and lost, and M-10 was damaged by a mine. Soviet submarines sank 12 ships (20,969 GRT), and damaged another (3,038 GRT). About ten Soviet SS were active but they did not sink or damage any major German warships which were busy giving naval gunfire support to retreating German troops.[461]

1945

During the winter of 1944—1945 the Soviets moved into naval bases in Finland under the Armistice terms. They established bases at Helsingfors, Hango and Abo. Submarine depot ships were sent to those ports. In early February they had ten SS ready for operations. By early May it was up to nineteen SS.

`From January through May 1945 when the German unconditional surrender was signed, the Soviet claimed 27 submarine sorties, 52 attacks, and indicated they fired 152 torpedoes. The Germans acknowledged the loss of 15 ships (67,504 GRT). However the Germans evacuated more than one million troops from the Eastern Front through the Baltic without loss to Soviet submarines.

There were two notable sinking's by a Soviet submarine during the year. On 30 January S-13 sank the *Wilhelm Gustloff* (25,484 GRT), with four torpedoes fired and three hits. The *Gustloff* was carrying 6,100 passengers, being evacuated ahead of the Soviet armies. Only 904 persons survived. On 10 February S-13 sank *General Steuben* (14,660 GRT) with one torpedo. She was carrying 3,000 evacuees. Only 300 survived.[462]

Northern Fleet Submarines

On 17 June 1941 German aerial reconnaissance of the Murmansk area increased markedly. The North Fleet Commander-in-Chief, Admiral A. G. Golovko, requested permission to use fighter planes to halt their activity. The Soviet High Command forbad any such aaction. However, when the German attack struck the western border of the Soviet Union on 22 June 1941, there were four Soviet submarines already on patrol along the northern coast of Norway. Two more were at sea off the Kola Inlet.

The German objective in the north was to capture the port of Murmansk by movement of ground forces across northern Norway. The German attack hung up at the Litsa River and that became the demarcation line between German and Soviet forces. It was about 35 miles west of Murmansk. The Germans never advanced east of the Litsa River. On 6 July a Soviet amphibious landing on the Rybachiy Peninsula helped secure the Litsa river line. There was no highway connecting northern Norway and northern Russia at that time. That meant that German forces had to be resupplied by sea.[463]

In the face of German air superiority the Soviet commander decided to use submarines rather than surface warships to attack the German resupply routes. Tromso and Honningsvaag were the staging bases for the German convoys. Transports would use the Norwegian skerrries to move from Tromso to Mageray Island.

On 7 July the Germans detected the first Soviet submarine off Vardo. The first German convoys were not well defended. The first German destroyers did not reach Kirkenes at Varanger Fjord until 10 July. U-boats did not become available until 19 July. However the Soviet Submarine Service was feeling its way along as well. During July and August the Germans detected some 3-4 Soviet subs from Hammerfest to Varanger Fjord.[464]

In July there were discussions between the USSR and the UK about sending a Royal Navy surface force up to assist the Soviets in dealing with the German offensive. Radm. Phillip L. Vian, RN went up to the Kola area to inspect and make recommendations. Noting German local air superiority, he advised against sending a group of surface ships. Vian had been involved in the Mediterranean Sea in the German battle to take Crete by air assault in May 1941. He had seen firsthand what Stuka dive bombers could do to RN ships. He recommended that submarines be used instead. In early August HMS Tigris and Trident arrived at the Kola Inlet to assist the Soviets.[465]

On 14 July SHCH-401 attacked a submarine chaser near Vardo unsuccessfully. SHCH—402 fired two torpedoes at steamer *Hanau* off Porsanger Fjord. She thought she had gotten a hit, but the torpedoes missed the target and exploded against rocks ashore. This phenomenon led to a number of erroneous sinking reports. By doctrine Soviet torpedoes were set to run at 5 meters (16 feet). Lightly loaded coastal ships rarely drew that much water. However doctrine was violated at great peril in the Soviet services.[466]

On 10 August U-251 sank guard ship *Zhemchug* off Svyatri Nos. During August and September there were a number of encounters between Soviet submarines and U-boats:

7 August	U-81 encountered an unidentified submarine off Rybachiy
23 August	M-172 encountered U-752 off Vardo
2 September	U-566 encountered an unidentified submarine off Cape Teriberskiy[467]

In August Northern Fleet was reinforced by the transfer of submarines from the Baltic by way of the Stalin (White Sea) river-canal system (K-3, K-21, K-23, S-101, S-102, and two incomplete subs (L-20 and L-22). The latter two were completed at Molotovsk/Severodvinsk shipyard in August and September.[468]

Only submarines K-1 and K-2 were able to lay mines. But unfortunately the mine inventory on hand for Northern fleet amounted to only 20 mines. By September the mine inventory had grown, and more K-class boats were available to start a mine laying campaign. On 10 September K-1 made a mine plant off Vardo. In early November K-23 made another at the entrance to Bok Fjord. On 5 November German minesweeper M-22 was badly damaged by a mine explosion. A Soviet M 08 mine was recovered nearby on 11 November.

On 12 September the first confirmed ship sinking by Soviet submarines took place. It was an unescorted Norwegian transport *Otto Jarl* off Tana Fjord, sunk by SHCH-422.

In late November the first Soviet submarine to operate as far west as North Cape was K-3. On 3 December she encountered and attacked

German steamer *Altkirch* but her torpedoes missed. K-3 was severely depth charged by the escorts. Her embarked division commander decided to surface and fight it out with guns. K-3 had two 100 mm deck guns plus two more 45 mm AA guns. She sank one submarine chaser and drove the other off. Subsequent to the battle, the division commander transferred to K-23, and K-3 returned to port surfaced. She was unable to dive.[469]

British submarines Tigris and Trident conducted three patrols each under Soviet operational control. They sank 5 to 6 German ships and two submarine chasers. In November they were relieved by HMS Sealion and Seawolf. They conducted several patrols but only remained at Polyarrnyy until December. At that time the Admiralty decided that the operational areas available were too small for the number of both British and Soviet submarines, and the RN contingent sailed home. There was some discussion about Soviet submarines operating elsewhere under RN opcon but nothing ever came of it.[470]

1942

In February 1942 at Porsanger Fjord an interesting encounter took place. A German minelayer *Brummer* came across SHCH-403. The submarine mistakenly identified the ship as friendly. An escort rammed SHCH-403. The submarine CO was trapped topside when the submarine dove and got away. He was taken prisoner. The escort, M-1503, did not do serious damage to SHCH—403 and she returned to port with an unusual deck log entry.

SHCH-402 suffered the embarrassment of running out of fuel while on patrol. She was rescued by K-21 which transferred fuel and lubricating oils to her.

In April and May there were more Soviet submarine patrols. The large submarines attacked targets off Nordkyn and Makkaur, while M-class boats were active in the Vardo area. They sank four German transports and engaged in some surface gun battles. On 10 April SHCH-421 suffered severe mine damage in Porsanger Fjord. K-22 was called to the scene and tried to tow her but was unsuccessful. K-22 then took her crew off and sank SHCH-421. On 24 April SHCH-401 was sunk by German surface ships off Tana Fjord.

K-23 was sunk off Okse Fjord on 12 May. SHCH-403 was damaged by dive bombing in Murmansk on 15 May. On 25 May S-101 escaped from depth charging off Tana Fjord.[471]

In July 1942 there was a great deal of convoy activity. The two convoys were PQ-17, headed for Murmansk, and QP-13, the return voyage. A number of Soviet submarines operated in support. They included: D-3, K-21, K-22, SHCH-402 and 403. German opposition included surface ships and twelve U-boats. Among the German surface detachment were battleship *Tirpitz*, heavy cruiser *Adm. Hipper*, pocket battleship *Lutzow*, seven destroyers and two MTB. K-21 sighted them as they exited a fjord near Ingoy Island. Their track took them right towards K-21 and she found herself in the middle of the formation. About 1600 K-21 fired four torpedoes at *Tirpiz* at a range of 3,150 meters (3,500 yards) from her stern and her trainable tubes and then went deep. Sonar reported two explosions at 2 minutes and fifteen seconds. At 1709 K-21 reported the attack. She was credited with damaging *Tirpitz*, but German records did not support the claim.[472]

In August K-2 was lost off northern Norway, probably to mines. In September the UK suspended convoys to Murmansk. There was too little shipping available, with the invasion of North Africa in the offing, as well as too much German opposition. Convoys resumed in November. Some 25 U-boats as well as many aircraft made their journeys exceedingly hazardous. At this time Soviet submarines were mostly involved in mine laying. During mid-November to early December the K-class boats and L-20 and L-22 laid mines in Varanger Fjord, and off Kirkenes and Petsamo.[473]

1943

On New Year's Day L-20 sank German transport *Muansa* in Tana Fjord, and also laid mines. In late January German radio intercepts indicated the sortie of at least four Soviet submarines. Between late-January and mid-February Soviet subs sank four ships (8,640 GRT) and damaged two more (1,406 GRT).

During spring and summer of 1943 at least four Soviet subs were on patrol from Vardo to the North Cape area. Between March and the end of August the Soviets lost K-3, SHCH-422 and M-106. In return they sank six cargo ships (5,140 GRT). Mine laying continued as usual. SHCH-402 and 403 landed sabotage detachments on Arnoy Island. On 7 October K-1 went missing in the Kara Sea.[474]

The Germans reported some 64 Soviet submarine attacks during 1943, with 119 torpedoes fired. Six cargo ships and seven escorts were claimed (22,500 GRT). Two more (6,109 GRT) were lost to mines. Four more were damaged (18,491 GRT). However the Germans moved six million GRT during 1943 from Narvik to Petsamo. Soviet subs sank only about 7/10th of one percent.[475]

1944

In July submarine V-1 (x-HMS Sunfish) was enroute the USSR from Great Britain. A Coastal Command Liberator bomber encountered her outside the prescribed transit lanes for her journey home. When V-1 dove, the bomber crew assumed she was German and attacked. V-1 was lost. V-1 had been provided with visual signals to indicate her identity.[476]

On 23 and 28 August S-103 employed electric torpedoes for the first time.

On 21 September SHCH-402 was sunk by Soviet aircraft in a "friendly fire" incident in the Barents Sea.

In September Finland signed an armistice with the USSR. German forces then withdrew into northern Norway, relieving the pressure on Murmansk. The Lyugen Fjord became the new front line. On 11 October the Germans began to run evacuation convoys from Petsamo. Eight to nine Soviet subs were deployed from Vardo to North Cape.

The Soviets claimed sinking fifteen cargo ships. The Germans acknowledged the loss of a sub chaser (SC) to S-104 on 12 October, and another SC to V-4 on 20 October. They also lost transport *Lume* to S-104 on 12 October. This marked the end of operational activity for submarines of Northern Fleet.[477]

Black Sea Fleet Submarines

At war's start the Black Sea Fleet had two submarine brigades and 47 submarines. Besides the two brigades there was a separate training division. The older Holland boats (A-1 through A-5) were in 2nd Brigade. They were all based at Sevastopol in the Crimea.

There were no German U-boats in the Black Sea. Rumania, a German ally, had one submarine, which had been launched back in 1931. Germany subsequently sent six small submarines overland to the Black Sea, as did Italy. The German surface contingent was quite large; 25 mine sweepers, 16 MTB, 26 submarine chasers, and 50 landing craft.

As soon as the German attack began on 22 June, four SS of 1ˢᵗ Brigade took station off the Rumanian ports of Constanta, Mangalia and Varna, and later off the Bosporus. 2ⁿᵈ Brigade had two boats off the Danube Estuary and the Caucasus coastline.

Rumanian submarine *Delfinul* operated near the Crimean shore and Caucasus coast between 10 July and 13 December. In August M-33 attacked her off Constanta but missed. That same month SHCH-210 made two attacks on her off Varna, but both missed.[478]

As the German air-ground attack went deep into Russia, Soviet forces were forced to retreat. They evacuated Nikolayla, a main shipbuilding site in mid-August. Three Soviet submarines under construction had to be destroyed on the ways, as well as material for two more. Five more, in "fitting out" status were moved to Sevastopol and ports further east. After October the Soviets had to evacuate Odessa. Meanwhile Soviet submarines were laying mines in the Dnepr River estuary, trying to block German movement by sea.

During 1941 Soviet submarines conducted 101 patrols and eight were lost: 6 to Rumanian mines off Bulgaria, 1 to a Rumanian destroyer, and 1 to an accident.[479]

Sevastopol came under siege by the Germans on 31 October 1941. It finally fell on 4 July 1942. Soviet submarines were pressed into transport duties to carry supplies in and evacuate the wounded out. Twenty-three submarines were used, including two obsolete A—class boats. They hauled 2,300 tons of ammunition; 1,100 tons of food; and 574 tons of fuel. They took out 1,400 wounded. Five Soviet subs were lost; SHCH-212 to a gasoline explosion at Sevastopol; S-32 was bombed; SHCH-214 was lost to an Italian MTB, and SHCH-208 was mined. In addition A-1 was scuttled at Sevastopol in June 1942.

1942

The Germans laid mine lines along the west coast of the Black Sea and the south coast of Crimea, using 5,000 mines. Some 1,700 were A/S mines, and 2,795 were floating anti-sweep mines.

By mid-July there were 34 Soviet subs including 14 new construction boats. Twenty were operationally ready. They had been reorganized into a single brigade. They were based at ports along the Caucasus, which meant they had long transits to their patrol areas.[480]

For the remainder of 1942 M-class boats operated off the Crimea and the northwest ports of the Black Sea. Larger subs were used to interdict shipping between the Crimea and Rumania, and off the Rumanian and Bulgarian coasts, and off the Bosporus. L-class laid anchored mines off Sevastopol and the Rumanian and Bulgarian coasts. Submarines were also used on special missions, to support partisans in the Crimea.[481]

During 1942 Soviet submarines sank only 13 ships (12,000 GRT). Only six of those were supporting German operations in the Crimea. During the second half of the year three subs were lost to mines, and two to A/S attacks.[482]

1943

On 1 January 1943 the Black Sea submarine brigade had 29 SS: 18 operational and 11 in refit. There was the very beginning of wolf pack tactics, with three boats deploying to a patrol area as a group. There also was some coordination between Soviet submarines and Soviet aircraft, although the aircraft reports of ship targets were often late or inaccurate.

On 20 April S-33 torpedoed and sank Rumanian cargo ship *Suceava* (6,700 GRT), a fine trophy in any submarine patrol area. However, Soviet submarines were hampered by comint. German intercept stations plotted their transmissions and either halted shipping traffic or rerouted it around them. Another problem lay in the fact that many targets were small coastal vessels with shallow drafts. Torpedoes tended to run under their hulls. During the summer of 1943 proximity fuses were introduced and they began to get better results. One must assume the new fuses were magnetic.

A German antisubmarine unit was established during the second half of 1943, the 1ˢᵗ A/S Flotilla. They sank five Soviet submarines by the end of the year. 1943 closed out with only 18 operational submarines left. They had conducted 139 patrols, and laid 120 mines.[483]

1944

The Soviet submarine threat to German shipping in the Black Sea was effectively neutralized by German A/S measures involving surface craft and air craft. In January the Germans sank L-23 with the Black Sea Fleet Submarine Brigade Commander embarked.

From mid-April to mid-May the evacuation of Sevastopol took place. The loss of Stalingrad in February 1943 and the stalemate during a massive tank battle at Kursk in July 1943 marked the high water mark of the German invasion of the USSR. Afterwards they were on the defensive and being pushed westward by increasingly strong Soviet armies.

The Sevastopol evacuation involved 32,000 men. Kuban was also evacuated, with 200,000 men and 60,000 horses being moved by ship. There was little interference by the Soviet Navy. On 24 August 1944 Rumania surrendered, ending German naval operations in the Black Sea. The Submarine Brigade had 16 operational boats left.[484]

Pacific Fleet Submarines

Between 1941 and early August 1945 there was a Non-Aggression Pact in effect between the USSR and Japan. Therefore the Soviet Pacific Fleet had no operational assignments other than training. The Soviet Union declared war on Japan on 8 August 1945 in accordance with the agreement between the United States, Great Britain and the USSR made in February 1945 during the Yalta Conference.[485]

There were 78 submarines available in the Soviet Pacific Fleet on the day the war began. On 14 August Japan announced that it would surrender. From 16 to 18 August the Soviet conducted an amphibious assault on Shimushu Island, the northernmost of the Kurile Islands. Submarine L-8 operated in support.

On 22 August Soviet submarines L-12 and L-19 were on patrol off the northwest coast of Hokkaido. They attacked and sank two Japanese ships evacuating people from Sakhalin Island, with large loss of life. L-19 was lost, apparently to a mine, while attempting to transit eastward through LaPerouse Strait on 22 August.

Overall Evaluation of Soviet Submarine Effectiveness

The Soviet Submarine Service was unequaled in its determination and steadfastness and courage. Nevertheless it was not very effective in the two theaters of operation in which it might have done well.

The Baltic was largely a write-off because of the geography. That geography lent itself to a mining campaign by the Germans and the Finns that effectively locked Soviet submarines in to the Gulf of Finland. Even when the Finnish Armistice freed Soviet submarines to use the Finnish skerrries to bypass the mine fields, they still failed to score against German shipping evacuating over a million troops from the Eastern front

However the Northern Fleet was not in the same position and it was facing enemy forces that relied exclusively on sea transport for support. Despite the opportunity Northern Fleet submarines failed to sink very many German support ships.

Black Sea Fleet submarines were in a similar situation. They were ineffective during the largely at-sea evacuations of Kuban and Sevastopol.

Although the Soviet Navy started the war with the largest number of submarines of all the nations involved, they were largely ineffective and contributed little to Soviet successes.

Chapter Eight—American Submarines

The German U-boat campaign of WW II had a clear objective almost from the beginning—to wage an unrestricted submarine campaign to cut the British Isles off from their Dominions and colonies thus strangling them economically. Germany tried that before in 1917-1918 and almost succeeded. The WW I U-boat campaign was finally defeated by the convoy system. Admiral Doenitz had devised tactics to counter the convoy system. It involved surfaced attacks at night by massed U-boats, the wolf packs. Doenitz began and ended the war as the *fuehrer der Uboote*. His "system" finally failed as the allies developed new technologies to offset his tactical innovations.

The American submarine campaign against Japan lacked the same singular focus by one individual with one purpose. It is safe to say that on December 6, 1941 few in the United States Navy or the U. S. Government would have agreed with the idea that the U.S. Submarine Service should wage an unrestricted submarine campaign in the event of war with Japan.

However, on December 8, one day after Japan's air attack on Pearl Harbor, the order was issued by the Navy Department to *"wage unrestricted air and submarine war on the Empire of Japan"*. It took a while for American submarine flotillas to focus on their part of that goal. Part of the problem was the separation of American submarines geographically and by command structure. Another element was the need to support defensive naval operations opposing the advance of Japanese forces in the Western Pacific during December 1941 and most of 1942.

Atlantic

For the United States the Atlantic theater was basically a safe training ground for new construction submarines. After June 1942 the U-boat threat to east coast shipping had been largely defeated although U-boats continued to operate in the Caribbean Sea. Upon completion of their training U.S. subs transited south to the Panama Canal, and then west to Pearl Harbor. There were some defensive submarine patrols in the eastern Atlantic.

During the summer of 1942 Prime Minister Churchill asked President Roosevelt for assignment of U.S. submarines to participate in the Battle of the Atlantic. Admiral King was opposed but he was overruled by the President. Six new fleet boats (Squadron 50) were selected to operate from Scotland. Squadron 50 was assigned to support Operation TORCH, the allied landings in North Africa in November 1942, and then would return to its base in Scotland to conduct patrols in the Bay of Biscay.[486]

Two of the six submarines assigned had H.O.R. high speed light weight diesel engines, whereas other fleet boats had either GM or FM engines installed. There was a peculiar problem with the engine gears in the H.O.R. engines. The steel used had cooled too rapidly at the steel mill, causing "snowflakes", a cleavage of internal integrity in the steel. Therefore the gears were very prone to failure. One of the six, USS Gurnard (SS-254) with H.O.R. engines, had early problems and could not transit with the remainder of the squadron. She went directly to Roseneath.

The other five deployed to North Africa. Another H.O.R. boat, USS Gunnel (SS-253), commanded by "Junior" McCain, lost the use of all four main engines and limped into Scotland on an auxiliary "dinky" engine.[487]

A "fix" for the defective gears was developed, but the Submarine Service developed a deep suspicion of H.O.R. engines.[488] No more were ever installed in U.S. submarines. Squadron 50 submarines, including two more H.O.R. engined boats, went on to conduct 27 patrols in European waters. They had no confirmed sinking's. Several boats including USS Herring (SS-233) and USS Shad (SS-235) reported torpedoes either duding or prematurely exploding[489]. In mid-1943 Squadron 50 redeployed to the Pacific.

In February 1943 Admiral King ordered that all H.O.R. engines be replaced (20 submarines). The last replacement took place in autumn 1944.[490]

Pacific

The real story about U.S. submarines in World War II began and ended in the Far East. It started in early 1941 in South East Asia with the U.S. Asiatic Fleet, and ended with a number of U.S. submarines present in Tokyo Bay in September 1945 as Japan's surrender was accepted aboard the battleship USS Missouri (BB-63) to mark the end of World War II.

U.S. submarines succeeded in isolating mainland Japan from her conquests in South East Asia (SEAsia) and thus her sources of oil and other vital raw materials. On December 7, 1941 there were a total of 56 U.S. submarines in the Pacific Ocean, split almost equally between the Asiatic Fleet in the Far East (29 SS) and the U.S. Pacific Fleet based at Pearl Harbor (27 SS). They were supported by the Submarine Base at Pearl Harbor, and by six submarine tenders (AS) or depot ships. Three AS were in the Philippines, two were on the west coast of the United States and one was in Hawaii.[491]

Asiatic Fleet Submarines

The U.S. Asiatic Fleet was small, and it was clear that it would not be able to withstand an all out attack by the Imperial Japanese Navy (IJN) in the event of war. Its traditional task was to conduct a fighting retreat, hopefully enabling U.S. Army forces to hold on in the Philippines until naval forces could push west from Pearl Harbor to relieve the defenders with reinforcements.

The Asiatic Fleet consisted of only three cruisers, thirteen destroyers, twenty-nine submarines, and a number of auxiliary ships.[492] The principal naval aviation assets in the Asiatic Fleet were several patrol squadrons, flying PBY Catalina flying boats. No aircraft carriers were assigned. Its main base was Manila Bay. It had been "beefed up" with additional submarines after General MacArthur's scheme for a defense of the Philippines was accepted by the Army in early 1941. In theory B-17s, operating from Philippine airfields, and a large number of U.S. submarines, would be able to deter a Japanese attack. If that failed, their common task was to sink the Japanese invasion fleet. Five of the submarines assigned were older S-class submarines dating from the early 1920s. The remainder consisted of modern "fleet boats".

In January 1941 U.S. Navy planners visited Manila and announced plans to reinforce the U.S. Asiatic Fleet, commanded by Admiral Thomas Hart. The prospective additions included an aircraft carrier, a cruiser division and a destroyer squadron. Admiral Hart was to command combined U.S. and British forces in the Far East. A month later the plan changed. There would be no surface ship reinforcements for Hart's fleet, but the United Kingdom would heavily reinforce their Eastern Fleet with battleships and cruisers. A Royal Navy admiral would command the combined forces. However, no formal combined planning actually took place.[493]

It was clear to senior U.S. Navy and Army officers that hostilities with Japan were likely. The official U.S. posture towards Japan and its war with China was to oppose Japan's activities, and to gradually attempt to reduce Japan's war making capabilities by throttling back on any war materials which Japan imported from the United States. The political objective was to induce Japan to withdraw from China. This laudable diplomatic goal was not adequately supported by U.S. military power in the Far East.

The Asiatic Fleet's submarine component consisted of 23 modern fleet submarines, and 6 S-boats. They were supported by submarine tenders, USS Canopus (AS-9) and USS Holland (AS-3), and a submarine rescue ship USS Pigeon (ASR-6). Merchant ship SS Otus was in the process of being converted to submarine tender capability.[494]

In the spring of 1941 Admiral Hart moved all U.S. naval forces from Manila to the southern Philippines, fearing a Japanese attack. Later Hart returned his forces to Manila Bay as fears subsided.

In June 1941 a new war plan emerged. General MacArthur, commander of U.S. Army and Philippine Army forces, came up with the idea that with 100 fighters, 100 B-17 bombers, and six months to train some 200,000 Filipino soldiers plus assistance from Hart's Asiatic Fleet with additional submarines—he could hold the Philippines against a Japanese amphibious assault until the relieving U.S. Pacific Fleet arrived in accordance with existing war plans.

Earlier, U.S. Army war planners had written off the Philippines, considering that it would not be possible to hold them in the event of war with Japan. However Secretary of War Stimson and Army Chief of Staff Marshall bought in to charismatic MacArthur's half baked scheme. Instead of abandoning the Philippines, they would be successfully defended by the new strategic bomber force of B-17s.

The key to this illusion was the demonstration by the *Luftwaffe* in the eastern Mediterranean Sea in early 1941 during the German airborne invasion of Crete that land-based aircraft could sink or inflict serious damage to warships. What Stimson and Marshall apparently did not comprehend was that the *Luftwaffe* had done most of the damage using Stuka dive bombers, not high altitude level bombers like the B-17. It looked as if General Billy Mitchell's remarkable demonstration of the sinking of a surrendered German battleship by U.S. Army Air Service bombers in 1921 would provide the model for the defense of the Philippines.

General Mitchell's demonstration was remarkable for a number of reasons. The bombs were dropped from low altitudes (about 1,000 feet), the targets were anchored and undefended by anti aircraft guns or fighters, and there were no crews on board the hulk to carry out damage control procedures or fire fighting.

Defense of the Philippines

General MacArthur's plan for the strategic defense of the Philippine Islands fell apart at the outset. Deterrence failed. MacArthur had forbidden pre-war reconnaissance flights over Japanese air bases on Taiwan (Formosa as it was then titled) by Army Air Force planes. On the Navy side Admiral Hart had authorized patrol plane reconnaissance over those same Japanese air fields.[495] From time to time Patrol Squadron Ten's PBYs overflew the fields, ducking into cloud cover when they were discovered and pursuit planes sent after them. In the days before radar installations, cloud cover was an adequate protection.

On December 8th those fields were "socked in" by weather and Japanese air commanders were concerned that their planes would be caught on the ground by B-17s from Clark Air Base. They need not have worried. Despite early warning about the Pearl Harbor attack, General MacArthur's air commander, Brigadier General Brereton, was unable to reach MacArthur to get permission to send an aerial reconnaissance mission to Taiwan as a prelude to a bombing attack. There is suspicion that MacArthur had some sort of breakdown on learning of the opening of hostilities. At any rate, about half the B-17s in the Philippines were sitting on the tarmac at Clark Air Base when the Japanese attacked around noon. They were destroyed, as were many of the AAF P-35 and P-40 fighter planes upon which a successful air defense of the islands depended.

Another part of the defense of the Philippines depended upon the large number of modern "fleet class" submarines assigned to the Asiatic Fleet. They were normally based at Manila, supported by submarine tender Canopus.

Asiatic Fleet submarines had not had any realistic training. There were no pre-war practice patrols such as were conducted by the British 4th submarine flotilla as described in Chapter Three. There were no long submerged periods to accustom their crews to possible wartime routines. When they went to sea to train, the Commodore, Captain Wilkes, was embarked in the submarine tender and divisions of submarines were maneuvered by flag hoist signals as if they were destroyers. Maintenance and upkeep were poor, and there were many material casualties. Those boats equipped with H.O.R. engines were in particularly bad condition. Their secure basing in Manila Bay was entirely dependent upon U.S. air superiority, which was the responsibility of the Army Air Forces. Although army and navy commanders received a "war warning" message on 27 November 1941, no submarines were sent to patrol stations.[496]

In routine training such heavy emphasis was placed upon not being detected that many commanding officers forwent periscope observations at close ranges and used passive sonar with approaches at a depth of 100 feet.[497]

On 10 December Japanese aircraft heavily bombed the Manila area and the naval repair faculties and support activities at Cavite Naval Station. They destroyed one fleet submarine which was in dock, USS Sea Lion (SS-195), and 233 Mk 14 submarine torpedoes.[498] The loss of torpedoes was very serious. The fleet boats had to depart Manila Bay. Thereafter they operated from Canopus at Corregidor.

On 14 December USS Seawolf (SS-197) fired four torpedoes at Japanese transports which were unloading troops at Aparri on the east coast of Luzon Island. Three torpedoes missed but one hit a transport. Unfortunately it was a "dud", and failed to explode.[499] On 15 December USS Swordfish (SS-193) sank *Atsutasan Maru* (8,663 tons) off Hainan Island.

A Japanese amphibious landing in Lingayan Gulf was predictable but only USS Stingray (SS-186) was off the Gulf on 21 December when the Japanese landing took place. After the fact Wilkes rushed several submarines there but it was too late to seriously interfere with the landing. The road to Manila was now open.[500]

On 22 December USS S-38 sank a merchant ship in Lingayan Gulf.[501] On 23 December USS Seal (SS-183) sank another. On 24 December the Asiatic Fleet Submarine Force commander moved to Corregidor. Submarine tender Canopus moved to Marivales on the Bataan Peninsula opposite Corregidor on 23 December. On 26 December Admiral Hart departed for Surabaya, Netherlands East Indies (NEI) aboard USS Shark (SS-174). On 31 December Capt. Wilkes decided to move his headquarters to Surabaya also. Submarine tender Holland and Internal Combustion Repair ship USS Otus (ARG-20) were sent to Darwin, Australia. Canopus stayed behind to tend the diminishing number of boats in the Philippines.

On 23 December the Japanese landing at Balikpapan on the east coast of the NEI island of Borneo began. USS Sturgeon (SS-187) fired at an amphibious convoy and reported hits. However they may have been premature detonations.[502]

The submarine component of the Asiatic Fleet split up. One part went to the Dutch naval port of Surabaya on the island of Java in the NEI, to operate in defense of the Malay Barrier. They joined some 15 RNN submarines in that task. Surabaya was first attacked by air on 2 February 1942. The air defenses of the NEI were inadequate to protect the port from bombing raids.[503] The other part of the Asiatic Fleet submarine component went to Darwin, Australia with USS Holland and Otus.

On 31 December Manila was evacuated. By the end of December the Asiatic Fleet submarine component had conducted 45 attacks and expended 96 torpedoes. Capt. Wilkes credited his force with 11 ships sunk including two destroyers. IJN records support only three ships sunk, all merchant ships.[504]

On 4 and 5 February USS Seadragon (SS-194) successfully evacuated Cast personnel from Corregidor. Station Cast was the Far East Naval Security Group station which targeted Japanese communications. Admiral King, the U.S. Chief of Naval Operations, specifically directed that they be taken out of harm's way lest they be captured and divulge comint secrets.[505]

On 6 May 1942 Corregidor was captured. USS Canopus and Pigeon were lost there.

Defense of the Malay Barrier

U.S. submarines left the Philippines and fell back to Surabaya, a Dutch naval port on the east end of Java, and patrolled from there. During January they were off Davao in the southern Philippines, the Mollucca Passage, the Makassar Strait and Camrahn Bay, Indo-China. Japanese records confirm that they sank three ships. During the two month period following the initial Japanese attacks, Asiatic Fleet submarines conducted 28 war patrols, and claimed six freighters. USS Shark (SS-174) and S-36 were lost, Shark to enemy action and S-36 in a grounding.[506] During the January-February 1942 period some 22 U.S. submarines were deployed in the vicinity of the Celebes. They accomplished very little.[507]

USS Holland and USS Otus escaped the very damaging air raid at Darwin that took place on 12 February 1942. By that time they were at Tjilatjap, on the south coast of Java in the NEI, servicing U.S. subs engaged in opposing Japanese naval forces.

On 8 February S-37 put a torpedo into IJN DD *Natsushio's* forward engine room. She sank 9 February while under tow. DD *Suzukase*, part of the Makassar Occupation Force, was damaged by a submarine torpedo on 8 February.[508]

Admiral Hart requested to be relieved of the ABDA naval command. He was replaced by Dutch Admiral Helfrich who presided over the final futile surface battles of the Java Sea before the Japanese conquered the NEI. Admiral Hart returned to Washington and joined the General Board of the Navy. From that position he continued to urge the building of small submarines similar to the S-class, and spoke out against the improvements in submarine habitability that characterized the new fleet boats. Fortunately Admiral King, a singularly strong minded individual, overrode Adm. Hart's recommendations and the fleet boats, with extremely long range and superior habitability and weapons capability continued to be built.[509]

Fall back to Australia

On 20 February USS Holland and destroyer tender USS Black Hawk (AD-9) and three subs departed Tjilatjap for Exmouth Gulf in northwestern Australia. Radm. Powell was embarked in Holland. On 28

February he inspected the Exmouth Gulf area and deemed it unsuitable as a submarine base. Holland then sailed on to Fremantle, escorted by USS Snapper (SS-185) and USS Sculpin (SS-191). Black Hawk and USS Stingray (SS-186) stayed at Exmouth Gulf temporarily to service other U.S. subs enroute Fremantle.

USS Sargo (SS-188) had a unique and memorable "welcome to Australia, mate" moment when she was bombed by a Royal Australian Air Force (RAAF) Hudson bomber. The bombs wrecked both periscopes and damaged her conning tower.[510] The irony that the bombs fell from an American-built aircraft, was probably lost on the Sargo crew. Such "blue on blue" encounters were rare but they could be deadly. In this case there were no personnel casualties.

Southwest Pacific Command (Commander Submarines, Southwest Pacific)

American submarines in Australia were based in two widely separated locations: Fremantle on the southwest coast of Western Australia; and Brisbane in Queensland in northeastern Australia. Operational control started, at the top, with General MacArthur, Commander Allied Forces Southwest Pacific at Melbourne. His naval commander, Vadm. Leary also at Melbourne, had two subordinates for submarine operations based respectively at Fremantle and Brisbane. Each reported separately to the Allied Forces Southwest Pacific's naval commander. In residence at Melbourne were the 75 men of Station Cast, rescued in two submarine loads from Corregidor.[511]

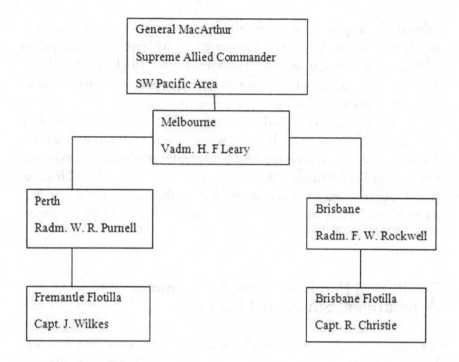

Brisbane Flotilla

American submarines based at Brisbane, Queensland, in eastern Australia, usually operated to the northeast near New Guinea and over in the Solomon Islands.

Admiral King had directed the transfer of S-boats from the Atlantic to the Southwest Pacific, perhaps influenced by Admiral Hart who was an enthusiast for small submarines. Capt. Ralph Christie, a torpedo specialist, was designated "in charge". On arrival at Panama he decided that the "20" series S-boats were not up to the long voyage. S-21, S-22, S-24, S-25 and S-29 were then loaned to the Royal Navy for use in training thus releasing more modern RN subs for combat duty. S-21, S-22, S-24 and S-29 were returned after the war. S-25 was recommissioned as HMS P-551, then loaned to Polish forces as *Jastrzab*. Unfortunately she was sunk by allied forces on 2 May 1942 off Norway. S-26 was lost in a collision off Panama while conducting training.

At the last minute Admiral King decided that most of the "30" series S-boats should go to the Aleutians and operate there under ComSubPac. They too would suffer from the weather but it was the extreme cold that they had to endure. That left six "40" series S-boats. USS Griffin (AS-13) carried Mk 14 torpedoes for the Fremantle based fleet boats and Mk 10 torpedoes for the older S-boats.[512]

Captain Ralph Christie arrived at Brisbane on 14 April in submarine tender Griffin with six S-boats. Five more joined his flotilla there from Fremantle. Four were sent off very shortly to support U.S. forces in the Coral Sea.

During the Coral Sea Battle in May 1942 four S-boats from the Brisbane flotilla (S-38, S-42, S-44 and S-47) made a total of five attacks on the periphery of the main battle area. The battle involved opposing carrier battle forces of the IJN and USN. S-42 sank Japanese minelayer *Okinoshima* off the south coast of New Britain Island.[513]

Six made patrols in May and five in June. Their patrol areas included Rabaul, Kavieng, Bougainville, Tulagi and other points in the Solomon Islands. The internal daytime temperatures in the submerged S-boats ranged from 105-120 degrees F. None had air conditioning except S-44, which had purchased a commercial set with private funds and which had been installed by her crew.

The S-boats were laid down from 1921 to 1924, were of riveted hull construction, and had an operational depth of 200 feet. They had four TT forward and fired the older Mk 10 torpedo which fortunately did not demonstrate the problems associated with the newer Mk 14 torpedo.

During her second patrol north of Guadalcanal S-44 sank converted gunboat *Keijo Maru* (2,262 tons). During her third patrol S-44 spotted four cruisers in line returning from the Battle of Savo Island. It was early morning of 10 August. The CO selected the last cruiser in line and fired four torpedoes at a range of 700 yards. Three hit and heavy cruiser *Kako* sank.[514]

Two days earlier S-38 spotted a Japanese troop convoy enroute Guadalcanal. There were six troop transports on their way to reinforce the Japanese garrison on Guadalcanal after the Marine landing. She made a submerged approach and sank *Meijo Maru* (5,600 tons).[515] The convoy turned around and headed back to port, giving the Marines a welcome break.

U.S. submarines from the ComSubPac larder patrolled near the IJN naval base at Truk. It was the northern point of a track to Rabaul and then south to Guadalcanal. Submarines sank 23 supply ships during the latter half of 1942.[516] Guadalcanal earned the bitter nickname "Starvation

Island" among Japanese troops. Several thousand literally starved to death there because of inability to resupply them in the face of American air and submarine attacks.

Christie convinced Admiral Leary that the S-boats were not adequate for the demands of the Solomons campaign. Leary directed that tender Griffin and the S-boats prepare to depart for the U.S. He ordered CSS2 (USS Holland) under Capt. James Fife to move from Fremantle to Brisbane. About this time Vadm. Leary was replaced by Radm. Carpender. This left Radm. Lockwood at Fremantle with only CSS 6 (Pelias) and eight SS. Christie was given command of CSS 2. About this time General MacArthur moved his headquarters to Port Moresby in Papua New Guinea. Radm. Carpender remained in Brisbane but sent Capt. Fife forward as a personal representative on MacArthur's staff. There were now a mix of fleet boats and S-boats patrolling the Solomons. As each new fleet boat showed up, an older S-boat was sent back to Pearl Harbor and the states.

Back in the United States in November 1942 torpedo production at Newport, Rhode Island was stagnating. Chief BuOrd asked that Capt. Christie be returned to serve as Inspector of Ordnance in Charge at Newport. Radm. Carpender picked James Fife to take over CSS 2. That took place on 22 December 1942.[517]

1943

In March 1943 a U.S. sub evacuated allied coast watchers and residual Australian Army personnel from Bougainville.[518]

During spring 1943, with Japanese code recovery complete, information was available about Japanese convoy routes to reinforce New Guinea and the Solomons area. A main convoy route was from Palau southeast to the equator, then to longitude 150 E, then south to Kavieng (on the north tip of New Ireland), then south to Rabaul. Another heavily traveled route was from the main IJN base at Truk to Kavieng. At the equator, escorts from Palau or Truk handed over their charges to escorts from Kavieng or Rabaul. Commodore Fife selected Lat 0/Longitude 150 east as a likely ambush position for submarines operating from Brisbane. He coordinated some pairs of subs, the first cut at wolf pack operations in the SW Pacific. There were no communications between the pair of submarines, with Fife playing "Doenitz" and moving them around based on comint data.[519]

During the first five months of 1943 Brisbane-based boats made 25 war patrols. They sank 18 ships. Four fleet boats were lost.[520]

From June through December 1943 Fife at Brisbane sent out 33 patrols. They sank 29 confirmed ships. In late November there was a cooperative attack on a five ship convoy by USS Gato (SS-212), USS Peto (SS-265), USS Ray (SS-271) and USS Raton (SS-270). They sank four ships. It was not an organized wolf pack, and there were no communications between the submarines. Neither Fife nor Christie organized any wolf packs.[521]

In October 1943 Fife established an advance base at Milne Bay, New Guinea with sub tender Fulton there to provide support. He also set up a refueling site at Tulagi Island, across "Iron Bottom" Sound from Guadalcanal, now safely in U.S. hands since the previous January.[522] Additional refueling points were established at Langemark Bay, Seeadler Harbor, Manus Island and Milne Bay.[523]

Fremantle Flotilla

From 1942 to 1945 the port of Freemantle, Western Australia was one of the largest and busiest submarine bases in the world. Over 170 allied submarines were based at Fremantle at various times. They made some 416 war patrols (USN—353, RN and RNN—63). The flotilla included American, Dutch, and British submarines. All were under American operational control.[524] However their missions also reflected national interests. The few Dutch submarines concentrated on inserting agents into the Japanese-occupied Netherlands East Indies, and extracting them. British submarines did the same for Malaya and North Borneo. American submarines also were involved in agent operations but their target was usually the Philippine Islands. American subs were the first entries into Freemantle, closely followed by three Dutch subs. As discussed in more detail in Chapter Four dealing with the Dutch Submarine Service, they were not in very good material condition. One was transferred to the RAN for use as a target for ASW training. Another was decommissioned as unfit for operational service. The third went on to Sydney for refit and then an operational role. Fairly late in the war, in September 1944, a flotilla of British submarines from Ceylon joined their allies in Fremantle.

American military forces in the Central Pacific came under Admiral Nimitz for operational control, and those in the Southwest Pacific were under General MacArthur. Their common superior was President

215

Roosevelt, since the Army and Navy could not agree upon an acceptable joint commander for the Pacific Theater. The president's direction came down through the Joint Chiefs of Staff organization.

In the case of submarine operations in the Pacific, the two sub-theaters operated independently, although with a good level of coordination. MacArthur was intent upon fulfilling his promise to return to the Philippines. Consequently they figured prominently in his axis of attack. There were a growing number of guerrilla organizations in the Philippines. That brought tasking from MacArthur to the two Australian-based submarine flotillas to conduct agent and guerilla resupply operations centered on the Philippines.

The two Australia-based flotillas had separate areas of operations, based on geography. The western Fremantle flotilla usually operated in the seas around the NEI and the South China Sea and in and around the Philippine Islands. The eastern Brisbane-based flotilla tended to operate to the northeast over in the New Guinea—Solomons area.

The first American subs arrived at Fremantle in company with USS Holland on 3 March 1942 after having been driven out of the NEI by overwhelmingly superior Japanese naval and air forces. Arrangements were made to take over sixteen warehouses and other buildings at dockside in Fremantle to set up repair shops, supply depots, and berthing spaces.[525]

On 6 March Commander U.S. Forces Southwest Pacific formally notified Australian government authorities of the intent to operate allied submarines from Fremantle. On 10 March, USS Otus, only partially converted into a submarine tender, arrived at Freemantle. By that time there were 12 U. S. subs there. On 15 March Holland and five SS arrived at Albany, in a move to disperse submarines. By 31 March some 25 U.S. subs were at Fremantle. They began patrols that day. All S-boats were sent around to Brisbane.

Captain John Wilkes was the first U.S. commander of the Fremantle flotilla. He set up a headquarters ashore in Fremantle with Otus moored nearby servicing submarines. Capt. Fife went south with USS Holland and a number of submarines to Albany, some 250 miles south of Fremantle, in a move to disperse submarines lest they all be wiped out in a Japanese air strike.

Wilkes and Fife put together a report on the U.S. submarine campaign to date. It highlighted torpedo problems, the fact that Japanese depth charges were too small and being set too shallow to inflict serious damage on our submarines, and H.O.R. engine problems

The report indicated that during 75 war patrols, 25 Asiatic Fleet submarines had made 146 attacks and fired 300 torpedoes. They claimed 36 ships sunk, however post-war Japanese records indicated that the score was only ten ships lost.

In response to this report, Admiral King directed that U.S. subs continue to operate from Australia. He assigned Wilkes an area of operations defined by Lat 10 S to 20 N, and Longitude 100 E to 130 E. This gave Fremantle based submarines almost three million square miles of ocean in which to operate. The northern latitude line bisected the Luzon Strait.[526]

Blair notes, in his splendid book about U.S. submarine operations, *Silent Victory*, that the Luzon Straits was a natural choke point through which all Japanese shipping from SEAsia to the home islands had to pass. Therefore he argues that submarines should have been concentrated there early in the war, to interdict Japanese shipping. He also argues that most of the fleet boats should have been concentrated at Pearl Harbor, under ComSubPac opcon, to more efficiently attack Japanese shipping. It is hard to disagree with Blair's theory.

Much later that course of action did come to pass. ComSubPac finally focused on wolf pack operations in the Luzon Straits areas and few Japanese convoys escaped unscathed. After a while, a long while, there was a supposed saying among Japanese Army personnel in Singapore that you could walk all the way from Singapore to Japan on the tops of American submarine periscopes and not get your feet wet. While not literally true it conveyed the menace of such a voyage.

On 15 March submarine tender Holland and a number of U.S. subs moved south to Albany as a dispersal measure to limit losses in the event of a Japanese carrier strike at Fremantle.[527] In mid-February a very damaging IJN carrier strike had hit Darwin and sunk a number of ships. By that time allied commanders had a healthy respect for Japanese naval airpower. Holland was replaced at Albany by USS Pelias (AS-14) in July 1942. There were 31 submarines in Albany, moored at Albany Jetty and the Quarantine Station. Later as fears of a Japanese raid faded, they moved back to Fremantle along with their tender. In March 1944 there was a temporary scare of an IJN air raid, and Pelias and Otus briefly departed for Albany until the scare subsided.[528]

Dutch submarine K-XII transited to Fremantle in early 1942. She then went to Melbourne, and later Sydney for maintenance work and dry docking. On 18 August 1942 she received orders to take an agent party to Java for insertion. She picked the group up at Cairn, then topped off fuel at Darwin, and transited to Java remaining submerged by day. She successfully inserted the party, and then sailed to Exmouth Gulf for fuel and on to Fremantle, arriving 23 September. This was just one of a series of special operations conducted by Dutch submarines during the war. In mid-November she embarked on more special operations, TIGER I and TIGER II, each name denoting a special landing party for insertion into Java. The round trip took about a month.

K-IX was not considered in good enough shape to undertake war patrols. She was transferred to the Royal Australian Navy for use in an ASW training role. K-VIII was in even worse material condition and she was decommissioned in May 1942.

By 31 March some 25 U.S. submarines reached Fremantle, and war patrols from Fremantle began very shortly. By the end of the year some 17, 513 tons of shipping had been sunk by Fremantle-based submarines. It was not a large score but it was a beginning. S-class boats, older, shorter range, and without air conditioning, were transferred to Brisbane.

In April 1942 USS Seawolf torpedoed IJN cruiser *Naka* off Christmas Island, south of the NEI. *Naka* had to be towed to Singapore for repairs.[529]

Capt. Wilkes was relieved as the Fremantle Flotilla commander in May 1942 by Radm. Charles Lockwood.[530] From May through August 1942 some 28 patrols originated at Fremantle. They sank 17 ships. The boats topped off fuel at Exmouth Gulf on the way north. There were no special efforts to target oil exports from the NEI to Japan. No patrols from Fremantle reached as far north as the Luzon Straits.[531]

Not long after Radm. Lockwood reached Fremantle and took command, USS Skipjack (SS-184) arrived back from a 50 day patrol off Cam Ranh Bay in French Indo-China. The CO submitted a patrol report stating that there were strong indications that the Mk 14 torpedo was running much deeper than set. Lockwood queried BuOrd by message. BuOrd replied, blaming misses on the COs and their fire control parties for firing with bad solutions.

While S-boats carried the older Mk 10 torpedo, the fleet boats all carried the new Mk 14 torpedo. It had entered service in 1938 and was a two speed torpedo. It had a range of 4500 yards at 46 knots, and 9000 yards at 31 knots. It also had two exploders. The first, designated Mk V, was purely a contact exploder that would operate to detonate the main explosive charge when the torpedo nose struck a target ship's hull. The second exploder, a Mk VI, was a magnetic influence exploder, which would operate to fire the main charge when passing under the hull of the target. If all went well the explosion and the gas bubble it generated would serve to break the keel of the enemy ship. The top secret Mk VI exploder was held in reserve ashore until the war started. Few commanding officers, torpedo officers and torpedo men's mates knew anything about the new device because of the secrecy surrounding it.[532]

Rather than accepting the Bureau's unfounded conclusion and letting the matter rest there, Lockwood directed that Capt. Fife at Albany run a series of torpedo trials using the remaining USS Skipjack torpedoes to establish their actual running depth. The tests began on 20 June 1942. By this time some 800 warshot torpedoes had been fired at Japanese ships with poor results.

Fife obtained a fisherman's net and moored it in Frenchman's Bay. The first torpedo fired was set for 10 feet running depth and fired at a range of 850 yards. The exercise head depth recorder showed that the torpedo ran at 25 feet, 15 feet deeper than set. The hole in the net confirmed that the torpedo ran at 25 feet. The following day two more torpedoes were fired at 700 yards. The first one, set at 10 feet, cut the net at 18 feet. The second set at 0 feet, cut the net at 18 feet. The data collected indicated that the Mk 14 torpedoes tested were running at least 11 feet deeper than set. Lockwood sent the results to BuOrd, which questioned the details of the trials, incidentally trials that BuOrd had never run in peacetime.

Lockwood told BuOrd that he would make the recommended trim adjustments and re-run torpedo trials, but he also requested that BuOrd have the Torpedo Station at Newport make its own tests and report the results.

On 18 July USS Saury (SS-189) fired three more torpedoes at ranges from 850 to 900 yards with depth set for 10 feet. They punched holes in the net at 21 feet.

About this time Admiral King got into action and put pressure on BuOrd. On 1 August Newport reported that its test firings indicated that the Mk 14 torpedo was running 10 feet deeper than set.[533]

On the Japanese side of wartime life there was ample proof that U.S. torpedoes were defective. More than one Japanese merchant ship arrived at its next port with an unexploded torpedo sticking in its hull plates. During the Guadalcanal campaign of late 1942 some twelve ships (87,000 tons) were hit by dud torpedoes. In July 1943 eight merchant ships (75,000 tons) reported dud hits.[534]

In January 1943, ComSubPac, Radm. English, died in an aircraft accident while flying from Pearl Harbor to the San Francisco area to inspect submarine facilities. Admiral King directed the Chief of Naval Personnel to order Radm. Charles Lockwood in as English's replacement. That in turn led to Capt. Christie taking command at Fremantle.

In January 1943 a very important conference was held at Casablanca in North Africa. Churchill and Roosevelt talked about European and Pacific strategies. There was no specific decision about a Pacific strategy, leaving somewhat vague any decision on the U.S. Navy's Central Pacific drive against MacArthur's "return to the Philippines" emphasis. What was not emphasized in any way shape or manner was a strategic submarine campaign to interdict Japan's commerce. Nor was any high level attention directed towards choking off the Japanese oil supply from the NEI and Borneo.[535] The Pacific submarine forces' commanders were left without any overall direction that might have focused them on two vital areas of activity.

In February 1943 TIGER III took place. From April to May 1943 K-XII carried out more special operations, TIGER IV and TIGER V. After return from that mission she was decommissioned because of her poor material condition.

During the period January through July 1943 Fremantle sent out 22 war patrols, an average of three per month. They had 23 confirmed sinking's. Nine patrols (41%) sank no ships. Two fleet boats were lost.[536] In February USS Gudgeon (SS-211) retrieved a small Australian force from the island of Timor.[537]

During summer 1943 the combined toll of submarines from Pearl Harbor, Brisbane and Fremantle reached an average of 100,000 tons of Japanese shipping per month. That represented some 70 submarines operating from the three bases. In response the IJN general staff requested 360 escorts for convoy protection. Only 40 were authorized. Planning began for a Central Convoy Escort Command.[538]

During the second half of 1943, newly promoted Radm. Christie at Fremantle received direction to concentrate on interdicting Japanese tankers moving oil from Borneo and Sumatra to the major naval base at Truk. U.S. code breakers were focused on tanker traffic. However tankers were not easy to sink. They had multiple compartments, making it easier for them to absorb torpedo hits. On the minus side, their cargo from Tarakan and Balikpapan was pure enough that it was very volatile, less so than refined gasoline but more so than ordinary crude oil, and thus fairly easy to set on fire.[539]

At the end of 1943 Vadm. Thomas Kinkaid relieved Vadm. Carpender as Commander 7th Fleet, and as MacArthur's naval component commander. Kinkaid, under pressure from Admiral King and Admiral Nimitz, then directed Radm. Christie to deactivate all Mk VI magnetic exploder devices used in the Mk 14 torpedo.[540] Christie did so, very grudgingly.

1944

On 1 January 1944 there were 16 submarines based in Western Australia. Ten were on patrol, and the remaining six were in refit at Fremantle. In early 1944 Radm. Christie changed target priorities to make tankers number one priority over IJN warships.[541] The tanker slaughter was about to begin.

That spring most submarines at Brisbane were transferred back to ComSubPac or transferred west to Fremantle. Capt. Wilkes was moved to OpNav in Washington to join Adm. King's planning staff. Capt. John Haines was placed in command of submarine operations from Brisbane-Milne Bay-Manus Harbor.[542]

On 10 August 1944 HMS Porpoise arrived at Fremantle, the first British submarine to join the allied ranks there. RN submarines and USN submarines conducted a number of special operations, landing, extracting, and resupplying agents and guerillas in North Borneo and the Philippines. Dutch submarines did the same for the NEI. The extraction operations were especially hazardous. If the agents were captured they would invariably be tortured to try to obtain information about how they got there and what were the arrangements for extraction. Thus a submarine had to approach an extraction rendezvous with extreme caution being alert for any signs of Japanese forces waiting in ambush.

On 28 August USS Orion departed Fremantle for Brisbane, with USS Euryale (AS-22) taking her post.

In September 1944 Radm. Christie sent USS Orion from Fremantle to *Mios Woendi*, a small island on the eastern end of Biak. That location served as an advance base for the Fremantle Flotilla. It was only about 1,000 nm from Saipan, where ComSubPac set up an advance base. The locations facilitated the interchange of fleet submarines between the two commands.

On 4 September 1944 HMS Maidstone, a British submarine depot ship, arrived at Fremantle, followed by the UK's 8th Submarine Flotilla with ten RN and RNN subs that had been released from the Mediterranean theater.

On 11 September HMS Porpoise departed for Operation RIMAU. RIMAU involved a small force of commandos, using semi-submersible motorized canoes to attack Japanese shipping in Singapore with limpet mines. The operation was abortive and thirteen men died during the attack or shortly thereafter. Ten were captured. They were tried by a Japanese court martial for espionage on 3 July, and beheaded on 7 Jul 1945.

On 6 October 1944 U-168 was enroute Surabaya. During that morning she was torpedoed and sunk by Dutch submarine *Zwaardvisch*. U-168 was enroute from France to Japan with technical information, radar, and plans for a new type submarine. U-168 settled to the bottom in about 150 feet of water. Twenty-eight of her crew managed to escape.[543] *Zwaardvisch* was part of RN Submarine Flotilla 8, based at Fremantle under operational control of Radm. Christie, USN. Eight days later *Zwaardvisch* sank IJN minelayer *Itsukshima*.

On 20 November 1944 USS Griffin (AS-13) departed Fremantle. Her billet was filled by USS Anthedon (AS-24).

That month Radm. Christie was replaced at Fremantle by newly promoted Radm. Fife. Christie's relief may have been as a result of Adm. Kincaid's annoyance at some of Christie's actions.[544]

On 18 December HMS Sea Rover had a collision with HMS Bunbury off Rotnest. This incident points out the fact that the hazards faced by submariners at sea did not all stem from enemy action. Storms, groundings, and collisions, all were intermittent dangers for seamen, whether on the surface or submerged.

On 31 December 1944 there were some 50 submarines at Fremantle.

1945

Fife in Fremantle, was focusing his patrols against the few IJN men-of-war left in southern waters. Two of these were carrier-battleships *Ise* and *Hyuga*, both at Singapore. On February 11th they sailed for home waters, each carrying thousands of drums of precious oil aboard. HMS Tantalus, off Singapore on patrol sighted them and sent off a contact report after Japanese aircraft prevented an attack. Fife alerted his many submarines in the South China Sea, some fourteen stretching from Indo-China to Hainan Island, to the intended track of *Ise* and *Hyuga*. All were unsuccessful for various reasons although some torpedoes were fired. After getting into ComSubPac's domain, they also eluded another twelve of Lockwood's boats, reaching home waters successfully.

On 11 April 1945 HMS Adamant and 4th Submarine Flotilla replaced HMS Maidstone and 8th Flotilla. Maidstone sailed for home waters. During June Fife had several British boats out seeking heavy cruiser *Ashigara*. HMS Trenchant (Hezlet) and HMS Stygian (Clarabut) were positioned just north of Bangka Strait. One of Fife's U.S. subs reported *Ashigara* departing Djakarta, but could not shoot. On 8 June Hezlet sighted a destroyer while on the surface. The destroyer fired and Hezlet submerged but remained in the area, waiting for expected *Ashigara*. She came along, hugging the coast off Sumatra. Hezlet fired six torpedoes at long range (4,700 yards) and got five hits. Ashigara sank later that day.

Dutch O-19 ran aground on a reef during passage from Fremantle to Subic Bay in July 1945. Her crew was rescued but she was a total loss. The last Dutch submarine patrol was conducted by O-21 off Java from 7 July to 8 August 1945.[545]

In August U.S. B-29s dropped atomic bombs on Hiroshima and Nagasaki. The Japanese government offered to surrender unconditionally on 2 September. Fremantle's time as a major submarine operating base for three allies was all over but for the final farewells as submarines departed in different directions.

Pacific Command (Commander Submarines U.S. Pacific Fleet)

In late 1941 prior to the Pearl Harbor attack, ComSubPac, Radm. Thomas Withers Jr., at Pearl Harbor sent several submarines off on practice war patrols to Midway and Wake islands, both U.S. possessions west of the Hawaiian Islands.[546] The Pacific Fleet was on short notice for war as tensions mounted. A Presidential exclusion zone had been declared around the entrance to Pearl Harbor, and any submerged submarine detected there was subject to instant attack with depth charges. There were submarine nets at the channel entrance to prevent a submarine from entering stealthily while submerged. When fleet units exited through the submarine net area, they went to "Condition Two", which meant that half their weapon batteries were manned. They remained at that advanced state of readiness until they passed the submarine nets on their way back into Pearl Harbor.[547]

The Pacific Submarine Force was as ready for war as doctrine and training permitted, which meant not very ready.[548] The doctrine in effect was that submarines would be utilized against enemy fleet units, not against merchant ships—in accordance with London Conference rules. Extensive training exercises in local waters with U.S. fleet units and aircraft had convinced many U.S. submarine commanding officers that periscope depth attacks were very dangerous to their naval careers. Getting sighted by "enemy" lookouts or aircraft meant low marks for the exercise, and perhaps even in fitness reports with longer term career consequences. As a result COs came to rely on passive sonar to solve the fire control problem of aiming torpedoes, and many firings took place at depths of 100 feet based entirely on sonar input. When on practice patrol, submarines would remain deep listening for targets on passive sonar, and only ascend to periscope depth to look around perhaps once an hour.

There was another problem, that of entirely inadequate torpedoes, but it was not known in advance. The Mark 14-3 torpedo was a "steam" torpedo which depended on a small turbine driven by an alcohol-air-water mixture at speeds up to 45 knots with a range of about 4500 yards. At a lower speed of 30 knots it had a longer range of 9,000 yards. Running depth was set into the torpedo before firing by a spindle that penetrated into the torpedo from the tube. Similarly gyro angle and depth were set by spindle action.

The warhead was activated by an exploder by either contact with a target hull, or preferably by a Top Secret magnetic sensor. The sensor read the magnetic signature around the torpedo warhead, and when it reached a certain level, the exploder detonated. If everything went as planned, the warhead would explode directly under the keel of the target ship—breaking the keel and sinking the ship. The only known deficiency was the presence of a visible wake on the surface that served to provide possible early warning to an alert lookout of a torpedo headed towards a ship, and that wake led back to the firing position. Unknown deficiencies included: a magnetic exploder that caused premature detonation or none at all; a depth mechanism that caused the torpedo to run as much as 12-18 feet deeper than set; and last but not least a contact exploder that was weak and could fail at many angles of incidence when the torpedo struck the target ship.

About six hours after the Japanese air attack at Pearl Harbor, the U.S. Pacific Fleet commander received the message from the Navy Department, "Execute unrestricted air and submarine warfare against the Empire of Japan." Adm. Kimmel directed Radm. Withers to send the majority of his available submarines to conduct reconnaissance of the Marshall Islands where the attackers were thought to have originated, with the others to Empire waters. Consequently four boats headed for the Marshalls and three to Empire waters. Two were held back for extensive repairs.[549] It was a small start.

Lcdr. Elton Grenfell in USS Gudgeon (SS-211) was sent off on the first patrol in Empire waters. They were 'terra incognita' to American submariners. Radm. Withers advised Grenfell to proceed with "extreme caution". He was to remain submerged in daylight when less than 500 nm from enemy air bases. At night he was to run only one of four engines in order to conserve fuel. Radio silence was in effect. He was to use only one or at most two torpedoes against enemy merchant ships because of a torpedo shortage.

During 1941 Japanese shipping losses to submarines were only 31,673 GRT.

1942

During 1942 the U.S. and its allies fell back from the Philippines and the Netherlands East Indies, and retreated to Australia, there to begin a buildup of U.S. Army forces for General MacArthurs campaign to return to the Philippines. Two major carrier battles were fought. The first at the Coral Sea in May was a tactical victory for the Japanese but a strategic defeat. It marked nearly the high water point of their expansion. At Midway in June the IJN suffered a crushing tactical and strategic defeat, losing four first line aircraft carriers and their embarked air groups. The U.S. landed at Guadalcanal in the Solomon Islands in August 1942 in a bold counter-stroke to Japanese plans to sever the sea lines of communications to Australia. Bitter fighting on Guadalcanal and its surrounding sea area took place during the remainder of the year. In New Guinea, Australian troops stopped the Japanese overland advance on Port Moresby. Subsequently Australian and U.S. forces set out to push the Japanese out of New Guinea.

On 2 January 1942 Gudgeon arrived off the *Bungo Suido*, the southern entrance to the Inland Sea of Japan after a 21.5 day transit. On 4 January Gudgeon attacked a small coastal freighter with two torpedoes at a range of 2,600 yards, and missed. On 9 January, on the surface at night, Gudgeon fired three torpedoes at a target at 2,500 yards range. After an explosion Grenfell claimed a 5,000 ton freighter.[550]

On 20 December 1941 Station Hypo (H for Hawaii in the phonetic code at that time) had regained contact with the IJN fleet. It had been lost due to Japanese security measures before the Pearl Harbor attack. Hypo focused on Japanese submarines. They were in daily communications to their operational commander. Noon positions, speed, intended tracks were among the data that Hypo could intercept. Another almost infallible clue was the propensity of IJN submarines to shell a land target just prior to heading home.

At this time there were three IJN submarines off the west coast of the U.S. They shelled an oil refinery near Los Angeles just prior to departing station. On 25 January they shelled Midway Island. Their intended track from Midway Island to Kwajalein was passed to Grenfell in Gudgeon. On 27 January along came I-173. Grenfell fired three torpedoes at it from periscope depth, hit and sank it. Gudgeon's diving officer lost depth control at a crucial moment so Grenfell did not observe the explosion. The sonar man reported hearing it 81 seconds after firing. Comint later confirmed the sinking. This was a very early example of the close coordination between comint activities and submarine operational commanders, which marked the American submarine campaign against Japan.[551]

After each submarine returned to Pearl Harbor its patrol report was reviewed in great detail by a Division Commander, a Squadron Commander, and finally by Commander Submarine Force, U.S. Pacific Fleet. The endorsements were often harsh and set policy, at least when they were issued by ComSubPac. They rapidly reversed operational tactics and procedures which had been in effect for years.

USS Argonaut (SS-166) CO was criticized for making a night sonar approach on a destroyer by the Division Commander who suggested a night periscope approach instead. ComSubPac in turn recommended a night surfaced attack.

CO USS Triton (SS-201)was chastised for a night sonar attack. The Squadron Commander recommended a night surface attack instead. The Squadron Commander also looked askance at indications that the CO was quick to dive at any sign of an enemy target and suggested he remain on the surface at night. These criticisms amounted to a major change in submarine operational policy.[552]

During the first three months of 1942 ComSubPac sent out 17 patrols. There did not seem to be any real strategy. Of 24 patrols since the Pearl Harbor attack, ten were to the Marshalls, Carolines, or Marianas islands with fourteen to Empire waters. There was some lost motion with subs pursuing comint targets. At this time no submarines were sent to the Luzon Straits, a natural choke point for Japanese merchant traffic from SEAsia to the home islands. Twenty-two sinking's were credited. That number was reduced to fifteen after the war when Japanese records were consulted.[553]

In May 1942 the Battle of the Coral Sea took place. Although the action was inside MacArthur's assigned theater of operations, it involved U.S. CVBGs which came under Admiral Nimitz. Nimitz and Admiral King, well aware of MacArthur's grandiose style of operations, were not about to let him have operational control of any fleet carriers. Japanese aircraft carrier *Shokaku* was damaged by air attack during the battle. Comint indicated that it would return to Japan for repairs, via Truk. CincPacFlt directed ComSubPac to intercept *Shokaku* and sink it.

ComSubPac attempted to intercept *Shokaku* off Truk, with four submarines. None detected her sortie from Truk on 11 or 12 May. Further north ComSubPac had four more submarines, off *Kii Suido*, the *Bungo Suido* and two off Okinawa. Several sighted *Shokaku* but could not gain a firing position.[554] Such hunts took place from time to time as high value targets, aircraft carriers and battleships, were tracked. In no case were they successful. They did chew up a lot of submarine time that might have been better spent searching for targets in assigned patrol areas.

From April through June ComSubPac, in addition to deployments for the Midway operation, sent 21 submarines on patrol. They sank 22 confirmed ships, with Drum scoring four and Triton five. Twelve COs were relieved because of poor performance. Radm. Withers was relieved as ComSubPac by Radm. English in early May.[555]

Radm. English was as much a drag on a solution to the growing torpedo problem as Withers had been. Despite continued reports and complaints from his COs, English refused to order any tests to see if the Mk 14 torpedo was running too deep as they claimed. He had a long list of "reasons" why they had missed. He insisted that the Mk 14 torpedo be set to run five feet deeper than the maximum draft of the target, thus depending upon the magnetic exploder to do its job.[556]

Comint revealed that the IJN intended to seize Midway Island, as a ploy to bring the remainder of the U.S. Pacific Fleet into action where it could be destroyed. The Midway operation had been triggered by the carrier raid against Tokyo and other major cities in Honshu when Doolittle's B-25s attacked in April. The unopposed attack was a great embarrassment to Japan's military leaders.

Midway operations overrode all other considerations for employment of U.S. submarines. ComSubPac positioned twelve submarines in the vicinity of Midway and seven others in two picket lines northwest of the Hawaiian Islands to give warning of any move against Pearl Harbor. Six others subs were on passage to or from patrol areas. USS Cuttlefish (SS-171), some 700 nm west of Midway, sighted an IJN oiler and reported it. She trailed as directed but then lost contact when dawn approached and she had to submerge.

There was a large concentration of U.S. and Japanese submarines having opposing roles in the Midway operation, some 19 U.S. and 16 Japanese. Both sides were attempting to use their submarines in the traditional role of fleet scouts, to nibble away at the enemy main body and reduce its strength before the main engagement.

As an example of classic naval tactics it was a total failure. Neither side's submarines sank any ships before the main engagement on 4-5 June. USS Nautilus (SS-168) fired two torpedoes at a battleship but missed. Later she got a shot in at an aircraft carrier, which had been badly damaged by air attack, but the torpedo was a dud. I-168 was more successful. She torpedoed and sank USS Yorktown, which had been badly damaged by an air attack but otherwise would have survived.

After the main exchange of air strikes during the battle, USS Tambor (SS-198) made an approach on several Japanese cruisers which intended to bombard Midway. Her periscope was sighted, and during evasive maneuvers two of the cruisers collided. One was later sunk by carrier aircraft as she tried to clear the area and the other badly damaged.[557]

On 6 June more B-17s had arrived on Midway and were sent out to attack IJN cruisers *Mogami* and *Mikumi* which had been involved in the collision and were limping away. That afternoon six B-17s reported attacking a "Japanese cruiser", dropping twenty 1,000 lb. bombs from 10,000 feet. They reported that they sank an IJN cruiser in 15 seconds. Several days later USS Grayling (SS-209) arrived in port and complained of being forced to crash dive because of a bomber attack at that same location.[558]

The Battle of Midway was a turning point in the Pacific War. The IJN lost four fleet aircraft carriers, all the aircraft of their assigned air groups, and many of the aircrew. A more rational enemy might have seriously begun negotiations at that point, but then a rational nation might not have chosen to attack another nation with ten times its own productive capacity.

Aleutians Interlude

As part of the Midway operation (MI), a Japanese carrier task force attacked Dutch Harbor in the Aleutian Islands just prior to the attacks on Midway. Intended as a diversion, it became somewhat compelling because Japanese troops landed on and took control of Attu and Kiska islands.[559] Strategically it was of little import since the Aleutian chain of islands were fog bound much of the time, and did not lend themselves as a reasonable avenue of attack for Japanese forces against the mainland United States. However, psychologically it focused American attention on the Aleutians and the "need" to retake lost territory. Both sides wasted a great deal of energy and material, and lives, in an area that had no real significance to the war.

In mid-June Adm. Nimitz directed Radm. English to send as many submarines as possible to Alaskan waters. Seven were sent under Capt.

Colclough. It was a mix of fleet boats and S-class submarines, based at Dutch Harbor. Operating conditions were generally horrible, with thick fog and little opportunity to obtain sun or star sights for navigation. There were no attacks on major IJN fleet units, most attacks being against Japanese destroyers or patrol vessels. The S-boats had no heating arrangements other than decaying engine heat after they submerged, so winter operations were as unpleasant as summer operations in the Solomon Islands without air conditioning.

In May 1943 submarines USS Nautilus and Narwhal (SS-167) transported 215 officers and men of the Army 7th Infantry Scout Company to Attu in advance of the main assault.[560] Attu was seized in an amphibious assault in May 1943.

In July 1943 USS Triton (SS-201) sank Japanese destroyer *Nenobi* on the 4th to celebrate Independence Day. The following day USS Growler (SS-215), off Kiska, attacked a group of IJN DDs. Her torpedoes sank HIJMS *Arare*, and seriously damaged *Shiranubu* and *Kasumi*[561]

The Japanese quietly withdrew their forces from Kiska Island in late July. When U.S. forces attacked in mid-August they found the island abandoned.

A total of thirteen S-boats had made some seventy war patrols in the Aleutians area during 1942 and 1943. They had sunk five confirmed ships. After the Aleutians campaign ended, they were withdrawn to training duty.

Central Pacific

In August 1942 the U.S. undertook an offensive of its own. The target was Guadalcanal in the Solomon Islands, where the Japanese were beginning construction of an air base. Once completed they planned to use land-based aircraft to move further south and interdict U.S. supply shipping to Australia and preclude it becoming a major factor in an allied move back up into the NEI.

Nimitz directed English to send submarines to invest the main Japanese naval base at Truk. Their tasks were to interdict Japanese shipping from Truk to the Solomon Islands and provide early warning to Commander Southwest Pacific (Vadm. Ghormley) of movements of IJN capital ships towards Guadalcanal. From July through September some eleven subs carried out these tasks. They sank eight confirmed ships. In addition they made three attacks on CVs and BBs, but achieved no sinking's.[562]

In August two large submarines, USS Nautilus and Argonaut, transported Marine Raiders under Colonel Evans Carlson to Makin Island in the Gilberts to conduct an attack. It was intended as a diversion to the Guadalcanal landings. They landed on 17 August. Both tactically and operationally it was a debacle. When the surviving Raiders re-embarked on their submarines, some 30 were unaccounted for. Nine were captured and later beheaded by the Japanese. The attack accomplished little except to direct Japanese attention to the poor state of their island defenses in the Gilberts. Later at Tarawa in 1943 the Marines would pay a heavy price for that unintended warning.[563]

During the period July through October the emphasis on Truk directed by the fleet commander, reduced the number of other patrols. There were only 20, some to Empire waters, others to the East China Sea and to the Aleutians.

USS Haddock (SS-231), assigned to Empire waters, during the period July-October, was among the first fleet boats fitted with the new SJ surface search radar. It was in addition to the older SD radar, a non-directional radar to warn of enemy aircraft. The SJ radar allowed the submarine to conduct a precision attack on the surface at night in darkness, rain, fog or snow. The radar provided target bearing and exact range. From those inputs the fire control plot could determine target course and speed. The torpedo data computer (TDC) then automatically calculated correct gyro angle to set in to the torpedoes to hit the target. Haddock used her SJ radar in two night surfaced attacks, sinking two freighters (6,251 tons).[564]

Japanese merchant ships had no electronic warning equipment so had no idea that a surfaced submarine was closing in, darkened and unseen, getting ready to fire. Even Japanese warships lacked electronic search measures (ESM) equipment at this stage of the war. It would cost them dearly. Earlier in the war expert Japanese lookouts had provided an edge in night combat. Radar was about to take that edge away. Galatin reported that the SJ radar installed in his submarine could even detect aircraft at ranges greater than 10,000 yards.[565]

In October 1942 Vadm. Halsey was sent in to relieve Vadm. Ghormley as Commander Southwest Pacific. Halsey requested that Nimitz send more fleet boats to operate from Brisbane in the hotly contested Solomons area. Nimitz agreed and directed English to send the bulk of his fleet boats to Brisbane. Most of CSS 8 and all of CSS 10 were sent. Along with more submarines went the Army 25th Infantry Division and some more B-17s.[566]

At this time USS Cachalot (SS-170), Cuttlefish (SS-171), Dolphin (SS-169), Nautilus and Narwhal were retired from war patrol duty due to their material condition. That left very few submarines for patrols in Empire waters. From October through December 1942 there were only ten Empire waters' patrols. Because of a shortage of torpedoes, several carried mines.[567]

During the second half of 1942 ComSubPac initiated 61 war patrols: 27 to the Truk area; 27 to the Empire or South China Sea; 3 to the Aleutians and 2 on special missions (Makin Island raid). A ship was sunk during only 34 patrols (57%). There were no sinking's in the Aleutians. Sinking's by area were:[568]

Empire	27 patrols	47 ships sunk
Truk	29 patrols	24 ships sunk

From 8 December 1941 through 1942 there were some 350 Pacific war patrols. Seven U.S. submarines were lost: three S-boats in groundings; Sea Lion damaged beyond repair by bombs on December 10th at Cavite; and three to enemy action. Subs carried out coastal defense, blockade, interception, commando raids, mine laying, reconnaissance, beacon and weather reporting, as well as shipping interdiction missions. They claimed 274 ships (1.6 million tons). Confirmed sinking were only 180 ships (725,000 tons).

Japanese bulk commodity imports for 1942 were roughly the same as they had been for 1941, some 20 million tons of coal, iron ore, bauxite, rice, lead, tin zinc, etc. Japan started the war with roughly 5.4 million tons of shipping excluding tankers. In December 1942 she still had some 5.2 mil tons, a loss of only 200,000 tons. In tanker stock Japan began the war with 575,000 tons. In December she had 686,000 tons, including an addition of 110,000 tons of new construction. Thus her net loss was 89,000 tons, a negligible amount.[569]

During 1942 there were only 54 Empire-oriented patrols, those in Japanese home waters. They sank 81 confirmed ships, for 45% of all confirmed sinking's.[570]

During the period December 1941 through December 1942, including the Battle of Midway and Truk Island interdiction campaign, U.S. submarines had the following record regarding major IJN fleet units:

Type	Attacks made	Results
5 BB	4	Slight damage to 1
18 CV	10	Slight damage to 3

U.S. submarines had also sunk the following lesser fleet units: HIJMS *Kako* (CA), HIJMS *Tenyu* (CL) and five SS[571]

During 1942 Japanese shipping losses to submarines were 612,039 GRT.

1943

During 1943 the Solomons Islands campaign and the fighting in New Guinea continued. In November Tarawa in the Gilberts was taken by amphibious assault, the first of many Marine Corps landings in the Central Pacific. Tarawa marked the beginning of the Navy-sponsored drive through the Central Pacific.

At Pearl Harbor as each submarine returned from patrol, a standard routine took place. The returning submarine had prepared a series of work requests for needed machinery repairs. These were handed over to the Repair Officer of the Submarine Base or Submarine Tender and work began immediately. The CO debriefed his patrol to the senior submarine commander on hand, with his comments and recommendations. A Relief Crew took over the submarine for a two week period, allowing the returning officers and men to take advantage of Rest and Recuperation (R&R) facilities.[572] In Hawaii it was the Royal Hawaiian Hotel, in Midway much more Spartan facilities. In Australia similar R&R facilities were established. Some personnel were transferred to new construction and replacements arrived and began their integration in to the crew.

After two weeks the original crew reported back and took over responsibility for supervising the repair work in progress. Some ship alterations (ShipAlts) and ordnance alterations (OrdAlts) as approved by the appropriate bureaus and by ComSubPac were also installed to update equipments. New equipments like surface search radars and electronic search receivers were installed or updated.

A short intensive training period at sea, under the supervision of a Division Commander, followed. New tactics were introduced if appropriate, based upon a distillation of all patrol reports and endorsements. After final loading and a briefing on the area assigned the submarine departed on patrol again.

Patrol report endorsements severely criticized sonar approaches and long range torpedo shots. These endorsements became policy documents. Night surface attacks were urged on all COs. However there were no specific attack doctrines mandated to the individual commanding officer. The tactics they chose to use were up to them.[573] The results were what counted.

In January 1943, Radm. English (ComSubPac) and several members of his staff were killed in an airplane crash in northern California while on a trip to visit submarine support facilities at Mare Island, California. Admiral King directed that the Chief of Naval Personnel name Radm. Lockwood to take over English's position. In related moves newly promoted Radm. Christie took over from Lockwood at Fremantle, and Capt. Fife took charge at Brisbane.[574]

In April 1943 more new fleet boats began to arrive at Pearl Harbor in large numbers from Electric Boat Company, Portsmouth Naval Shipyard, Manitowoc Shipbuilding Company and Mare Island Naval Shipyard.[575] Lockwood now had about 50 fleet boats. Some he sent to Australia to maintain a force of about 20 fleet boats there, as directed by Admiral King.

Target priorities for submarines were set by CincPacFleet. The highest priority was aircraft carriers, followed by battleships, and then lesser fleet units. Oil tankers from Sumatra and Borneo to Japan and the island bases were assigned as priority #3 in mid-1943, after CVs and BBs.[576] Fifteen tankers were sunk during the period September-December 1943 but the Japanese tanker fleet was still larger than it had been at the start of the war.

Admiral *Koga*, at Truk with major fleet units, was a focus of attention for CincPacFleet and ComSubPac. Lockwood also sent boats to the Marshalls, the Marianas and Palau's—all bases for resupply of Japanese forces in the Solomon Islands.

On 21 May Mush Morton (USS Wahoo CO) returned from his 3rd patrol, complaining loudly and bitterly to Lockwood about prematures and duds with the Mk 14. These complaints added to those of Lowrance (CO

Kingfish), Scott (CO USS Tunny) and Thomas (CO Pompano), finally destroyed Lockwood's trust in the worth of the magnetic exploder.[577]

During the afternoon of 10 June, Roy Benson in USS Trigger (SS-237) made a submerged attack on IJN CV *Hiyo* as it steamed out of Tokyo Bay. Benson fired a full salvo forward, six Mk 14 torpedoes equipped with magnetic detonators at 1200 yards. *Hiyo's* bridge watch spotted the wakes and turned left. The first two torpedoes missed ahead. Torpedo #3 had a premature detonation. #4 hit the chain locker resulting in slight damage. #5 hit but was a dud. #6 hit and caused major engineering damage. *Hiyo's* boiler rooms flooded and she lost propulsion. Comint informed ComSubPac that *Hiyo* had been seriously damaged but not sunk.[578] It is fairly clear that if # 3 through #6 had all exploded as designed, aircraft carrier *Hiyo* probably would have been sunk on the spot.

That was the final straw. After Benson returned to Pearl Harbor and debriefed, Radm. Lockwood ordered deactivation of all magnetic exploders, in a message signed by Adm. Nimitz. However Radm. Christie in Australia was under Vadm. Carpender and not under Nimitz. He declined to deactivate the magnetic exploders in his area arguing that they sometimes worked. It was not until November 1943 when Vadm. Kincaid took over as Commander 7th fleet in Australia that things changed. Under pressure from Admiral King and Admiral Nimitz, Kincaid directed Christie to deactivate the unreliable magnetic exploder once and for all.[579]

In July 1943 Dan Daspit was on patrol in USS Tinosa (SS-283) off Truk with orders to interdict tanker traffic between Palau and Truk. Although the U.S. side was not as focused on a final decisive battle as the IJN, its planners were well aware of the limitations that sinking tankers would have on IJN fleet mobility. Daspit's Mk 14 torpedoes were equipped with contact exploders, with the magnetic feature disabled.

During the morning of 24 July Tinosa intercepted a very large whale factory ship, *Tonan Maru* (19,000 tons), enroute Truk without escort, heavily loaded with oil and making 13 knots. Daspit fired four torpedoes and saw two splashes forward where torpedoes hit the hull. As the apparently undamaged target turned away, Daspit fired two more. One hit aft and smoke was spotted. The target stopped and settled somewhat by the stern. Daspit then set up and fired a number of torpedoes at the helpless target at close range, keeping careful records of each shot;

#7—Hit starboard side, large splash, no explosion (time 1009 local)

#8   Hit, no effect (time 1011)

#9   Hit, no effect (time 1014)

#10—# 14 All hits, no effect.

After the last torpedo hit without effect, Daspit cleared the area and took home his last, unfired torpedo to Pearl Harbor.[580] One can only imagine the story that the whale ship/tanker crew had to tell after their safe arrival at Truk.

Daspit's patrol report clearly indicated a third systemic problem with the Mk 14 torpedo—the contact exploder. The two earlier problems, the depth and magnetic exploder problems, had helped conceal a problem with the contact exploder. Lockwood directed his staff to investigate.

Capt. Swede Momsen proposed a simple test: fire warshots at a vertical cliff at Kahoolawe Island; wait until a dud occurred, then recover it and examine it to find out what went wrong. It was easier said than done since the dud warhead contained 685 pounds of TNT, and by definition no one knew why it had not gone off.

On 31 August USS Muskallunge (SS-262) fired three warshots at the cliff. The first two exploded but the third was a dud. An intrepid boatswain's mate free dove to 55 feet and shackled a line to the tail of the torpedo. It was carefully brought aboard USS Widgeon (ASR-1) and examined. The nose of the torpedo was crushed, and an examination of the exploder indicated that the firing plunger had traveled all the way up the guide lines and actually struck the fulminate cap—but too lightly to set it off.

Follow-on tests were conducted in Pearl Harbor Naval Shipyard. Torpedo dummy warheads with exploders, less explosives, were dropped vertically on to a steel plate. Various angles of incidence were tried. The tests showed that a perfect 90 degree impact would always fail to detonate. Those at striking angles of 45 degrees had a 50% failure rate.

Torpedo experts at Pearl Harbor set to work to design a firing mechanism that would work 100% of the time. They were successful. USS Halibut (SS-232) went back to Kahoolawe and fired torpedoes fitted with the modified exploders. There were six explosions and one dud. Radm. Lockwood ordered enough manufactured to replace all the current firing devices. The modified exploders were issued and deployed that month (October 1943). He advised the COs at sea to try for a glancing shot using the torpedoes that were on board. He also advised BuOrd of the problem and its solution. The Newport Torpedo Station then conducted tests against submerged steel plates and confirmed Pearl Harbor's findings. It then officially redesigned the firing mechanism.[581]

It had taken twenty-one months since the war began to identify and fix the three major problems in the Mk 14 torpedo. Each fix had been over the protestations of the Bureau of Ordnance. Perhaps a stint in Portsmouth Naval Prison for several senior personnel of BuOrd might have had a chastening effect on the organization. The German Navy did just that to a Rear Admiral and several senior civilian personnel in their torpedo development organization after the torpedo problems of the Norwegian Campaign of 1940 came to light (see Chapter One).

During 1943 the U.S. submarine focus on Japanese merchant shipping began to sharpen. At this time Japan had about 500,000 tons above the minimum to support her war industry. On the other side of the equation, new U.S. submarines were being produced at the rate of five per month. After initial shakedown and training they proceeded to Pearl Harbor for briefings and advanced training. Some boats watched Palau, Truk or the Marshalls, but the majority went against the Empire SLOC. By August 1943 an average of 18 were on patrol constantly.

Fitted with surface search radar they could maneuver at 20 kts. to attack at night, and could conduct "end around" runs to place themselves on the convoy track (which comint information provided them) in a position to make a submerged attack in day light.

Back in January USS Wahoo (SS-235) had attacked a convoy near New Guinea and in a two hour battle, sank three ships (12,000 tons each) and damaged a fourth. In March Wahoo sank nine ships (nearly 20,000 tons) in the Yellow Sea.

About September 1943 the first new Mk XVIII electric torpedo arrived at Pearl Harbor. It was a reverse engineered copy of the German G7e torpedo. It was 10-15 knots slower than the Mk 14 but was wake less, a major advantage. German U-boat COs used the G7e wake less electric torpedo in submerged attacks in daylight, and saved their G7a steam torpedoes for night use when the wake was less likely to be noticed. Now U.S. sub COs had the same opportunity. The electric torpedo speed was directly affected by sea water temperature and the time since the charge was topped off. A test and trial program was rapidly instituted to train COs and fire control parties to use the new weapon.

U.S. submarine tactics, as well as torpedoes, were about to undergo a significant change. Lockwood's subordinates were busy persuading him to consider wolf packs. Until September all patrols were individual. Japanese convoys were increasing in size and numbers of escorts. More firepower was needed to break up a larger convoy.

In September USS Trigger (SS-237), operating on her own in the East China Sea, sank four ships (26,000 tons).

In October 1943 Capt. Swede Momsen, CSS2, embarked in USS Cero (SS-225) as the first wolf pack commander appointed by ComSubPac. The pack included USS Grayback (SS-208) and USS Shad (SS-235). Prior to sailing Momsen and his three COs gamed their intended tactics on the dance floor of the Submarine Base Officers' Club. They then went to sea and tried out their tactics using a friendly convoy running between Pearl Harbor and the west coast as a practice target

They established some general rules: the first boat to spot a convoy, attacks and then drops back to trail and report. The other two would close, one on each side, alternately attacking and trying to push the convoy towards the other sub. High frequency voice radio was used for coordination. In Doenitz's wolf pack attacks in the Atlantic, it was a free for all with no rules. Communications were Doenitz to U-boat and reply only. The German wolf packs did not normally communicate within the wolf pack. Doenitz accepted the small risk of one U-boat torpedoing another. In fact that never happened although there was a collision or two.

Momsen's wolf pack headed for the China Sea to interdict the Honshu to Formosa Straits' traffic. They reportedly sank five ships (38,000 tons) and damaged eight (63,000 tons). Post-war analysis reduced the toll to three sunk (23,500 tons).[582]

In October 1943 Freddy Warder was sent out to command the second ComSubPac wolf pack sent on patrol. It consisted of USS Harder (SS-257), USS Snook (SS-279), and USS Pargo (SS-264) with Warder embarked as wolf pack commander. The wolf pack claimed nine ships for 58,000 tons. The confirmed kills were seven ships (31,500 tons). Communications encountered were poor and coordination inadequate. On return Warder recommended that the senior submarine CO act as wolf pack commander, dispensing with a separate embarked commander.[583]

German wolf packs were large, sometimes up to 40 U-boats, whereas ComSubPac wolf packs rarely exceeded 4-5 subs. Admiral Doenitz actively directed each German wolf pack by radio. Radm. Lockwood established each wolf pack and ensured it was provided with up to date comint information on convoy location and intentions, but otherwise normally kept his hands off.

British or allied convoys were large, from 40 to 80 ships. Japanese convoys were usually small, from 5 10 ships. British or allied convoys were well defended from 1942 on, while Japanese convoy defense, especially merchant convoys, was spotty. Allied long range air cover with radar was able to drive U-boats down by day or night by mid-1943, whereas Japanese air cover was generally not as significant a factor.

By the fall of 1943 the importance of the Luzon Strait as a shipping bottleneck had become apparent to ComSubPac operations staff. From September through December ComSubPac sent 89 war patrols from Midway and Pearl Harbor, averaging 22 per month.[584] Thirty-nine had zero scores (44%), but the others sank 99 ships, greater than one ship per patrol.[585]

Typically Japanese convoys consisted of 4-5 ships with about the same number of escorts (destroyers or lesser escorts). They sailed close inshore in shallow water when possible. At night they would transit in the open sea. During 1943 no Japanese ships or aircraft had radar. IJN escorts had active sonar, but they usually left a submerged contact after an initial attack with depth charges, and hurried after the convoy.

1943 Japanese ship losses averaged just over 100,000 tons per month. In November 1943 the figure rose steeply to 231,000 tons. Some 300 ships were sunk. In addition seventeen escorts were sunk by U.S. submarines. Japanese forces sank 15 U.S. subs during the year but that represented only a three months production run at the rate that U.S. shipyards were turning out new fleet boats. The Japanese built 800,000 tons of new shipping but lost 1,800,000 tons during the year, a net loss of one million tons. At the end of 1943 the total of Japanese shipping available was 7.5% less than they had at the start of the war.[586]

Japanese shipping was being sunk at a rate that exceeded possible replacement, and their ASW measures were inadequate to deal with the mounting submarine attack. If it continued Japan would be isolated from her oil and raw materials in SEAsia.

Patrol reports from 1943 clearly indicated the increasing advantage of night surfaced attacks using radar. The fleet submarines' 20 kts. surfaced speed gave them a huge advantage over the much slower 8-kt. convoys, and older escorts.[587]

Although comint provided very good locating information on Japanese shipping, actual interceptions were subject to the uncertainties of navigation at sea by both sides. Each side could think it was at the same exact Lat/Long but be off by 4—6 miles, not uncommon when using sextants to shoot stars or sun lines to obtain a position in the days before GPS. Some Japanese traits helped searching submarines locate convoys. One was the IJN tendency to use active sonar to search for submarines as the escorts steamed along. The distinctive active sonar "ping" could be heard from a greater distance than the more muffled noise from the convoy ships' propellers. In daytime smoke from old or faulty boilers in freighters could be seen a long ways away.[588]

During 1943 ComSubPac sent out only two wolf packs. As the IJN reorganized its convoy system ComSubPac increased the number of wolf packs it sent out. Some six would be used in the spring 1944.

In November 1943 during the U.S. attack on the Gilbert Islands, ten U.S. subs supported the invasion by weather reporting and life guard operations. This was a diversion from the interdiction campaign against Japanese shipping from SEAsia to the home islands.[589]

During 1943 there were some 350 U.S. submarine patrols. They claimed 335 sinking's (about 1.5 million tons including 400,000 tons of tankers). Japan's tanker tonnage was 686,000 tons at the end of 1942. At the end of 1943 it was 863,000 tons, a net increase of 177,000 tons. A statistical breakdown showed the following results:

0.95 ships claimed sunk per patrol
4,286 tons claimed sunk per patrol[590]

Fourteen per cent of submarine commanding officers were relieved during 1943 because of low productivity. This compared with 30% during 1942. As noted earlier there were 350 war patrols and 335 ships claimed sunk, with 3,937 torpedoes expended, a ratio of 11.2 torpedoes per ship sunk. On the bright side, the torpedo problem had been solved, surface search radar was now installed in all fleet submarines, and officers and men were experienced and tested.[591] With the relatively low level of Japanese ASW readiness it was not a good omen for Japan.

During 1943 Japanese shipping losses to submarines were 1,312,353 GRT.

1944

During 1944 the Central Pacific drive of the Navy continued. The Marshalls were attacked in February, and the Marianas in June. The seizure of the Marianas Islands gave the USAAF a secure base for its B-29 bombers to strike mainland Japan. In October the U.S. landed at Leyte in the Philippine Islands.

In January 1944 the Japanese merchant marine had fallen below 5,000,000 tons. During the first five months of the year merchant ship losses of 212 ships (about 1 million tons) were experienced at the hands of U.S. submarines.[592]

From January 1944-on there were enough U.S. submarines available in the Pacific to support U.S. fleet operations and also interdict Japanese shipping through the Luzon Strait. Regular patrols and wolf packs were established there. The expression "convoy college" was used to refer to the various submarine patrol areas near the Luzon Straits.

In early 1944 USS Sandlance (SS-381) was conducting a patrol in the Kurile Island region, near Soviet territory of the Kamchatka Peninsula. A ship that had no markings and was not in a "safe conduct" lane came along. Sandlance sank it thinking it was Japanese. It turned out to be the *Bella Russa*, a Soviet ship, sunk in error. USS Sawfish (SS-276) and USS Permit (SS-178) had also sunk Soviet ships in error in those waters.[593]

In February Radm. Lockwood flew to Majuro Atoll in the Marshall Islands to set up an advanced submarine base. Majuro was turned into a major fleet anchorage. USS Sperry (AS-12) moved to Majuro from Midway with Squadron Ten. Another submarine tender, USS Bushnell (AS-15) also moved to Majuro and set up shop there. USS Kingfish (SS-234) was the first sub to go through a refit at Majuro in April.[594]

In April the fourth ComSubPac wolf pack, led by George Peterson (CSD 141) and consisting of USS Parche (SS-384), USS Bang (SS-385) and USS Tinosa (SS-283) ran wild in the Luzon Strait. They sank seven confirmed ships (35,300 tons). Wolf pack #5 also operated in the Luzon Straits in April. It consisted of USS Picuda (SS-382), USS Peto (SS-265) and USS Perch II (SS-313). It was led by Mike Fenno, CO Picuda. The results were very poor. Only one gunboat, 1,200 tons was sunk.[595]

During the May-June period "Blair's Blasters" (USS Shark (SS-174), USS Pilotfish (SS-386) and USS Pintado (SS-381)) sank 35,000 tons.[596] Although the wolf pack scheme was originally intended to closely coordinate individual attacks, it morphed into a closely coordinated search scheme, followed by *ad hoc* individual attacks.

The Japanese were losing about 50 ships (200,000 tons) a month to U.S. submarines. Japanese shipbuilders were unable to make up the losses. Oil shortages began to be noticed. There was a shortage of escort vessels for convoys, and a shortage of experienced merchant seamen.[597]

In July-August "Donk's Devils" (USS Picuda, USS Redfish (SS-395) and USS Spadefish (SS-411)) sank thirteen ships (64,000 tons) north of Luzon. The toll included one destroyer and most of the convoy.

During the July-August period two parallel thrusts towards the Philippines were underway. Nimitz was getting ready to attack the Palau's and MacArthur was set to invade Morotai. At this time there were about 140 fleet submarines in the Pacific, 100 at Pearl Harbor and 40 in Australia.

In August USS Ray (SS-271), Haddo (SS-255), Harder (SS-257), Guitarro (SS-363)and Raton (SS-270) encountered a twelve ship convoy with five escorts and air cover. They sank five ships (28,000 tons)[598]

In January and February some 21 tankers were sunk, which was three times the tanker building rate. As a result, in April and May, all tankers were placed in convoy. In May 1944 oil imports fell to 50% of the January 1944 figures. Wartime oil consumption in Japan was about 300% of peacetime consumption, much larger than expected. Most of the tanker losses were at the hands of submarines operating in the South China Sea, from Fremantle.[599]

In April CincPacFleet placed Japanese destroyers as #4 priority on submarine target lists, after CVs, BBs and heavy cruisers (CAs). Five DDs had been sunk since January. Twenty-five more were sunk during the year. USS Harder alone sank four Japanese destroyers with "down the throat" torpedo shots at close range.[600]

In late April-early May a Japanese troop convoy departed Shanghai, China enroute New Guinea via Manila. USS Jack (SS-259) sank 5,425 ton transport *Yoshida Maru I* carrying an Army regiment of three thousand men, off the NW coast of Luzon. The convoy continued on to Manila and then went south into the Celebes Sea. There, USS Gurnard (SS-254) sank three freighters. The convoy was diverted into Halmahera vice continuing on to New Guinea. The two submarines had effectively eliminated two Japanese Army divisions from combat at a crucial time.

Operation FORAGER was the planned attack on the Marianas Islands in June 1944. After massive carrier air attacks on Japanese air bases in the Marianas Islands; first Saipan, then Guam and finally Tinian would be invaded. Control of the Marianas Islands would position U.S. forces for moves against the Palau's, the Philippines, Formosa, Okinawa and the Bonin Islands. The USAAF wanted bases in the Marianas for use by B-29 bombers against mainland Japan. Their existing bases in Chengdu China were too distant from their targets and the logistical support of those bases too expensive to be practical.[601] For U.S. submarines, the capture of the Marianas would provide an advanced base 3,300 nm beyond Pearl Harbor and only 1,500 nm from the Luzon Straits bottle neck.

Admiral Nimitz arranged a merger of Halsey's 3rd Fleet with Spruance's 5th Fleet. All their fast carrier battle groups were placed in Task Force X8 under Radm. Mitscher. When Halsey was in command, the organization was 3rd Fleet and TF 38. When Spruance took command it became 5th Fleet and TF 58. Only the fleet commanders and their immediate staffs would rotate from ship to shore. When not in active command, the "idle" fleet commander and his staff were busy planning the follow-on operation, which they would then execute. The ships and their crews stayed at sea throughout.

Spruance was selected to lead Operation FORAGER. His forces included 535 warships and auxiliaries; and 128,000 troops (1/3 Army, 2/3 Marines). Air power included fifteen CVs and CVLs and their air groups, as well as shore-based USN and USAAF aviation operating from the Gilbert Islands.[602]

During FORAGER in June 1944 Admiral *Ozawa* put plan *A-Go* into effect. It called for IJN aircraft carrier strikes from outside the range of the U.S. carriers, supplemented by aerial attacks by Japanese aircraft at bases in the Marianas. His intention was to strike the American carriers first and then recover his aircraft ashore, and refuel and rearm them for a second strike. However the highly sophisticated and technically advanced radar direction system of air defense for U.S. carrier battle groups defeated the Japanese air attacks over the open ocean. No U.S. ship suffered any damage from air attack. U.S. submarines reported IJN movements throughout the battle, and sank two fleet carriers.

Admiral Christie's submarines interfered with vital Japanese naval air training off Tawi Tawi. They sank seven warships and 24 merchantmen. In addition code breakers led U.S. ASW forces to sink nine out of twelve Japanese submarines which had been positioned for operations. USS England (DE-635), operating with comint information, sank six IJN submarines.[603]

During summer 1944 Lockwood sent eight wolf packs to the Luzon Strait. They sank 56 ships (250,000 tons), including two CVEs that were assigned to convoy protection duties. At this time many of Lockwood's submarines were operating from advance bases at Majuro and Saipan.[604]

During August two wolf packs went to the Luzon Strait. One, "Ed's Eradicators" (USS Barb (SS-220), USS Tunny and USS Queenfish (SS-393)), was badly harassed by Japanese aircraft equipped with radar. On 1 September Tunny was on the surface after dark. She was attacked from the air and nearly destroyed. Her hull was dished in by the bombs. It was an example of how potent air ASW could be in that area.[605]

Operati on STALEMATE II was set for September 1944. It involved the invasion of the Paulau Islands. Admiral Halsey requested extensive submarine support. Lockwood wanted to focus on interdicting shipping through the Luzon Strait but in this case Admiral Nimitz overruled him. Twelve SS were diverted to support the invasion forces. After his carrier strikes on the Manila area on 22 September, Halsey released nine SS that had operated between the Philippines and the Palau's. They moved up into the Luzon Straits area as three wolf packs. However the extensive air strikes had halted most convoy traffic. There were only a few targets at sea in late September and early October.[606]

On 21 November USS Sealion II (SS-315) was on patrol at the north end of the Formosa Strait at night. She picked up a large radar contact at 20 nm headed north. The contact turned out to be two battleships with destroyer escorts. They were HIJMS *Kongo* and *Haruna*, enroute from Brunei Bay to Japan. On the surface Sealion fired six Mk XVIII (electric) torpedoes from 3,000 yards. She obtained three hits on the target BB. She then fired three torpedoes from her after tube nest at the second BB. One hit and sank destroyer *Urakaze*. Battleship *Kongo* was badly damaged by the first three torpedoes. She slowed down and dropped out of the formation. At 0524 she blew up just as Sealion was preparing to fire another salvo. It was the first battleship sinking of the war for a U.S. submarine.[607]

On 28 November 1944 USS Archerfish (SS-311) was on patrol off Tokyo Bay. She detected a new IJN aircraft carrier, HIJMS *Shinano*, escorted by four destroyers, departing Tokyo Bay for the Inland Sea. *Shinano* had recently been "completed" but was still in a very precarious state, with many shipyard workers still aboard and almost no training accomplished for her crew in damage control procedures. After a lengthy tracking period, early on 29 November Archerfish fired her six bow tubes at a range of 1,500 yards, followed by two more torpedoes from her stern tubes. A pair of destroyers immediately attacked and held Archerfish down. *Shinano* continued on her way at a reduced speed, attempting to deal with the four torpedo hits she had suffered. Some watertight doors had not been installed, others had leaky gaskets. Gradually, despite all her relatively untrained crew could do, she kept flooding and sank. *Shinano* was the largest warship sunk by a U.S. submarine, 59,000 displacement tons.[608] The Archerfish only claimed damage but comint later revealed the loss of *Shinano*.

During the last quarter of 1944 (October-December), 43 submarines sank just over 300,000 tons of Japanese shipping. The Japanese merchant marine fell to 50% of its starting tonnage. Many ships were sunk by air attack while trying to reinforce Luzon. Most losses to submarines occurred in the South China Sea and near Formosa. Submarines were sinking from 2/3rds to 3/4ths of each convoy's total tonnage.[609]

From May through December some 60 wolf packs of three subs apiece operated, but 50% of all U.S. subs were still mounting solitary patrols in the Far East. In November Guam became available as an operational submarine base, reducing transit time from base to patrol area, and increasing patrol duration from 23 to 27 operational days. In December sinking's fell off although the number of subs on patrol had significantly increased. The reason was simple: most of the Japanese merchant marine had been sunk. During December a wolf pack consisting of USS Flasher (SS-249), USS Hawkbill (SS-366) and USS Becuna (SS-319) sank four tankers (42,868 tons) and two escorting destroyers in the South China Sea. That particular convoy never made it as far north as the Luzon Straits[610]

1944 was a very bad year for the Japanese merchant marine. There were 520 submarine war patrols, claiming 849 ships (5.1 million tons). Post war records confirmed 603 ships sunk (2.7 million tons). During 1943, 16.4 million tons of bulk commodities reached the Japanese home islands. During 1944 that fell to only 10 million tons. At the start of

1944, total merchant tonnage amounted to 4.1 million tons. At the end of the year only 2 million tons were left afloat, excluding tankers.

After the invasion of Mindoro Island in the Philippines in September 1944 the oil flow from SEAsia was sharply reduced as U.S. air power was able to reach and sink oil tankers from the NEI and Borneo.

In addition to the damage done to the Japanese merchant marine, U.S. subs sank: one battleship, seven aircraft carriers, two heavy cruisers, seven light cruisers, about 30 destroyers, and seven submarines. Nineteen U.S. subs were lost, 13 of Lockwood's, and six of Christie's. USS Tang (SS-306) and USS Tullibee (SS-284) were victims of their own torpedoes that ran circular, hit and sank them. USS Seawolf was lost in a mistaken attack by U.S. ASW forces. USS Darter (SS-227) stranded and could not get off the reef she had struck. USS Robalo (SS-273) hit a mine in the Balabac Strait. The 14 others were either sunk by Japanese ASW forces or hit mines. Thirty-five sub COs were relieved for low productivity (14%), the same percentage as the previous year. Some 6,092 torpedoes were fired by U.S. submarines during the year.[611]

During 1944 Japanese shipping losses to submarines were 2,388,709 GRT.

1945

During 1945 U.S. subs continued their patrols but the "pickings" were getting slimmer and slimmer. By March 1945 the Japanese ceased all convoys. Japan was cut off from South East Asia. Soon submarines, and aerial mines dropped by B-29s, would cut her off from Korea and Manchuria. The U.S. had slowly backed itself into a strategic submarine campaign, and it worked very well. By December 1944 Japan had been defeated, largely by submarines. However, it would take another eight months, much bloodshed, and two atomic bombs to make the point that the war was over.

During 1945 Japanese shipping losses to submarines were 420,826 GRT.

During the war U.S. submarines sank 1,314 ships (5.3 million tons), 55% of all ships sunk and 57% of Japanese shipping tonnage losses. USS Tang (SS-306) under Dick O'Kane had the highest score: 24 ships for 93,824 tons sunk. Fifty-two subs were lost, 44 of them to enemy action. The United States began the war with 99 submarines and added another

203. Some 14,748 torpedoes were fired by U.S. subs during the war.[612] van der Vat notes that the U.S. Submarine Service had the highest ratio of ships sunk per submarine lost: 29.2:1. The British Submarine Service was next with a ratio of 9.3:1. The U.S. Strategic Bombing Survey (Pacific) noted that "Submarines accounted for the majority of vessel sinkings (sic) and the greatest part of the reduction in tonnage."

Japanese ASW and Convoy Escort Measures

Although Japan went to war in late 1941 with the United States, Great Britain and the Netherlands specifically to obtain the resources of South East Asia, particularly oil—in order to pursue its political goals of conquering China, its leaders seemed to ignore the logistic problems involved. The oil of the Dutch East Indies, and tin and rubber, could only be brought back to the home islands of Japan by ship, a journey of thousands of miles.[613] The United States had the third largest submarine force in the world, exceeded only by the Soviet Union and Italy, some 99 submarines. Many of them were modern 'fleet' submarines, capable of very long range operations. The expanded U.S. Navy building programs of 1940 authorized the construction of 71 new submarines.[614] That sort of information was available publically and the Japanese naval attaché in Washington would have been derelict if he had not reported promptly to Tokyo about it.

The Imperial Japanese Navy planning staff failure to critically examine the logistical elements of the exploitation of the soon to be captured resources of Southeast Asia is hard to understand.[615] The IJN had exercised a number of its submarines in a commerce destruction exercise in October 1940. IJN "enemy" submarines were on station in the *Tsushima* Straits between Korea and Japan, the *Bungo* Strait at the southeastern entrance to the Inland Sea, and the *Uraga* Strait leading to Tokyo Bay. During a five day period they constructively "sank" 133 Japanese merchant ships. Rather than drawing the obvious conclusions about the need for strong ASW measures and a coordinated convoy system to protect Japanese shipping against submarines, the IJN's conclusion was that "enemy" submarine radio transmissions rendered them vulnerable to detection and attack.[616] While perhaps accurate, it concentrated on one tree and missed the "forest" entirely.

A few years after the war ended, in June 1952, the U.S. Naval Institute Proceedings published two fascinating articles dealing with the subject. One was by former IJA Major, *Y. Horie*, who served as a liaison officer with the IJN in matters regarding transportation of troops and material. The second was by former IJN Captain *Asushi Oi*, who served as Operations Officer, Grand Escort Command Headquarters. Their accounts substantiate the conclusions the author has drawn from other material.

The problem lay in the basic approach of the Imperial Japanese Navy to warfare. The "decisive battle" was the focal point of its strategy and operational training.[617] All else was considered inconsequential. Aviation training was focused on supporting the decisive battle in lieu of reconnaissance and convoy protection roles. Submarines were also almost entirely focused on the anti-fleet role rather than being employed against enemy merchant shipping. The potential threat to Japan's sea lanes was studiously ignored.

IJN experience in naval warfare was somewhat limited during WW I. It did participate in limited coordinated ASW operations in the Mediterranean Sea, contributing a squadron of destroyers to oppose German and Austrian submarines. However the overall implications of the German unrestricted submarine warfare campaign of 1917 and 1918 appeared to have escaped Japanese planners. Their main focus was on the Battle of Jutland, vice the unrestricted German U-boat campaign of 1917-1918.

In 1929 the IJN chief of staff Admiral Kanji Kato made a Memorial to the Throne about protecting Japan's sea lanes. However there were no subsequent specific proposals for naval force structure to provide for commerce protection. There were probably several reasons for this situation. They included budgetary problems during the 1920s and 1930s; mirror imaging of IJN plans for submarine wartime operations focused against an enemy fleet and ignoring enemy commercial shipping; and a basic limitation on what were considered vital sea lanes for Japan—pre 1941 plans called for protection north of the Formosa (Taiwan) Straits and along the north east Asia littoral. The China Sea and Micronesia were only provisionally included.

The principal IJN focus was on a final decisive battle between the Japanese fleet and an enemy fleet, reflecting previous Japanese experience during the Sino—Japanese War of 1894—1895 and the Russo-Japanese

War of 1904-1905. In the latter encounter the Japanese fleet decisively defeated Russia's Baltic Fleet in the momentous Battle of Tsushima Straits, effectively ending the war in Japan's favor. The focus on a decisive sea battle between surface ships seemed to preclude much thought to other possibilities and vulnerabilities.

The 1928 Nomura Report relegated coastal defense, including commerce protection, to overage warships in service rather than proposing an effective convoy system with modern escorts. The 1936 Imperial Defense Policy document was very weak in the area of sea lane protection. During the summer of 1941 the Cabinet Planning Board, which was civilian, warned of potential shipping losses in wartime exceeding Japan's capability to replace, a warning unheeded by the IJN. In *Kaigun*, Evans and Peattie state that the IJN had an ". . . official disdain for commerce protection", and Japanese naval officers had ". . . no interest in learning what seemed to be a marginal and unrewarding trade".[618]

At the risk of exceeding the author's credentials in the field of amateur cultural psychology, I offer the suggestion that the pre-war prototypical IJN officer saw himself as a modern samurai warrior. In feudal Japan society was split into three social classes, underneath the *daimyos* (feudal lords). They were in order of rank: first—samurai warriors, second—peasant farmers, and last and certainly least—merchants. Commerce and those who engaged in it did not have much respect from the samurai. I suspect that this deep-seated cultural disdain for commerce may have lapped over into the thought that protecting commerce was somehow beneath the dignity of a "fighting man". Certainly IJN officers, who were otherwise thoroughgoing professionals in most fields of naval endeavor, left ASW and convoy escort work to officers at the bottom of the professional barrel until far too late.

In November 1941 the Emperor queried the Navy Chief of Staff, Admiral *Nagano*, about the ability to transport oil from the Netherlands East Indies in the face of the threat from planes and submarines based in Australia. *Nagano* indicated that there was no problem.

The Japanese Navy General Staff estimated in its pre-war studies, that shipping losses would be 800,000 to 1,100,000 gross tons during the first year. After that during the second and third years of war they would not exceed 700,000 to 800,000 gross tons. The extra losses during the first year took into consideration the fact that antisubmarine (A/S) measures would not be fully developed at that time.[619]

There was no naval high command which had exclusive responsibility for planning convoy escort and ASW activity. To the extent that there was any responsibility it rested in the 2nd Defense Section (Defense Planning) of the Operations Division of the Navy General Staff. One officer handled Rear Area Defense which included Commerce Protection. He was also an *aide-de-camp* to the Emperor.

At the beginning of the war the IJN had 14 old destroyers, 210 auxiliary escorts, and 100-odd MTB, submarine chasers and the like available for escort duty.

A major line command for commerce protection was not established until March 1942, albeit with inadequate forces. A fully fledged escort force was not established until 1943. *Shimushu* vessels (DE equivalents) had been reduced from a planned 1200 ton hull to 860 tons in order to fully fund construction of battleships *Yamato* and *Mushashi*. Fourteen were ordered but none were in commission when the war began.

In 1943 the IJN finally set up a convoy system. It included, on paper: 360 escorts and 2,000 ASW aircraft.[620]

Until mid-1943 Second Base Force at Balikpapan, a major oil port in the captured NEI, had only three submarine chasers to protect vital oil traffic through the Makassar Straits.

North China forces included some auxiliary patrol craft, two converted merchant ships and a modified former Chinese Customs Cruiser. China Area Fleet had eight MTB and three old destroyers. The home islands areas were almost undefended. In March 1943 USS Wahoo (SS-238) sank nine merchant ships in the Yellow Sea without any serious threat from escorts.

Another factor may have entered into IJN planners' calculations. They apparently thought that American submarine personnel were not up to the task of long submerged operations, not being as tough as their own submariners. They only gave U.S. submarines credit for making two week patrols at maximum.[621] The inclusion of air conditioning in U.S. fleet submarines was viewed as a sign of weakness rather than a reasonable measure to deal with high humidity and consequent electrical equipment problems while submerged.

There were a few dissenting voices. In January 1941 Admiral *Shigeyoshi Inoue*, the chief of the Navy Ministry's Naval Aviation Department, attended a Naval Staff-Ministry consultation dealing with revising the Circle Five naval construction plan. *Inoue* startled the group by attacking the basis of the Circle Five plan. Several weeks later he addressed a memorandum to the Navy Ministry pointing out that while Japan could not destroy the United States, the United States was capable of blockading Japan's home islands and destroying Japan. That pointed to the need for protection of Japan's sea lanes and a convoy escort scheme. He noted that rather than engage in the "decisive battle" that Japanese naval strategists expected, the U.S. Navy was far more likely to roll up Japanese island garrisons one by one, and to attack Japan's sea lanes with her large force of submarines.[622] As prescient as *Inoue* was, his memo had no effect on future events.

The Imperial Japanese Navy General Staff was a tightly closed circle, chary of letting outsiders have access to information. A classic example is the fact that the Japanese Prime Minister, General *Tojo*, was not informed of the Navy's Pearl Harbor attack plan until November 1941. After the disaster at Midway in June 1942, information about the loss of four IJN fleet aircraft carriers was withheld from General *Tojo* for a month.[623]

Conceptually, the task of putting together an integrated convoy escort and ASW protection plan to ensure the safe arrival of raw materials from Southeast Asia to Japanese ports is rather simple. Although the distances are long, almost 3,000 nautical miles, the basic tracks are all within reach of medium range land-based aircraft. Unlike the North Atlantic where U-boats could operate in a "black hole" beyond the reach of all but very long range aircraft, U.S. submarines would have been well within range of Japanese airbases all along the way. That meant that they could not safely transit on the surface in daytime or even at night if the IJN acquired airborne radar. Good aerial coverage of the convoy routes, along with a strong convoy organization could have precluded the terrible destruction that the U.S. Submarine Service wreaked on the Japanese merchant fleet in 1943 and 1944. However, the IJN seemed obvious to the history of unrestricted submarine warfare in the Atlantic, both in WW I and during the period 1939-1941.

The U.S. Submarine Service may have led the IJN down the garden path by its relatively inept performance after the Pearl Harbor attack and during 1942. Faulty tactics, incompetent or timid commanding officers, and most of all—badly deficient torpedoes probably helped keep the IJN leadership from focusing on the grave danger to Japan that lurked along the 3,000 nautical mile supply route from Singapore to Yokohama.

The roughly 600,000 tons of Japanese shipping sunk by U.S. submarines during 1942 despite their disabilities was a portent that the

IJN failed to heed. When the U.S. torpedo problems were resolved in mid-1943, there were finally enough U.S. submarines to carry out a devastating anti-shipping campaign. In a sense it was a perfect storm for which the IJN was unprepared. Focused narrowly on a final decisive surface battle, its leaders overlooked the fact that defeat could come in another fashion. At the end of the war the 6.4 million tons of pre-war Japanese shipping had been reduced to about 1.5 million tons, 60% of it lost to American submarines.[624]

Each Japanese service had its own shipping control office, which is understandable. Less understandable is the fact that there was almost no cooperation between them. In February 1944 when the IJN had information about a pending U.S. carrier strike at Truk, it failed to pass that information on to the IJA—with the result that a large number of Army ships were sunk. The IJA had been indiscrete enough to criticize IJN convoy escort techniques in the presence of the Emperor, a deadly insult that the IJN General Staff never forgave. A subsequent IJA proposal for a sea transport liaison committee fell on deaf ears in the Naval General Staff.[625]

The pre-war Japanese Cabinet Planning Board had calculated that the Japanese civilian economy required three million tons of shipping, including: for coal fuel—1.8 mil tons; for foodstuffs—450 ktons; and for steelmaking—300 ktons. During the war the U.S. Board of Economic Warfare estimated that 4-5 million tons was required for the Japanese economy assuming: IJA and IJN cooperation; full utilization of SEAsia shipyards; and use of cargo space would be maximized. None of these assumptions held true.[626] Furthermore the Southern Resources Area in South East Asia (Borneo, Malaya and the Dutch East Indies) was remote from the fighting areas which were over towards New Guinea and the Solomon Islands. Hence it was not practical for Japanese shipping to carry arms and ammunition to resupply the fighting areas and then return with raw materials for Japanese industry.[627]

In 1940 the oil fields under the Dutch and British produced a total of 9 million tons of petroleum (Dutch fields—8 mil tons, British fields—1 mil tons). Japanese estimates were that once these fields were captured they would be producing 4.5 mil tons within three years. Although some destruction of the fields and equipment was carried out by Dutch and British forces, the fields were producing at 78% of pre-war production (7.02 mil tons) in two years. So, production was not a problem. The oil fields that were the principal target of the Japanese move into SEAsia were secure and producing handsomely.

The problem was *transportation*. Pre-war Japanese studies indicated that Japan would require 4-4.5 mil tons of petroleum, with the military forces using the bulk of the total. Once the war started it was apparent that the estimates were too conservative. The IJN alone needed 50% more. Some 6-7 mil tons was a more realistic estimate of Japan's wartime needs.[628]

During the first year of the war (December 1941-December 1942) Japanese shipping losses were roughly in accordance with predicted figures, although shipping losses off Guadalcanal to allied aircraft were high. So far there was no cause for alarm.

In April 1942 the First and Second Escort Units were established by IJN to escort shipping to the central and southwest Pacific areas. The number and quality of the escort ships would turn out to be sadly inadequate. In the spring of 1942 the Combined Fleet Headquarters had to detach two light cruisers and a motor torpedo boat squadron to protect oil drilling rigs and crews in the NEI. Combined Fleet HQ suggested that a special escort unit be formed rather than the Naval General Staff tasking Combined Fleet for such matters. The Army was concerned over escort preparations, and proposed a joint general staff for escort operations. In November 1942 the Naval General Staff established an escort operations office (12th section) staffed with six officers and a Section Chief.

Prior to 1943 there were few Japanese convoys, with the exception of military troop transports. During the first two years the problems that U.S. submarines were experiencing allowed the IJN ample time to organize its ASW forces to protect vital shipping. However the IJN did not take advantage of this period. Convoys were instituted in 1943, although some had no escort forces assigned. Normal convoy size was five merchant ships, but a "large" convoy might be as big as 10-15 ships. Atlantic convoys were as large as 70-100 ships, for comparison.[629]

First Escort Force consisted of ten old destroyers, two MTB, five gunboats (converted merchant ships), and was responsible for the 2,500 nm route from Japan to. Singapore. It only protected the routes from Moji to Takao to Manila to Singapore.[630] The usual convoy was 10-20 ships plus escorts. Independent sailers had no protection at all. Second Escort Force covered the 2,000 nm from Yokosuka, a major naval port on

Tokyo Bay, to Truk. It consisted of four old destroyers, one MTB, and two converted gunboats.[631]

In September 1943 losses of 180,000 tons of shipping were experienced, twice those of August of 1942.

In November 1943 The Naval General staff established a Grand Escort Headquarters (GE HQ) under Admiral *Koshiro Okawa*. He was a former Navy Minister and senior to Combined Fleet Commander Admiral *Mineichi Koga*.[632] However the staffing of the new escort headquarters was poor. None of the staff officers were acquainted with escort operations. Some staff officers were convalescents. The air staff officer was only a part-time appointment. The designated Chief of Staff didn't even have information on when he was supposed to report for duty.

The GE HQ could task naval districts, guard districts, and First and Second Escort Units for convoy escort work. Combined Fleet and China Area Fleet retained authority over frontline fleet units and some Chinese areas. GE HQ was located in Tokyo in the same building as the Naval General Staff. Certainly there was no physical impediment to close liaison between the two staffs. In August 1944 GE HQ established an Escort of Convoy Headquarters to assist in the resupply of the Micronesia islands. It organized convoys and provided escort commanders for convoys.[633]

In December 1943 the 901st Air Unit was established. In mid-January 1944 it was ordered to active duty, without time for ASW training. Once on station, 10% to 33% of the unit pilots were returned home for instruction in operation of the radar and MAD equipment, and tactics to pursue. They were expected to train the other personnel upon return.[634]

In March 1944 the loss of shipping to submarines fell to only 133,000 tons, about half the normal monthly loss. GE HQ personnel were very happy. During the first half of April, only 31,000 tons were lost. GE HQ thought that the submarine problem had been solved. The real reason was that U.S. subs had been diverted from anti-shipping roles to conduct search and rescue (SAR) in support of carrier raids. During the second half of April, losses rose to 63,000 tons. In May some 230,000 tons were lost.

The fate of the *Take* (Bamboo) convoy is instructive. Ten troop transports departed Shanghai on 17 April 1944, to take the IJA 32nd and 35th infantry divisions to New Guinea, where MacArthur's forces were on the offensive. Northwest of Luzon USS Jack sank *Yoshida Maru* (5,245 tons) and most of the troops embarked were lost. The convoy arrived at Manila Bay on 29 April. It was now in Combined Fleet's AOR.

The convoy departed on 1 May. On 6 May, near Halmahera Island, a submarine wolf pack attacked and sank three troop transports without being detected by the escorts. At that point the Japanese Prime Minister, General *Tojo*, stepped in and directed that the surviving troops be off loaded at Halmahera. They were then transported, very slowly, to Biak by barge. They arrived too late to affect the operations in progress.[635]

In June 1944 the American assault on the Marianas Islands took place. Admiral *Ozawa's A-Go* plan for a decisive battle was sabotaged by U.S. submarines. Almost all of his fleet movements from Singapore to Tawi Tawi were reported by U.S. subs. Seven warships, including a light cruiser and six destroyers, were sunk by submarines. In addition they sank six tankers, four troop transports, and fourteen freighters. Many other merchant ships were damaged.[636]

The Battle of the Marianas cost the IJN three fleet aircraft carriers and over three hundred first line naval aircraft. Two of the three fleet carriers lost were sunk by submarine torpedoes. Because of the severe loss of Japanese aircraft with very low losses to American aircraft, the air battle was disparaging termed "The Marianas Turkey Shoot". The loss caused General *Tojo's* Cabinet to fall.

The Battle of the Philippine Sea was a "decisive battle" for which the IJN had long prepared. There were a large number of submarines involved on each side: Japanese—24; U.S.—25. Japanese submarines accomplished little.

U.S. subs sighted and reported Adm. *Ozawa's* forces enroute the battle. Early in battle USS Albacore (SS-218) torpedoed and sank IJN CV *Taiho*, the fleet flagship, with one very lucky torpedo hit. Some aviation fuel tanks were damaged and a bad damage control decision led to a buildup of explosive fumes in the hangar deck. *Taiho* literally blew up. USS Cavalla (SS-244) put four torpedoes into another IJN CV, *Shokaku*, and she also sank.[637]

The capture of Saipan marked the first loss of pre-war Japanese territory to the Americans. Imperial General Headquarters order number 33 placed GE HQ and all shipping protection units under Combined Fleet Headquarters as of 9 August 1944. Combined Fleet HQ was focused as always on the "decisive battle", not realizing that another *decisive battle* was being waged against the Japanese merchant marine.

In October 1944 the invasion of the Philippine island of Leyte took place. When this happened Combined Fleet placed all ASW escorts into surface combat roles. It was a disaster for the escort function. The escorts were second rate warships as it was, and there was no way they could reasonably undertake surface combat against first rate U.S. ships and aircraft. Combined Fleet even sent specially equipped ASW aircraft into battle with U.S. carrier air groups. All of 901 Air Unit's radar equipped aircraft were destroyed.[638]

As of August 1944 there were four escort fleets. They did not have assigned geographic areas of responsibility. Each was assigned to a specific convoy. Each escort fleet had its own command structure and used different ships for each assignment. There was no development of standard ASW tactics and procedures within the IJN. A better recipe for failure would be hard to describe.

In November 1944 the 101st Flotilla was established with training ship *Kashii* and six coast defense ships. Two weeks later it left Japan to escort a convoy through the South China Sea. On 9 January 1945 an escorted convoy of four tankers and six supply ships departed Saigon. U.S. subs promptly sank all the tankers, three of the supply ships, *Kashii* and three escorts. A few days later the remaining three supply ships were sunk.[639]

During 1944 the IJN outfitted some ASW aircraft with magnetic airborne detection (MAD) equipment. The 1945 models had an increased range of plus or minus 300 yards (900 feet). Assuming an aircraft altitude of 200 feet above the ocean, the MAD gear could detect a magnetic disturbance as deep as 700 feet, far deeper than submarines of that era were capable. However the planes lacked retro-rockets so they were unable to launch a depth bomb that would fall on the spot that the MAD gear had noted. The equipment was thus adequate only for search and detection but not for attack.[640]

In January 1945 Halsey's carriers raided Hong Kong and Formosa during a ten day period. They sank 25 oil tankers. No tankers arrived in Japan after March 1945. The oil spigot of SEAsia had been turned off for good. All convoys were halted that month

In spring 1945 the Japanese Naval General Staff established a General Naval Command with all naval forces including escorts under its command. GE HQ thus gained in theory but this action was too late to save the Japanese merchant marine.

During 1945 sinking's by U.S. submarines fell off appreciably due to lack of targets at sea. They sank slightly less than 500,000 tons. However, aircraft and aerial mines accounted for nearly 1.5 million tons. From

January-on fuel shortages, and lack of ships and escorts, halted most seaborne traffic.

In February "Loughlin's Loopers", a wolf pack operating off Formosa, hit a convoy of seven tankers, five freighters and eight escorts, enroute from Japan to Singapore. Loughlin's group sank four ships. The convoy then entered port at Takao in Formosa but lost two freighters and two tankers to carrier air strikes while in port. It continued on to Hong Kong and lost several more ships there to carrier attacks. Two ships plus four escorts continued south. A sub sank one escort off Malaya, and only one ship and the remaining three escorts reached Singapore.

During June 1945 nine U.S. submarines penetrated submerged through extensive Japanese mine fields into the Sea of Japan using frequency modulated (FM) active sonar to detect and evade the mines. Once inside the Sea of Japan they sank twenty-eight ships. One sub was lost.[641] Not long after that extensive B-29 aerial mining shut down the Japanese ports on the Sea of Japan, and all imports from the Asian continent ceased.

40% of all Japanese merchant mariners died at sea during the war. In 1944 over 25 % of Japanese merchant crews were novices. By 1945 most crewmembers were teenagers.[642]

From 1943 through 1945 some 1.1 million tons of Japanese tanker shipping was sunk. Aircraft sank 366,000 tons while submarines sank the rest. The 734,000 tons of tankers sunk by sub was 44% more than Japan had in December 1941.[643]

U.S. subs sank 1,113 Japanese merchant ships of all classifications during the war. It amounted to over 60% of all shipping lost to enemy action. In addition they sank 201 warships of 540,192 displacement tons. Mines sank about 500,000 tons of shipping. Aerial attack accounted for 2.5 million tons of shipping.[644]

The Japanese Government reported to the Diet, immediately after Japan's surrender, that the greatest cause of defeat was the loss of shipping.[645]

Introduction of dedicated CVEs for ASW

The IJN decided to adopt the American-British ASW CVE concept to help reduce shipping losses. On 8 August 1944 the first CVE departed Japan with a ten-ship merchant ship convoy under her protection. She was sunk on 18 August in the Luzon Straits. One month later, her sister ship

Unyo was sunk there also. The third CVE, *Shinyo,* was sunk in the Yellow Sea. The fourth CVE was still in the shipyard when the war ended.

Comint role in the destruction of the Japanese merchant marine by submarines

In submarine warfare the first and largest problem is to locate ships that you intend to sink or capture. The second problem is to overcome convoy defenses if any. In the Atlantic Battle the overriding value of comint was shown by the fact that only one convoy in ten was attacked by U-boats, due to evasive routing used by controlling authorities to avoid U-boat concentrations. That evasive routing was based upon comint, specifically the breaking of the German Enigma radio traffic from Admiral Doenitz's headquarters to his U-boats at sea, and their replies.

In the actual battles between allied escorts and U-boats in the Atlantic the value of comint was also clearly shown in the statistic that escorts provided with comint information had three times the kill rate over U-boats that escorts had when they lacked comint information.[646] In warfare, as in gambling, it is extremely valuable to be able to sneak a peek at your opponent's cards.

U.S. submarines were usually provided with very accurate locating information on Japanese shipping and convoys moving through their assigned patrol areas. That capability dated back to before the start of the war. Prior to the Pearl Harbor attack, the USN kept track of IJN tankers by intercepting and decrypting their weather reports. The tankers were important because no task force could move far at sea without tanker support.[647]

U.S. Navy communications intelligence organizations broke the "*Maru*" code, the code that provided operational information of great value. During fighting in the Solomons area documents were captured that enabled the U.S. to read the IJN oceanographic grid references. The IJN broadcast predicted noon positions for their convoys and sent time tables to all interested Japanese commands.[648] Thus USN authorities were privy to this information. A "hot line" between the code breakers at CincPacFlt headquarters and ComSubPac headquarters ensured that ComSubPac operations personnel had this information. It was sent out each night to patrolling submarines' commanding officers.

In August 1942 concerns were raised about the Americans reading Japanese merchant marine transmissions. The IJN General Staff, the Foreign Ministry, the Transportation Ministry and Communications Ministry all met to discuss the issue. They decided that their codes were secure, but to assign all communications regarding shipping to IJN communications channels as an added precaution. Two years later the Imperial Japanese Army ordered an end to shipping administrative offices sending out information regarding ship movement by radio, but the Navy and the Civil Government that controlled far more tonnage, did not follow suit.

The Japanese believed, like the Germans, that their codes were unbreakable. They ascribed increasing losses of merchant shipping to: spy networks, convoy smoke, disloyal Japanese, POW signals, allied agents in IJA shipping headquarters, etc. Comint information also provided after action reports by Japanese commanders, mine barrier locations, and data on tankers.[649]

The ability to decrypt Japanese shipping information promoted economy of force in the use of U.S. submarines, greatly increasing their effectiveness. Vadm. Lockwood estimated that U.S. submarines sank 30% more targets because of comint.[650] In *War Plan Orange*, Miller refers to the United States Strategic Bombing Survey, and states that 50% of all sinking's of Japanese merchant ships resulted from intercepting Japanese communications.[651]

Mines and the Japanese Merchant Marine

Mines were used throughout the war to destroy Japanese warships and merchant shipping. Early in the war when torpedoes were scarce, U.S. submarines were often sent on mine laying missions. They were never popular since they called for close-in work near a harbor, in waters that were minable by definition hence very dangerous. The probability that the submarine would be given credit for ships destroyed by the mines it laid was low. All in all it was not attractive duty. Be that as it may, mines were and are useful tools to shut down seaborne commerce.

In late March 1944 the island of Palau was mined by air. All sea traffic ceased for nine days while sweep gear was flown in. The critical oil port of Balikpapan in the NEI was shut down for 24 days in an 8-week period by mines. Over 40% of all ships of over 1,000 tons struck mines in that area. After November 1944 all steel hull ships avoided Balikpapan because of the mine danger.

The aerial mining of the Shimonoseki Straits by B-29s was very damaging. That strait separates the southernmost main island of Japan, Kyushu, from Honshu. The interruption to coal supplies from Kyushu to industry in the Kobe-Osaka region of Honshu was devastating. Japanese industry depended primarily upon coal to operate. Despite the introduction of additional AAA batteries and fighters, B-29s continued to mine the strait and the Inland Sea until the end of the war.[652]

Mine sweepers were only able to remove 15% of the mines laid in Japan's coastal waters. Near the end of the war all shipping traffic had to be routed to ports on the Sea of Japan side. The ports of Osaka and Kobe were empty, as were the ports of Tokyo, Yokohama and Nagoya. By July 1945 aerial mining had also saturated the Sea of Japan port areas with mines. Japan's sea commerce was at all stop.

GLOSSARY

AA Anti-aircraft (referring to a gun)

AAA Anti-aircraft artillery

AAFAC Army Air Forces Antisubmarine Command

ABDA American, British, Australian, Dutch (combined) Command (Java 1941-1942)

Acoustic torpedo One that homes on a ship's propeller noise

AG American Holland (designation of a class of Russian, later Soviet, submarines built in North America

AOR Area of Responsibility

A/S Anti Submarine

Asdic Active sonar (RN term)

ASV Air to surface (ship) radar (British designation)

ASW Antisubmarine warfare

BC Bomber Command (RAF)

B-Dienst The German functional equivalent of Bletchley Part, tasked with breaking Allied codes and ciphers and providing operational information to German commanders

BdU German U-boat Command Headquarters

Bee Patrol aircraft (U-boat slang)

Betasom Italian submarine base in Bordeaux

BP Bletchley Park

Billet RN Submarine Service term for patrol area assigned

Blue on blue Deadly force used against own or friendly forces, sometimes called "friendly fire"

Bold A German evasion device that gave off gas bubbles simulating a U-boat hull

Bombe Device used at GC & CS to break enciphered Enigma traffic

BuOrd U.S. Naval Bureau of Ordnance

CA Heavy cruiser (8" guns)

CC Coastal Command (RAF)

CF Combined Fleet (Imperial Japanese Navy)

CHOP Change of Operational Control

CL Light cruiser (6" guns)

CSF Caribbean Sea Frontier

CO Commanding Officer

Combined Operations or planning between the military services of two separate countries

COMINCH Commander in Chief (USN)

Comint Communications intelligence

CSS Commander Submarine Squadron

CV Aircraft carrier, fleet

CVBG Aircraft carrier Battle Group

CVE Aircraft carrier, escort

CVL Aircraft carrier, light

DD Destroyer

DE Destroyer Escort (somewhat smaller and cheaper than a destroyer and optimized for ASW operations)

Depot ship An auxiliary ship used for repair and maintenance of submarines or destroyers, called a Submarine (AS) or Destroyer Tender (AD) in USN usage.

Depth bomb Depth charge in an aerodynamic shape for more accurate bombing of submerged submarines by aircraft

Depth charge A cylindrical canister dropped or projected over the side of a surface escort, equipped with a hydrostatic fuse

DM Destroyer-minelayer

E-boats Fast German motor torpedo/gun boats

Eel German U-boat slang for torpedo

Electroboote High speed advanced diesel-electric U-boats

Enigma German cryptographic machine

ESF Eastern Sea Frontier (U.S. East Coast)

ESM Electronic search equipment

FAA Fleet Air Arm (Great Britain)

Fido U.S. acoustic homing torpedo

FM Fairbanks Morse diesel engine

FM Frequency modulated sonar

Force 136 SOE group operating in the Indian Ocean area

Foxer Allied acoustic decoy

FW *Focke Wulf* (aircraft)

G-7a German "steam" torpedo
G7e German electric torpedo
GC & CS Government Code & Cipher School (Great Britain's WW II NSA)
GE HQ Grand Escort Headquarters (Imperial Japanese Navy)
GHQ General Headquarters
GM General Motors' diesel engine
GPS Global Positioning System (based on satellites)
GSF Gulf Sea Frontier (Gulf of Mexico)
Hedgehog An ahead thrown contact-fused projectile used against submerged U-boats
HF High frequency
HF/DF Radio direction finder (literally high frequency/direction finding)
H_2S Airborne radar used by Bomber Command for targeting (functionally identical to ASV installed in long range aircraft engaged in ASW)
HHMS His Hellenic Majesty's Ship (Greek naval ship)
HIJMS His Imperial Japanese Majesty's Ship
HMS His Majesty's Ship (Royal Navy)
H.O.R. Hooven, Owens, Rentschler diesel engine
HUK Hunter Killer (ASW group)
IJA Imperial Japanese Army
IJN Imperial Japanese Navy
Joint Operations or planning between two different military services within a single country
KIA Killed in action
Ktons Kilo tons (thousands of tons)
Leigh light Aircraft searchlight
LRA Long range aircraft
MAD Magnetic Airborne Detection
Metox ESM equipment (German)
MF Medium frequency
Milchkuh German resupply submarine
MOMP Mid-Ocean Meeting Point
MTB Motor Torpedo Boat
NANCF North Atlantic Naval Coastal Frontier (later renamed ESF)
NEFIS Netherlands East Indies Forces Intelligence Service
NEI Netherlands East Indies (current Indonesia)

NSA National Security Agency (U.S.), charged with breaking foreign communications and ciphers

OIC Operational Information Center (central plot of U-boats and ASW forces and convoys)

OKM *Oberkammando der Marine* (German Navy headquarters)

OODA Observation-Orientation-Decision-Action

Opcon Operational control

PBY Catalina flying boat

Pig Italian Navy slang for a manned guided torpedo (*Miali* in Italian)

Pillenwerfer See Bold

POW Prisoner of War

RAAF Royal Australian Air Force

RAF Royal Air Force (Great Britain)

RCN Royal Canadian Navy

RDF Radio Direction Finder

RHN Royal Hellenic Navy (Greece)

RN Royal Navy (Great Brittan)

RNN Royal Netherlands Navy

SC Submarine chaser (smaller than a DE)

Skerrries Small offshore islands and reefs

SLOC Sea Lines of Communications

SOE Special Operations Executive (a WW II British organization that oversaw and coordinated *guerrilla* warfare inside occupied Europe)

SubDiv Submarine Division (fraction of a squadron)

SS Steam ship or diesel-electric submarine

Stuka German dive bomber, Ju-87

SubRon Submarine Squadron

Supermarina Italian Navy headquarters

Type XXI Streamlined U-boat (1600 tons) with high-capacity batteries, capable of much higher submerged speeds than a typical Type VII U-boat. Also referred to as *Electroboot*

Type XXIII Similar to a Type XXI boat but significantly smaller (230 tons) in displacement, intended for operations in coastal waters

UK United Kingdom

USAAF United States Army Air Forces (successor to Army Air Corps)

VLR Very long range (aircraft—usually referring to a Liberator bomber)

V-1 German Luftwaffe cruise missile

V-2 German Army tactical ballistic missile

WA Western Approaches (to British isles)
Walter boat Hydrogen peroxide propelled U-boat, capable of sustained high submerged speeds
WATU Western Approaches Tactical Unit
WRNS Women's Royal Naval Service
Zaunkonig German homing torpedo (T5)

BIBLIOGRAPHY

Books

Abbot, Willis J., *Aircraft and Submarines* (G. P. Putnam's Sons, New York and London, 1918)

Alden, John D. *The Fleet Submarine in the U.S. Navy* (Naval Institute Press, Annapolis, Maryland, 1979)

Bagnasco, Erminio, *Submarines of World War Two*, (Naval Institute Press, Annapolis, Maryland, 1973)

Barnett, Correlli, *The Audit of War* (Macmillan, London, 1986)

Barnett, Correlli, *Engage The Enemy More Closely* (W.W. Norton & Company, New York, 1991)

Beach, Edward L., *Submarine!* (Naval Institute Press, Annapolis, Maryland, 1946)

Blair, Clay, *Hitler's U-boat War: The Hunters, 1939-1942* (Modern Library, New York, 2000)

Blair, Clay, *Hitler's U-boat War, The Hunted, 1942-1945* (Random House, New York, 1998)

Blair, Clay, *Silent Victory*, (Naval Institute Press, Annapolis, Maryland, 1975)

Boyd, Carl, *Hitler's Japanese Confidant* (University Press of Kansas, Lawrence, Kansas, 1993)

Boyd, Carl and Yoshida, Akihiko, *The Japanese Submarine Force and World War II* (Naval Institute Press, Annapolis, Maryland, 1995)

Bradford, Ernle, *Siege Malta 1940-1943*, (William Morrow And Company, Inc., New York, 1986)

Cairn, Lynne, *Fremantle's Secret Fleets* (Western Australia Maritime Museum, Fremantle, Australia, 1995)

Calvert, Vice Admiral James F., *Silent Running* (John Wiley & Sons, Inc., New York, 1995)

Ciano, Galeazzo Count, *The Ciano Diaries, 1939-1943* (Doubleday & Company, Inc., Garden city, New York, 1946)

Compton-Hall, Richard, *The Underwater War, 1939-1945* (Blandford Press, Poole, Dorset, England, 1982)

Craven, Wesley Frank and Cate, James Lea, Eds., *The Army Air Forces in World War II, Vol. I, Plans and Early Operations, January 1939-August 1942* (The University of Chicago Press, Chicago, 1948)

Craven, Wesley Frank and Cate, James Lea, Eds., The Army Air Forces in World War II, Vol. II, Europe: Torch to Pointblank, August 1942-December 1943 (The University of Chicago Press, Chicago, 1949)

Doenitz, Karl Grand Admiral, *Memoirs*, (Da Capo Press, 1997)

Dull, Paul S., *A Battle History of The Imperial Japanese Navy* (United States Naval Institute, Annapolis, Maryland, 1978)

Evans, Dr. David C., Editor, *The Japanese Navy in World War II* (Naval Institute Press, Annapolis, Maryland, 1969)

Evans, David C. and Peattie, Mark R., *KAIGUN*, (Naval Institute Press, Annapolis, Maryland, 1997)

Fluckey, Admiral Eugene B. USN (Ret.), *Thunder Below!* (University of Illinois Press, Urbana and Chicago, 1992)

Frank, Richard B., *Guadalcanal* (Penguin Books, New York, 1990)

Galatin, Admiral I. J., USN (Ret.), *Take Her Deep!* (Algonquin Books, Chapel Hill, 1987)

Gannon, Michael, *Black May* (HarperCollins Publishers, New York, 1998)

Gannon, Michael, *Operation Drumbeat*, (Harper Perennial, New York, 1991)

Gannon, Robert, *Hellions of the Deep—The Development of American Torpedoes in World War II* (The Pennsylvania State University Press, University Park, Pennsylvania, 1996)

Giese, Otto and Wise, James E. Jr., *Shooting The War* (Bluejacket Books, Naval Institute Press, Annapolis, Maryland, 1994)

Gray, Edwyn, *The Devil's Device* (Seely, Service and Co. Ltd., London, 1975)

Harris, Brayton, *The Navy Times Book of Submarines* (Berkley Books, New York, 1997)

Hezlet, Vice Admiral Sir Arthur, *Electronics and Sea Power* (Stein And Day, New York, 1975)

Hezlet, Vice Admiral Sir Arthur, *The Submarine and Sea Power* (Stein And Day, New York, 1967)

Howarth, Stephen and Law, Derek, eds., The Battle of the Atlantic 1939-1945, The 50th Anniversary International Naval Conference (Naval Institute Press, Annapolis, MD, 1994)

Hurst, Doug, The Fourth Ally: The Dutch Forces in Australia in WW II (Doug Hurst, 2001)

Januszewski, Tadeusz, *Japanese Submarine Aircraft* (Stratus, UK, 2002)

Keegan, John, *Intelligence In War* (Vintage Books, New York, 2004)

Keegan, John, *The Second World War* (Viking, New York, 1990)

Kemp, Paul, *Midget Submarines of the Second World War* (Chatham Publishing, London, 1999)

Knox, MacGregor, *Hitler's Italian Allies* (Cambridge University Press, Cambridge, England, 2000)

Korzh, Victor, *Red Star Under the Baltic* (Pen & Sword Books Ltd., Barnsley, South Yorkshire, England S70 2AS, 2004)

Layton, Rear Admiral Edwin T., *"And I Was There"* (William Morrow and Company, INC., New York, 1985)

Lenton, H. T., Navies of the Second World War: German Submarines 1 and 2 (Doubleday & Company, Inc., Garden City, New York, 1967

Macintyre, Donald, *The Battle for the Mediterranean* (W.W. Norton & Company, INC., New York, 1964)

Mahnken, Thomas G., *Uncovering Ways of War*, (Cornell University Press, Ithaca and London, 2002)

Mars, Alastair, *British Submarines At War 1939-1945* (William Kimber, London, 1971)

Marshall, George C., *War Reports* (J.B. Lippincott Company, Philadelphia and New York, 1947)

Miller, Edward S., *War Plan Orange* (Naval Institute Press, Annapolis, Maryland, 1991)

Morison, Samuel Elliot, History of United States Naval Operations in World War II, Volume 1, The Battle of the Atlantic September 1939-May 1943 (University of Illinois Press, Urbana and Chicago, 2001)

Morison, Samuel Elliot, History of United States Naval Operations in World War II, Volume 4, Coral Sea, Midway and Submarine Actions May 1942-August 1942 (University of Illinois Press, Urbana and Chicago, 2001)

Murray, Williamson and Millet, Allan R., Eds., *Military Innovation in the Interwar Period* (Cambridge University Press, Cambridge UK, 1996)

Neufeld, Michael J., *The Rocket and the Reich* (The Free Press: New York, 1995)

O'Neill, Richard, *Suicide Squads* (Lansdowne Press, London, 1981)

Papadopoulos, Sarandis, *Feeding the Sharks: The Logistics of Undersea Warfare, 1935-1945* (UMI, Ann Arbor, MI, 1999) (GWU Doctoral dissertation)

Parillo, Mark P., *The Japanese Merchant Marine in World War II* (Naval Institute Press, Annapolis, Maryland, 1993)

Payne, Stanley G., *Franco and Hitler: Spain, Germany and World War II* (Yale University Press, New Haven and London, 2008)

Polmar, Norman and Noot, Jurrien, *Submarines of the Russian and Soviet Navies 1718-1990* (Naval Institute Press, Annapolis, Maryland, 1991)

Porter, David, World War II Data Book: *The Kreigsmarine 1935-1945* (Amber Books Ltd., London, 2010)

Roberts, William R. and Sweetman, Jack, (Ed) *New Interpretations in Naval History*, Ninth Naval History Symposium 18-20 October 1989, Naval Institute Press, Annapolis, Maryland, 1991.

Rohwer, Jurgen, Allied Submarine *Attacks of World War II European Theater of Operations 1939-1945* (Naval Institute Press, Annapolis, Maryland, 1997)

Rohwer, Jurgen, *Axis Submarine Successes of World War II* (Naval Institute Press, Annapolis, Maryland, 1999)

Roskill, RN, Captain S. W., The *War At Sea 1939-1945, Volume I, The Defensive* (Her Majesty's Stationery Office, London, 1954)

Sakaida, Henry, Nila, Gary and Takaki, Koji, *I-400* (Hikoki Publications Limited, East Sussex, England, 2006)

Schmeelke, Karl-Heinz and Michael, *German U-Boat Bunkers* (Schiffer Military/Aviation History, Atgen, PA, 1999)

Shirer, William L., *Berlin Diary* (Alfred A. Knopf, New York, 1941)

Shirer, William L., *The Collapse Of The Third Republic* (Simon and Schuster, New York, 1969)

Showell, Jak Mallmann, *The U-Boat Century* (Chatham publishing, London, 2006)

Stille, Mark, *Imperial Japanese Navy Submarines 1941-1945* (Osprey Publishing, Oxford, England, 2007)

Tarrant, V. E., *The U-Boat Offensive 1914-1945* (Arms and Armour Press, London, 1989)
Tillman, Barrett, *Clash of the Carriers* (New American Library, New York, 2005)
Van der Vat, Dan, *The Pacific Campaign* (Simon & Schuster Paperbacks, New York, 1991)
Williamson, Gordon, *U-Boat Bases and Bunkers* (Osprey Publishing, London, 2003)
Wilson, Michael, *A Submariners' War, The Indian Ocean 1939-45* (Spellmount, Gloucestershire, England, 2008)(

Magazines

U.S. Naval Institute Proceedings, Vol. No. 78, No. 6, June 1952
Horie, Y. The Failure of the Japanese Convoy Escort, (pp. 1073-1081)
Oi, Atsushi Why Japan's Anti-Submarine Warfare Failed (pp. 587—601

Pamphlets

The U-boat Commander's Handbook (High Command of the Navy (German), 1943. (Thomas Publications, Gettysburg, PA., 1989)

END NOTES

1 Doenitz Memoirs, p. 46. *Doenitz states* that there were 56 U-boats in commission at the beginning of the war. However in Appendix 6 he lists 57 U-boats in commission.

2 Porter, Kreigsmarine, p. 30

3 Doenitz, Memoirs, pp. 1 – 4.

4 The interested reader is referred to the author's The Effectiveness of Airpower in the 20th Century, Part One (1914 – 1939), which deals at length with pre-Hitler rearmament efforts in Germany.

5 Gannon, Hellions of the Deep, p. 47

6 Vause, Wolf, P. 25

7 Doenitz, Memoirs, pp. 12 - 13

8 Vause, Wolf, p. 27

9 Doenitz, Memoirs, pp. 13 - 15

10 In the U.S. Submarine Service diving time was measured from the second blast of the diving alarm (when the chief of the watch started opening main vent valves) to keel depth of 48 feet, which meant that the highest point of the periscope shears was under water. Average diving time for most U.S. fleet subs was 45 seconds. The author served in two converted fleet boats, a troop transport sub (Perch) and a guided missile sub (Barbero), each having a large hangar topside and additional lead ballast to compensate for the buoyancy of the hangar. Average diving time for these two boats was 30 seconds. One memorable dive in Perch with the author as diving officer was recorded at 19 seconds.

11 Papadopoulos, Sarandis, Feeding the Sharks, p. 45 & 47

12 Lenton, German Submarines I, p. 87

13 Doenitz, Memoirs, p. 14

14 The U-boat Commander's Handbook, p. 24 B.I.21

15 Hezlet, Electronics and Sea Power, p. 164

16 Hezlet, Electronics and Sea Power, pp. 179 - 180

17 Doenitz, Memoirs, pp. 22 - 23

18 Williams, Secret Weapon, p. 60
19 Hezlet, The Submarine and Sea Power, pp. 118 -119
20 Williams, Secret Weapon, p. 85
21 Hezlet, The Submarine and Sea Power, pp. 118 – 119.
22 Brown, Anthony Cave, "C", pp. 182 - 184
23 Blair, Hitler's U-Boat War, p. 110
24 Hezlet, Electronics and Sea Power, pp. 175 – 176
25 Vause, ,Wolf, pp. 29 - 30
26 Terraine, Business in Great Waters, pp. 239 - 240
27 Gannon, Drumbeat, p. 43
28 Doenitz, Memoirs, pp. 132 – 133
29 Blair, Hitler's U-Boat War, p. 48
30 Doenitz, Memoirs, p. 21
31 Usually one-third of a submarine force is in transit to or from an operational area, another one-third is in repair status, leaving the final one-third on patrol. These ratios are necessary to support sustained operations at sea.
32 Terraine, In Great Waters, p 222. In the case of HMS Courageous - two of her four destroyer escorts had been detached to assist a merchantman, leaving only two destroyers left to perform ASW screen duties, an entirely inadequate number.
33 Doenitz, Memoirs, pp. 73 – 74. On 30 November 1939 U-56 fired three torpedoes at battleship HMS Nelson. All three impacted Nelson's hull but failed to detonate. Nelson had an escort of twelve destroyers at the time.
34 During WW I a German court-martial convicted a British civilian ship master of violating the Laws of War by attempting to ram a U-boat. The offender was convicted and shot the same day.
35 British bombers were enjoined not to allow their bombs to fall on German soil lest that begin a mutual bomber attack between the countries.
38 Roskill, The War At Sea, p. 21
39 Roskill, The War At Sea, p. 103
40 Doenitz, Memoirs, p. 229
41 Roskill, The War At Sea, pp. 73 - 74
42 Roskill, The War At Sea, p. 78
43 Roskill, The War At Sea, p. 94
44 Roskill, The War At Sea, p. 90
45 Roskill, The War At Sea, pp. 132-133

46 Roskill, The War At Sea, p. 190
47 German parachute troops came under Luftwaffe control as did antiaircraft artillery units.
48 Doenitz, Memoirs, p. 62
49 Doenitz, Memoirs, p. 71
50 Wake less electric torpedoes were normally used in daylight. Steam torpedoes were usually used after dark when their wake was less likely to alert a target's lookouts.
51 Doenitz, Memoirs, p.p. 432 – 435, Appendix 3
52 Submariners are aware of the buildup of air pressure inside the submarine hull while submerged. When surfacing after a number of hours submerged the conning tower hatch has to be "cracked" (opened) slowly to let excess pressure bleed off. If opened too rapidly the person opening the hatch is apt to find himself propelled upward at high speed into whatever lies immediately above the hatch. Serious injury can occur.
53 Doenitz, Memoirs, p. 110
54 See Williamson's U-Boat Bases and Bunkers 1941 – 45 for a complete description of the construction and its resistance to bombs.
55 Feeding the Sharks, p. 72
56 Ibid, p 83
57 Doenitz, Memoirs, p. 101
58 Feeding the Sharks, pp. 412 - 413
59 Feeding the Sharks, p. 142
60 Roskill, The Navy at War, pp. 92 - 93
61 Doenitz, Memoirs, p. 102
62 The U-boat was really a submersible, using its relatively high surface speed to hunt for and hunt down targets. Enemy air cover was a very serious threat to U-boat operations. Aircraft drove U-boats beneath the surface where they had great difficulty in sighting and closing on targets.
63 Doenitz, Memoirs, p. 131. Normal U-boat routine in its patrol area was to operate on the surface to maximize its visual horizon, using lookout binoculars as its primary sensor. Any aircraft sighting normally called for a fast dive to avoid detection. After submerging the U-boat would raise a periscope and monitor the aircraft behavior.
64 Doenitz, Memoirs, pp. 104 - 105
65 Doenitz, Memoirs, pp. 275, 291
66 Roskill, The War at Sea, pp. 308-320
67 Doenitz, Memoirs, pp. 104 - 106

68 Doenitz, Memoirs, pp. 115 - 117

69 Roskill, The War at Sea, p. 490

70 Roskill, The War at Sea, pp. 349 - 351

71 Doenitz, Memoirs, p.p. 132 - 133

72 Roskill, The War at Sea, pp. 338 - 339

73 Roskill, The Navy at War, p. 121

74 Doenitz, Memoirs, p. 141

75 Roskill, The War at Sea, p. 462

76 Roskill, The Navy at War, pp. 126 - 127

77 Brown, "C", pp. 334 - 335

78 Roskill, The Navy at War, pp. 139 - 140

79 Feeding the Sharks, pp. 330 - 334

80 Roskill, The War at Sea, p. 458

81 Roskill, The Navy at War, p. 139

82 Gannon, Drumbeat, p. 348

83 Bagnasco, Submarines of World War Two, p. 75

84 Doenitz, Memoirs, p. 219

85 Roskill, The War at Sea, p. 470 See also Terraine, Business in Great Waters, p. 359, who supports this statement.

86 Roskill, The War at Sea, p. 143

87 Roskill, The War at Sea, p. 467

88 Roskill, The War at Sea, pp. 473 - 474

89 Doenitz, Memoirs, p. 140

90 Roskill, The Navy at War, p. 146

91 Doenitz, Memoirs, p. 375. Also see Roskill, The War at Sea, pp. 534 - 535

92 Terraine, Business in Great Waters, pp. 358 - 361

93 Terraine, Business in great Waters, p. 400

94 Roskill, The War at Sea, p. 141

95 Roskill, The Navy at War, p. 145

96 Gannon, Drumbeat, p. 267

97 Roskill, The Navy at War, pp. 146-147

98 Terraine, Business in Great Waters, p. 428

99 Doenitz, Memoirs, p. 159

100 In these days of nuclear powered submarines with submerged speeds of up to 30 knots a current of four or five knots is merely an inconvenience, something to be taken into account but not a major factor. When you are operating a battery powered diesel-electric submarine with a submerged

speed of perhaps seven knots at maximum such currents are a major problem.

[101] Barnett. Engage the Enemy More Closely, pp. 440 - 441
[102] Barnett, Engage the Enemy More Closely, pp. 276 - 277
[103] Barnett, Engage the Enemy More Closely, p. 476
[104] Gannon, Drumbeat, p. 313
[105] Gannon, Drumbeat, p. 199
[106] Gannon, Drumbeat, p. 142
[107] Gannon, Drumbeat, p. 211
[108] Barnett, Engage the Enemy More Closely, pp. 463 - 467
[109] Doenitz, Memoirs, p. 325. Doenitz states ""And to this day, as far as I know, we are not certain whether or not the enemy did succeed in breaking our ciphers during the war." The British GC&CS, with the aid of the French and Polish Intelligence Services had been breaking the Enigma cipher since 1939.
[110] Brown, "C", pp. 420 - 421
[111] Doenitz, Memoirs, p. 206
[112] During summer 1941 with Germany controlling most of Europe and Japan on the march in China, the U.S. Congress only extended the existing draft act by one vote in the House of Representatives.
[113] NANCF would be renamed Eastern Sea Frontier (ESF) in February 1942.
[114] Craven & Cate, AAF in WW II, pp. 519 - 523
[115] Barnett, Engage the Enemy More Closely, p. 442
[116] Barnett, Engage the Enemy More Closely, p. 443
[117] Doenitz, Memoirs, p. 203
[118] Gannon, Black May, pp. 84 - 85
[119] Gannon, Drumbeat, p. 378
[120] Gannon, Drumbeat, pp. 340 - 341
[121] Terraine, Business in Great Waters, p. 466
[122] Gannon, Drumbeat, p. 386
[123] Gannon, Black May, pp. 336 - 337
[124] Morison, The Battle of the Atlantic (September 1939 – May 1943), pp. 242 - 243
[125] Morison, The Battle of the Atlantic, Vol. I, p. 241
[126] Gannon, Drumbeat, p. 367
[127] Gannon, Drumbeat, pp. 380 - 381
[128] Morison, The Battle of the Atlantic, Vol. I, p. 245

[129] Gannon, Drumbeat, pp. 151-152

[130] Gannon, Drumbeat, p. 379

[131] Gannon, Drumbeat, p. 388

[132] Doenitz, Memoirs, p. 271

[133] Terraine, Business in Great Waters, p. 429

[134] Terraine, Business in Great Waters, p. 454

[135] Terraine, Business in great Waters, p. 442. See also Roskill, The Navy at War, pp. 195 - 196

[136] Terraine, Business in Great Waters, p. 435

[137] Terraine, Business in Great Waters, p. 432

[138] Terraine, Business in Great Waters, p. 501

[139] Doenitz, Memoirs pp. 244 - 245

[140] Doenitz, Memoir p. 237

[141] Gannon, Black May, pp. 74 - 75

[142] Roskill, The Navy at War, p. 225

[143] Terraine, Business in Great Waters, p. 502

[144] Doenitz, Memoirs, p. 265

[145] Doenitz, Memoirs, pp. 232 - 233

[146] Doenitz, Memoirs, p. 233

[147] Doenitz, Memoirs, p. 221

[148] Gannon, Drumbeat, p. 393

[149] Oil was pumped overland from Iraq to Syria via pipeline.

[150] Roskill, The Navy at War, p. 212

[151] Barnett, Engage the Enemy More Closely, p. 556

[152] Doenitz, Memoirs, p. 277

[153] Terraine, Business in Great Waters, p. 515 and p. 581.

[154] Terraine, Business in Great Waters, p. 515.

[155] Terraine, p. 517. Underlining supplied by author.

[156] Roskill, The Navy at War, p. 270

[157] Roskill, The Navy at War, p. 270. Some 300 aircraft of lesser capability were available.

[158] Roskill, The Navy at War, pp. 271 - 272

[159] Roskill, The Navy at War, pp. 272 – 274. The author comments that "... very near to disrupting communications between the New World and the Old."

[160] Doenitz, Memoirs, pp. 340 – 341. See also Roskill, The Navy at War, p. 277

[161] Gannon, Black May, pp. 66 - 67

162 Gannon, Black May, p. 101
163 Gannon, Black May, pp. 70 - 71
164 Gannon, Black May, pp. 238 - 239
165 The author used a more modern version successfully in an exercise off San Diego in 1967 in which a destroyer squadron was "working up" for a Westpac deployment. He was successful in penetrating a five DD escort screen undetected, "shooting" the main target, and leaving several false contacts behind to occupy the escorts while his boat, USS Spinax (SS-489), went under the formation and out the opposite side.
166 Gannon, Black May, p. 129
167 Gannon, Black May, p. 344
168 Doenitz, Memoirs, pp. 406 - 407
169 Doenitz, Memoirs, pp. 416 - 417
170 Feeding the Sharks, p. 346
171 Roskill, The Navy at War, pp. 304 - 305
172 Barnett, Engage the Enemy More Closely, pp. 612 - 613
173 Gannon, Black May, pp. 377 - 378
174 Morison, The Atlantic Battle Won, Vol. 10, p. 128
175 Terraine, Business in Great Waters, p. 627
176 Roskill, The Navy at War, pp. 281 – 282, p. 284
177 Roskill, The Navy at War, p. 336
178 Morison, The Atlantic Battle Won, Vol. 10, p. 95
179 Porter, *Kreigsmarine*, p. 30
180 Terraine, Business in Great Waters, pp. 637 - 638
181 Roskill, The Navy at War, p. 307
182 Morison, The Atlantic Battle Won, Vol. 10, p. 247
183 Roskill, The Navy at War, pp. 351 – 353
184 Blair, Silent Victory, pp. 689 – 690. Information about "Ultra", that is intelligence derived from code breaking was Top Secret, compartmented information. Only those with an absolute need to know were briefed. The captured U-505 is on display at the Chicago Museum of Science and Industry.
185 Japanese submarines were engaged in transporting scarce raw materials to Germany and taking back advanced German technology and weapons systems in exchange.
186 Wilson, A Submariners' War, pp. 198 - 199
187 Roskill, The Navy at War, pp. 404 - 405
188 Hezlet, Submarines and Seapower, pp. 213 - 214

189 In the 1950s and 1960s U.S. Guppy-class submarine snorkels had rubberized coatings applied to further reduce the small radar signature of the snorkel head valve assembly.

190 Terraine, Business in Great Waters, pp. 653 - 654

191 Morison, The Atlantic Battle won, Vol. 10, p. 328

192 U.S. CVEs had similar problems with aircraft detection of snorkel boats in April- May 1945 as will be related later

193 Terraine, Business in Great Waters, pp. 662 - 663

194 Morison, The Atlantic Battle Won, Vol. 10, pp. 346 – 356

195 Morison, The Atlantic Battle Won, Vol. 10, p. 363

196 O'Connell, Submarine Operational Effectiveness in the 20th Century, Part One (1900 – 1939), p. 190. During WW I U-boats sank or captured 6,196 ships totaling 12,438,262 tons.

197 Morison, The Atlantic Battle Won, Vol. 10, p. 361

198 Wilson, A Submariners' War, p. 43

199 Wilson, A Submariners' War, p. 26 and pp. 43 - 44

200 Blair, Hitler's U-boat War, pp. 74 -75

201 Wilson, A Submariners' War, p. 19

202 Roskill, The War at Sea, Vol. I, p. 31

203 O'Connell, The Effectiveness of Air Power in the 20th Century, Part Two (1939 – 1945), pp. 1 - 2

204 Jones, Experiment at Dundee, NSL Review, January 2010

205 Mars, British Submarine at War, p. 65

206 Wilson, A Submariners' War, p. 43

207 Mars, British Submarines at War, p. 80

208 Roskill, The War at Sea, p. 318. See also Barnett, Engage the enemy More Closely, pp. 204 - 205

209 Wilson, A Submariners' War, pp. 46 - 47

210 Roskill, The War at Sea, p. 517

211 Wilson, A Submariners" War, pp. 46 - 47

212 Wilson, A Submariners' War, pp. 49 - 50

213 Wilson, A Submariners' War, pp. 50 - 51

214 Boyd, Hitler's Japanese Confidant, pp. 53 – 54. Germany was trying to persuade Japan to establish a naval base on Madagascar to attrite British shipping from India to the Middle East. Churchill was aware of this initiative through Magic, the interception of messages from Japanese ambassador Oshima in Berlin to Tokyo, and chose to act to preclude

such an action. Actually Japan had too much on its plate after the Battle of Midway and was highly unlikely to take action re Madagascar.

215 Wilson, A Submariners' War, pp. 51 - 53

216 Morison, Operations in North Africa, p. 98

217 Blair, The Hunted, p. 93

218 Morison, Operations in North Africa, p. 252

219 Barnett, Engage the Enemy More Closely, p. 569

220 Morison, Operations in North Africa, p. 240

221 Mars, British Submarines at War, p. 87

222 Mars, British Submarines at War, p. 39

223 Wilson, A Submariners' War, p. 17

224 None of the "O", "P" or "R" class submarines had air conditioning, having been built during the 1920s. Operations in the temperate latitudes were tolerable but during tropical operations conditions rapidly became bad.

225 Wilson, A Submariners' War, p. 19

226 Mars, British Submarines at War, pp. 61 - 62

227 Wilson, A Submariners' War, p. 55

228 van der Vat, The Pacific Campaign, p. 125

229 Hezlet, The Submarine and Seapower, pp. 193 - 194

230 Dull, The Imperial Japanese Navy, p. 41

231 Wilson, A Submariners' War, p. 57

232 Young, One of Our Submarines. pp. 304 - 305

233 The interested reader is referred to Correlli Barnett's fascinating book about the backwardness of British industry The Audit of War. See p.168 in which Barnett describes "...a disharmony between scientific genius and industrial backwardness."

234 Wilson, A Submariners' War, pp. 22 - 23

235 Wilson, A Submariners' War, p. 22

236 Wilson, A Submariners' War, p. 26

237 Roskill, The Navy at War, p. 186

238 Roskill, The Navy at War, pp. 187 - 188

239 Roskill, The Navy at War, p. 342

240 Wilson, A Submariners' War, pp. 59 - 61

241 Wilson, A Submariners' War, pp. 120 - 121

242 Wilson, A Submariners' War, pp. 121 - 122

243 Wilson, A Submariners' War, pp. 122 -124

244 Wilson, A Submariners' War ,p. 126

245 Wilson, A Submariners' War, p. 127

246 Wilson, A Submariners 'War, p. 176
247 Wilson, A Submariners' War. P. 130
248 Wilson, A Submariners' War, p. 167
249 Wilson, A Submariners' War, pp. 178 - 179
250 Mars, British Submarines at War, p. 29
251 Roskill, The Navy at War, p. 58
252 Much of the material about 9th Submarine Flotilla was derived from a series of three articles by Mark C. Jones which were published in The Submarine Review in October 2009 and January and April 2010.
253 Jones, Experiment at Dundee, NSL Review, Oct. 2009, pp. 54 -56
254 O'Connell, The Effectiveness of Air Power during the 20th Century, Part Two (1939 – 1945). See the section on the Norwegian Campaign for a description of the limitations on allied airpower and its consequences.
255 Mars, British Submarines at War, pp. 104 -105. Mars discusses torpedo fire control as part of the PCO or as the Brits called it the "Perisher" Course. It stood for periscope course, but also referred to the fact that not all candidates survived the course. He relates that selecting 90 degree angles was soon banned because of gyro failures.
256 Compton-Hall, The Underwater War, 1939 – 45, p. 59. The official name for the Fruit Machine was Submarine Torpedo Director Mk. II.
257 Mars, British Submarines at War, pp. 69 - 70
258 Both Germany and Great Britain started the war by trying to observe the London Conference rules of not sinking ships without warning. .On the day after the Pearl Harbor attack the U.S. Navy Department issued an order to conduct unrestricted air and submarine warfare against the Empire of Japan.
259 Mars, British Submarines at War, p. 73
260 Mars, British submarines at War, p. 76
261 Roskill, The Navy at War, p. 98
262 Mars, British Submarines at War, p. 113
263 Roskill, The Navy at War, p. 142
264 Mars, British Submarines at War, p. 121
265 Mars, British submarines at War, p. 121
266 Mars, British Submarines at War, pp. 101 - 102
267 Mars, British submarines at War, pp. 204 - 205
268 Mars, British Submarines at War, pp. 80 - 81
269 Mars, British Submarines at War, p. 87
270 Macintyre, Battle for the Mediterranean, p. 89

271 Macintyre, Battle for the Mediterranean, PP. 86 - 88
272 Macintyre, Battle for the Mediterranean, P. 89
273 Mars, British Submarines at War, p. 90
274 Macintyre, Battle for the Mediterranean, pp. 104 - 105
275 Mars, British Submarines at War, p. 93
276 Macintyre, Battle for the Mediterranean, p. 106
277 Macintyre, Battle for the Mediterranean, p. 109
278 Ciano Diaries, p. 416
279 Macintyre, Battle for the Mediterranean, p. 85
280 Macintyre, Battle for the Mediterranean, pp. 135 - 136
281 Macintyre, Battle for the Mediterranean, pp. 86 - 87
282 Ciano Diaries, pp. 484 - 485
283 Roskill, The Navy at War, p. 212
284 Roskill, The Navy at War, p. 235
285 Roskill, The Navy at War, p. 237
286 Macintyre, Battle for the Mediterranean, p. 96
287 Ciano Diaries, pp 525 - 526
288 Macintyre, The Battle for the Mediterranean, p. 203
289 Compton-Hall, The Underwater War, p. 79. *Dolfijn* was a former U-class British submarine transferred to the Royal Netherlands Navy.
290 Roskill, The Navy at War, pp. 281 – 284
291 Mars, British Submarines at War, p. 175
292 Bragadin, The Italian Navy in World War II, pp. 235 - 236
293 Bragadin, The Italian Navy in World War II, p. 248
294 Wilson, A Submariners' War, p. 68
295 Hurst, The Fourth Ally, p. 12
296 Hurst, The Fourth Ally, p. 13
297 Hurst, The Fourth Ally, p. 38
298 Hurst, The Fourth Ally, p. 11
299 In the 1920s and early 1930s Dutch submarines intended for operations in European waters carried the "O" designation (*Onderzeeboot*) while those intended for colonial use were designated "K" (*Kolonien*). The K class boats were bigger and longer range as suited Pacific operations. After 1937 all Dutch submarines were designated "O".
300 Wilson, A Submariners' War, p. 55
301 Dull, The Imperial Japanese Navy, p. 42. Dull reports that K-XVI sank IJN destroyer *Sagiri* on 24 December, and also damaged three transports.

302 Hezlet, Submarines and Seapower, pp. 193 - 194
303 van der Vat, The Pacific Campaign, p. 125
304 Dull, The Imperial Japanese Navy, pp 63, and 68 - 69
305 Hurst, The Fourth Ally, pp. 10 - 11
306 Dull, The Imperial Japanese Navy, p. 62
307 Dull, A Battle History, p. 53
308 Dull, The Imperial Japanese Navy, p. 41. Dull reports that K-XVI was lost to a British mine.
309 Dull, A Battle History, p. 72
310 Wilson, A Submariners' War, p. 57. See also Cairn's Fremantle's Secret Fleets, p. 20
311 Bragadin, The Italian Navy in WW II, pp. 324 - 325
312 Know, Hitler's Italian allies, pp. 61 - 62
313 Wilson, A Submariners' War, p. 29. U.S. submarines used dichlorodifluoromethane, a much safer refrigerant fluid.
314 Ciano Diaries, pp. 151 - 152
315 Bragadin, The Italian Navy in WW II, pp. 19 - 20
316 Bragadin, The Italian Navy in World War II, p. 117
317 Bragadin, The Italian Navy in World War II, p. 275
318 The Ciano Diaries, p. 256
319 Winton, Ultra at Sea, p. 9
320 Roskill, The War at Sea, Vol. I, p. 61
321 Bagnasco, Submarines of World War Two, p 132. Bagnasco indicates that Italy had 115 subs with eight in the Red Sea, leaving her 107 in the Med.
322 Doenitz, Memoirs, pp. 144 - 145
323 Howarth. The Battle of the Atlantic, p. 324
324 Blair, Hitler's U-boat War, p. 196
325 Blair, Hitler's U-Boat War, pp. 164 - 165
326 Barnett, Engage the Enemy More Closely, p. 219
327 Winton, Ultra at Sea, p. 11
328 Hezlet, The Submarine and Sea Power, pp. 137 - 138
329 Bragadin, The Italian Navy in World War II, p. 297
330 Bragadin, The Italian Navy in WW II, p. 7
331 Howarth, The Battle of the Atlantic, p. 324
332 U.S. fleet boats had the same problem with extensive superstructure. Early in the Pacific fighting the bridge-conning tower arrangements were modified to reduce the visible silhouette of the submarine.

333 Blair, Hitler's U-Boat War, pp. 204 – 205
334 Knox, Hitler's Italian Allies, p. 60
335 Doenitz, Memoirs, pp. 146 - 147
336 Doenitz, Memoirs, pp. 147 - 150
337 Bragadin, The Italian Navy in World War II, p. 41
338 Howarth, The Battle of the Atlantic, pp. 325 - 326
339 Wilson, A Submariners' War, pp. 29 - 30
340 Wilson, A Submariners' War, p. 31. *Galilei* was commissioned in the Royal Navy as HMS X2 and used as a training target.
341 Wilson, A Submariners' War, pp. 34 35
342 Wilson, A Submariners' War, pp. 33 - 34
343 Wilson, A Submariners' War, p. 36
344 Wilson, A Submariners' War, pp. 27 - 28
345 Roskill. The War at Sea, p. 426
346 Bragadin, The Italian Navy in World War II, p. 30
347 Mars, British Submarines at War, p. 86
348 Bragadin, p. 55
349 Mars, British Submarines at War, pp. 98 - 99
350 Roskill, The War at Sea, p. 347
351 Bragadin, The Italian Navy in World War II< p. 73
352 Bagnasco, Submarines of World War Two, p. 153
353 Doenitz, Memoirs, pp. 148 - 149
354 Bragadin, The Italian Navy in World War II, p. 83
355 The guided torpedoes were called '*maiale*', literally "hogs" in Italian.
356 Bragadin, The Italian Navy in World War II, p. 282
357 Howarth, The Battle of the Atlantic, p. 327
358 Roskill, The War at Sea, p. 538
359 Doenitz, memoirs, pp. 155 - 156
360 Ciano Diaries, pp. 383 – 386
361 Bragadin, The Italian Navy in World War II, p. 123
362 Winton, Ultra at Sea, pp. 99 - 100
363 Bragadin, The Italian Navy in World War II, p. 131
364 Bragadin, The Italian Navy in World War II, p. 138
365 Howarth, The Battle of the Atlantic, pp. 327 328
366 Bragadin, The Italian Navy in World War II, pp. 284 - 285
367 Bragadin, The Italian Navy in World War II, p. 145
368 Bragadin, The Italian Navy in World War II, pp. 168 - 169
369 Blair, Hitler's U-Boat War, p. 508

370 Bragadin, The Italian Navy in World War II, pp. 286 - 287

371 Bragadin, The Italian Navy in World War II, p. 289. MAS was an abbreviation for *Mezzi d'Assalto*, or assault vehicle

372 Bragadin, The Italian Navy in World War II, p. 170

373 Ciano Diaries, p. 498

374 Bragadin, The Italian Navy in World Aar II, pp. 177 - 178

375 Bragadin, The Italian Navy in World War II, p. 173

376 HMS Cairo and HMS Kenya each had the capability of directing air interceptors to protect the convoy. Cairo sank, and Kenya had to depart leaving the convoy without any ship-borne fighter direction capability. It suffered as a result.

377 Bragadin, The Italian Navy in World War II, pp. 205 – 207, and 209 - 210

378 Blair, The Hunted, p. 102

379 Bragadin, The Italian Navy in World War ii, pp. 293 - 294

380 Bragadin, The Italian Navy in World War II, p. 239

381 Bragadin, The Italian Navy in World War II, p. 227

382 Howarth, The Battle of the Atlantic, pp. 332 - 333

383 Howarth, Battle of the Atlantic, p. 333

384 Bragadin, The Italian Navy in World War II, p. 255

385 Howarth, The Battle of the Atlantic, pp. 328 - 329

386 Bragadin, The Italian Navy in World War II, p. 295

387 Bragadin, The Italian Navy in World War II, p. 344

388 Bragadin, The Italian Navy in World War II, p. 347

389 Hezlet, The Submarine and Sea power, pp. 156 - 157

390 Boyd & Yoshida, The Japanese Submarine Force and WW II, p. 45 (later JapSubForce)

391 Evans and Peattie, pp. 428 - 429

392 Boyd & Yoshida, JapSubForce, p. 55

393 Evans and Peattie, Kaigun, pp. 431 – 432. See also Evans, The Japanese Navy in WW II, p. 118 and p. 511. Evans quotes a retired IJN Vice Admiral who says he "never saw exercises with warfare against or in defense of maritime lines of communication."

394 Evans, The Japanese Navy in WW II, p. 117

395 Boyd and Yoshida, JapSubForce, p. 55 - 61

396 Evans, The Japanese Navy in WW II, p. 51

397 Evans, The Japanese Navy in WWW II, pp. 25 - 28

398 Evans, The Japanese Navy in WW II, pp. 32 - 33

399 During my tour as Defense Attaché and Naval Attaché Tokyo (1978 – 1981) I had occasion to visit the Naval Academy at Eta Jima and see the memorial to them.

400 Boyd & Yoshida, JapSubForce, pp. 55 - 59

401 van der Vat, The Pacific Campaign, p. 178

402 van der Vat, The Pacific Campaign, pp. 143 - 144

403 Boyd & Yoshida, JapSubForce, pp. 69 - 70

404 van der Vat, The Pacific Campaign, p. 152

405 Boyd & Yoshida, JapSubForce, pp. 65 - 68

406 Barnett, Engage the Enemy More Closely, pp. 412 - 413

407 Boyd & Yoshida, JapSubForce, pp. 70 - 71

408 Boyd & Yoshida, JapSubForce, p. 72

409 Evans, The Japanese Navy in WW II, p. 110

410 Boyd & Yoshida, JapSubForce, pp. 76 - 77

411 Roskill, The Navy at War, p. 210

412 Boyd & Yoshida, JapSubForce, pp. 111 - 112

413 Cairn, Freemantle's Secret Fleets, p. 12

414 Cairn, Freemantle's Secret Fleets, pp. 12 - 13

415 Boyd & Yoshida, JapSubForce, pp. 90 - 91

416 Hurst, The Forth Ally, p. 67

417 Boyd & Yoshida, JapSubForce, pp. 87 - 88

418 Hurst, The Fourth Ally, pp. 77 - 78

419 Evans, The Japanese Navy in WW II, p. 127

420 Evans, The Japanese Navy in WW II, p. 124

421 Evans, The Japanese Navy in WW II, p. 148

422 Blair, Silent Victory, p. 238

423 Dull, The Imperial Japanese Navy (1941-1945), p. 134

424 Boyd & Yoshida, JapSubForce, pp. 86 - 88

425 Boyd & Yoshida, JapSubForce, pp. 109 - 111

426 Boyd & Yoshida, JapSubForce, pp. 77 - 81

427 Boyd & Yoshida, JapSubForce, pp. 92 - 93

428 Boyd & Yoshida, JapSubForce, pp. 96 - 98

429 Boyd & Yoshida, JapSubForce, p. 99. See also van der Vat, The Pacific Campaign, p. 225 – 226. They disagree on exactly how many torpedoes struck Wasp.

430 USS Yorktown was sunk after the Battle of Midway had already been decided.

431 Boyd & Yoshida, JapSubForce, p. 105

432 Boyd & Yoshida, JapSubForce, p. 114
433 van der Vat, The Pacific Campaign, p. 245
434 Boyd & Yoshida, JapSubForce, pp. 114 - 115
435 van der Vat, The Pacific Campaign, pp. 279 - 280
436 Boyd & Yoshida, JapSubForce, pp. 116 - 117
437 Boyd & Yoshida, JapSubForce, pp. 116 - 117
438 Boyd & Yoshida, JapSubForce, p. 117
439 van der Vat, The Pacific Campaign, p. 276
440 Boyd & Yoshida, JapSubForce, pp. 122 - 123
441 Boyd & Yoshida, JapSubForce, pp. 120 - 121
442 Boyd & Yoshida, JapSubForce, p. 121
443 Boyd & Yoshida, JapSubForce, pp. 134 - 135
444 Boyd & Yoshida, JapSubForce, pp. 136 - 137
445 van der Vat, The Pacific Campaign, p. 321
446 Boyd & Yoshida, JapSubForce, pp. 158 - 160
447 Evans, The Japanese Navy in WW II, p. 329. Adm. Ozawa's detailed combat report noted both the direct threat and indirect threat (fuel shortages) caused by U.S. submarine operations.
448 Boyd & Yoshida, JapSubForce, p. 160
449 Evans, The Japanese Navy in WW II, pp. 32 - 33
450 Boyd & Yoshida, JapSubForce, pp. 167 - 171
451 Evans and Peattie, Kaigun, p. 497
452 van der Vat, The Pacific Campaign, p. 271
453 Polmar and Noot, Soviet Subs, p. 101
454 Polmar and Noot, Soviet Subs, p. 102
455 Polmar and Noot, Soviet Subs, p. 102
456 Polmar and Noot, Soviet Subs, p. 102. Jurgen Rohwer, Allied Submarine Attacks, p. 80.
457 Polmar and Noot, Soviet Submarines, pp. 102 - 103
458 Korzh, Red Star Under the Baltic, p. 30
459 Polmar and Noot, Soviet Submarines, pp. 103 - 106
460 Polmar and Noot, Soviet Submarines, pp. 107 - 108
461 Polmar and Noot, Soviet Submarines, p. 108
462 Polmar and Noot, Soviet Submarines, p. 109. The *Gustloff* loss was the greatest loss of life ever in a marine disaster.
463 Polmar and Noot, Soviet Submarines, pp. 111 - 112
464 Polmar and Noot, Soviet Submarines, p. 112

465 Polmar and Noot, Soviet Submarines, pp. 112 – 113. See also O'Connell, The Effectiveness of Airpower in the 20ᵗʰ Century, Part Two, pp. 37 - 40

466 Polmar and Noot, Soviet submarines, p. 113

467 Polmar and Noot, Soviet Submarines, p. 113

469 Polmar and Noot, Soviet submarines, p. 114

470 Polmar and Noot, Soviet Submarines, p. 114

471 Polmar and Noot, Soviet Submarines, p. 115

472 Polmar and Noot, Soviet Submarines, p. 115

473 Polmar and Noot, p. 116

474 Polmar and Noot, Soviet Submarines, pp. 116 - 117

475 Polmar and Noot, Soviet Submarines, p. 117

476 When Italy left the war in 1943, a number of her warships were allotted to the Allies. However it was not possible to move them from Italy to the USSR because of German forces. Instead a number of UK and U.S. warships were substituted.

477 Polmar and Noot, Soviet Submarines, pp. 118 - 119

478 Polmar and Noot, Soviet Submarines, pp. 121 - 122

479 Polmar and Noot, Soviet submarines, p. 122

480 Polmar and Noot, Soviet Submarines, p. 123

481 Polmar and Noot, Soviet Submarines, p. 123

482 Polmar and Noot, Soviet submarines, p. 124

483 Polmar and Noot, Soviet Submarines, p. 124

484 Polmar and Noot, Soviet Submarines. pp. 124 = 125

485 The first atomic bomb had been dropped on Hiroshima on 6 August; the second was dropped on Nagasaki on 9 August.

486 Blair, Silent Victory, pp. 263 - 266

487 "Junior " McCain was the son of Radm. John Sidney McCain, then an aviator commanding a CVBG in the Pacific. Later "Junior" McCain would reach four star rank and serve as USCINCPAC during the Vietnam War. His son, John McCain III, was shot down and did time in the "Hanoi Hilton", and later became a U.S. Senator.

488 The "fix" consisted of flame-hardening spare gears to restore their quality, and replacing the original gears.

489 Morison, The Atlantic Battle,Won, Vol. 10, p. 87

490 Feeding the Sharks, pp. 189 - 190

491 Feeding the Sharks, p. 367

492 Roskill, The War at Sea, p. 560

493 Blair, Silent Victory, p. 81

494 Cairn, Fremantle's Secret Fleets, pp. 11 - 12

495 There was no overall area commander. Hart and MacArthur reported to their respective Service Secretaries, both Cabinet officers. Over them was the President.

496 Blair, Silent Victory, pp. 156 - 157

497 Calvert, Silent Running, p. 51

498 Feeding the Sharks, p. 453

499 Dull, The Imperial Japanese Navy, p. 31

500 Blair, Silent Victory, p. 159

501 van der Vat, The Pacific Campaign, p. 160

502 van der Vat, The Pacific Campaign, p. 127

503 Cairn, Fremantle's Secret Fleets, pp. 11 12

504 Blair, Silent Victory, p. 155

505 Blair, Silent Victory, pp. 173 - 174

506 Blair, Silent Victory, p. 171

507 Blair, Silent Victory, p. 167 map showing their patrol stations.

508 Dull, The Imperial Japanese Navy, p. 53

509 Feeding the Sharks, pp. 117 - 119

510 Cairn, Fremantle's Secret Fleets, p. 17

511 Blair, Silent Victory, pp. 218 - 219

512 Blair, Silent Victory, P. 217

513 Blair, Silent Victory, p. 222

514 Dull, The Imperial Japanese Navy, p. 193

515 Dull, The Imperial Japanese Navy, p. 184

516 Hezlet, The Submarine and Seapower, pp. 198 - 199

517 Blair, Silent Victory, p. 348

518 van der Vat, The Pacific Campaign, p. 235

519 Blair, Silent Victory, pp. 386 - 387

520 Blair, Silent Victory, p. 387

521 Blair, Silent Victory, p. 485

522 Blair, Silent Victory, p. 475

523 Feeding the Sharks, p. 379

524 The British had operational control of allied operations in the Indian Ocean and the Malacca Straits, while the United States had operational control of most of the Pacific. This division was settled at the Combined Chiefs of Staff level and held during the war.

525 Cairn, Fremantle's Secret Fleets, p. 3

526 Blair, Silent victory, pp. 197 - 203
527 Cairn, Fremantle's Secret Fleets, p. 8
528 Cairn, Fremantle's Secret Fleets, p. 28
529 Dull, The Imperial Japanese Navy, p. 104
530 Cairn, Fremantle's Secret Fleets, pp. 17 - 19
531 Blair, Silent Victory, pp. 292 - 293
532 Feeding the Sharks, p. 423 & 451
533 Blair, Silent Victory, p 275. The author had occasion to fire a warshot Mk 14-5 torpedo at a target ship in 1966. The torpedo ran deep, underneath the target.
534 Parillo, The Japanese Merchant Marine, p. 204
535 Blair, Silent Victory, pp. 398 - 399
536 Blair, Silent Victory, p. 390 - 391
537 Hurst, The Fourth Ally, p. 80. There were no RN submarines at Fremantle at this time, and the RAN had only one training submarine.
538 Blair, Silent Victory, p. 424
539 Blair, Silent Victory, pp. 486 – 487.
540 Blair, Silent Victory, p. 564
541 Calvert, Silent Running, p. 115
542 Blair, Silent Victory, p. 610
543 Griese, Shooting the War, pp. 210 - 211
544 Blair, Silent Victory, p. 814
545 Wilson, A Submariners' War, pp. 69 - 70
546 On 7 December the submarines of the Pacific Fleet were officially part of Scouting Force, U.S. Pacific Fleet. Shortly thereafter they shifted to Submarine Force, US Pacific Fleet. See Galatin, Take Her Deep, p. 39
547 During the early morning hours of December 7th, USS Ward, on patrol in the exclusion area sighted a midget submarine periscope and immediately attacked in accordance with the existing rules of engagement. The midget submarine was attempting to penetrate Pearl Harbor as part of the Japanese Navy attack plan.
548 During his tour as COMSUBPAC (1964 – 1966) Radm. Fluckey remarked one day about how unprepared they had been for war.
549 Blair, Silent Victory, pp. 106 – 107. See also Galatin, Take Her Deep, p. 15.
550 Blair, Silent Victory, pp. 109 112.
551 Blair, Silent Victory, pp. 117 - 118
552 Blair, Silent Victory, pp. 119 - 120

553 Blair, Silent Victory, p. 216
554 Blair, Silent Victory, pp. 230 - 233
555 Blair, Silent Victory, pp. 254 - 255
556 Blair, Silent Victory, p. 227
557 Hezlet, The Submarine and Seapower, p. 196. See also Blair, Silent Victory, pp. 243 - 244
558 Morison, WW II, Part Fur, pp. 150 - 151
559 Morison, Vol. 4, p. 181. According to Morison Japanese transports reported an unsuccessful attack by an American submarine on 8 June as they were offloading troops at Attu Island.
560 Blair, Silent Victory, p. 417
561 Dull, The Imperial Japanese Navy, p. 261
562 Blair, Silent Victory, pp. 307 - 310
563 Blair, Silent Victory, pp. 317 - 318
564 Blair, Silent Victory, pp. 321 - 322
565 Galantin, Take Her Deep, p. 95
566 van der Vat, The Pacific Campaign, p. 229
567 Blair, Silent Victory, p. 335
568 Blair, Silent Victory, p. 337
569 Blair, Silent Victory, p. 359
570 Blair, Silent Victory, p. 361
571 Blair, Silent Victory, pp. 360 - 361
572 Calvert, Silent Running, p. 91
573 Calvert, Silent Running, pp. 54 - 55
574 Blair, Silent Victory, pp. 365 - 368
575 There were two basic fleet boat designs: Electric Boat and Portsmouth. They were similar but not identical. Manitowoc built to the EB design and MINSY to the Portsmouth design.
576 Hezlet, The Submarine and Seapower, p. 218
577 Blair, Silent Victory, pp. 426 - 427
578 Blair, Silent Victory, pp. 429 - 431
579 van der Vat, The Pacific Campaign, p. 334. Also see Blair, Silent Victory, p. 55. The magnetic exploder project, G-53, started in 1922, with Christie very much involved. He was a "true believer" in its worth, and very reluctant to accept evidence of its problems.
580 Blair, Silent Victory, pp. 435 - 437
581 Blair, Silent Victory, p. 43
582 Blair, Silent Victory, pp. 541 - 544

583 Blair, Silent Victory, pp. 543 - 544
584 There was a submarine tender at Midway to provide refit facilities. R&R facilities were minimal, and a given submarine was guaranteed that the next patrol would end at Pearl Harbor.
585 Blair, Silent Victory, pp. 509 - 510
586 Hezlet, The Submarine and Seapower, pp. 215 - 216
587 Calvert, Silent Running, p. 109
588 Calvert, Silent Running, pp. 60 - 61
589 Hezlet, The Submarine and Seapower, p. 200
590 van der Vat, The Pacific Campaign, pp. 332 - 333
591 Blair, Silent Victory, p. 553
592 Roskill, The Navy at War, p. 349
593 Blair, Silent victory, p. 594
594 Blair, Silent Victory, p. 561
595 Blair, Silent Victory, pp. 597 – 599
596 Each wolf pack usually acquired a nickname, having some connection with the name of the pack leader.
597 Blair, Silent Victory, p. 688
598 Hezlet, The Submarine and Seapower, pp. 218 - 219
599 Hezlet, The Submarine and Seapower, p. 218
600 Hezlet, The Submarine and Seapower, pp. 201 - 202
601 All aviation fuel had to be flown in to Chengdu from India. It took about seven tanker loads over the Himalayas to provide fuel for one B-29 mission to southern Japan.
602 Blair, Silent Victory, p. 642. It is interesting to see this huge armada in the Pacific at the same time that the allies were mounting the invasion of Normandy on the Atlantic side. It was a clear indication of the overwhelming industrial strength of the United States.
603 Blair, Silent Victory, p. 641
604 Blair, Silent Victory, p. 721
605 Blair, Silent Victory, p. 707
606 Blair, Silent Victory, pp. 724 - 725
607 Blair, Silent Victory, pp. 775 - 776
608 Blair, Silent Victory, pp. 778 - 780
609 Hezlet, The Submarine and Seapower, p. 219
610 Hezlet, The Submarine and Seapower, p. 219
611 Blair, Silent Victory, pp. 816 - 817

612 van der Vat, The Pacific Campaign, pp. 376 – 377. Also see Blair, Silent Victory, pp. 878 – 879.
613 From Singapore to Yokohama is 2,858 nautical miles.
614 Alden, The Fleet Submarine in the U.S. Navy, Appendix 3. See also Dull, The Imperial Japanese Navy, p. 4
615 Evans and Peattie, *Kaigun*, p. 409
616 Evans and Peattie, *Kaigun*, p. 430
617 Parillo, The Japanese Merchant Marine, p. 11. Also see Oi, pp. 58 - 588
618 Evans and Peattie, *Kaigun*, pp 434 -
619 Oi, Why Japan's Anti-Submarine Warfare Failed, p. 589
620 van der Vat, The Pacific Campaign, p. 290
621 Evans and Peattie, Kaigun, p. 599, footnote 30
622 Evans and Peattie, Kaigun, pp. 482 - 486
623 Parillo, The Japanese Merchant Marine, p. 21
624 Evans and Peattie, Kaigun, p. 495
625 Parillo, The Japanese Merchant Marine, p. 23
626 Parillo, The Japanese Merchant Marine, pp. 34 - 35
627 Parillo, The Japanese Merchant Marine, pp. 37 - 38
628 . Parillo, The Japanese Merchant Marine, p. 45
629 Parillo, The Japanese Merchant Marine, p. 134
630 Moji is a port at the Shimonoseki Strait separating Kyushu from Honshu. Takao is the Japanese name for Kaohsiung, Taiwan
631 Parillo, The Japanese Merchant Marine, pp. 96 - 97
632 Parillo, The Japanese Merchant Marine, pp. 67 - 68
633 Parillo, The Japanese Merchant Marine, pp. 69 – 70
634 Parillo, The Japanese Merchant Marine, p. 117
635 Parillo, The Japanese Merchant Marine, pp. 138 - 141
636 Blair, Silent Victory, p. 641
637 Dull, The Imperial Japanese Navy, pp. 307 - 311
638 Oi, Why Japan's Anti-Submarine Warfare Failed, pp. 600 - 601
639 Parillo, The Japanese Merchant Marine, pp. 70 - 71
640 Parillo, The Japanese Merchant Marine, p. 111
641 Hezlet, pp. 221 - 223
642 Parillo, The Japanese Merchant Marine, p. 151
643 Parillo, The Japanese Merchant Marine, p. 205
644 Parillo, The Japanese Merchant Marine, p. 207
645 *Oi*, Why Japan's Anti-Submarine Warfare Failed, p. 601
646 Parillo, The Japanese Merchant Marine, p. 85

647 The key to defeating an enemy's comint efforts is radio silence. The IJN CVBG that attacked Pearl Harbor was on strict radio silence.

648 Parillo, The Japanese Merchant Marine, pp. 88 - 90

649 Parillo, The Japanese Merchant Marine, pp. 91 92

650 Hezlet, Electronics, p. 233

651 Miller, War Plan Orange, pp. 352 - 353

652 Parillo, The Japanese Merchant Marine, pp. 196 - 197

Index

Gulf of Finland
  A/S net barriers 191
  mine barrier 190
Gulf Sea Frontier 45

H

HF/DF 61
HMS Audacity 37
HMS Barham 18, 35, 38, 82, 146
HMS Fiji 29, 82
HMS Galatea 35
HMS Illustrious 84
HMS Medway 56
HMS Parthian 82

I

I Bomber Command 42
IRONSIDE 83
Italian Air Force
  little or no coordination with the
    Navy's activities 130
Italian ciphers
  being read by the British 131
Italian Navy
  lack of a naval air arm 129
  lack of fuel oil 129
  lack of radar aboard Italian ships 129
  planned an occupation of Malta 130
  \"special warfare\" units 131
Italian submarines
  Admiral Doenitz was somewhat
    skeptical 132
  air conditioning machinery 129
  Bagnolini 133
  German requests for naval
    cooperation 130
  in the Red Sea 137
  Italian submarine base was set up at
    Bordeaux 133
  lack of an independent main
    induction valve 136
  pressed into service to carry
    cargoes 145

successful Italian submarine
    commanding officers 142
  trained for daylight submerged at-
    tacks only 132
Italy
  Count Ciano 130
  declared war on Greece 136
  Mussolini 130
  Mussolini and the Italian High
    Command were ignorant of
    naval matters 137

J

Japan
  Admiral Nobumasa Suetsugu 156
  desired defensive perimeter 156
  Operation \"K\" 166
  planned invasion of Midway 166
Japanese submarines
  coordinated midget submarine at-
    tack 163
  drawn into resupply missions in the
    Solomons 173
  Force \"Z\" was sighted and re-
    ported 161
  Four IJN mine laying submarines 164
  I-6 160
  I-19 171
  I-25 sent a reconnaissance seaplane
    over Sydney 165
  I-26 170
  I-58 181
  I-168 167
  I-172 160
  I-400 class submarines 181
  Kaiten 183
  midget sub 158
  off Guadalcanal 170
  patrols off the U.S. west coast 168
  patrols off the west coast 159
  Pearl Harbor attack 157
  sank aircraft carriers Yorktown and
    Wasp 172
Joseph Stalin 52, 186

L

Leningrad
  key German objective 188
  under siege 189
London Naval Agreement 8
London Submarine Agreement 13
Luftwaffe long-range FW Condor
  aircraft 34

M

Maginot Line 15
Malay Barrier 127
Mers-el-Kebir 81

N

North Atlantic convoy campaign 72

O

Observation-Orientation-
  Decision-Action 6
Operational Intelligence Center 8
Operation BELLRINGER 83
Operation CATAPULT 81
Operation MENACE 82
Operation SEA WOLF 73

P

Paukenschlag (Attack on the U.S.) 39
Phony War 13
Pillenwerfer. See Bold; See Bold
Plan Dog 42
Plan Orange 42
Plan Z 10
Polish Intelligence Service 32
Prize Ordinance 13

R

RAF
  Bomber Command 51
  Coastal Command 51
Rainbow Five 42
Room 40 7

S

Shipping Defense Advisory
  Committee 8
snorkel capability
  snorkel equipped U-boats 69
Soviet operational control
  British submarines Tigris and
    Trident 196
  HMS Sealion and Seawolf 196
Soviet submarine bases
  Baltiski Port 187
  Helsingfors, Hango and Abo 193
  Leningrad 187
  Libau 187
  Revel 187
Soviet submarines
  K-2 197
  K-3 195
  K-21 197
  K-23 197
  M-95 190
  M-96 193
  M-97 189, 190
  S-9 192
  S-12 192
  S-13 193
  S-103 198
  S-104 198
  SHCH-307 189
  SHCH-317 189
  SHCH-323 189, 192
  SHCH-401 195, 196
  SHCH -402 195
  SHCH-402 196, 198
  SHCH-403 196, 197
  SHCH-422 195, 197
Soviet submarines were already on
  patrol stations when the war
  started 187
V-1 198
V-4 198
SS Athenia 16
Submarine Tracking Room 36, 45

300